JavaBeans™ Programming
from the Ground Up

About the Authors ...

Joseph O'Neil works at AT&T Laboratories in New Jersey where he builds system prototypes using Java and other new software technologies. In his more than 20 years experience designing and developing software for communication services and products, Joe managed a development team that built call processing and system management software for several voice and data switching systems. He also represented AT&T in an international effort to define new software architectures for the next generation Intelligent Network.

In his spare time, Joe teaches classes on Java and JavaScript programming. He worked with Herb Schildt to write Osborne/McGraw-Hill's *Java Programmer's Reference* and served as technical reviewer for other Osborne books on JavaScript, ActiveX, the Microsoft Foundation Classes, and Java. His next book is now in preparation.

Joe has degrees in electrical engineering from Stanford University and Cooper Union.

Herb Schildt is the world's leading programming author. He is an authority on the C and C++ languages, a master Windows programmer, and an expert on Java. His programming books have sold over two million copies worldwide and have been translated into all major foreign languages. He is the author and co-author of numerous best-sellers, including *C: The Complete Reference, C++: The Complete Reference, C++ from the Ground Up, Windows NT 4 Programming from the Ground Up, Java 1.1: The Complete Reference*, and many others. Herb is a member of both the ANSI C and C++ standardization committees. His contribution as a developmental editor to this book ensures the highest level of quality and the most accurate information available.

JavaBeans™ Programming
from the Ground Up

Joseph O'Neil
Edited by Herb Schildt

Osborne **McGraw-Hill**

Berkeley   New York   St. Louis   San Francisco
Auckland   Bogotá   Hamburg   London   Madrid
Mexico City   Milan   Montreal   New Delhi   Panama City
Paris   São Paulo   Singapore   Sydney
Tokyo   Toronto

Osborne/**McGraw-Hill**
2600 Tenth Street
Berkeley, California 94710
U.S.A.

For information on translations or book distributors outside the U.S.A., or to arrange bulk purchase discounts for sales promotions, premiums, or fund-raisers, please contact Osborne/**McGraw-Hill** at the above address.

JavaBeans™ Programming from the Ground Up

1234567890 DOC DOC 901987654321098

ISBN 0-07-882477-X

Publisher
Brandon A. Nordin

Editor-in-Chief
Scott Rogers

Acquisitions Editor
Megg Bonar

Developmental Editor
Herb Schildt

Project Editor
Janet Walden

Editorial Assistant
Stephane Thomas

Technical Editor
Martin Rinehart

Copy Editors
Jan Jue
Claire Splan
Judith Brown

Proofreader
Emily Wolman

Indexer
David Heiret

Computer Designer
Mickey Galicia

Illustrator
Lance Ravella

Series Design
Peter F. Hancik

Cover Design
John Nedwidek, emdesign

This book is dedicated to Jennifer Casto, John Casto, and Matthew Mitchell.

Contents at a Glance

Table of Contents

Foreword

by Herbert Schildt

The rise of the Internet was the catalyst that finally moved to the forefront one of software engineering's long sought-after goals: reusable software components. For years, component software lingered on the edges of mainstream computing. Although widely recognized as a potentially powerful solution to several fundamental problems, including that of software reliability, component software was simply not very compatible with the non-networked, stand-alone computing environment which was common for so many years. The key benefits of component software are best realized when a component can be acquired on demand, as needed; that is, when it can be dynamically downloaded. This requires a vast, online universe populated with such components, with the user free to pick and choose. But for years, such a universe did not exist and component software remained an elusive dream. Then, with a resounding roar, the Internet and the World Wide Web changed computing forever. And in the process, set the stage for component software—and JavaBeans.

This book is about JavaBeans, which are reusable software components written in Java. JavaBeans are not the only way to write component software.

They are, however, the easiest. Because Java compiles to portable code, the JavaBeans that you create can run in nearly any computing environment that can connect to the Internet. While it is too early to say with certainty, JavaBeans may become the "lingua franca" of component software development. In any event, JavaBeans defines an entirely new class of commercial software which will be delivered primarily over the Internet. Frankly, the creation of component software using JavaBeans offers a great opportunity to those programmers with the foresight to take advantage of it.

This book is written by Joe O'Neil, a top-notch programmer, Java expert, and long-time associate. While this is Joe's first book, it is not his first writing effort. He has helped in the revision of two of my own programming books and co-authored the *Java Programmer's Reference*. When Joe invited me to edit this book I was delighted. I knew that the JavaBeans technology could best be advanced by a well-written, practical guide. And, I knew that Joe was just the person to do it. As you will discover, this book is packed with interesting Beans, insider tips, and step-by-step instructions. I am certain that you will be pleased with the result.

Acknowledgments

I especially thank my acquisitions editor, Megg Bonar, for her help in resolving some contract issues for this project. Without her efforts in this area, the book could not have been published. Thanks are also due to Scott Rogers, Stephane Thomas, Janet Walden, Robin Small, and the many other people at Osborne/McGraw-Hill who handle all the details of creating a book.

Herb Schildt's encouragement and guidance have been invaluable through the many months it took to complete this task. I enjoy reading his books and frequently consult them when building software. He has a unique style of organization and writing that makes difficult topics easy to understand.

Marty Rinehart did an excellent job as the technical reviewer for the book. His critical reading and feedback helped eliminate some ambiguities and sources of error.

Finally, congratulations to the team at Sun Microsystems for inventing and developing the Java programming language and JavaBeans. It is a pleasure to work with this technology!

Introduction

Beans are software components written in Java. They represent an important and exciting advance in software technology. It is now possible to create applications by integrating platform-independent components from multiple vendors. That is, you can create a new application by connecting various off-the-shelf software components. This approach provides substantial benefits of reuse and interoperability.

JavaBeans also ushers in a new category of programmer: the component developer. No longer do we need to think of applications as large, monolithic systems. Instead, an application can be viewed as a framework upon which various software components can be attached, removed, and reattached, as needed. While the story of component software is just now beginning, software components will have a long-term effect on computing. And, JavaBeans is the technology that is leading the way.

Who Is the Audience for This Book?

This book is intended for anyone who wants to design, develop, and use Java software components. There is a strong emphasis on how to apply the classes and interfaces defined in the JavaBeans API. Simple examples are provided early in the book so you can easily grasp the concepts that are being described. More complex and interesting components are given later.

It is assumed that you are familiar with the basics of Java programming. If you need to brush up on your Java skills, I recommend *Java 1.1: The Complete Reference, Second Edition*, by Herbert Schildt and Patrick Naughton. It is a valuable resource for any Java programmer. This book is also available from Osborne/McGraw-Hill.

What's in This Book?

This book is first and foremost a practical guide to the JavaBeans technology. While it includes complete discussions of the theory and philosophy behind each feature of JavaBeans, its emphasis is on using them. Throughout this book are numerous examples that you can use as-is or use as starting points for your own Bean development. Step-by-step instructions are provided throughout.

The book consists of the 14 chapters summarized here:

Chapter 1, "An Overview of JavaBeans," introduces the concept of a software component and explains how it provides the advantages of reusability and interoperability. You will see how to use the Bean Development Kit (BDK) and some of the simple Beans that are provided with it. Java Archive (JAR) files are also discussed. Beans and their supporting files are packaged in JAR files.

Chapter 2, "Building Simple Beans," guides you step-by-step through the process of building a Bean and testing it with the BDK. The naming conventions that can be used to identify the properties of a Bean are described. Other Bean examples are included.

Chapter 3, "Events," outlines the delegation event model. The material in this chapter is a prerequisite to understanding all of the examples that are included later in the book. Adapter classes are also described, as are inner classes, an important enhancement to the Java language. This chapter shows how to deal with all of the events that can be generated by the various AWT widgets.

Chapter 4, "Persistence," covers the basics of object serialization and deserialization. Examples are also provided to illustrate that threads and images cannot be serialized and how to deal with that fact. Object versioning is also addressed.

Chapter 5, "Reflection and Introspection," defines these important features. Code examples then show how a Bean developer may explicitly designate the properties, events, and methods that are presented via an application builder tool.

Chapter 6, "Bean Examples," integrates some of the concepts that have been described in the preceding chapters. This is done by building several examples. First, a Bean is built that displays a sequence of images from a JAR file. Second, a set of components simulate the operation of instruments you would find in an electronics laboratory, such as a sine wave generator, meter, and plotter. Finally, a Bean to generate and display a moving 3-D surface is included as an example.

Chapter 7, "Bound and Constrained Properties," explains how bound and constrained properties provide a mechanism by which changes to properties in one Bean may be coordinated with other components. A brief overview of the HotJava™ Browser Beans from Sun Microsystems is also provided. These provide an excellent example of how to use bound properties.

Chapter 8, "Applets, Applications, and Beans," shows how to build Beans that are applets and how to build applications that use Beans from JAR files.

Chapter 9, "Property Editors and Customizers," discusses the process of developing custom property editors and customizers for a Bean. These can be very important to differentiate your product from that of a competitor.

Chapter 10, "Remote Method Invocation (RMI)," introduces the main concepts of RMI with some simple application examples. The chapter then presents a Bean that makes use of RMI to communicate with a server.

Chapter 11, "Building Multicast Beans," begins with some simple application examples to introduce the main concepts of multicast. It then presents some Beans that make use of multicast. For example, one Bean transmits random numbers that have a Gaussian distribution. Another Bean receives this data and plots the frequency distribution of the numbers. Over time, it makes a nice plot!

Chapter 12, "Internationalization," shows how to construct a Bean so that it can operate in different locales with minimum effort. The recent enhancements for dealing with text, date, time, and other locale-sensitive information are outlined. An example shows how to build a calendar viewer that displays month and day information in a locale-sensitive manner.

Chapter 13, "Building Electronic Mail Beans," demonstrates how Beans are built that act as SMTP and POP3 clients. There are also components that provide user interfaces for testing the SMTP and POP3 clients.

Chapter 14, "Integrating Key Concepts," shows how to write a very simple tool that can create and connect several Beans. This is an interesting case study of how to work with JAR files, write class loaders, use introspection, and design a user interface for such a tool.

What You'll Need

The instructions and examples in this book use the Java Developer Kit (JDK) and Bean Development Kit (BDK) from Sun Microsystems. These are available free-of-charge on the Web at **http://java.sun.com**. Several vendors provide development environments for working with Java software. It should be straightforward to apply the information in this book to those environments.

Code on the Web

The source code for all of the programs in this book is available free-of-charge on the Web at **http://www.osborne.com**. In addition, all supporting files such as image files and manifest template files are also available on that site. The code for each example is held in a separate subdirectory. This is consistent with the conventions used for naming Java packages.

CHAPTER 1

An Overview of JavaBeans

JavaBeans is the software component architecture for Java. It is an exciting and important new technology that allows you to efficiently construct applications by configuring and connecting components called *Beans*. You can create these reusable Beans or get them in binary form from vendors. In addition, these software building blocks need to be designed, coded, and tested only once. Then they can be reused in multiple applications. This approach substantially improves productivity and quality.

A Bean is a reusable software component written in Java.

A Bean is a software component written in Java that follows the JavaBeans specification. That standard defines the mechanisms by which components perform common tasks such as communicating with each other, interacting with tools, and saving/restoring their configuration. You will see in this book that although JavaBeans is a sophisticated and powerful software technology, it is straightforward to use. In fact, writing a Bean is no harder than creating any other type of Java program.

This chapter provides an overview of the JavaBeans technology. It begins by briefly describing the reuse and interoperability problems that have plagued the software industry for many years. Monolithic applications are compared with systems constructed from a set of components. An example is used to explain how properties, events, and methods are fundamental to understanding and using components. Another example outlines how a simple web browser can be built from free components that are available today. (A later chapter will tell you how to obtain these components.)

Any discussion of JavaBeans must also consider the builder tools that allow you to visually configure and connect a set of Beans to construct an application. The Bean Developer Kit (BDK) is an example of a very simple builder tool. It can be downloaded without charge from the JavaSoft web site (**http://java.sun.com**). You will see how to use this tool and some of the demonstration code that comes with it.

Finally, a summary of the major advantages of Java components is presented. This sets the stage for the detailed discussion that follows in the remaining chapters of the book.

 REMEMBER: This book assumes that you know how to program in Java. If you need to build your Java skills, we recommend *Java 1.1: The Complete Reference,* by Naughton and Schildt (Osborne/McGraw-Hill, 1998). It provides a comprehensive description of the Java language.

Background

Engineers who work with other technologies are able to select and purchase components from a paper or online catalog. These building blocks can be integrated to construct a system. For example, an electrical engineer who designs *hardware* systems can use discrete components (for example, resistors, capacitors, inductors) and integrated circuits (for example, digital signal processors, counters, multiplexers, digital/analog converters) to build a product. Someone knowledgeable about this technology can read the associated specifications and learn how the parts can be connected to provide a solution. The available components provide enough diversity of capability, cost, and size so it is unusual for expensive custom development to be required.

Unfortunately, *software* designers have been unable to achieve such benefits of reuse and interoperability. Until recently, there has not been a standard definition of what constitutes a software component. A common mechanism for connecting pieces of software had been lacking. The procedures to configure programs so they operate as desired in a particular application environment have been created ad hoc. Thus, the ways to store and retrieve this important configuration data can be different for each part of a system. Because of these incompatibilities, it had not been possible to use a builder tool to visually configure and interconnect software supplied by multiple vendors. JavaBeans remedies this situation.

Until JavaBeans was created, the programmer paid a stiff price to gain access to the world of component software. Competing technologies defined highly complex mechanisms by which components interacted. You will see in this book that Beans are considerably easier to work with than software built with other languages and architectures.

Software Components

Many software systems today are structured as large, monolithic applications. The situation is represented in Figure 1-1. That diagram shows a system that is composed of parts X, Y, and Z. These pieces interact with each other by using proprietary mechanisms. They are tightly joined. The connections among them are shown as thick lines to symbolize that these links are very difficult to change or enhance.

A system constructed with software components is represented in Figure 1-2. Here the system is composed of components C1 through C5. The arrows that

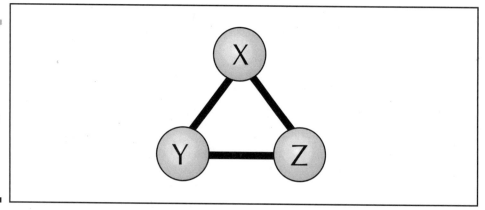

The connections between the pieces of a monolithic application are very difficult to change or enhance

Figure 1-1.

originate from a component represent events that it generates. These are objects that depict some state change in that component. Events are the standard mechanism by which objects interact. The arrows are shown as thin lines to indicate that it is easy to add additional components that should receive events. Components that receive an event are loosely coupled with the source of that event.

Do not make any assumptions about the appearance, capabilities, complexity, or size of a software component. A component such as a button is visible to a user, but a software timer is invisible. Components can be as simple as a label

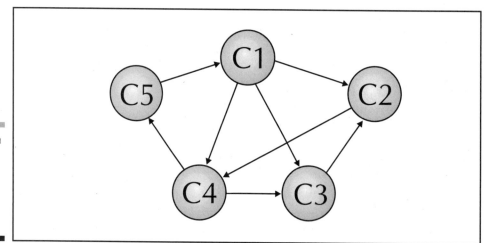

An application built with components can easily be modified

Figure 1-2.

that displays a string or as complex as software that encodes and decodes a multimedia stream in real time, or that uses artificial-intelligence techniques to filter large quantities of data and to make decisions.

Properties, Events, and Methods

Properties, events, and methods are fundamental to understanding and using components. This section outlines a simple example to explain these terms.

A *property* is a subset of a component's state. You may change the behavior of that component by modifying its properties. Consider a Bean that generates and displays a real-time graph to track incoming data. It may have a number of properties that determine exactly how that plot appears. Examples of properties include

A property describes some aspect of a component.

- ◆ Title of the graph
- ◆ Color, font style, and font size of the title
- ◆ Position of the title
- ◆ Labels used for the horizontal and vertical axes
- ◆ Color, font style, and font size of these axis labels
- ◆ Scale for the horizontal and vertical axes
- ◆ Style in which the data values are presented (dots, solid lines, dotted lines)
- ◆ Color used for the data points

Many other properties can be imagined that allow the user to control the behavior of that component so it operates as desired.

An *event* is a notification that is generated by a component when there is some change in its state. Consider a Quote Bean that receives real-time price information from a stock exchange and watches for changes in a specific security. When the price changes, the Bean generates an event and sends it to other components that need this information. For example, the Quote Bean can send events to the Graph Bean. Each of these event objects contains the latest price of the security.

An event is a notification generated by a component.

Methods can be invoked to execute code in a component. The Graph Bean has a method that can be invoked to add a new data point to the graph. This code receives the new value, adds it to its internal state, and updates the display.

To connect the Quote and Graph components, you must map the event generated by the Quote Bean to the appropriate method of the Graph Bean. In this manner, the real-time data received from the stock exchange can be monitored on a graph. The situation is represented here:

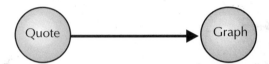

It is easy to add more components that can receive and process events. For example, it may be necessary to log the price data for later analysis. This can be done by sending events from the Quote Bean to both the Graph and Log Beans, as shown here:

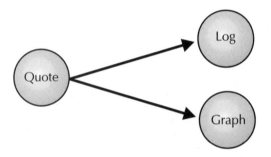

Note that the latter two components do not know about each other. Each performs a specific role in the overall application. The functionality provided by each of these components is generic, so it may be used in very different application environments.

In Chapter 3 of this book, you will see that user activities such as typing at the keyboard, dragging the mouse, or adjusting a scroll bar also generate events.

Introspection and Builder Tools

Assume that you have just downloaded a set of Beans from the Web and installed these on your computer. You now wish to configure these components and visually connect them to construct a working system. To do this you will use a builder tool. In addition to other things, the builder tool tells you about the properties, events, and methods provided by each of those

Beans. The builder tool uses a mechanism called *introspection* to obtain this information. Therefore, introspection is absolutely required for the JavaBeans technology.

In the previous section, we described how the Quote, Graph, and Log Beans could be integrated together. In that example, the tool would use introspection to identify their specific properties. You could then modify those properties to affect the behavior of that component. The tool would also use introspection to identify the events that can be generated by a component. Then you could map an event to a method invocation on another Bean.

Introspection is designed so minimal effort is required on the part of a Bean developer. Standard naming patterns are defined for properties, events, and methods. If these are followed, the introspection facilities work without any additional effort by you. A Bean developer also has the ability to explicitly designate which properties, events, and methods are presented by a builder tool. These techniques are explained later in this book.

Example: A Web Browser Built with Components

Let's consider a specific example to illustrate how an application can be built from components. Figure 1-3 outlines how a simple web browser might be constructed in this manner. There are five components shown in this diagram. These are described in the following list:

◆ The *HTML Parser and Renderer* can accept a Uniform Resource Locator (URL) and fetch the corresponding file from the Web. It can then parse this data and display the web page for a user. If the page is too large to fit in the available display area, scroll bars are automatically provided so the user can view the entire page. If the user clicks on a hyperlink, another page is fetched and displayed. Each time a new URL is fetched, an event is generated and sent to the History List and the Text Field. The HTML Parser and Renderer also maintains a cache of the most recently accessed pages.

◆ The *Text Field* allows a user to enter and edit a URL specification. When the ENTER key is pressed, an event is sent to the HTML Parser and Renderer. That event object contains the string typed by the user.

◆ The *History List* maintains an ordered list of the URLs that have been fetched and displayed by the HTML Parser and Renderer. These URLs are

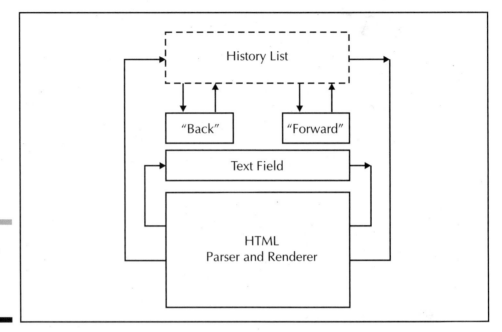

A simple
web browser
built with
components

Figure 1-3.

obtained from the events generated by the HTML Parser and Renderer. The History List also sends events to the buttons to enable or disable them based on its contents. (Figure 1-3 shows the History List with a dashed border because that component is an invisible Bean. It does not appear in the graphical user interface of this application.)

◆ One *Button* is labeled "Back." This allows a user to move backward in the sequence of pages maintained by the History List. An event is generated by this button and is received by the History List. In response to this event, the History List sends another event to the HTML Parser and Renderer directing it to display the page.

◆ Another *Button* is labeled "Forward." This allows a user to move forward in the sequence of pages maintained by the History List. An event is generated by this button and is received by the History List. In response to this event, the History List sends another event to the HTML Parser and Renderer directing it to display the page.

In this example, you can see that a very useful application has been put together by interconnecting a set of software components.

Another benefit of component software is that it is straightforward to enhance its functionality. Assume that we want to build a web browser that also accepts spoken commands. That is, a user can speak into the microphone on his or her PC and provide a desired URL, or tell the browser to move back or forward in the History List.

Figure 1-4 shows a set of six components that can provide this functionality. Five of these are identical to the previous diagram. In addition, a Speech-to-Text Converter accepts spoken input from the user and generates events that are sent either to the History List or to the HTML Parser and Renderer. If the user selects Back or Forward, an event is sent to the History List. Otherwise, an event is sent to the HTML Parser and Renderer. That event object contains the text equivalent of the speech input. The Speech-to-Text Converter is an invisible Bean.

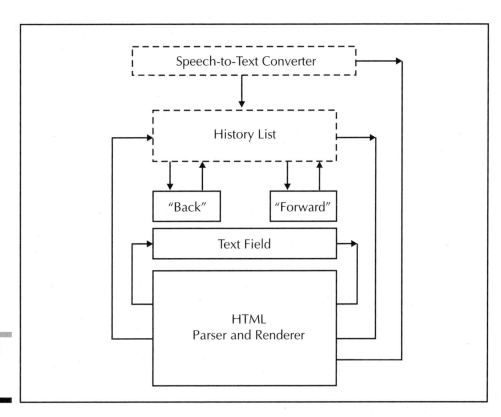

An enhanced
web browser

Figure 1-4.

In this example, you can see that there has been substantial software reuse. We were able to just "drop" the speech recognition component into our original design. The HTML Parser and Renderer, Text Field, History List, and Buttons are used unchanged from their previous application. Thus, it was possible to enhance the user interface provided by our simple browser by adding a component, rather than reengineering the entire application.

The trend to break down large monolithic applications into a set of components is an important one in the software industry today. This will make it possible to reuse major pieces of functionality such as the HTML parsing and rendering component.

The Bean Developer Kit (BDK)

The Bean Developer Kit (BDK) is a tool that may be downloaded free of charge from the JavaSoft site at **http://java.sun.com**. It allows you to configure and interconnect a set of Beans. Using it, you can change the properties of a Bean, link two or more Beans, and watch Beans execute. Therefore, the BDK provides an easy way for you to test Beans that you write and to explore the capabilities of Beans written by others. The BDK also includes a set of demonstration components and their source code. These are valuable examples from which you can learn. Since you will use the BDK extensively as you work your way through this book, an overview of the BDK and its use is given here.

NOTE: Several vendors also supply tools that allow you to work with Beans. The user interface for those utilities is different from that of the BDK. If you are using one of those products, you will need to consult its documentation to determine how to request the same operations. However, this should be straightforward. Our primary goal in this book is to teach you how to build Java software components. This information is applicable to any tool environment.

The BDK is a Java application. Therefore, it is necessary that you also install the Java Developer Kit (JDK) on your computer. Check that the JDK tools are accessible from your path. The BDK cannot work otherwise.

Also, the source code for the BDK itself is included in the set of files that you install on your computer. By studying that program, you can get some insight into how a builder tool is constructed.

In the sections that follow, several of the BDK's example Beans are examined. The same general mechanism that you use to connect and configure these Beans will also apply to Beans that you write.

NOTE: The instructions provided here are for a Windows 95/NT environment. Check the documentation on the JavaSoft site for details about other platforms. It is also assumed in this chapter that the BDK was installed in the default installation directory (that is, c:\bdk).

Starting the BDK

Follow these steps to start the BDK:

1. Type **cd c:\bdk\beanbox** to change to the correct directory.

2. Type **run** to execute a batch file that starts the BDK. The three windows shown in Figure 1-5 appear.

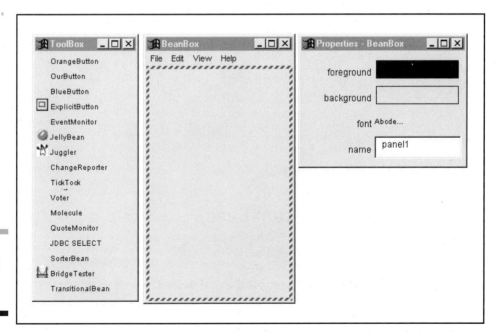

The Bean
Developer Kit
(BDK)

Figure 1-5.

The Duke logo is a trademark or registered trademark of Sun Microsystems, Inc. in the United States and other countries.

The ToolBox window lists the demonstration Beans that have been provided with the BDK. The BeanBox window provides an area in which you may connect these components. The Properties window provides an interface through which you may configure a Bean.

The Juggler Bean

The **Juggler** Bean presents an animation that shows the Java mascot doing a juggling act. Follow these steps to experiment with this component:

1. Position your cursor on the ToolBox entry labeled "Juggler," and click the left mouse button. Observe that the cursor changes to a cross.

2. Move the cursor to approximately the center of the BeanBox, and click the left mouse button. Observe that a rectangular area appears containing the animation. Also note that there is a hatched border surrounding this area. This indicates the Bean is currently selected and may be configured via the Properties window.

3. Move the cursor so it is positioned directly over the hatched border. Observe that the cursor now appears as two bidirectional arrows. This indicates you can reposition the Bean by pressing the left mouse button and dragging. Practice this technique until you are comfortable with it.

4. Observe that the Properties window presents five different properties for **Juggler**. For the moment, let's work with the **animationRate** property. Its default value is 125. Position the cursor in the text field for this property and change it to **60**. Observe that the Java mascot now juggles at a faster rate. This is a very important point: Changing a Bean property causes an immediate change in the behavior of that component. These are live components!

Figure 1-6 shows the BDK windows.

The OurButton Bean

The **OurButton** Bean provides a push button. Follow these steps to experiment with this component:

1. Create an instance of the **OurButton** Bean in the BeanBox.

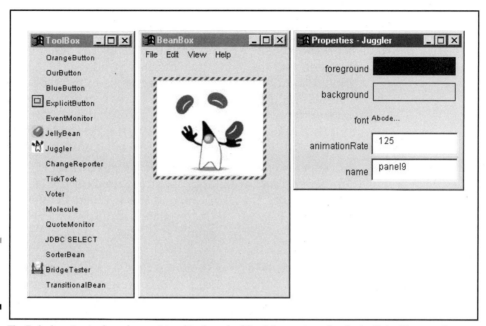

The Duke logo is a trademark or registered trademark of Sun Microsystems, Inc. in the United States and other countries.

2. The Properties window contains several properties that affect the behavior of the Bean. Let's experiment with changing some of these values. Place the cursor in the text field for the **label** property. Change the string from "press" to **stop**. Observe that the label on the button also changes.

3. The **background** and **foreground** properties determine the colors that are used to display the button. These properties are not represented as a text field, but are instead shown in the Properties window as rectangular regions filled with a specific color.

   To change the **background** property, position the cursor over the rectangular region, and click the left mouse button. A new dialog box titled "ColorEditor" appears, as shown here:

You can change the color by entering its red, green, and blue values in the text field. Alternatively, you can select a color from the choice element on the right side of the dialog box. In either case, observe that the small filled rectangle on the left side of the dialog box changes color. Also note that the colored rectangle in the Properties window representing the background color changes. Finally, the background color of the component in the BeanBox changes. When you are done with the ColorEditor dialog box, click the Done button to close it. Practice with this technique until you are comfortable with it.

Also experiment with changing the **foreground** property of the button. This determines the color of the string used for the label. The dialog box used to modify a property such as this is called a *custom property editor*. It provides an easy way to manipulate a property.

4. The **font** property determines the name, style, and size of the font that is used to display the button label. This property is not represented as a text field, but is instead shown in the Properties window as a rectangular region filled with some sample text presented in the selected font.

To change the **font** property, position the cursor over the rectangular region, and click the left mouse button. A new dialog box, FontEditor, appears.

You may modify the font name, style, or size by using the three choice elements in the dialog box. Observe that the size of the characters in the button increases and that the overall dimensions of the button expand to accommodate the larger text. When you are done with the FontEditor dialog box, click the Done button to close it.

Connecting the Juggler and OurButton Beans

Since the true power of Beans (and component software in general) is found when two or more are joined, this section describes how to build a simple application by connecting three Beans. Two instances of the **OurButton**

Bean are created. The first is labeled "Start," and the second is labeled "Stop." These are used to control the operation of the **Juggler** Bean. The buttons can generate several types of events. The type of event that is generated when the button is clicked is an *action event*. (You will learn about events in detail later in this book.) You need to map the action events generated by the **OurButton** Beans to method invocations on the **Juggler** Bean.

Follow these steps to perform this experiment:

1. Create an instance of the **Juggler** Bean in the BeanBox.
2. Create two instances of the **OurButton** Bean in the BeanBox. Change the **label** property of one button to **Start** and the other to **Stop**.
3. Click the left mouse button on the Stop button. This action selects that component and causes a hatched border to appear around it.
4. Select the Edit | Events | action | actionPerformed options from the BeanBox menu bar. When you make these selections and release the mouse button, a red line extends from the Stop button to the cursor position. As you move the cursor, one end of the red line moves to track its position. The other end remains fixed at the button.
5. Position the mouse inside the **Juggler** Bean, and click the left mouse button. A new dialog box, EventTargetDialog, appears (see Figure 1-7). Observe that it lists the public methods of the **Juggler** Bean.
6. Select the entry titled "stopJuggling," and click the OK button at the bottom of the dialog box. Observe that the dialog box disappears. A message box appears momentarily reporting that the tool is "Generating and compiling adapter class." The *adapter class* is the code that maps an action event from the button to a method invocation on the **Juggler** Bean.
7. Click the Stop button and observe that the animation stops.
8. Click the left mouse button on the Start button to select it. Map its action event to the startJuggling method of the **Juggler** Bean. The procedures to do this are similar to those you just followed for the Stop button.
9. Click the Start button and observe that the animation starts again.

The preceding example demonstrates the essence of component software. You were able to reuse two standard components (**Juggler** and **OurButton**). By connecting them, you formed a simple application. No matter how complex your component software applications grow, they utilize these basic concepts.

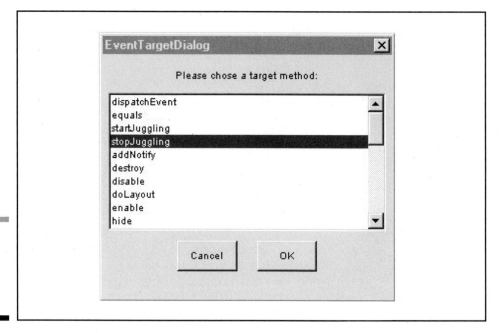

Selecting a
target method
of the **Juggler**
Bean

Figure 1-7.

The Molecule Bean

The **Molecule** Bean displays a visual representation of a molecule. The following substances are available: benzene, buckministerfullerine, cyclohexane, ethane, hyaluronic acid, and water. Follow these steps to experiment with this component:

1. Create an instance of the **Molecule** Bean in the BeanBox.
2. The Properties window allows you to configure this component. It has a choice element that allows you to select a value for the **moleculeName** property. Choose a different entry, and observe that the Bean's appearance also changes. Figure 1-8 shows the appearance of the BDK windows.

The TickTock Bean

The **TickTock** Bean generates an event at regular intervals. These events can be mapped to method invocations on other Beans. In this manner, **TickTock** can be used as a type of sequencer or timer to cause other Beans

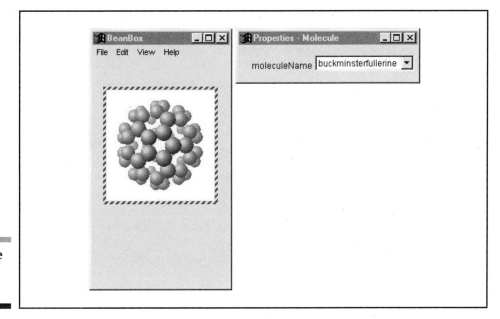

The **Molecule**
Bean
Figure 1-8.

to perform actions at regular intervals. Follow these steps to experiment with this component:

1. Create an instance of the **TickTock** Bean in the BeanBox. Unlike the other Beans we have looked at so far, the function of **TickTock** is not to act as an element in a graphical user interface. Therefore, it does not provide a visual representation of itself. For the component to be visible in the BeanBox, the BDK generates a visual representation of it. This consists of a rectangular region that contains the name of the Bean (that is, "TickTock"). A Bean such as this is called an *invisible Bean*. You may hide invisible components by selecting View | Hide Invisible Beans from the BeanBox menu bar. Choose View | Show Invisible Beans to make such components visible.

2. Observe that the Properties window presents only one property for this component. The **interval** property determines the number of seconds that elapse between the events fired by this Bean. The type of event generated by this component is known as a *property change event*.

Figure 1-9 shows the BDK windows.

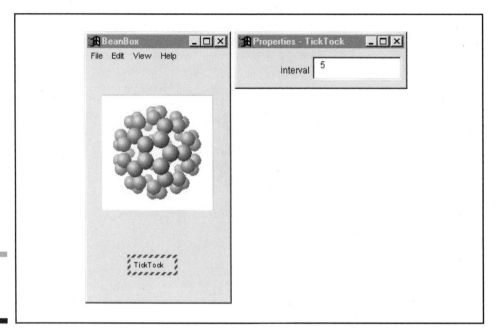

Connecting the Molecule and TickTock Beans

This section presents another example that shows how to connect several Beans to build an application. Two instances of the **TickTock** Bean are created. These fire events to a **Molecule** Bean that cause it to rotate its molecule in space. One instance of **TickTock** causes rotation about the X axis, and the other causes rotation about the Y axis. Follow these steps to perform this experiment:

1. Create an instance of the **Molecule** Bean.

2. Create two instances of the **TickTock** Bean.

3. Select one of the **TickTock** components. Select the Edit I Events I propertyChange I propertyChange options from the BeanBox menu bar. A red line extends from the **TickTock** component to the cursor position.

4. Position the mouse inside the **Molecule** Bean, and click the left mouse button. A new dialog box, EventTargetDialog, appears. Select the entry titled "rotateOnX," and click the OK button at the bottom of the dialog box. The dialog box disappears and an adapter class is generated.

5. Observe that the molecule slowly rotates about one of its axes.

6. Select the other **TickTock** component. Adjust its **interval** property to **2**. Map its property change events to the rotateOnY method of the **Molecule** Bean.

7. Observe that the molecule now slowly rotates about both the X and Y axes.

The Benefits of Java Components

The following list summarizes the primary benefits of constructing components in Java. It provides a preview of the topics that are fully addressed in the remaining chapters of the book.

◆ A Bean has all the benefits of the "write once, run anywhere™" paradigm that is the foundation of Java.

◆ A set of Beans, supporting classes, and associated resources can be packaged into a Java Archive (JAR) file. This provides a convenient mechanism to deliver software components to users.

◆ A builder tool can use introspection to dynamically determine the properties, events, and methods that are provided by a software component. This makes it possible for you to install Beans on your machine and to connect them with other components.

◆ A Bean developer can explicitly control the properties, events, and methods that are presented to the user via a builder tool. This helps the user focus on the essential features of your component and not be distracted or confused by other capabilities.

◆ Property editors and customizers can be provided for users. These help a user configure a complex component. Providing an outstanding user interface for these items is one way that a Bean developer can differentiate his or her product from competitors' products.

◆ Standard mechanisms are used to save the state of a Bean to a file. This information can later be retrieved. This is essential for saving the configuration information of a Bean.

◆ A component can be designed so it operates correctly in different locales. The strings used to communicate with the user can be correct for that region or culture. The conventions used to format date, time, numbers, and currency can be followed. This makes a Bean usable by an international audience.

◆ A Bean can be written that provides access to legacy code. This makes it possible to build applications that combine functionality written in Java with existing systems.

◆ A Bean can cooperate with other distributed software by using the networking classes. In addition, distributed components can use sockets, Remote Method Invocation (RMI), or other technologies to communicate with each other.

◆ Components developed as JavaBeans can be integrated with software built with other architectures such as CORBA (Common Object Request Broker Architecture) and ActiveX.

CHAPTER 2

Building
Simple Beans

This chapter discusses the essential features of a Bean and shows you how to build several simple ones. Although Beans have significant similarities to applets, Beans must fulfill several additional requirements. For example, Beans must support the introspection mechanism. Also, the precise procedure that you will use to build and test Beans is a little different than that used to develop applets. Even though the Beans described in this chapter are quite simple, they illustrate the foundation of Beans programming, so a careful reading is advised.

The chapter begins by constructing a simple Bean. Instructions are provided to lead you step-by-step through the entire process of building, packaging, and testing a Java software component. Next, the introspection mechanism is introduced. As explained in Chapter 1, this feature can dynamically examine a Bean and determine its properties. The easiest way to support introspection is to follow the simple naming conventions described here.

Next, four more example Beans are presented. In some cases, the code developed here is integrated with Beans introduced in the previous chapter. After you have seen these examples, we can begin to discuss the distinction between a Bean and any other class.

Finally, Java Archive (JAR) files are discussed in detail. JAR files are important because tools such as the BDK require that Beans be stored in JAR files. The JDK provides a command-line utility called **jar** to create and manage these archive files. Several examples are presented here to illustrate the use of this tool.

Your First Bean

Before discussing any theory, let's build a simple Bean. This section leads you step-by-step through the process of constructing a Bean called **Spectrum**. The component displays a square 100 pixels wide and 100 pixels high, and fills it with the colors of the spectrum. The component has one **boolean** property named **vertical**. If this property is **true**, the colors are arranged in a vertical direction. Otherwise, the colors are oriented in a horizontal direction.

Follow the instructions in the following sections to develop and test this Bean.

Create a Directory for the Bean

Create a directory named **spectrum** anywhere on your computer.

Create the Source Code

Enter the source code shown in the listing at the end of this section. You must name this file **Spectrum.java** and place it in the spectrum directory. The package statement at the beginning of the file places this class in a package named **spectrum**. (Each example in this book is placed in its own package to avoid naming conflicts.)

The class is named **Spectrum** and is a subclass of **Canvas**. The private boolean variable named **vertical** is one of its properties. The constructor initializes that property to **true** and sets the size of the component.

NOTE: Every Bean must have a zero-argument constructor. The builder tool creates an instance of the component by using that constructor.

The methods to access the property are **getVertical( )** and **setVertical( )**. Because the property itself is a private instance variable, code outside this class does not have direct access to that data. Instead, all reads and writes of the data can only be done through these access methods. Note that when the property is changed via the **setVertical( )** method, the **repaint( )** method is invoked to update the display.

The **paint( )** method fills the square with the colors of the spectrum. A specific color can be uniquely represented by its hue, saturation, and brightness. Each of these parameters is a **float** and ranges from 0.0 to 1.0f. In this code, the saturation and brightness are set to 1.0f and the hue is varied from 0.0 to 1.0f. This is the mechanism used to compute the complete range of colors.

The **getSize( )** method is invoked to determine the dimensions of this Bean. The **vertical** property is then checked to determine if the colors should change in the vertical or horizontal dimension.

If **vertical** is **true**, the square is filled by drawing horizontal lines of different colors. The hue of each line is calculated by scaling its y coordinate to a value between 0.0 and 1.0f. The **getHSBColor( )** static method of the **Color** class accepts hue, saturation, and brightness parameters for a color and returns a reference to a **Color** object. That object is used to set the current color of the graphics context. Then a horizontal line of that color is drawn.

If **vertical** is **false**, the square is filled by drawing vertical lines of different colors. The logic to do this is analogous to that described in the previous paragraph, except that the hue of each line is calculated by scaling its x coordinate to a value between 0.0 and 1.0f.

```java
package spectrum;
import java.awt.*;

public class Spectrum extends Canvas {
  private boolean vertical;

  public Spectrum() {
    vertical = true;
    setSize(100, 100);
  }

  public boolean getVertical() {
    return vertical;
  }

  public void setVertical(boolean vertical) {
    this.vertical = vertical;
    repaint();
  }

  public void paint(Graphics g) {
    float saturation = 1.0f;
    float brightness = 1.0f;
    Dimension d = getSize();
    if(vertical) {
      for(int y = 0; y < d.height; y++) {
        float hue = (float)y/(d.height - 1);
        g.setColor(Color.getHSBColor(hue, saturation, brightness));
        g.drawLine(0, y, d.width - 1, y);
      }
    }
    else {
      for(int x = 0; x < d.width; x++) {
        float hue = (float)x/(d.width - 1);
        g.setColor(Color.getHSBColor(hue, saturation, brightness));
        g.drawLine(x, 0, x, d.height - 1);
      }
    }
  }
```

```
      }
  }
```

Compile the Source Code

Change to the parent directory of spectrum and type

    javac spectrum\Spectrum.java

Check that the .class file has been created in the spectrum directory.

 NOTE: Each code example in this book exists in a separate package. Java requires that the directory hierarchy mirror the package hierarchy. Therefore, you must always be in the parent directory when compiling a code example with **javac** or executing an application with **java**. Your **CLASSPATH** environment variable must include this parent directory. This is necessary so the .class files can be found.

Create the Manifest Template File

All Beans must be specified in a manifest template file. This file is used in the next step by the tool that packages your Bean into a JAR file. In this example, you must create a manifest template file in order to indicate that Spectrum.class is a Bean. The contents of this file are shown in the following listing. Note that a manifest template file always uses forward slashes in the path name of a file. Name the file **spectrum.mft** and place it in the spectrum directory.

```
Name: spectrum/Spectrum.class
Java-Bean: True
```

Manifest files are examined in detail at the end of this chapter. Briefly, a *manifest template file* is the basis for a manifest file, which is the first element in a JAR file and describes its contents.

In the next chapter, you will see how to package several Beans into one JAR file. In those situations, the manifest template file includes a separate entry for each Bean.

NOTE: Each code example in this book exists in a separate directory. For convenience, the manifest template file (if any) for that example is also located in the same directory. Its prefix is the same as the directory name. For example, spectrum.mft is located in the spectrum directory. However, this naming convention is not required by the **jar** utility.

Create a JAR File

All Beans must be stored within a JAR (Java Archive) file. Change to the parent directory of spectrum and enter the following command to create a JAR file containing the **Spectrum** Bean:

```
jar cfm c:\bdk\jars\spectrum.jar spectrum\*.mft spectrum\*.class
```

This command creates a JAR file named spectrum.jar and places it in the C:\bdk\jars directory. This is the directory in which the BDK looks for JAR files. The manifest template file and the .class files in the spectrum directory are used. Later in this chapter we will examine JAR files in detail.

Start the BDK

Type **cd c:\bdk\beanbox** to get to the appropriate directory. Then type **run** to start the BDK. You should see the Toolbox, BeanBox, and Properties windows. Toolbox should have an entry labeled "Spectrum."

Test the Spectrum Bean

Create an instance of **Spectrum** in the BeanBox. You should see a square with the colors of the spectrum oriented in a vertical direction. Figure 2-1 shows how your component should appear.

Use the Properties window to change the **vertical** property to **false**. Observe that the display changes immediately. You may create several instances of Spectrum in BeanBox. The **vertical** property for each can be changed independently.

The Properties window also presents several other properties for this Bean (for example, **background**, **foreground**, and **font**). These properties are defined by the **Component** class. Since our Bean is a subclass of **Component**, it also has these properties. However, the values of these properties are not relevant to this Bean because it completely fills the square

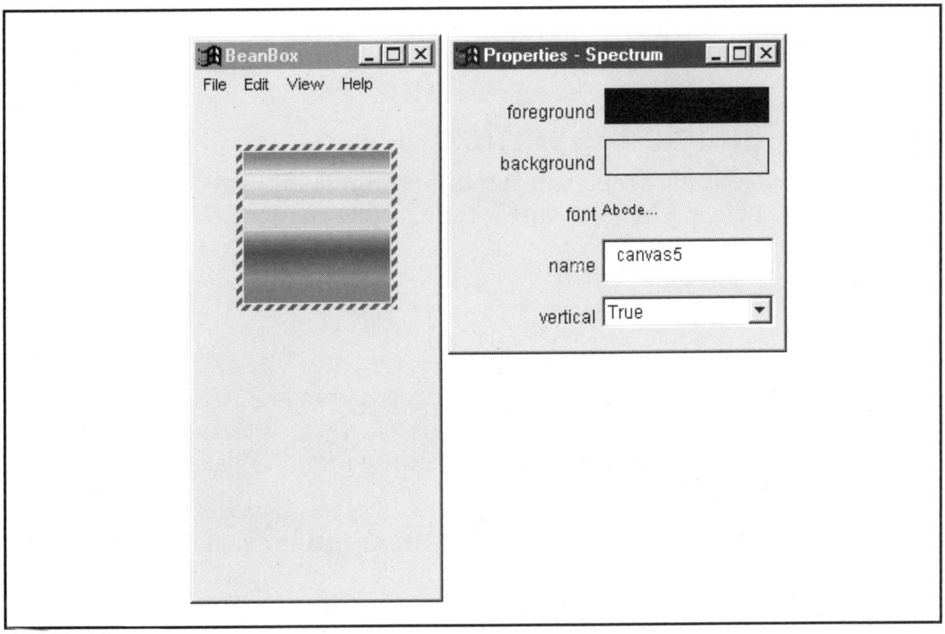

The **Spectrum**
Bean
Figure 2-1.

with colors and does not display text. (In Chapter 5 you will see how a Bean developer can explicitly specify which properties are presented to a user by a builder tool.)

In this example, the BDK used introspection to examine your new Bean and to automatically infer that **vertical** was one of its properties. This was possible because the access methods **getVertical( )** and **setVertical( )** followed a simple naming pattern. The next section describes these conventions.

Introspection Naming Conventions

As noted in the previous chapter, a property is a subset of a Bean's state. You may affect the behavior of a component by changing its value. The previous chapter described how this is done via the Properties window of the BDK.

The BDK uses the process of introspection to determine the properties of a Bean. The JavaSoft designers made this process very simple. If you follow some rules for naming the methods that read and write properties, the introspection facilities can examine your Bean and determine the names of its properties. This section describes these conventions. It defines simple,

boolean, and indexed properties and provides an example to illustrate each of these.

Simple Properties

A simple property refers to a single value.

A simple property contains one value that may be either a simple type or an object. The following naming patterns are used for its access methods:

public *T* get*N*( )

public void set*N*(*T value*)

Here, *T* is the type of the property and *N* is its name. A property typically has both of these access methods. However, a read-only property has only the **get*N*( )** method and a write-only property has only the **set*N*( )** method.

The following listing shows a class that has three read/write simple **float** properties named **amplitude**, **frequency**, and **phase**.

```
public class SignalGenerator {
  private float amplitude, frequency, phase;

  public SignalGenerator() {
    amplitude = 0f;
    frequency = 100f;
    phase = 0f;
  }

  public float getAmplitude() {
    return amplitude;
  }

  public void setAmplitude(float amplitude) {
    this.amplitude = amplitude;
  }

  public float getFrequency() {
    return frequency;
  }

  public void setFrequency(float frequency) {
    this.frequency = frequency;
  }
```

2

```
public float getPhase() {
  return phase;
}

public void setPhase(float phase) {
  this.phase = phase;
}
}
```

Boolean Properties

A *boolean*
property may be
true or **false**.

A **boolean** property contains one value that may be either **true** or **false**. The following naming patterns are used for its access methods:

public boolean is*N*( )

public boolean get*N*( )

public void set*N*(boolean *value*)

Here, *N* is the name of the property. The first or second form can be used to read the property. (If both exist, the first is used.) The third form is used to write the property. A read-only property has only the **is*N*( )** and/or **get*N*( )** method. A write-only property has only the **set*N*( )** method.

The following listing shows a class that has one read/write **boolean** property named **open**.

```
public class Switch {
  private boolean open;

  public Switch() {
    open = true;
  }

  public boolean isOpen() {
    return open;
  }

  public boolean getOpen() {
    return open;
  }

  public void setOpen(boolean open) {
```

```
    this.open = open;
  }
}
```

Indexed Properties

An indexed property contains several values that may be either simple types or objects. The following naming patterns are used for its access methods:

public *T* getN(int *index*)

public *T*[ ] getN( )

public void setN(int *index*, *T value*)

public void setN(*T values*[ ])

Here, *T* is the type of the property and *N* is its name. The first form reads one value where *index* identifies which entry is wanted. All values may be retrieved with the second form. The third form writes one value. The argument *index* identifies which entry to change, and the argument *value* is the new value for that property. All values may be updated with the fourth form. The argument *values* is an array that contains the new values for the property. A read-only property has only the **getN( )** method, and a write-only property has only the **setN( )** method.

The following class has an indexed property named **inputs**.

```
public class Decoder {
  private final static int NUMINPUTS = 16;
  private boolean inputs[];

  public Decoder() {
    inputs = new boolean[NUMINPUTS];
    for(int i = 0; i < NUMINPUTS; i++) {
      inputs[i] = false;
    }
  }

  public boolean getInputs(int index) {
    return inputs[index];
  }

  public boolean[ ] getInputs() {
```

```
      return inputs;
  }

  public void setInputs(int index, boolean value) {
    inputs[index] = value;
  }

  public void setInputs(boolean values[]) {
    inputs = values;
  }
}
```

NOTE: The Properties window of the BDK does not handle indexed properties. However, as shown in Chapter 9, you can build custom property editors or customizers so the user can do this.

More Simple Beans

Now that you know how to build a Bean and understand the introspection naming conventions, let's look at several more example Beans.

The Text Bean

This section describes a Bean that displays a string. It has several properties. The **boolean** property **border** indicates if a box is drawn around the string. The **String** property **message** is the text to be displayed. The **Font** property **font** determines the font that is used. The appearance and size of the Bean change dynamically as these properties are modified.

The following listing shows the source code for this Bean. It is placed in a package named **text** and is a subclass of **Canvas**. There are two **int** constants, **XPAD** and **YPAD**, that define the space in pixels between the text and border. The instance variables **message** and **border** are the properties. (The **font** property is handled by the **Component** class.)

The constructor initializes **message** to "Hello". There are access methods for the **border** and **message** properties. Note that when the **message** property is modified, the **adjustSize( )** method is invoked. A method **setFont( )** is called when that property is updated. Note that it calls the **setFont( )** method of its superclass. This is needed so that the appropriate code in the

Component superclass is invoked. The **adjustSize( )** method is also invoked when **font** is modified because this action may affect the size of the Bean.

The **getPreferredSize( )** method returns a **Dimension** object that indicates the preferred size of the Bean. The method begins by getting the current **Graphics** and **FontMetrics** objects. The **stringWidth( )** method of the **FontMetrics** object is used to obtain the width of the **message** property in pixels. Its **getHeight( )** method is used to obtain the height of the **message** property in pixels. By use of some simple calculations, the overall preferred size of the component is calculated and returned.

The **adjustSize( )** method is used to change the size of the Bean. It begins by calling the **getPreferredSize( )** method to obtain the desired dimensions. This data is then used to provide arguments to the **setSize( )** method. To cause this component to actually change its appearance and size, the container in which this Bean exists must be issued commands to lay out its components. The **getParent( )** method returns the component that contains this Bean. The **invalidate( )** and **doLayout( )** methods are called to cause the necessary layout operations to occur. (The **adjustSize( )** method is also used for other examples in this book.)

The **paint( )** method displays the **message** property by calling the **drawString( )** method. It then checks the **border** property to determine if the **drawRect( )** method should be called to draw a border around this text.

```
package text;
import java.awt.*;

public class Text extends Canvas {
  private final static int XPAD = 10;
  private final static int YPAD = 10;
  private String message;
  private boolean border;

  public Text() {
    message = "Hello";
  }

  public boolean getBorder() {
    return border;
  }

  public void setBorder(boolean border) {
```

2

```java
    this.border = border;
    repaint();
  }

  public void setFont(Font font) {
    super.setFont(font);
    adjustSize();
  }

  public String getMessage() {
    return message;
  }
  public void setMessage(String message) {
    this.message = message;
    adjustSize();
  }

  public Dimension getPreferredSize() {
    Graphics g = getGraphics();
    FontMetrics fm = g.getFontMetrics();
    int w = fm.stringWidth(message) + 2 * XPAD;
    int h = fm.getHeight() + 2 * YPAD;
    return new Dimension(w, h);
  }

  private void adjustSize() {
    Dimension d = getPreferredSize();
    setSize(d.width, d.height);
    Component parent = getParent();
    if(parent != null) {
      parent.invalidate();
      parent.doLayout();
    }
  }

  public void paint(Graphics g) {
    Dimension d = getSize();
    int w = d.width;
    int h = d.height;
    FontMetrics fm = g.getFontMetrics();
    int x = (d.width - fm.stringWidth(message))/2;
    int y = (d.height + fm.getMaxAscent() -
      fm.getMaxDescent())/2;
    g.drawString(message, x, y);
    if(border) {
```

```
        g.drawRect(0, 0, w - 1, h - 1);
      }
   }
}
```

Follow the same sequence of steps as described for the **Spectrum** Bean: compile the source code, create a manifest template file, create a JAR file, start the BDK, and create an instance of your component.

Figure 2-2 shows how your Bean should look after changing the text string.

The Greeting Bean

This section describes a Bean that displays a greeting. The string that is presented depends on the current time. For example, in the afternoon, "Good afternoon" might be displayed.

The component has several properties. The **boolean** property **border** indicates if a box is drawn around the greeting. The **String** property **morning** is presented if the current time is between midnight and noon. The **String** property **afternoon** is presented if the current time is between noon and 7 P.M. Otherwise, the **String** property **evening** is presented. As in the previous example, a **Font** property **font** also exists. The appearance and size of the Bean changes dynamically as these properties are modified.

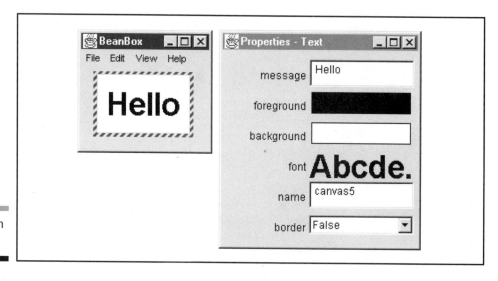

The **Text** Bean

Figure 2-2.

The following listing shows the source code for this Bean. It is placed in a package named **greeting** and is a subclass of **Canvas**. The instance variables **morning**, **afternoon**, **evening**, and **border** are properties. (The other properties are handled by the **Component** class.)

The constructor initializes the instance variables. The access methods read and write the properties and invoke the **adjustSize( )** method when any property is changed. The **getPreferredSize( )** method is similar to that of the previous example, except that the **selectGreeting( )** method is used to select the appropriate greeting based on the current time. The **adjustSize( )** method is identical to that of the previous example. The **paint( )** method is similar.

```java
package greeting;
import java.awt.*;
import java.util.*;

public class Greeting extends Canvas {
   private final static int XPAD = 10;
   private final static int YPAD = 10;
   private String morning, afternoon, evening;
   private boolean border;

   public Greeting() {
     morning = "Good morning";
     afternoon = "Good afternoon";
     evening = "Good evening";
     border = true;
   }

   public String getMorning() {
     return morning;
   }

   public void setMorning(String morning) {
     this.morning = morning;
     adjustSize();
   }

   public String getAfternoon() {
     return afternoon;
   }

   public void setAfternoon(String afternoon) {
```

```
    this.afternoon = afternoon;
    adjustSize();
}

public String getEvening() {
  return evening;
}

public void setEvening(String evening) {
    this.evening = evening;
    adjustSize();
}

public boolean getBorder() {
  return border;
}

public void setBorder(boolean border) {
    this.border = border;
    repaint();
}

public void setFont(Font font) {
    super.setFont(font);
    adjustSize();
}

public Dimension getPreferredSize() {
    Graphics g = getGraphics();
    FontMetrics fm = g.getFontMetrics();
    int w = fm.stringWidth(selectGreeting()) + 2*XPAD;
    int h = fm.getHeight() + 2*YPAD;
    return new Dimension(w, h);
}

private void adjustSize() {
    Dimension d = getPreferredSize();
    setSize(d.width, d.height);
    Component parent = getParent();
    if(parent != null) {
      parent.invalidate();
      parent.doLayout();
    }
}
```

2

```
public void paint(Graphics g) {
  String greeting = selectGreeting();
  Dimension d = getSize();
  FontMetrics fm = g.getFontMetrics();
  int x = (d.width - fm.stringWidth(greeting))/2;
  int y = (d.height + fm.getMaxAscent() -
    fm.getMaxDescent())/2;
  g.drawString(greeting, x, y);
  if(border) {
    g.drawRect(0, 0, d.width - 1, d.height - 1);
  }
}

private String selectGreeting() {
  Calendar calendar = Calendar.getInstance();
  int hour = calendar.get(Calendar.HOUR_OF_DAY);
  if(hour < 12) {
    return morning;
  }
  else if(hour < 19) {
    return afternoon;
  }
  else {
    return evening;
  }
}
}
```

Follow the same sequence of steps as described for the **Spectrum** Bean: compile the source code, create a manifest template file, create a JAR file, start the BDK, and create an instance of your component.

Figure 2-3 shows how your Bean should appear. The string that appears depends on the current time.

The Counter Bean

This section describes a Bean that acts as a counter. There are four methods that control its operation. First, **increment( )** increases the value by one. Second, **reset( )** sets the value to zero. Third, **stop( )** causes the Bean to ignore any subsequent requests to increment the value. Finally, **start( )** causes the Bean to process any subsequent requests to increment the value.

The only properties of the Bean are those inherited from the **Component** class. Note that the background and foreground colors of the **Counter** Bean

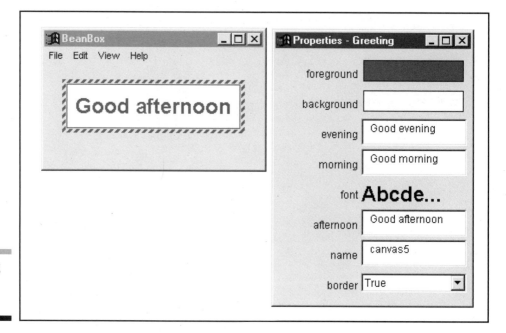

can be changed. The font used to display the counter value can also be changed. This causes the overall size of the Bean to adjust to contain the text.

The following listing shows the source code for this Bean. It is placed in a package named **counter** and is a subclass of **Canvas**. There are two **int** constants, **XPAD** and **YPAD**, to define the space in pixels between the text and border. The **int** instance variable **count** contains the value to be displayed. The **boolean** instance variable **operate** affects the behavior of the **increment( )** method. The constructor initializes these variables.

The **reset( )** method sets **count** to zero and invokes **repaint( )**. The **start( )** and **stop( )** methods set **operate** to **true** and **false**, respectively. The **increment( )** method also invokes **adjustSize( )** and **repaint( )** to update the display if **operate** is **true**. The **getPreferredSize( )**, **adjustSize( )**, and **paint( )** methods are similar to the code seen in the previous examples.

```
package counter;
import java.awt.*;

public class Counter extends Canvas {
```

```
private final static int XPAD = 10;
private final static int YPAD = 10;
private int count;
private boolean operate;

public Counter() {
  count = 0;
  operate = true;
}

public void reset() {
  count = 0;
  repaint();
}

public void start( ) {
  operate = true;
}

public void stop() {
  operate = false;
}

public synchronized void increment() {
  if(operate) {
    ++count;
    adjustSize();
    repaint();
  }
}

public void setFont(Font font) {
  super.setFont(font);
  adjustSize();
}

public Dimension getPreferredSize() {
  Graphics g = getGraphics();
  FontMetrics fm = g.getFontMetrics();
  int w = fm.stringWidth("" + count) + 2 * XPAD;
  int h = fm.getHeight() + 2 * YPAD;
  return new Dimension(w, h);
}

private void adjustSize() {
```

```
    Dimension d = getPreferredSize();
    setSize(d.width, d.height);
    Component parent = getParent();
    if(parent != null) {
      parent.invalidate();
      parent.doLayout();
    }
  }

  public void paint(Graphics g) {
    Dimension d = getSize();
    FontMetrics fm = g.getFontMetrics();
    int x = (d.width - fm.stringWidth("" + count))/2;
    int y = (d.height + fm.getMaxAscent() -
      fm.getMaxDescent())/2;
    g.drawString("" + count, x, y);
    g.drawRect(0, 0, d.width - 1, d.height - 1);
  }
}
```

To experiment with the **Counter** Bean, use the **TickTock** and **OurButton**
Beans to control its operation.

Create an instance of the **TickTock** and **Counter** components in the
BeanBox. Map the property change events generated by **TickTock** to the
increment( ) method of **Counter**. You should see the value increase.
Modify the **interval** property of **TickTock** and change its value from
5 to 1. Observe that the count increases at a faster rate.

Now create three instances of the **OurButton** Bean. Change their labels to
Reset, **Start**, and **Stop**. Map the action events generated by these buttons
to the **reset( )**, **start( )**, and **stop( )** methods of **Counter**.

If you click the Reset button, the count changes to zero but then continues to
increment. The Stop button causes the counter to maintain its value until the
Start button is clicked.

Figure 2-4 shows how your Bean should appear.

The StockWatcher Bean

This section describes a Bean that retrieves and displays the current price of a
stock. In addition to the Bean, a simple Java application that generates
simulated stock prices is described. This is an example of a Bean that uses
sockets to communicate with another application.

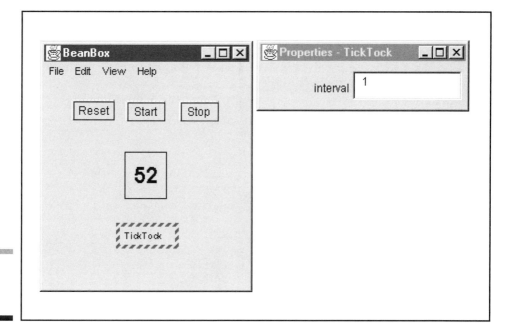

The **Counter**
Bean
Figure 2-4.

There are three properties that control its operation. First, **hostname** is a **String** containing the name or address of the machine from which the simulated stock data can be obtained. Second, **port** is a **String** identifying the software port on that machine. Third, **symbol** is a **String** identifying the stock.

In addition, the Bean inherits properties from the **Component** class. Specifically, the background and foreground colors can be changed. The font used to display information can also be changed. This causes the overall size of the Bean to adjust to contain the text.

The following listing shows the source code for this Bean. It is placed in a package named **stock** and is a subclass of **Panel**. Two instance variables hold references to **Label** objects. These are **symbolData** and **priceData**. String variables **hostname**, **port**, and **symbol** contain the property values. The constructor initializes all of these instance variables. A 2x2 grid layout is used to arrange the labels.

The **refresh( )** method provides the main processing of this Bean. It creates a **Socket** object to communicate with the remote application that has the simulated stock price information. The **hostname** and **port** properties are used to calculate the arguments to the **Socket** constructor. Input and output streams are obtained for the socket. **BufferedReader** and **PrintWriter** objects are then created from these streams. A message containing the symbol of the desired stock is sent to the server. The server returns a message with the price. This data is passed as an argument to the **setText( )** method of the **priceData** object.

```java
package stock;
import java.awt.*;
import java.io.*;
import java.net.*;

public class StockWatcher extends Panel {
  private Label symbolData, priceData;
  private String hostname, port, symbol;

  public StockWatcher() {
    setFont(new Font("Helvetica", Font.BOLD, 18));
    setLayout(new GridLayout(2, 2, 5, 5));
    Label symbolLabel = new Label("Symbol:", Label.RIGHT);
    add(symbolLabel);
    symbolData = new Label("");
    add(symbolData);
    Label priceLabel = new Label("Price:", Label.RIGHT);
    add(priceLabel);
    priceData = new Label("");
    add(priceData);
    hostname = port = symbol = "";
  }

  public String getHostname() {
    return hostname;
  }

  public void setHostname(String hostname) {
    this.hostname = hostname;
  }

  public String getPort() {
    return port;
  }

  public void setPort(String port) {
    this.port = port;
  }
```

```
public String getSymbol() {
  return symbol;
}

public void setSymbol(String symbol) {
  this.symbol = symbol;
  repaint();
}

public void paint(Graphics g) {
  Dimension d = getSize();
  g.drawRect(0, 0, d.width - 1, d.height - 1);
  symbolData.setText(symbol);
}

public Insets getInsets() {
  return new Insets(5, 5, 5, 5);
}

public void refresh() {
  try {
    Socket socket =
      new Socket(hostname, Integer.parseInt(port));
    InputStream is = socket.getInputStream();
    OutputStream os = socket.getOutputStream();
    PrintWriter pw = new PrintWriter(os, true);
    pw.println(symbol);
    BufferedReader br =
      new BufferedReader(new InputStreamReader(is));
    String line = br.readLine();
    priceData.setText(line);
    socket.close();
  }
  catch(Exception ex) {
    ex.printStackTrace();
  }
}
}
```

The code for the server is shown in the following listing. It opens a server socket on port 5000 and waits for an incoming request. (The selection of port 5000 is arbitrary.) A request contains the stock symbol. This data is passed to the **getInstance( )** static method of the **Stock** class. It returns a reference to the **Stock** object corresponding to that symbol. The **getPrice( )** instance method is used to obtain the price of the stock. This value is written back to the Bean via the **println( )** method of the **PrintWriter** object.

```
package stock;
import java.io.*;
import java.net.*;

public class StockServerApp {
  private final static int PORT = 5000;

  public static void main(String args[]) {
    try {
      ServerSocket ssocket = new ServerSocket(PORT);
      while(true) {
        Socket socket = ssocket.accept();
        InputStream is = socket.getInputStream();
        BufferedReader br =
          new BufferedReader(new InputStreamReader(is));
        OutputStream os = socket.getOutputStream();
        PrintWriter pw = new PrintWriter(os, true);
        String symbol = br.readLine();
        Stock stock = Stock.getInstance(symbol);
        if(stock != null) {
          pw.println("" + stock.getPrice());
        }
        socket.close();
      }
    }
    catch(Exception ex) {
      ex.printStackTrace();
    }
  }
}
```

Finally, the next listing contains the code for the **Stock** class. The class has one static variable named **stocks**. This holds a reference to a **Vector** object that contains references to all **Stock** objects that are created. (This technique of having the class keep track of its instances is commonly used in object-oriented programming.) There is one static method called **getInstance( )**. It accepts one **String** argument that is the symbol of the desired stock and returns a **Stock** object. If a **Stock** object already exists with that symbol, the **change( )** instance method is called to update its price. If a **Stock** object does not already exist with that symbol, such an object is created.

2

The **Stock** constructor initializes the symbol and price instance variables for that object. A random value is chosen for the price. Notice that the fractional component of the price is some multiple of 1/8. The last line of the constructor adds this object to the **stocks** vector that is a static variable of the class. This is the mechanism that allows the class to keep track of its instances.

The **change( )** method introduces some variability in the price. It is invoked each time a request is handled. The change in price is between −10 percent and +10 percent. Again, the fractional component of the price is some multiple of 1/8.

```
package stock;
import java.util.*;

public class Stock {
  private static Vector stocks = new Vector();
  private String symbol;
  private float price;

  public static Stock getInstance(String s) {
    Enumeration e = stocks.elements();
    while(e.hasMoreElements()) {
      Stock stock = (Stock)e.nextElement();
      if(stock.getSymbol().equals(s)) {
        stock.change();
        return stock;
      }
    }
    return new Stock(s);
  }

  public Stock(String symbol) {
    this.symbol = symbol;
    int i = (int)(100 * Math.random());
    int j = (int)(8 * Math.random());
    price = i + j * 0.125f;
    stocks.addElement(this);
  }

  public String getSymbol() {
    return symbol;
  }

  public float getPrice() {
```

```
      return price;
    }

  private void change() {
    int i = (int)price;
    int delta = (int)(i * 0.1 * Math.random());
    if(Math.random() < 0.5) {
      i += delta;
    }
    else {
      i -= delta;
    }
    int j = (int)(8 * Math.random());
    price = i + j * 0.125f;
  }
}
```

To build this software, follow these steps:

1. Change to the parent directory of **stock**, and type **javac stock*.java** at the command line.
2. Create a manifest template file to indicate that **StockWatcher** is a Bean.
3. Enter the command **jar cfm c:\bdk\jars\stock.jar stock*.mft stock*.class** to create a JAR file containing all the .class files.

 NOTE: This example contains multiple source files. For simplicity, you can instruct the **jar** utility to package all of the .class files in the JAR file even if they might not be used by the Bean. This approach avoids any problems that might be caused by missing files.

To test this software, follow these steps:

1. Open a DOS window and type **java stock.StockServerApp** to start the server application.
2. Open another DOS window and start the BDK.
3. Create instances of the **StockWatcher** and **TickTock** Beans.
4. Configure **StockWatcher**. Set **hostname** to **127.0.0.1**. (This represents the IP address of the current machine.) Set **port** to **5000**. Set **symbol** to your favorite stock symbol.

5. Map the property change event of **TickTock** to the **refresh( )** method of **StockWatcher**. Observe that the price data appears and changes.

6. Decrease the **interval** property of **TickTock**, and observe that the price changes more frequently.

7. Create additional instances of **StockWatcher** to observe the simulated price changes in other securities. (Note: If you create two instances of **StockWatcher** to observe the same stock, you will find that their prices are always different. This is because the server application changes a stock's price on each request. This application could be designed so that multiple observers who are monitoring the price of a stock always see the same value. Techniques to provide this behavior are discussed later in the book.)

Figure 2-5 shows how the **StockWatcher** and **TickTock** Beans work together.

What Is the Difference Between a Bean and Any Other Class?

Beans must supply zero-argument constructors.

Beans must provide access methods to properties.

Beans must support introspection.

The preceding sections have shown you five specific examples of Beans. At this point, you may be asking: What is the distinction between a Bean and an applet? Or between a Bean and any other Java class? In essence, what is it that makes a Bean a Bean?

A complete answer to this question will have wait until later in this book. Nonetheless, there are some comments that can be made at this point. First, every Bean requires a zero-argument constructor. The reason can be seen in how the BDK operates. A user selects a component from ToolBox and then clicks the mouse in BeanBox to request that the component be instantiated. At that point, no properties have been specified by the user. The BDK cannot make any assumptions about their values. The only way to create an instance of this component is to use a zero-argument constructor. That constructor can initialize the properties. If those values are not correct, the user may modify them.

Second, a Bean does not have public member variables. Instead, it provides access methods so that its properties may be read and written.

Third, a Bean must provide support for introspection. As shown in the examples, the easiest way to do this is by following the introspection naming conventions.

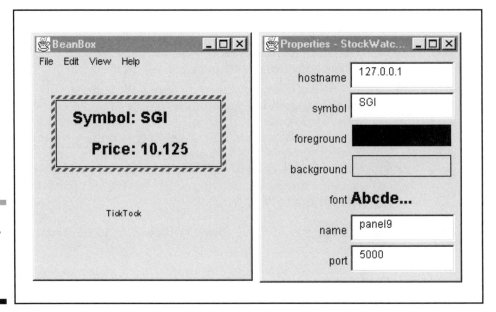

The
StockWatcher
and **TickTock**
Beans
Figure 2-5.

Contrary to what you might expect, there is not a single class from which all Beans must inherit. This was done deliberately. The goal was to make it easy for programmers who are familiar with Java to build reusable components. However, there are some subtle points about Beans that make use of sockets, threads, images, and certain other classes that will be examined later.

A Closer Look at JAR Files

Beans must be contained within JAR files.

Java Archive (JAR) files provide a standard mechanism to compress and package a set of files for distribution to users. You can create a single JAR file that contains several Beans and any associated files. For example, assume that you have developed a set of Beans to receive and transmit streaming audio and video on the Internet. The following files may be packaged into one JAR file:

◆   The Beans

◆   Any supporting .class files

◆   .txt and .html files that provide help to the user

◆   Static images

◆   Audio and video clips

◆   Configuration data

◆   Any other files required for the software to operate

It is much easier for a user to receive and install one deliverable than to handle multiple files.

The elements in a JAR file are compressed by using the industry standard ZIP algorithms. This makes it much faster to download a package of software over the Internet.

Each of the files in the archive may have an associated digital *signature.* Think of a digital signature as analogous to a handwritten signature. It indicates that the file was produced by a specific individual or organization. In addition, it is also used to check that the file was not altered after the time it was signed. In many execution environments, files that are digitally signed are trusted and can be given extra capabilities, such as the ability to read or write sensitive data.

The first element in a JAR file is always a *manifest file.* This is a plain text file that contains information about all of the other files in the archive. The manifest file indicates which of the .class files are JavaBeans. It also has any digital signature information for those files. You will see the contents of a manifest file shortly.

The jar Utility

The **jar** utility provided with the JDK allows you to create and manage JAR files. This command-line tool is located in the same directory as the Java compiler and other JDK tools. Its syntax is

jar *options files*

The following table lists the allowed options and their meanings:

Option	Meaning
c	Create an archive.
f	The first element in *files* is the name of the archive to be created.
m	The second element in *files* is the name of the manifest file.
t	Tabulate the contents of the archive.

Option	Meaning
v	Provide verbose output.
x	Extract files from the archive. (If *files* has only one element, that is the name of the archive, and all its contents are extracted. If *files* has more than one element, the first one is the name of the archive, and the others are the names of the specific files to be extracted.)
0	Do not use compression.
M	Do not create a manifest file.

The following sections look at some examples of using the **jar** utility.

Tabulating the Contents of a JAR File

This section describes how to list the contents of a JAR file. Follow these steps to become familiar with the command:

1. Type **cd c:\bdk\jars** to change to the directory in which the BDK looks for JAR files. Any Beans that you produce must be packaged in JAR files and placed in this directory so that the BDK can find them.

2. Type **dir** to list the contents of that directory. Observe that there is a set of JAR files. These files contain the demonstration Beans included with the BDK. For example, juggler.jar contains the **Juggler** Bean and molecule.jar contains the **Molecule** Bean.

3. Type **jar tvf juggler.jar** to tabulate the contents of the **Juggler** Bean. You should see output similar to this:

```
1247 Sun Apr 06 15:00:58 EDT 1997 META-INF/MANIFEST.MF
3266 Sun Apr 06 15:00:56 EDT 1997
sunw/demo/juggler/Juggler.class
 482 Sun Apr 06 15:00:56 EDT 1997
sunw/demo/juggler/JugglerBeanInfo.class
3090 Tue Apr 01 11:54:44 EDT 1997
sunw/demo/juggler/Juggler0.gif
3090 Tue Apr 01 11:54:44 EDT 1997
sunw/demo/juggler/Juggler1.gif
3290 Tue Apr 01 11:54:44 EDT 1997
sunw/demo/juggler/Juggler2.gif
3360 Tue Apr 01 11:54:44 EDT 1997
sunw/demo/juggler/Juggler3.gif
```

```
3067 Tue Apr 01 11:54:44 EDT 1997
sunw/demo/juggler/Juggler4.gif
 955 Tue Apr 01 11:54:46 EDT 1997
sunw/demo/juggler/JugglerIcon.gif
```

The first entry in the JAR file is the manifest file. It is listed as "META-INF/ MANIFEST.MF." The archive includes **Juggler.class**, which is the Bean class. **JugglerBeanInfo.class** is a supporting class. **JugglerIcon.gif** is the icon for this Bean that is shown next to its entry in ToolBox. The five image files that are necessary to provide the animation are also contained in the JAR.

Try tabulating the contents of some of the other JAR files in the C:\bdk\jars directory. For example, the molecule.jar file contains not only .class files but also some data files that are needed to present a visualization of the various molecules. These elements are hyaluronicAcid.xyz, benzene.xyz, buckministerfullerine.xyz, cyclohexane.xyz, ethane.xyz, and water.xyz.

NOTE: If you tabulate the contents of select.jar or quote.jar, you will see that there are .class files named with an embedded dollar sign character. For example, quote.jar contains QuoteMonitor$DialogOKHandler.class. These are examples of inner classes, a topic that is covered in Chapter 3.

Extracting Files from a JAR File

This section describes how to extract files from a JAR file. Follow these steps to become familiar with the command:

1. Create a new directory anywhere on your machine.
2. Copy C:\bdk\jars\juggler.jar to the new directory.
3. Change to the new directory.
4. Type **jar xvf juggler.jar** to extract the contents of the JAR file. You should see output similar to that shown in the following listing. The first file in the JAR file is its manifest file.

```
extracted: META-INF\MANIFEST.MF
extracted: sunw\demo\juggler\Juggler.class
extracted: sunw\demo\juggler\JugglerBeanInfo.class
extracted: sunw\demo\juggler\Juggler0.gif
extracted: sunw\demo\juggler\Juggler1.gif
extracted: sunw\demo\juggler\Juggler2.gif
extracted: sunw\demo\juggler\Juggler3.gif
```

```
extracted: sunw\demo\juggler\Juggler4.gif
extracted: sunw\demo\juggler\JugglerIcon.gif
```

The **jar** utility created the necessary subdirectories and extracted these files from the archive.

Examining a Manifest File

In the previous section we extracted all of the files in the juggler.jar archive. The first element in that JAR file was its manifest file. It should now be in META-INF\MANIFEST.MF. This is an ordinary text file that can be viewed with an editor such as Notepad. Its contents are shown in the following listing. The first line of the manifest file provides version information. The other lines provide information about each of the elements in the JAR file.

The path name of each file in the archive directory tree is given. Also included are the algorithms that were used to compute its message digests. In this manifest file, you can see that Secure Hash Algorithm (SHA) and Message Digest (MD5) were used.

One of the most important items to note in this file is the fourth line, `Java-Bean: True`. This designates that the file Juggler.class is a Bean and is the mechanism by which the BDK determines the entries in ToolBox. The other .class files in this manifest do not have this designation.

```
Manifest-Version: 1.0

Name: sunw/demo/juggler/Juggler.class
Java-Bean: True
Digest-Algorithms: SHA MD5
SHA-Digest: HvNgDbu0tEItNQrN2FxtnLHUB/g=
MD5-Digest: lodCaNW4vjtpiyVtqQojAg==

Name: sunw/demo/juggler/JugglerBeanInfo.class
Digest-Algorithms: SHA MD5
SHA-Digest: aVi52xkXvbrqrBBkW4lmI9GJvSo=
MD5-Digest: cy2MF8RT8c8AncXB7ZKtVA==

Name: sunw/demo/juggler/Juggler0.gif
Digest-Algorithms: SHA MD5
SHA-Digest: BoXVBkl+aKR7/2+f80rqxYbltTc=
MD5-Digest: SOLrOrGbrm+3aJNgJgIwdQ==

Name: sunw/demo/juggler/Juggler1.gif
Digest-Algorithms: SHA MD5
SHA-Digest: BoXVBkl+aKR7/2+f80rqxYbltTc=
```

2

```
MD5-Digest: SOLrOrGbrm+3aJNgJgIwdQ==

Name: sunw/demo/juggler/Juggler2.gif
Digest-Algorithms: SHA MD5
SHA-Digest: vf+oWwJoCJXwd0FTwIAOqBwShc8=
MD5-Digest: 0UQOpDSyiy7ziKGuk8o2xQ==

Name: sunw/demo/juggler/Juggler3.gif
Digest-Algorithms: SHA MD5
SHA-Digest: 5ngCVC3l4zj4zefuY5V0zWjGKAM=
MD5-Digest: 0XIiV4Hs97ZLE6Vh5wYH3g==

Name: sunw/demo/juggler/Juggler4.gif
Digest-Algorithms: SHA MD5
SHA-Digest: 7/z73JtPbxHmsn61TQp1q2cvuDs=
MD5-Digest: GY6JSNxiIabXhvoK2ZjjYQ==

Name: sunw/demo/juggler/JugglerIcon.gif
Digest-Algorithms: SHA MD5
SHA-Digest: Irqj25Pd5hgucribaj3QUIU3UAc=
MD5-Digest: BS0b0MJ3J+/tI4G/NFxVEw==
```

Creating a JAR File

There are two ways to create a JAR file. First, you may issue a command that does not specify a manifest file template. For example, the following command combines all of the GIF files in the current directory into an archive named images.jar.

```
jar cf images.jar *.gif
```

In this case, a manifest file is automatically created that provides information about all of the GIF files in the archive.

Second, you may issue a command that does specify a manifest file template. For example, the following command combines all of the .class and GIF files in the current directory into an archive called animator.jar:

```
jar cfm animator.jar animator.mft *.class *.gif
```

The file animator.mft would contain the following:

```
Name: Animator.class
Java-Bean: True
```

A manifest file template is used as a starting point by the **jar** utility as it builds a manifest file to describe all of the elements in a JAR file. It is required for any JAR file that contains a Bean.

Concluding Comments

This chapter presented the detailed steps to build and package a Bean. Be sure you are comfortable with these procedures. They are used many times in the remainder of this book. Remember that all source code and manifest template files are available at the Osborne web site (**http://www.osborne.com**).

CHAPTER 3

Events

In Chapter 1 you saw how events generated by one Bean can be mapped to method invocations on other Beans. One Bean generates an event, and one or more other Beans receive it. This is the primary mechanism by which Java components interact with each other. In the previous chapter, several simple Beans were developed that could receive events, but none could generate them. In this chapter you will learn how a Bean can generate an event and more about events in general.

This chapter begins by discussing the delegation event model and considers the classes and interfaces that are available in the **java.awt.event** package. Numerous code examples illustrate how to construct Beans that generate and receive the AWT events.

This chapter also examines two important, recent additions to the Java language: adapter and inner classes. They make it easier to write code that processes events. Finally, you will see how to generate and receive your own custom events.

The Delegation Event Model

The delegation event model handles events using event sources and event listeners.

When Java was first invented, it provided a mechanism for handling events based upon the class inheritance hierarchy. The original event model was inefficient and was replaced by the delegation event model when Java 1.1 was released. Since the delegation event model was not part of the original specification for Java, many readers might not be familiar with it. For that reason it is discussed here at some length.

The *delegation event model* provides a standard mechanism for a *source* to generate an event and send it to a set of *listeners*. The listeners must register with the source to receive notifications about specific types of events. Let's look first at events and then examine the specific responsibilities of sources and listeners.

Events

An event describes a change in the state of its source.

An *event* is an object that describes some state change in a source. It can be generated when a person interacts with an element in a graphical user interface. For example: pressing a button, moving the slider in a scroll bar, typing characters into a text field, dragging the mouse, or closing a window. In addition, events may also be generated that are not directly caused by user input. For example: arrival of incoming data, expiration of a software timer, overflow of a buffer, or conclusion of some processing.

Sources

An event
source
generates
events.

An event *source* generates events. It has three main responsibilities. First, it must provide methods that allow listeners to register and unregister for notifications about a specific type of event. Second, it must generate the event. Finally, it must send the event to all registered listeners. If a notification is sent to multiple listeners, this is known as *multicasting* the event. If it is sent to only one listener, this is known as *unicasting* the event.

3

The methods implemented by a source that allow listeners to register and unregister for events are shown next:

    public void add*Type*Listener(*Type*Listener *el*)

    public void add*Type*Listener(*Type*Listener *el*) throws
       TooManyListenersException

    public void remove*Type*Listener(*Type*Listener *el*)

Here, *Type* is the type of the event, and *el* is the event listener. The first form allows several listeners to register for the same type of event. The second form is provided if only one listener may be registered to receive that type of event. The last form allows a listener to unregister for notifications about a specific type of event.

An example of an event source is an AWT button. It generates an action event when it is pressed. The registration and unregistration methods provided by the **Button** class are shown next:

    void addActionListener(ActionListener *al*)

    void removeActionListener(ActionListener *al*)

Here, *al* is the *action listener*.

It is possible for a source to generate several types of events. In that case, multiple registration/unregistration methods would be provided.

Listeners

An event
listener receives
events.

An event *listener* receives event notifications. It has three main responsibilities. First, it must register to receive notifications about specific events. It does so by calling the appropriate registration method of the source. Second, it must implement an interface to receive events of that type.

Finally, it must unregister if it no longer wants to receive notifications about a specific type of event. It does so by calling the appropriate unregistration method of the source.

For example, the **ActionListener** interface provides one method to receive action events. Its form is shown next:

> void actionPerformed(ActionEvent *ae*)

Here, *ae* is the **ActionEvent** object generated by the source. Buttons generate action events. When a button is pressed, the **actionPerformed( )** method of all registered listeners is invoked, and the event is passed as an argument to that method.

Event Classes

A set of classes is provided to represent the various types of AWT events. The relationships among these classes are shown in Figure 3-1. The most commonly used classes are discussed in this chapter.

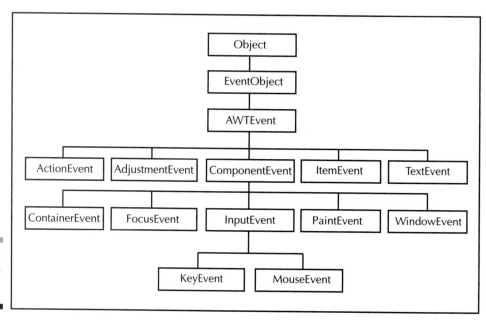

The Java **Event** class hierarchy

Figure 3-1.

EventObject

The **EventObject** class extends **Object** and is part of the **java.util** package. Its constructor has the following form:

EventObject(Object *source*)

Here, *source* is the object that generates the event.

It has the two methods shown here:

Object getSource( )

String toString( )

The **getSource( )** method returns the object that generated the event, and the **toString( )** method returns a string equivalent of the event.

AWTEvent

The abstract **AWTEvent** class extends **EventObject** and is part of the **java.awt** package. All of the AWT event types are subclasses of **AWTEvent**. These events are discussed throughout the rest of this chapter.

One of its constructors has the following form:

AWTEvent(Object *source*, int *id*)

Here, *source* is the object that is generating the event, and *id* identifies the type of the event. The possible values of *id* are described in the examples section of this chapter.

Two frequently used methods are shown here:

int getId( )

String toString( )

The **getId( )** method returns the type of the event, and the **toString( )** method returns the string equivalent of the event.

Listener Interfaces

The **EventListener** interface is part of the **java.util** package. It does not define any constants or methods, but exists only to identify those interfaces that process events. All event listener interfaces must extend this interface. Table 3-1 shows the relationship between the AWT event types and the listener interfaces that define the methods to process those events.

Exploring the AWT Events

This section examines the event classes and event listener interfaces that are provided in the **java.awt.event** package. Each of the primary event types is considered separately. Its most commonly used constants and methods are briefly outlined. Then the listener interface which receives events of that type is discussed. Finally, code examples are provided to illustrate how you can write Beans that generate and receive such events.

Action Events

Action events are generated when a button is pressed, a list item is double-clicked, or a menu item is selected. The **ActionEvent** class defines several **int** constants, some of which are shown in Table 3-2.

Event Class	Listener Interface(s)
ActionEvent	ActionListener
AdjustmentEvent	AdjustmentListener
ComponentEvent	ComponentListener
ContainerEvent	ContainerListener
FocusEvent	FocusListener
ItemEvent	ItemListener
KeyEvent	KeyListener
MouseEvent	MouseListener, MouseMotionListener
TextEvent	TextListener
WindowEvent	WindowListener

AWT **Event** Classes and Listener Interfaces

Table 3-1.

Some
Constants
Defined by
ActionEvent
Table 3-2.

Constant	Key Pressed to Generate Event
ALT_MASK	ALT key
CTRL_MASK	CTRL key
META_MASK	META key
SHIFT_MASK	SHIFT key

Two frequently used methods of **ActionEvent** are shown here:

String getActionCommand( )

int getModifiers( )

The **getActionCommand( )** method returns a string that names the event, and the **getModifiers( )** method returns a bit mask indicating if the ALT, CTRL, META, or SHIFT key was pressed when it was generated.

The **ActionListener** interface is implemented by objects that receive action events. It defines one method whose form is shown next:

void actionPerformed(ActionEvent *ae*)

Here, *ae* is the **ActionEvent** object that was generated by the source.

The following example develops three Beans to illustrate how action events can be generated and processed. **ActionSource1** extends **Button**, which generates an action event each time it is pressed. **ActionSource2** extends **List**, which generates an action event each time an entry is double-clicked. **ActionReceiver** receives and displays the events.

The source code for **ActionSource1** is shown in the following listing. It extends **Button**. Since a **Button** object generates an action event each time the button is pressed, **ActionSource1** inherits this ability and also generates an action event when its button is pressed. The label on the button is "ActionSource1."

```
package actionevents;
import java.awt.*;

public class ActionSource1 extends Button {
```

```
public ActionSource1() {
    super("ActionSource1");
  }
}
```

The source code for **ActionSource2** is shown in the following listing. It extends **List**, which generates an action event each time a list item is double-clicked. Since **ActionSource2** inherits **List**, it too generates an action event each time the list is double-clicked.

```
package actionevents;
import java.awt.*;

public class ActionSource2 extends List {
  public ActionSource2() {
    add("Item 1");
    add("Item 2");
    add("Item 3");
  }
}
```

The source code for **ActionReceiver** is shown in the following listing. It extends **Panel** and implements the **ActionListener** interface. A text area is created and added to the panel. Information about events is displayed in the text area.

```
package actionevents;
import java.awt.*;
import java.awt.event.*;

public class ActionReceiver extends Panel
implements ActionListener {
  private TextArea ta;

  public ActionReceiver() {
    setLayout(null);
    ta = new TextArea();
    ta.setBounds(0, 0, 200, 300);
    add(ta);
    setSize(200, 300);
  }

  public void actionPerformed(ActionEvent ae) {
    String ac = ae.getActionCommand();
```

```
    int modifiers = ae.getModifiers();
    String s = ac;
    if((modifiers & ActionEvent.ALT_MASK) != 0) {
      s += ", ALT_MASK";
    }
    if((modifiers & ActionEvent.CTRL_MASK) != 0) {
      s += ", CTRLT_MASK";
    }
    if((modifiers & ActionEvent.META_MASK) != 0) {
      s += ", META_MASK";
    }
    if((modifiers & ActionEvent.SHIFT_MASK) != 0) {
      s += ", SHIFT_MASK";
    }
    ta.append(s + "\n");
  }
}
```

There are three Beans in this example. Therefore, the manifest template file must contain three entries as shown next:

```
Name: actionevents/ActionSource1.class
Java-Bean: True

Name: actionevents/ActionSource2.class
Java-Bean: True

Name: actionevents/ActionReceiver.class
Java-Bean: True
```

Many of the other examples in this chapter also contain multiple Beans, and this must be reflected in the manifest template files.

Follow these steps to experiment with the components:

1. Create an instance of **ActionReceiver** in BeanBox.
2. Create an instance of **ActionSource1** in BeanBox, and map its action event to the **actionPerformed( )** method of **ActionReceiver**.
3. Select the button. Observe that an action event is displayed by **ActionReceiver**.
4. Create an instance of **ActionSource2** in BeanBox, and map its action event to the **actionPerformed( )** method of **ActionReceiver**.

5. Double-click one of the list items. Observe that an action event is displayed by **ActionReceiver**.

Figure 3-2 shows how these three Beans appear in BeanBox.

There is one important point to make about the preceding example. Notice that there is no direct linkage between **ActionSource1**, **ActionSource2**, and **ActionReceiver**. Only when they are connected by use of the BeanBox do events generated by the sources get received by the **ActionReceiver**. This is a critical point. Beans are reusable software components that may be hooked together. The sources **ActionSource1** and **ActionSource2** may be used to send events to any listener—not just to **ActionReceiver**. The opposite also applies. **ActionReceiver** may receive action events from any action event source—not just from the sources shown here. These same principles apply to the rest of the examples as well.

Adjustment Events

Adjustment events are generated when a scroll bar is manipulated. The **AdjustmentEvent** class defines several **int** constants. Table 3-3 describes some of these constants.

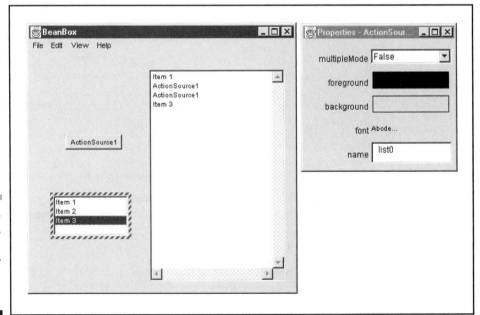

ActionSource1, **ActionSource2**, and **ActionReceiver** Beans

Figure 3-2.

Constant	Description
BLOCK_DECREMENT	The mouse was clicked in the region between the slider and lower bound button.
BLOCK_INCREMENT	The mouse was clicked in the region between the slider and the upper bound button.
TRACK	The slider is being dragged.
UNIT_DECREMENT	The lower bound button was pressed.
UNIT_INCREMENT	The upper bound button was pressed.

Some Constants Defined by **Adjustment-Event** **Table 3-3.**

3

Three frequently used methods of **AdjustmentEvent** are shown here:

    Adjustable getAdjustable( )

    int getAdjustmentType( )

    int getValue( )

The **getAdjustable( )** method returns a reference to the object that generated this event. The **getAdjustmentType( )** method returns one of the constants defined in Table 3-3. The current value of the **Adjustable** object is returned by the **getValue( )** method.

The **AdjustmentListener** interface is implemented by objects that receive adjustment events. It defines one method whose form is shown next:

    void adjustmentValueChanged(AdjustmentEvent *ae*)

Here, *ae* is the **AdjustmentEvent** object that was generated by the source.

The next example develops two Beans to illustrate how adjustment events can be generated and processed. **AdjustmentSource** generates adjustment events, and **AdjustmentReceiver** receives and displays them.

The source code for **AdjustmentSource** is shown in the following listing. It extends **Scrollbar** and overrides the **getPreferredSize( )** method.

```
package adjustmentevents;
import java.awt.*;

public class AdjustmentSource extends Scrollbar {
```

```
  public AdjustmentSource() {
  }

  public Dimension getPreferredSize() {
    return new Dimension(20, 200);
  }
}
```

The source code for **AdjustmentReceiver** is shown in the following listing. It extends **Panel** and implements the **AdjustmentListener** interface. A text area is created and added to the panel. Information about the events is displayed in the text area.

```
package adjustmentevents;
import java.awt.*;
import java.awt.event.*;

public class AdjustmentReceiver extends Panel
implements AdjustmentListener {
  private TextArea ta;

  public AdjustmentReceiver() {
    setLayout(null);
    ta = new TextArea();
    ta.setBounds(0, 0, 200, 300);
    add(ta);
    setSize(200, 300);
  }

  public void adjustmentValueChanged(AdjustmentEvent ae) {
    int type = ae.getAdjustmentType();
    int value = ae.getValue();
    if(type == AdjustmentEvent.BLOCK_DECREMENT) {
      ta.append("block decrement, value = " + value + "\n");
    }
    else if(type == AdjustmentEvent.BLOCK_INCREMENT) {
      ta.append("block increment, value = " + value + "\n");
    }
    else if(type == AdjustmentEvent.TRACK) {
      ta.append("track, value = " + value + "\n");
    }
    else if(type == AdjustmentEvent.UNIT_DECREMENT) {
      ta.append("unit decrement, value = " + value + "\n");
    }
```

```
        else if(type == AdjustmentEvent.UNIT_INCREMENT) {
          ta.append("unit increment, value = " + value + "\n");
        }
    }
}
```

3

To experiment with these Beans, map the adjustment events generated by **AdjustmentSource** to the **adjustmentValueChanged( )** method of **AdjustmentReceiver**.

Figure 3-3 shows how these two Beans appear in BeanBox.

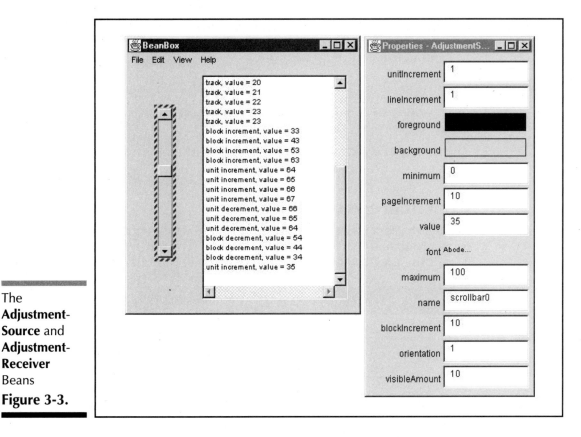

The
**Adjustment-
Source** and
**Adjustment-
Receiver**
Beans
Figure 3-3.

Constant	Description
COMPONENT_HIDDEN	A component was hidden from view.
COMPONENT_MOVED	A component was moved.
COMPONENT_RESIZED	A component was resized.
COMPONENT_SHOWN	A component became visible.

Component Events

A *component* event is generated when a component is hidden, moved, resized, or shown. The **ComponentEvent** class defines several **int** constants. Table 3-4 (above) describes some of these constants.

One frequently used method of **ComponentEvent** is shown next:

    Component getComponent( )

This method returns a reference to the source of the event.

As previously shown in Figure 3-1, **ComponentEvent** is the superclass of several other event classes.

An example of a Bean that receives component events can be seen in the section that discusses window events.

Container Events

Container events are generated when a component is added to or removed from a container. The **ContainerEvent** class defines several **int** constants. Two of these are listed next:

Constant	Description
COMPONENT_ADDED	A component was added to the container.
COMPONENT_REMOVED	A component was removed from the container.

Two frequently used methods of **ContainerEvent** are shown here:

    Component getChild( )

Container getContainer( )

The **getChild( )** method returns the component that was added or removed. The **getContainer( )** method returns the container.

The **ContainerListener** interface is implemented by objects that receive container events. It defines two methods whose forms are shown next:

void componentAdded(ContainerEvent *ce*)

void componentRemoved(ContainerEvent *ce*)

Here, *ce* is the **ContainerEvent** object that was generated by the source.

The next example develops two Beans to illustrate how container events can be generated and processed. **ContainerSource** generates container events, and **ContainerReceiver** receives and displays them.

The source code for **ContainerSource** is shown in the following listing. It extends **Panel** and displays a maximum of nine buttons arranged in a 3x3 grid layout. The **addButton( )** method causes a new button to be added to the container. The **removeButton( )** method causes a button to be removed from the container. Note that both of these methods invoke **doLayout( )** to force the layout manager to update the appearance of the container.

```
package containerevents;
import java.awt.*;
import java.awt.event.*;

public class ContainerSource extends Panel {
  private final static int MAXBUTTONS = 9;
  private Button buttons[];
  private int index;

  public ContainerSource() {
    setLayout(new GridLayout(3, 3));
    buttons = new Button[MAXBUTTONS];
    index = 0;
  }

  public Dimension getPreferredSize() {
    return new Dimension(320, 80);
  }

  public void paint(Graphics g) {
```

```
    Dimension d = getSize();
    g.drawRect(0, 0, d.width - 1, d.height - 1);
  }

  public void addButton() {
    if(index >= MAXBUTTONS) {
      return;
    }
    buttons[index] = new Button("Button" + index);
    add(buttons[index]);
    ++index;
    doLayout();
  }

  public void removeButton() {
    if(index == 0) {
      return;
    }
    --index;
    remove(buttons[index]);
    doLayout();
  }
}
```

The source code for **ContainerReceiver** is shown in the following listing. It extends **Panel** and implements the **ContainerListener** interface. A text area is created and added to the panel. Information about events is displayed in the text area.

```
package containerevents;
import java.awt.*;
import java.awt.event.*;

public class ContainerReceiver extends Panel
implements ContainerListener {
  private TextArea ta;

  public ContainerReceiver() {
    setLayout(null);
    ta = new TextArea();
    ta.setBounds(0, 0, 150, 300);
    add(ta);
    setSize(150, 300);
```

```
  }

  public void componentAdded(ContainerEvent ce) {
    ta.append("component added\n");
  }

  public void componentRemoved(ContainerEvent ce) {
    ta.append("component removed\n");
  }
}
```

3

Follow these steps to experiment with these components:

1. Create an instance of **ContainerSource** and **ContainerReceiver** in BeanBox.

2. Map the component-added event generated by the source to the **componentAdded( )** method of the receiver.

3. Map the component-removed event generated by the source to the **componentRemoved( )** method of the receiver.

4. Create an instance of **OurButton** in BeanBox.

5. Change its label to **Add**, and map its action event to the **addButton( )** method of **ContainerSource**.

6. Create another instance of **OurButton** in BeanBox.

7. Change its label to **Remove**, and map its action event to the **removeButton( )** method of **ContainerSource**.

8. Press the Add button. Observe that a new button is added to the grid in the sender and that the receiver displays a container event. Add some more buttons to the container.

9. Press the Remove button. Observe that a button is removed from the grid in the sender and that the receiver displays a container event. Remove some more buttons from the container.

Figure 3-4 shows how these components appear in the BeanBox.

Focus Events

Focus events are generated when a component gains or loses keyboard focus. The **FocusEvent** class defines several **int** constants, including those shown in the following table:

Constant	Description
FOCUS_GAINED	The component gained focus.
FOCUS_LOST	The component lost focus.

One frequently used method of **FocusEvent** is shown here:

boolean isTemporary( )

This method returns **true** if the focus loss is temporary. Otherwise, it returns **false**. A temporary loss of focus can occur when the focus is given to an element on a graphical user interface such as a scroll bar or pop-up menu.

The **FocusListener** interface is implemented by objects that receive focus events. It defines two methods whose form is shown next:

void focusGained(FocusEvent *fe*)

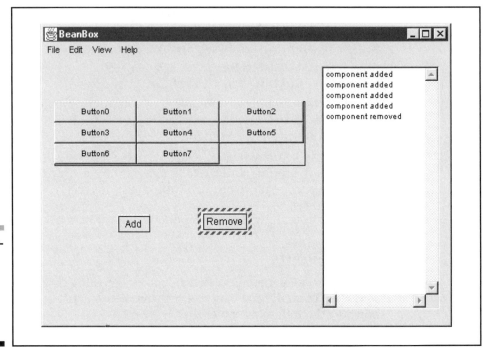

The **Container-Source** and **Container-Receiver** Beans

Figure 3-4.

void focusLost(FocusEvent *fe*)

Here, *fe* is the **FocusEvent** object that was generated by the source.

The next example develops two Beans to illustrate how focus events can be generated and processed. **FocusSource** extends **TextField**, which generates a focus event each time it gains or loses focus. **FocusReceiver** receives and displays the events.

The source code for **FocusSource** is shown next:

```
package focusevents;
import java.awt.*;

public class FocusSource extends TextField {
  public FocusSource() {
    super(10);
  }
}
```

The source code for **FocusReceiver** is shown in the following listing. It extends **Panel** and implements the **FocusListener** interface. A text area is created and added to the panel. Information about events is displayed in the text area.

```
package focusevents;
import java.awt.*;
import java.awt.event.*;

public class FocusReceiver extends Panel
implements FocusListener {
  private TextArea ta;

  public FocusReceiver() {
    setLayout(null);
    ta = new TextArea();
    ta.setBounds(0, 0, 150, 300);
    add(ta);
    setSize(150, 300);
  }

  public void focusGained(FocusEvent fe) {
    ta.append("focus gained\n");
  }
```

```
public void focusLost(FocusEvent fe) {
  ta.append("focus lost\n");
 }
}
```

To experiment with the Beans, follow these steps:

1. Create an instance of **FocusReceiver** in BeanBox.

2. Create two instances of **FocusSource** in BeanBox.

3. Map the focus-gained event from each source to the **focusGained( )** method of **FocusReceiver**.

4. Map the focus-lost event from each source to the **focusLost( )** method of **FocusReceiver**.

5. Change the keyboard focus from one source to the other. Observe that the receiver displays focus events.

Figure 3-5 shows how these two Beans appear in BeanBox.

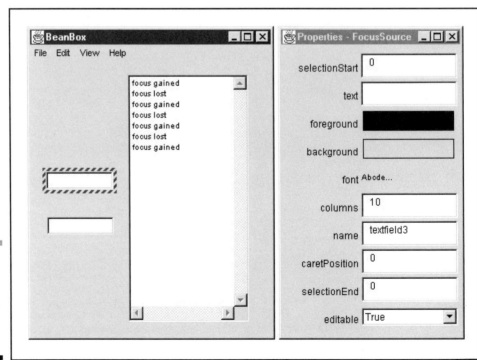

The
FocusSource
and
FocusReceiver
Beans

Figure 3-5.

Constant	Keypress Used to Determine
ALT_MASK	the ALT key
BUTTON1_MASK	the first mouse button
BUTTON2_MASK	the second mouse button
BUTTON3_MASK	the third mouse button
CTRL_MASK	the CTRL key
META_MASK	the META key
SHIFT_MASK	the SHIFT key

Some Constants Defined by **InputEvent** **Table 3-5.**

Input Events

The **InputEvent** class is the superclass of **KeyEvent** and **MouseEvent**. It defines several **int** constants. Table 3-5 (above) describes some of these constants.

Table 3-6 describes some commonly used methods of **InputEvent**.

These methods can be used by any subclass of **InputEvent**.

Method	Description
int getModifiers( )	Returns information about any modifiers that apply for this input event.
boolean isAltDown( )	Returns **true** if the ALT key was pressed. Otherwise, returns **false**.
boolean isControlDown( )	Returns **true** if the CTRL key was pressed. Otherwise, returns **false**.
boolean isMetaDown( )	Returns **true** if the META key was pressed. Otherwise, returns **false**.
boolean isShiftDown( )	Returns **true** if the SHIFT key was pressed. Otherwise, returns **false**.

Some Methods Defined by **InputEvent** **Table 3-6.**

Item Events

Item events are generated when a choice selection is made, a checkable menu item is selected or deselected, or a list item is selected or deselected.

The **ItemEvent** class defines several **int** constants, including the following:

Constant	Description
DESELECTED	The item has been deselected.
ITEM_STATE_CHANGED	The item state changed.
SELECTED	The item has been selected.

Some commonly used methods of **ItemEvent** are shown here:

    Object getItem( )

    ItemSelectable getItemSelectable( )

    int getStateChange( )

The **getItem( )** method returns a reference to the item. The **getItemSelectable( )** method returns a reference to the source of the event (for example, a list). The last method returns DESELECTED or SELECTED.

The **ItemListener** interface is implemented by objects that receive item events. It defines one method whose form is shown next:

    void itemStateChanged(ItemEvent *ie*)

Here, *ie* is the **ItemEvent** object that was generated by the source.

The next example develops two Beans to illustrate how item events can be generated and processed. **ItemSource** extends **List**, which generates an item event each time an item is selected or deselected. **ItemReceiver** receives and displays the events.

The source code for **ItemSource** is shown in the following listing:

```
package itemevents;
import java.awt.*;
import java.awt.event.*;
```

```
public class ItemSource extends List {

  public ItemSource() {
    add("One");
    add("Two");
    add("Three");
    add("Four");
    setMultipleMode(true);
  }
}
```

The source code for **ItemReceiver** is shown in the following listing:

```
package itemevents;
import java.awt.*;
import java.awt.event.*;

public class ItemReceiver extends Panel
implements ItemListener {
  private TextArea ta;

  public ItemReceiver() {
    setLayout(null);
    ta = new TextArea();
    ta.setBounds(0, 0, 150, 300);
    add(ta);
    setSize(150, 300);
  }

  public void itemStateChanged(ItemEvent ie) {
    int sc = ie.getStateChange();
    Object obj = ie.getItem();
    if(sc == ItemEvent.DESELECTED) {
      ta.append("deselected " + obj + "\n");
    }
    else {
      ta.append("selected " + obj + "\n");
    }
  }
}
```

To experiment with these Beans, map the item events from **ItemSource** to the **itemStateChanged( )** method of **ItemReceiver**.

Figure 3-6 shows how these two Beans appear in BeanBox. As you select and deselect entries in the list, you can see the **ItemReceiver** Bean report the item events that occur.

Key Events

Key events are generated when a key is pressed or released. In addition, a key event occurs when a Unicode character is entered. The **KeyEvent** class defines many **int** constants. The most commonly used are KEY_PRESSED, KEY_RELEASED, and KEY_TYPED. These respectively indicate that a key was pressed, released, or typed. If an alphanumeric key is typed, three key events (pressed, typed, and released) are generated. If a modifier key (for example, HOME, END, PAGE UP, PAGE DOWN) is pressed and released, only two key events (pressed and released) are generated.

In addition to these constants, **VK_A** through **VK_Z** and **VK_0** through **VK_9** represent the letters and numbers, respectively. Some of the other

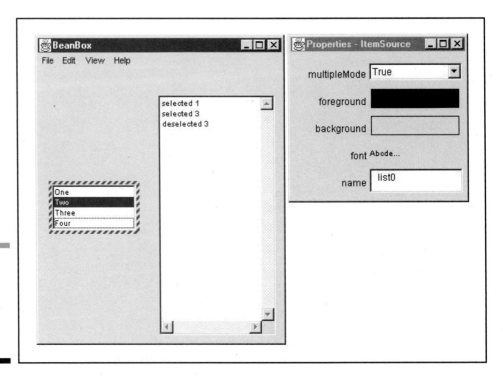

The
ItemSource
and
ItemReceiver
Beans
Figure 3-6.

commonly used constants are **VK_ENTER**, **VK_DELETE**, **VK_INSERT**, **VK_TAB**, **VK_ESCAPE**, and **VK_BACK_SPACE** to represent those keys.

Two commonly used methods of **KeyEvent** are shown here:

char getKeyChar( )

int getKeyCode( )

The first method returns the character that was entered, and the second returns the code for the key that was pressed.

The **KeyListener** interface is implemented by objects that receive key events. It defines three methods whose forms are shown next:

void keyPressed(KeyEvent *ke*)

void keyReleased(KeyEvent *ke*)

void keyTyped(KeyEvent *ke*)

The next example develops two Beans to illustrate how key events can be generated and processed. **KeySource** extends **TextField**, which generates a key event when there is keyboard activity. **KeyReceiver** receives and displays the events.

The source code for **KeySource** is shown here:

```
package keyevents;
import java.awt.*;

public class KeySource extends TextField {

  public KeySource() {
    super(10);
  }
}
```

The source code for **KeyReceiver** is shown here:

```
package keyevents;
import java.awt.*;
import java.awt.event.*;
```

```
public class KeyReceiver extends Panel
implements KeyListener {
  private TextArea ta;

  public KeyReceiver() {
    setLayout(null);
    ta = new TextArea();
    ta.setBounds(0, 0, 150, 300);
    add(ta);
    setSize(150, 300);
  }

  public void keyPressed(KeyEvent ke) {
    ta.append("key pressed\n");
  }

  public void keyReleased(KeyEvent ke) {
    ta.append("key released\n");
  }

  public void keyTyped(KeyEvent ke) {
    ta.append("key typed: " + ke.getKeyChar() + "\n");
  }
}
```

To experiment with these Beans, map the key events of **KeySource** to the appropriate method of **KeyReceiver**. Figure 3-7 shows how these two Beans appear in BeanBox. As you type in the text field, you can see the **KeyReceiver** Bean report the key events that occur. Notice that when you type a character or number, three key events (namely, pressed, typed, and released) are sent to the receiver.

Mouse Events

Mouse events are generated when the mouse is clicked, dragged, moved, pressed, or released. In addition, mouse events occur when the mouse enters or exits a component. The **MouseEvent** class defines many **int** constants. Table 3-7 describes some of these constants.

The most commonly used methods of **MouseEvent** are shown here:

Point getPoint( )   int getY( )

int getX( )

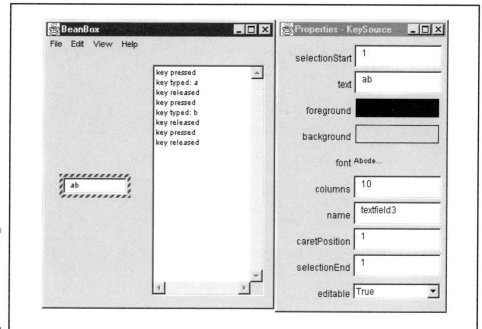

The **KeySource**
and
KeyReceiver
Beans
Figure 3-7.

3

The **getPoint( )** method returns a **Point** object encapsulating the position of the mouse. The **getX( )** and **getY( )** methods return the x and y coordinates of the mouse.

Some
Constants
Defined by
MouseEvent
Table 3-7.

Constant	Description
MOUSE_CLICKED	The mouse was clicked.
MOUSE_DRAGGED	The mouse was dragged.
MOUSE_ENTERED	The mouse entered the source component.
MOUSE_EXITED	The mouse exited from the source component.
MOUSE_MOVED	The mouse was moved.
MOUSE_PRESSED	The mouse was pressed.
MOUSE_RELEASED	The mouse was released.

There are two listener interfaces, **MouseListener** and **MouseMotion-Listener**, that receive mouse events.

The **MouseListener** interface defines five methods whose forms are shown next:

> void mouseClicked(MouseEvent *me*)

> void mouseEntered(MouseEvent *me*)

> void mouseExited(MouseEvent *me*)

> void mousePressed(MouseEvent *me*)

> void mouseReleased(MouseEvent *me*)

In all cases, *me* contains the mouse event object. The **mouseClicked( )** method is called when a mouse button is pressed and released at the same position. The **mouseEntered( )** and **mouseExited( )** methods are called when the mouse enters and exits a component. The **mousePressed( )** and **mouseReleased( )** methods are called when the mouse is pressed and released.

The **MouseMotionListener** interface defines two methods whose forms are shown next:

> void mouseDragged(MouseEvent *me*)

> void mouseMoved(MouseEvent *me*)

The **mouseDragged( )** method is called when the mouse is moved when a button is pressed, and **mouseMoved( )** is called when the mouse is moved with no button pressed. In both cases, *me* contains the mouse event.

The next example develops two Beans to illustrate how mouse events can be generated and processed. **MouseSource** extends **Canvas** and can generate all of the possible mouse events. **MouseReceiver** receives and displays the events.

The source code for **MouseSource** is shown in the following listing. The constructor sets the size of the component, and the **paint( )** method draws a border around this area.

```
package mouseevents;
import java.awt.*;

public class MouseSource extends Canvas {

  public MouseSource() {
    setSize(100, 100);
  }

  public void paint(Graphics g) {
    Dimension d = getSize();
    g.drawRect(0, 0, d.width - 1, d.height - 1);
  }
}
```

The source code for **MouseReceiver** is shown in the following listing. It implements both the **MouseListener** and **MouseMotionListener** interfaces.

```
package mouseevents;
import java.awt.*;
import java.awt.event.*;

public class MouseReceiver extends Panel
implements MouseListener, MouseMotionListener {
  private TextArea ta;

  public MouseReceiver() {
    setLayout(null);
    ta = new TextArea();
    ta.setBounds(0, 0, 150, 300);
    add(ta);
    setSize(150, 300);
  }

  public void mouseClicked(MouseEvent me) {
    ta.append("mouse clicked\n");
  }

  public void mouseEntered(MouseEvent me) {
    ta.append("mouse entered\n");
  }
```

```
public void mouseExited(MouseEvent me) {
  ta.append("mouse exited\n");
}

public void mousePressed(MouseEvent me) {
  ta.append("mouse pressed\n");
}

public void mouseReleased(MouseEvent me) {
  ta.append("mouse released\n");
}

public void mouseDragged(MouseEvent me) {
  ta.append("mouse dragged\n");
}

public void mouseMoved(MouseEvent me) {
  ta.append("mouse moved\n");
}
}
```

To experiment with these Beans, map the mouse events from **MouseSource** to the appropriate method of **MouseReceiver**. Figure 3-8 shows how these two Beans appear in BeanBox. As **MouseSource** generates events, you can see **MouseReceiver** report the events that occur. Observe that when the user clicks the mouse, three events are generated (pressed, released, and clicked).

Text Events

Text events are generated when the characters in a text area or field change.

The **TextEvent** class defines the **int** constant **TEXT_VALUE_CHANGED**. A text event object does not contain the characters in a text area or text field. You must use the methods provided by those objects to retrieve that information.

The **TextListener** interface is implemented by objects that receive text events. It defines one method whose form is shown next:

    void textValueChanged(TextEvent *te*)

Here, *te* is the **TextEvent** object that was generated by the source.

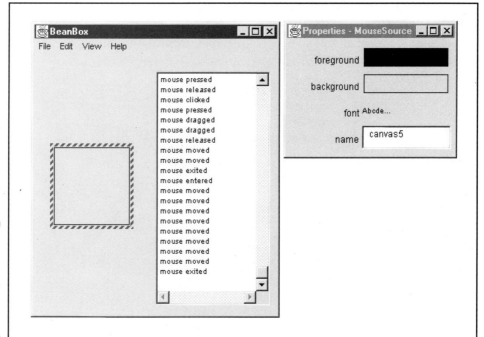

The
MouseSource
and
MouseReceiver
Beans
Figure 3-8.

The next example develops two Beans to illustrate how text events can be generated and processed. **TextSource** extends **TextField**, which generates a text event each time the text entry changes. **TextReceiver** receives and displays the events.

The source code for **TextSource** is shown in the following listing. It extends **TextField**, which generates a text event each time the string is changed.

```
package textevents;
import java.awt.*;

public class TextSource extends TextField {

  public TextSource() {
    super(10);
  }
}
```

The source code for **TextReceiver** is shown in the following listing. It extends **Panel** and implements the **TextListener** interface. A text area is created and added to the panel. Information about events is displayed in the text area.

```
package textevents;
import java.awt.*;
import java.awt.event.*;

public class TextReceiver extends Panel
implements TextListener {
  private TextArea ta;

  public TextReceiver() {
    setLayout(null);
    ta = new TextArea();
    ta.setBounds(0, 0, 150, 300);
    add(ta);
    setSize(150, 300);
  }

  public void textValueChanged(TextEvent te) {
    ta.append("text value changed\n");
  }
}
```

To experiment with these Beans, map the text event of **TextSource** to the **textValueChanged( )** method of **TextReceiver**. Figure 3-9 shows how this component appears in the BeanBox.

Window Events

Window events are generated when a window is activated, closed, closing, deactivated, deiconified, iconified, or opened. The **WindowEvent** class defines several **int** constants. Table 3-8 describes some of these constants.

The most commonly used method is shown next:

Window getWindow( )

This method returns the window that was the source of the event.

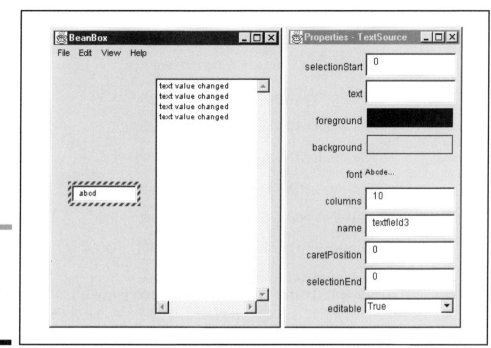

The
TextSource
and
TextReceiver
Beans
Figure 3-9.

3

Constant	Description
WINDOW_ACTIVATED	The window was activated.
WINDOW_CLOSED	The window was closed.
WINDOW_CLOSING	A request to close this window has been received.
WINDOW_DEACTIVATED	The window is no longer active.
WINDOW_DEICONIFIED	The window was deiconified.
WINDOW_ICONIFIED	The window was iconified.
WINDOW_OPENED	The mouse was opened.

Some
Constants
Defined by
WindowEvent
Table 3-8.

The **WindowListener** interface is implemented by objects that receive window events. It defines seven methods whose forms are shown next:

    void windowActivated(WindowEvent *we*)

    void windowClosed(WindowEvent *we*)

    void windowClosing(WindowEvent *we*)

    void windowDeactivated(WindowEvent *we*)

    void windowDeiconified(WindowEvent *we*)

    void windowIconified(WindowEvent *we*)

    void windowOpened(WindowEvent *we*)

Here, *we* is the **WindowEvent** object that was generated by the source. The **windowActivated( )** and **windowDeactivated( )** methods are called when a window is activated or deactivated. The **windowClosing( )** method is called when a user requests that a window be closed. (The application should call **setVisible( )** or **destroy( )** on the associated **Window** object in response to this event.) The **windowClosed( )** method is called after a **Window** object has been closed via a **setVisible( )** or **destroy( )** method invocation. The **windowDeiconified(**) and **windowIconified( )** methods are called after a window is iconified or deiconified. The **windowOpened( )** method is called when a window is first opened.

The next example develops a Bean named **WindowReceiver** that creates a window. The component and window events generated by that window are received and displayed by **WindowReceiver**. The Bean also has a button that can be pressed to make the window appear and disappear. Figure 3-10 shows how this component appears in BeanBox.

The source code for **WindowReceiver** is shown in the following listing. The Bean implements the **ComponentListener** and **WindowListener** interfaces to receive those events from the window. It also implements the **ActionListener** interface to receive action events generated by its own Show/Hide button.

The constructor creates the window and registers the **WindowReceiver** object to receive component and window events generated by the window. A button labeled "Show" is created, and the **WindowReceiver** object is

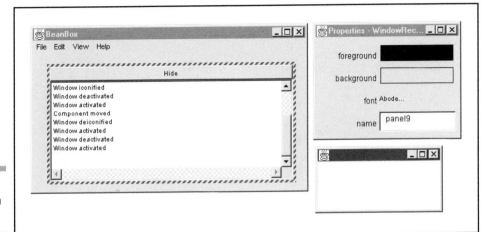

registered to receive the action events generated when that button is pressed. Finally, a text area is created in which event notifications are displayed.

The **actionPerformed( )** method is invoked when the button is pressed. If the label of the button is "Show," the **setVisible( )** method is invoked to make the window appear and change the button label to "Hide." If the label of the button is "Hide," the **setVisible( )** method is invoked to make the window disappear and change the button label to "Show."

The other methods in **WindowReceiver** process the events from the window by appending a string to the text area.

```
package windowevents;
import java.applet.*;
import java.awt.*;
import java.awt.event.*;

public class WindowReceiver extends Panel implements
ActionListener, ComponentListener, WindowListener {
  private Frame f;
  private Button b;
  private TextArea ta;

  public WindowReceiver() {
    setLayout(new BorderLayout());
    f = new Frame();;
    f.setSize(200, 100);
```

```
    f.addComponentListener(this);
    f.addWindowListener(this);
    b = new Button("Show");
    b.addActionListener(this);
    add("North", b);
    ta = new TextArea();
    add("Center", ta);
  }

  public void actionPerformed(ActionEvent ae) {
    if(ae.getActionCommand() == "Show") {
      f.setVisible(true);
      b.setLabel("Hide");
    }
    else {
      f.setVisible(false);
      b.setLabel("Show");
    }
  }

  public void componentHidden(ComponentEvent ce) {
    ta.append("Component hidden\n");
  }

  public void componentMoved(ComponentEvent ce) {
    ta.append("Component moved\n");
  }

  public void componentResized(ComponentEvent ce) {
    ta.append("Component resized\n");
  }

  public void componentShown(ComponentEvent ce) {
    ta.append("Component shown\n");
  }

  public void windowActivated(WindowEvent we) {
    ta.append("Window activated\n");
  }

  public void windowClosed(WindowEvent we) {
    ta.append("Window closed\n");
  }

  public void windowClosing(WindowEvent we) {
```

```
      ta.append("Window closing\n");
      f.dispose();
    }

    public void windowDeactivated(WindowEvent we) {
      ta.append("Window deactivated\n");
    }

    public void windowDeiconified(WindowEvent we) {
      ta.append("Window deiconified\n");
    }

    public void windowIconified(WindowEvent we) {
      ta.append("Window iconified\n");
    }

    public void windowOpened(WindowEvent we) {
      ta.append("Window opened\n");
    }
}
```

If you experiment with this Bean, you will see that one user operation can cause several events. For example, if you minimize a window, both an iconified and deactivated event are generated. If you maximize a window, three notifications (moved, deiconified, and activated) occur. When you close an active window, three events (closing, deactivated, and closed) are generated in sequence.

Adapter Classes

An adapter class provides an empty implementation of all the methods defined by an interface.

An *adapter class* provides empty implementations of all methods defined in a specific event listener interface. An adapter class is useful if you want to process only a subset of the events that are received by a particular interface. You need only define those methods that you are actually using. The empty implementations provided by the adapter class will handle the others. That is, you don't have to provide implementations for the methods that you aren't using.

For example, the **MouseListener** interface has five methods. Assume that you only want to process the **mouseClicked( )** method. First, define a new class that extends **MouseAdapter** and overrides that method. Second, create an instance of that new class. Third, register that object to receive the mouse events. You don't need to provide implementations for the other methods defined by **MouseListener**.

Table 3-9 lists the adapter classes that are provided in the **java.awt.event** package and the event listener interfaces they implement.

The following example illustrates how this is done. A Bean named **Dot** is developed that displays a 200x200-pixel square filled with the background color. Each time the user clicks the mouse in that square, a 4x4-pixel square filled with the foreground color is displayed at the position where the mouse was clicked.

The **Dot** constructor sets the size of the component and initially positions the dot at the center of the Bean. The **addMouseListener( )** method is invoked to register an instance of **MyMouseAdapter** for mouse events generated by **Dot**. Notice that the **Dot** object is passed as an argument to the **MyMouseAdapter** constructor.

The **changePoint( )** method creates a new **Point** object whose position is determined by the information in the **MouseEvent** object. The **repaint( )** method is then called to update the display. The **paint( )** method draws a border around the Bean and draws a 4x4-pixel square filled with the foreground color centered at position **p**.

MyMouseAdapter extends **MouseAdapter**. It can access only the public members of **Dot**. Its constructor accepts a **Dot** object. This is saved for later use. When any mouse event occurs, it is processed by the **MyMouseAdapter** object. Recall that **MouseAdapter** provides an empty implementation of all mouse event handlers. Here, only **mouseClicked( )**

Adapter Class	Event Listener Interface
ComponentAdapter	ComponentListener
ContainerAdapter	ContainerListener
FocusAdapter	FocusListener
KeyAdapter	KeyListener
MouseAdapter	MouseListener
MouseMotionAdapter	MouseMotionListener
WindowAdapter	WindowListener

Adapter
Classes
Table 3-9.

has been overridden. It invokes the **changePoint( )** method of the **Dot** object and passes the **MouseEvent** object as an argument to that method. Empty implementations of the other methods defined by **MouseListener** are provided by the **MouseAdapter** class.

```java
package adapter;
import java.awt.*;
import java.awt.event.*;

public class Dot extends Canvas {
  private Point p;

  public Dot() {
    setSize(200, 200);
    p = new Point(100, 100);
    addMouseListener(new MyMouseAdapter(this));
  }

  public void changePoint(MouseEvent me) {
    p = new Point(me.getX(), me.getY());
    repaint();
  }

  public void paint(Graphics g) {
    Dimension d = getSize();
    g.drawRect(0, 0, d.width - 1, d.height - 1);
    g.fillRect(p.x - 2, p.y - 2, 4, 4);
  }
}

class MyMouseAdapter extends MouseAdapter {
  private Dot dot;

  public MyMouseAdapter(Dot dot) {
    this.dot = dot;
  }

  public void mouseClicked(MouseEvent me) {
    dot.changePoint(me);
  }
}
```

Figure 3-11 shows how this component appears in BeanBox.

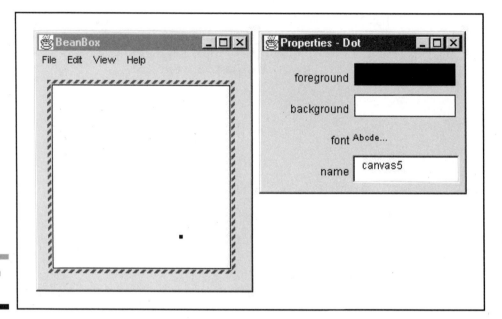

The **Dot** Bean
Figure 3-11.

Inner Classes

Inner classes are defined within the scope of another class.

In the original version of Java, one class could not be defined within another. When Java 1.1 was released, this restriction was lifted. Java 1.1 added a feature called the inner class. An *inner class* is one that is defined within the scope of another class or expression. This capability can be very useful when you're writing code to process events. Consider the Bean in the following listing. Its behavior is identical to that in the previous section. However, it has been rewritten to illustrate how inner classes can be used.

MyMouseAdapter extends **MouseAdapter** and is defined within the scope of **Dot2**. Therefore, it has access to all of the variables and methods of **Dot2**. Its **mouseClicked( )** method can directly invoke the **changePoint( )** method. It is not necessary to define a **MyMouseAdapter** constructor that stores a reference to **Dot2**.

In the **Dot2** constructor, the **addMouseListener( )** method is passed a reference to the **MyMouseAdapter** object that is instantiated.

```
package inner;
import java.awt.*;
import java.awt.event.*;
```

```
public class Dot2 extends Canvas {
  private Point p;

  public Dot2() {
    setSize(200, 200);
    p = new Point(100, 100);
    addMouseListener(new MyMouseAdapter());
  }

  public void changePoint(MouseEvent me) {
    p = new Point(me.getX(), me.getY());
    repaint();
  }

  public void paint(Graphics g) {
    Dimension d = getSize();
    g.drawRect(0, 0, d.width - 1, d.height - 1);
    g.fillRect(p.x - 2, p.y - 2, 4, 4);
  }

  class MyMouseAdapter extends MouseAdapter {
    public void mouseClicked(MouseEvent me) {
      changePoint(me);
    }
  }
}
```

Anonymous Inner Classes

An anonymous inner class does not have a name.

An *anonymous inner class* is one that does not have a name. This capability can be very convenient when you're writing code to process events. Consider the Bean in the following listing. Its behavior is identical to that in the previous section. However, it has been rewritten to illustrate how anonymous inner classes can be used.

There is one top-level class in this program named **Dot3** that extends **Canvas**. The constructor sets the size of the component, initializes the instance variable, and invokes **addMouseListener( )**. The argument to this method is an expression that defines and instantiates an anonymous inner class.

The expression new MouseAdapter( ) { ... } is the key to understanding inner classes. This syntax tells the Java compiler that the code between the braces defines an anonymous inner class that extends

MouseAdapter. An instance of this new class is automatically created when the expression is executed. It has access to all of the variables and methods of the **Dot3** class.

```java
package anonymous;
import java.awt.*;
import java.awt.event.*;

public class Dot3 extends Canvas {
  private Point p;

  public Dot3() {
    setSize(200, 200);
    p = new Point(100, 100);
    addMouseListener(new MouseAdapter() {
      public void mouseClicked(MouseEvent me) {
        changePoint(me);
      }
    });
  }

  public void changePoint(MouseEvent me) {
    p = new Point(me.getX(), me.getY());
    repaint();
  }

  public void paint(Graphics g) {
    Dimension d = getSize();
    g.drawRect(0, 0, d.width - 1, d.height - 1);
    g.fillRect(p.x - 2, p.y - 2, 4, 4);
  }
}
```

Custom Events

The previous sections in this chapter showed how to work with AWT events. You may also define your own types of events. Custom events are useful when one of your objects wants to notify other objects about a change in its state.

There are six steps to accomplish this:

1. You must define a new class to describe the event. This new class must extend **EventObject**.

2. You must define a new interface for listeners to receive this type of event. This new interface must extend **EventListener**.

3. The source must provide methods that allow listeners to register and unregister for event notifications.

4. The source must provide code to generate the event and send it to all registered listeners.

5. The listener must implement the interface to receive the event.

6. The listener must register/unregister to receive the notifications.

The following example demonstrates a custom event. It has two Beans. The **Painter** Bean displays a square filled with a color. The **Selector** Bean provides a graphical user interface that allows a user to choose a color. The **Painter** registers for **ColorEvent** notifications that are generated by the **Selector**.

To experiment with these Beans, map the color event from **Selector** to the **colorChange( )** method of **Painter**. Manipulate the three scroll bars, and observe that the color displayed by **Painter** changes.

Figure 3-12 show how these two Beans appear in the BeanBox.

There are four source files for this example. The code for **ColorEvent** is shown in the following listing. That class extends **EventObject**. Its

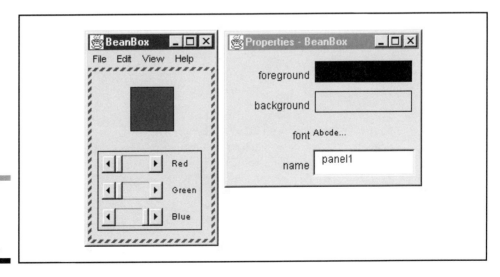

The **Selector** and **Painter** Beans

Figure 3-12.

constructor accepts two arguments. The first is the source of the event. The second is the color. The constructor uses **super** to pass the source to the **EventObject** constructor. The **getColor( )** method returns the color value.

```
package cselector;
import java.awt.*;
import java.awt.event.*;
import java.util.*;

public class ColorEvent extends EventObject {
  private Color color;

  public ColorEvent(Object source, Color color) {
    super(source);
    this.color = color;
  }

  public Color getColor() {
    return color;
  }
}
```

The code for **ColorListener** is shown in the following listing. That interface extends **EventListener**. It contains one method, **changeColor( )**, which accepts a **ColorEvent** object as its argument.

```
package cselector;
import java.util.*;

public interface ColorListener extends EventListener {
  public void changeColor(ColorEvent ce);
}
```

The code for **Painter** is shown in the following listing. It defines the Bean that implements the **ColorListener** interface to receive **ColorEvent** objects. The **changeColor( )** method receives a **ColorEvent** as its argument. The information in that event is saved in the **color** instance variable. The **repaint( )** method is then invoked to update the display.

```
package cselector;
import java.awt.*;

public class Painter extends Canvas implements ColorListener {
  private Color color;

  public Painter() {
    color = Color.white;
    setSize(50, 50);
```

```
    }

    public void paint(Graphics g) {
      Dimension d = getSize();
      int w = d.width;
      int h = d.height;
      g.setColor(color);
      g.fillRect(0, 0, w - 1, h - 1);
      g.setColor(Color.black);
      g.drawRect(0, 0, w - 1, h - 1);
    }

    public void changeColor(ColorEvent ce) {
      this.color = ce.getColor();
      repaint();
    }
}
```

The code for **Selector** is shown in the following listing. It defines the Bean that provides a graphical user interface to generate **ColorEvent** objects. There are five instance variables. The current color is stored in **color**. References to the registered listeners are kept in the **listeners** variable. The other variables hold references to the scroll bars.

The constructor begins by initializing **listeners** and creating the elements of the user interface. Note that the **addAdjustmentListener( )** method is called for each scroll bar. A reference to the current object (that is, the **Selector** object) is passed as its argument. This causes the **adjustmentValueChanged( )** method to be invoked every time any scroll bar is manipulated. The access methods for the **color** property follow the constructor.

The **paint( )** method simply draws a border around the Bean. The **adjustmentValueChanged( )** method reads the values of all three scroll bars and instantiates a **Color** object. A **ColorEvent** object is created. The first argument to that constructor is a reference to the current object, and the second argument is a reference to the **Color** object. The **fireColorEvent( )** method is then invoked to multicast this event to all registered listeners.

The **addColorListener( )** and **removeColorListener( )** methods allow listeners to register and unregister for event notifications. The **fireColorEvent( )** method performs the event notification function. It begins by cloning the vector that references the registered listeners. This is done inside a **synchronized** block to ensure that an element is not removed from or added to the list during the clone operation. When the cloned list is complete, the **changeColor( )** method is invoked on each of its members.

```java
package cselector;
import java.awt.*;
import java.awt.event.*;
import java.beans.*;
import java.util.*;

public class Selector extends Panel
implements AdjustmentListener {
  private Color color;
  private Vector listeners;
  private Scrollbar rScrollbar, gScrollbar, bScrollbar;

  public Selector() {

    // Initialize listeners vector
    listeners = new Vector();

    // Initialize GUI elements
    setLayout(new GridLayout(3, 2, 5, 5));
    rScrollbar =
      new Scrollbar(Scrollbar.HORIZONTAL, 255, 10, 0, 265);
    add(rScrollbar);
    rScrollbar.addAdjustmentListener(this);
    Label rLabel = new Label("Red", Label.LEFT);
    add(rLabel);
    gScrollbar =
      new Scrollbar(Scrollbar.HORIZONTAL, 255, 10, 0, 265);
    add(gScrollbar);
    gScrollbar.addAdjustmentListener(this);
    Label gLabel = new Label("Green", Label.LEFT);
    add(gLabel);
    bScrollbar =
      new Scrollbar(Scrollbar.HORIZONTAL, 255, 10, 0, 265);
    add(bScrollbar);
    bScrollbar.addAdjustmentListener(this);
    Label bLabel = new Label("Blue", Label.LEFT);
    add(bLabel);
  }

  public Insets getInsets() {
    return new Insets(5, 5, 5, 5);
  }
```

```java
public Color getColor() {
  return color;
}

public void setColor(Color color) {
  this.color = color;
}

public void paint(Graphics g) {
  Dimension d = getSize();
  g.drawRect(0, 0, d.width - 1, d.height - 1);
}

public void adjustmentValueChanged(AdjustmentEvent ae) {
  Scrollbar source = (Scrollbar)ae.getSource();
  int value = ae.getValue();
  source.setValue(value);
  int r = rScrollbar.getValue();
  int g = gScrollbar.getValue();
  int b = bScrollbar.getValue();
  color = new Color(r, g, b);
  fireColorEvent(new ColorEvent(this, color));
}

public void
addColorListener(ColorListener cl) {
  listeners.addElement(cl);
}

public void
removeColorListener(ColorListener cl) {
  listeners.removeElement(cl);
}

public void fireColorEvent(ColorEvent ce) {
  Vector v;
  synchronized(this) {
    v = (Vector)listeners.clone();
  }
  for(int i = 0; i < v.size(); i++) {
    ColorListener cl = (ColorListener)v.elementAt(i);
    cl.changeColor(ce);
  }
}
}
```

In this example, you have seen that a custom event can be generated and sent to a registered listener. You may wish to experiment with these components further by confirming that a **Selector** Bean can multicast **ColorEvent** objects to multiple **Painter** Beans.

NOTE: This example contains two Beans and a supporting class. For correct operation, the manifest template file must contain entries for both Beans. Also check that the JAR file contains all three .class files. The file **ColorEvent.class** is needed by the Beans and must be in the JAR file. For the simple examples in this book, it is easiest to always package all .class files associated with an example into the JAR file.

CHAPTER 4

Persistence

Y ou have seen how software can be built by selecting, configuring, and connecting a set of Beans. After a developer has completed this work, it is necessary to save this information in a file before exiting from the builder tool. Later, the tool can be restarted, and the data in that file can be used to restore the objects. The feature of Beans that allows you to do this is *persistence*.

This chapter discusses how persistence is provided by Java. It begins by defining the serialization and deserialization mechanisms that allow you to save and restore the state of a set of objects. You will see the interfaces and classes that provide this functionality.

In many cases, the default serialization and deserialization mechanisms are sufficient to save/restore your Beans. However, there are situations that require you to customize this process. Several examples are provided to illustrate how this is done. Customized serialization features are essential when you are designing production quality Beans.

A section is included here about object *versioning*, which allows you to handle different versions of a class where serialization is concerned. Specifically, you will see how to update a class and read serialized objects generated with a previous version of that class.

Saving and Restoring Beans in the BDK

To better understand persistence, let's begin with an example:

1. Start the BDK and create an instance of the **Spectrum** Bean from Chapter 2. Its **vertical** property is initially **true**. Change this value to **false**. You will see an immediate change in the appearance of the Bean.

2. Now select the File | Save menu options in BeanBox. A file dialog box titled "Save As" appears. Press the Save button to serialize this Bean to the default file beanbox.tmp. Select the File | Exit menu options to exit the BDK.

3. Start the BDK again. Select the File | Load options in BeanBox. A file dialog box titled "Open" appears. Press the Open button to restore the Bean from the default file beanbox.tmp. Observe that the component appears, and its **vertical** property is **false**.

This exercise demonstrates how a simple Bean with one property could be serialized and deserialized. It demonstrates the essence of persistence—the ability to save the state of a Bean and restore it later.

Now let's save two Beans and their connections:

1. Create an instance of the **Counter** Bean from Chapter 2. Also create an instance of **TickTock**. Change its **interval** property to **1**, and map its property change events to the **increment( )** method of **Counter**. You should see the counter incrementing. Wait until the count equals 30.

2. Select the BeanBox by clicking the mouse button in a empty region of that window. Repeat the steps previously outlined in order to save and restore **Counter** and **TickTock**.

Observe that the restored counter does not begin counting at 0. Instead, the count value was saved/restored as part of the serialization/deserialization process. Therefore, the Bean resumes with a nonzero value. (This behavior may not be what the customer wants from the **Counter** Bean. Instead, it may be desirable to have the counter resume counting from zero. This chapter will discuss how to provide this behavior.)

4

Serialization and Deserialization

Serialization is the process of saving an object's state.

Serialization is the ability to *save* the state of several objects to a stream. The stream is typically associated with a file. This allows an application to start execution, create a set of objects, save their state in a file, and terminate.

Deserialization is the process of restoring an object's state.

Deserialization is the ability to *restore* the state of several objects from a stream. This allows an application to start execution, read a file, restore a set of objects from the data in that file, and continue.

If an object contains references to other objects, these are also saved. This is done automatically. The process is recursive, so an attempt to serialize one object can result in the serialization of many other objects. The serialization mechanisms are designed to correctly handle sets of objects that have circular references to each other.

Only the nonstatic and nontransient parts of an object's state are saved by the serialization mechanisms. Static fields of an object are not saved, because they are considered part of the state of the class, not the state of an object. In addition, static fields are sometimes initialized by static initialization blocks that are executed when the class is loaded. Transient fields of an object are not saved, since they contain temporary data not needed to correctly restore that object later. In addition to the object state data, some type information is saved so the object can be reconstructed properly.

It is important to understand that when an object is deserialized, none of its constructors is invoked. Instead, memory is allocated and the variables are set directly from the data that is read from the serial stream. If your constructors perform actions that are essential to getting an object running correctly (for example, starting threads), you will need to follow the techniques explained later in this chapter.

Object Graphs

Consider the collection of objects shown in Figure 4-1. There are five objects that hold references to each other as depicted by the arrows. This arrangement is called an *object graph*. Note that there are cycles in the graph. That is, it is possible to reach some objects by more than one path. For example, D can be reached by starting at A and following the references labeled "2," "6," and "8." It can also be accessed by starting at A and following the references labeled "2" and "5." You can also traverse the references labeled "1" and "3" to access D.

If you attempt to serialize A, the references among these objects cause all of them to be saved.

Although an object may be encountered several times during this process, it is extremely important that it be saved only once in the serial stream. Otherwise, multiple copies of the same object will be created during deserialization. The Java persistence mechanisms have been designed to operate in this manner. When an object is encountered a second time,

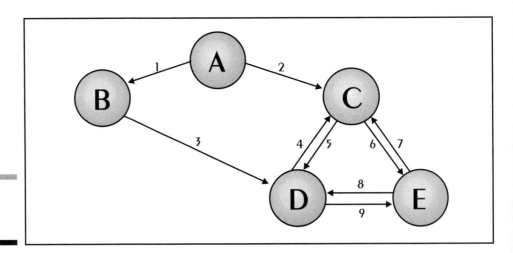

An object
graph

Figure 4-1.

another complete copy of it is not written to the stream. Instead, a *handle* is written. This is a compact reference to an object that has already been written to the stream.

Serializable

Serializable is the interface that indicates a class may be serialized.

The **Serializable** interface in the **java.io** package defines no constants or methods. It exists simply to designate that an object may be saved to and restored from a serial stream. An object can be serialized only if its class implements this interface. A **java.io.NotSerializableException** is generated if an attempt is made to serialize any object whose class has not been defined in this manner.

4

Many classes provided with the JDK libraries have been designed to be serializable. The **Component** class is an example. Therefore, any component you create that inherits from this class can be serialized. This capability is invaluable for Beans that present a graphical user interface. They can be saved to and restored from persistent storage. Many other classes that we have been working with, such as **Color**, **Font**, **Rectangle**, and **String**, are serializable. The class **Number** is defined to implement **Serializable**. Therefore, its subclasses such as **Float** and **Integer** are also serializable. This is very important because Bean properties are frequently of these types, and you want to save that information.

However, there are many other types in the Java class library that are not serializable. For example, objects of class **Thread** cannot be saved in persistent storage. The reason is that the implementation of threads is tightly coupled with the particular platform on which the JVM (Java Virtual Machine) is running. Think about the complexities of "freezing" a group of threads. All of the internal information used to manage each of those threads, such as its stack, priority, and current status, would need to be correctly saved. Now imagine the complexity of trying to correctly "unfreeze" each of these threads on a different platform. The task becomes unmanageable.

Almost none of the classes in the **java.io** package are serializable. Consider the class **RandomAccessFile**. Internally, it acquires file handles and keeps track of the read and write positions in the file. It would not be possible to "freeze" this transient state information and hope to use it at a later time, even on the same machine. For much the same reason, many classes in the **java.net** package are not serializable. In particular, instances of **ServerSocket**, **Socket**, **DatagramSocket**, and **MulticastSocket** cannot be saved.

The class **Runtime** is not serializable because it encapsulates a variety of platform-dependent system functions. **Process** represents a program that is external to the JVM. Therefore, it is not serializable.

If you want to serialize an object that has instance variables of these types, those variables must be designated as **transient**. Later sections of this chapter provide examples to illustrate this point.

A Serializable Bean

This section develops a Bean called **Graph** that shows six nodes positioned at the corners of a hexagon. You can create a link between two nodes by moving the mouse to a node, pressing the mouse button, dragging the mouse to another node, and then releasing it. This Bean is serializable because all of its classes either directly or indirectly implement the **Serializable** interface. It illustrates several issues relating to persistence.

Figure 4-2 shows how the **Graph** Bean appears in BeanBox.

The source code for the example is located in three files.

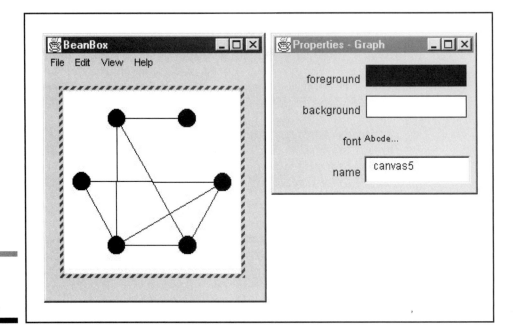

The **Graph** Bean

Figure 4-2.

4

The **Graph** class is defined in the following listing. It extends **Canvas** and implements **MouseListener** and **MouseMotionListener**. The **Graph** class is serializable because it inherits from the **Component** class, which implements the **Serializable** interface. References to the **Node** and **Link** objects that make up the graph are maintained in vectors named **nodes** and **links**. Variables **node1** and **node2** are used only when the user is drawing a link between two nodes. They are **transient** because we do not want to store this data as part of the serialization process. Variables **x** and **y** are used only to track the current position of the mouse as it is being dragged. These are also **transient** variables because we do not want to store this data as part of the serialization process.

The constructor begins by setting the size of the Bean to 200x200 pixels and initializing the **nodes** and **links** vectors. The object registers itself to receive mouse and mouse motion events. Finally, the **makeNodes( )** method is called to create the six nodes at the appropriate positions.

Implementations are provided for all of the methods in the **MouseListener** and **MouseMotionListener** interfaces.

The **doMousePressed( )** method checks if the mouse is positioned within a node. If so, the variable **node1** is set to reference that node. Otherwise, **node1** is set to **null**.

The **doMouseDragged( )** method updates the **x** and **y** variables to track the position of the mouse and invokes **repaint( )** so that a rubber-band line can be drawn from the center of the first node to the current mouse position.

The **doMouseReleased( )** method checks if **node1** has been set. If so, it then checks if the mouse is positioned within a node. If so, **makeLink( )** is called to create a **Link** object connecting **node1** and **node2**. In any case, **node1** and **node2** are set to **null**, and **repaint( )** is called to update the display.

The **paint( )** method draws the nodes, links, and a rubber-band line if needed.

The **makeNodes( )** method generates a display that shows the nodes of the graph and adds these to the **nodes** vector.

The **makeLink( )** method returns if a link already exists between **node1** and **node2**. Otherwise, it creates a new **Link** object and adds it to the **links** vector.

The **linkExists( )** method returns **true** if a link already exists between two specified nodes. Otherwise, it returns **false**.

```
package graphs;
import java.awt.*;
import java.awt.event.*;
import java.io.*;
import java.util.*;

public class Graph extends Canvas
implements MouseListener, MouseMotionListener {
  private final static int NNODES = 6;
  private Vector nodes;
  private Vector links;
  private transient Node node1, node2;
  private transient int x, y;

  public Graph() {
    setSize(200, 200);
    nodes = new Vector();
    links = new Vector();
    addMouseListener(this);
    addMouseMotionListener(this);
    makeNodes();
  }

  public void mouseClicked(MouseEvent me) {
  }

  public void mouseEntered(MouseEvent me) {
  }

  public void mouseExited(MouseEvent me) {
  }

  public void mousePressed(MouseEvent me) {
    doMousePressed(me);
  }

  public void mouseReleased(MouseEvent me) {
    doMouseReleased(me);
  }

  public void mouseDragged(MouseEvent me) {
    doMouseDragged(me);
  }

  public void mouseMoved(MouseEvent me) {
```

```
    }

    public void doMousePressed(MouseEvent me) {
      // Check if node1 should be initialized
      x = me.getX();
      y = me.getY();
      Enumeration e = nodes.elements();
      while(e.hasMoreElements()) {
        node1 = (Node)e.nextElement();
        if(node1.contains(x, y)) {
          return;
        }
      }
      node1 = null;
    }

    public void doMouseDragged(MouseEvent me) {
      x = me.getX();
      y = me.getY();
      repaint();
    }

    public void doMouseReleased(MouseEvent me) {
      // Make a link between node1 and node2
      x = me.getX();
      y = me.getY();
      if(node1 != null) {
        Enumeration e = nodes.elements();
        while(e.hasMoreElements()) {
          node2 = (Node)e.nextElement();
          if(node2.contains(x, y)) {
            makeLink(node1.getId(), node2.getId());
            break;
          }
        }
        node1 = node2 = null;
        repaint();
      }
    }

    public void paint(Graphics g) {
      // Draw nodes
      Enumeration e = nodes.elements();
      while(e.hasMoreElements()) {
        ((Node)e.nextElement()).draw(g);
```

```
      }
      // Draw links
      e = links.elements();
      while(e.hasMoreElements()) {
        ((Link)e.nextElement()).draw(g);
      }
      // Draw rubber band line (if any)
      if(node1 != null) {
        g.drawLine(node1.getX(), node1.getY(), x, y);
      }
    }

    private void makeNodes() {
      // Initialize nodes variable
      Dimension d = getSize();
      int width = d.width;
      int height = d.height;
      int centerx = width/2;
      int centery = height/2;
      double radius =
        (width < height) ? 0.4 * width : 0.4 * height;
      for(int i = 0; i < NNODES; i++) {
        double theta = i * 2 * Math.PI/NNODES;
        int x = (int)(centerx + radius * Math.cos(theta));
        int y = (int)(centery - radius * Math.sin(theta));
        nodes.addElement(new Node(x, y));
      }
    }

    private void makeLink(int id1, int id2) {
      // Return if a link already exists between these nodes
      if(linkExists(id1, id2)) {
        return;
      }
      // Otherwise, create a new link
      Node n1 = (Node)nodes.elementAt(id1);
      Node n2 = (Node)nodes.elementAt(id2);
      links.addElement(new Link(n1, n2));
    }

    private boolean linkExists(int i, int j) {
      // Check if a link exists between nodes i and j
      Enumeration e = links.elements();
      while(e.hasMoreElements()) {
        Link link = (Link)e.nextElement();
```

```
        int id1 = link.getNode1().getId();
        int id2 = link.getNode2().getId();
        if((id1 == i && id2 == j) || (id1 == j && id2 == i)) {
          return true;
        }
      }
    }
    return false;
  }
}
```

The source code for the **Node** class is shown in the following listing. Note that this class must implement **Serializable**. Because the **Graph** object holds references to **Node** objects, any attempt to serialize the Bean will also cause the **Node** objects to be serialized.

The radius of the node is defined by an **int** constant **NODERADIUS**. Each **Node** object has an instance variable named **id** that contains a unique value to identify that node. The **Node** class has a static variable named **count** that is incremented each time a **Node** object is created. This is the mechanism used to assign a unique **id** value for each node. The **x** and **y** variables define the center position of the node.

The constructor initializes the instance variables. Note that the **id** variable is set from the current value of the static **count** variable. Access methods for the **x**, **y**, and **id** variables follow the constructor.

The **contains( )** method returns **true** if a point is within the node. Otherwise, it returns **false**. The **draw( )** method displays the node.

```
package graphs;
import java.awt.*;
import java.io.*;

public class Node implements Serializable {
  private final static int NODERADIUS = 10;
  private static int count = 0;
  private int x, y, id;

  public Node(int x, int y) {
    this.x = x;
    this.y = y;
    id = count++;
  }

  public int getX() {
```

```
    return x;
  }

  public int getY() {
    return y;
  }

  public int getId() {
    return id;
  }

  public boolean contains(int x, int y) {
    int deltax = this.x - x;
    int deltay = this.y - y;
    int a = deltax * deltax + deltay * deltay;
    int b = NODERADIUS * NODERADIUS;
    return (a <= b);
  }

  public void draw(Graphics g) {
    int w = 2 * NODERADIUS;
    int h = w;
    g.fillOval(x - NODERADIUS, y - NODERADIUS, w, h);
  }
}
```

The source code for the **Link** class is shown in the following listing. Note
that this class must be **Serializable**. Because the **Graph** object holds
references to **Link** objects, any attempt to serialize the Bean will also cause
the **Link** objects to be serialized.

The **node1** and **node2** variables hold references to the two nodes connected
by this link. The **getNode1( )** and **getNode2( )** methods provide access to
these variables. The **draw( )** method draws a line connecting the centers of
the two nodes.

```
package graphs;
import java.awt.*;
import java.io.*;

public class Link implements Serializable {
  private Node node1, node2;

  public Link(Node node1, Node node2) {
    this.node1 = node1;
```

```
      this.node2 = node2;
  }

  public Node getNode1() {
    return node1;
  }

  public Node getNode2() {
    return node2;
  }

  public void draw(Graphics g) {
    int x1 = node1.getX();
    int y1 = node1.getY();
    int x2 = node2.getX();
    int y2 = node2.getY();
    g.drawLine(x1, y1, x2, y2);
  }
}
```

Note that the **Link** objects have references to **Node** objects. Furthermore, a given **Node** object may be referenced by more than one **Link** object. This example has illustrated that object graphs are correctly saved and restored. To confirm this, try saving and restoring the state of this Bean.

The Serialization Streams

Java provides several stream classes that aid in the serialization of Beans. Three are **ObjectOutputStream**, **ObjectInputStream**, and **ObjectStreamClass**. They are described here along with several examples that illustrate their use.

ObjectOutputStream

The **ObjectOutputStream** class in the **java.io** package provides methods to serialize objects, arrays, and simple types to an output stream. These methods are summarized in Table 4-1. All of these methods can throw an **IOException**.

Two of these methods deserve special mention. The **writeObject( )** method is used to serialize an object and all other objects that are directly or indirectly referenced by it. The **defaultWriteObject( )** method is frequently used during custom serialization.

Method	Description
void close( )	Closes the stream
void defaultWriteObject( )	Writes the nonstatic and nontransient fields of the current object to the stream
void flush( )	Flushes the stream
void reset( )	Resets the stream
void write(int *i*)	Writes *i* to the stream
void write(byte *b*[ ])	Writes the array *b* to the stream
void write(byte *b*[ ], int *index* int *num*)	Writes *num* bytes starting at *index* in array *b* to the stream
void writeBoolean(boolean *b*)	Writes *b* to the stream
void writeByte(int *b*)	Writes *b* to the stream
void writeBytes(String *str*)	Writes *str* to the stream
void writeChar(int *ch*)	Writes *ch* to the stream
void writeChars(String *str*)	Writes *str* to the stream
void writeDouble(double *d*)	Writes *d* to the stream
void writeFloat(float *f*)	Writes *f* to the stream
void writeInt(int *i*)	Writes *i* to the stream
void writeLong(long *l*)	Writes *l* to the stream
void writeObject(Object *o*)	Writes *o* to the stream
void writeShort(short *s*)	Writes *s* to the stream
void writeUTF(String *str*)	Writes *str* to the stream in UTF format

Methods Defined by **ObjectOutput-Stream**
Table 4-1.

ObjectStreamClass

The **ObjectStreamClass** class in the **java.io** package encapsulates information about a serialized object. It contains the name of the class and a **long** named **serialVersionUID**. (This latter variable is described later in this chapter.) Instances of this object are created and stored in the serial stream. This is the mechanism by which type information is saved.

ObjectInputStream

The **ObjectInputStream** class in the **java.io** package provides methods to deserialize objects, arrays, and simple types from an output stream. The most commonly used methods are summarized in Table 4-2. All of these methods

Method	Description
int available( )	Returns the number of bytes that are available for reading.
void close( )	Closes the stream.
void defaultReadObject( )	Reads the nonstatic and nontransient fields of the current object from the stream.
int read( )	Returns a **byte** from the stream. Blocks if no data is available.
int read(byte *b*[ ], int *index*, int *num*)	Reads a maximum of *num* bytes from the stream into array *b* starting at *index*. Blocks if no data is available. Returns the number of bytes actually read or –1 at the end of the stream.
boolean readBoolean( )	Reads a **boolean** from the stream.
byte readByte( )	Reads a **byte** from the stream.
char readChar( )	Reads a **char** from the stream.
double readDouble( )	Reads a **double** from the stream.
float readFloat( )	Reads a **float** from the stream.
int readInt( )	Reads an **int** from the stream.
long readLong( )	Reads a **long** from the stream.
Object readObject( )	Reads an object from the stream.
short readShort( )	Reads a **short** from the stream.
String readUTF( )	Reads a UTF format string from the stream.
int readUnsignedByte( )	Reads an unsigned **byte** from the stream.
int readUnsignedShort( )	Reads an unsigned **short** from the stream.
int skipBytes(int *num*)	Skips a maximum of *num* bytes in the stream. Returns the number of bytes actually skipped.

Some Methods Defined by **ObjectInput-Stream**

Table 4-2.

can throw an **IOException**. The **defaultReadObject( )** method can also throw a **ClassNotFoundException** or **NotActiveException**. The methods to read specific data types can also throw an **EOFException**.

Two of these methods deserve special mention. The **readObject( )** method is used to deserialize an object and all other objects that are directly or indirectly referenced by it. The **defaultReadObject( )** method is frequently used during custom deserialization.

Some Simple Serialization Examples

This section shows some simple applications that perform serialization and deserialization by using the classes just described.

Saving and Restoring Objects

The first example shows how to save and restore a set of objects. This example consists of two programs: one that saves the objects and one that restores them. The program shown next saves the set of objects to a file. It begins by creating a **Vector** object containing **Integer**, **Rectangle**, and **String** objects as its elements. These objects are then serialized and saved to a file named save1.data in the current directory. An **ObjectOutputStream** object is created, and its **writeObject( )** method is used to perform the serialization. The **Vector** object is provided as the argument to this method. All of the other referenced objects are automatically serialized.

```
package serial;

import java.awt.*;
import java.io.*;
import java.util.*;

public class Save1 {
  public static void main(String args[]) {
    try {
      Vector v = new Vector();
      v.addElement(new Integer(-7));
      v.addElement(new Rectangle(20, 20, 100, 50));
      v.addElement("Hello");
      System.out.println(v);
      FileOutputStream fos;
      fos = new FileOutputStream("save1.data");
      ObjectOutputStream oos;
      oos = new ObjectOutputStream(fos);
```

```
      oos.writeObject(v);
      oos.flush();
      fos.close();
    }
    catch(Exception ex) {
      System.out.println("Exception: " + ex);
    }
  }
}
```

To test this program, type the following on the command line:

    java serial.Save1

The output from this program is shown here:

```
[-7, java.awt.rectangle[x=20,y=20,width=100,height=50], Hello]
```

The next program deserializes objects from the data in save1.data. In it, an **ObjectInputStream** object is created. Its **readObject( )** method is used to perform the deserialization. All of the other objects referenced by the vector are automatically deserialized.

```
package serial;
import java.io.*;

public class Restore {
  public static void main(String args[]) {
    try {
      FileInputStream fis = new FileInputStream(args[0]);
      ObjectInputStream ois = new ObjectInputStream(fis);
      Object obj = ois.readObject();
      fis.close();
      System.out.println(obj);
    }
    catch(Exception ex) {
      System.out.println("Exception: " + ex);
    }
  }
}
```

To test this program, type the following on the command line:

    java serial.Restore save1.data

The output is shown next:

```
[-7, java.awt.rectangle[x=20,y=20,width=100,height=50], Hello]
```

Note that this output is identical to that of the **Save1** application. It was possible to save/restore each of these four objects because their classes are defined as **Serializable**.

Serializing Your Own Objects

Let us now look at an example that illustrates how to save your own types of objects. The following listing shows an application that saves a set of objects to a file. The program begins by creating a **Vector** object containing three **Person** objects as its elements. These objects are then serialized and saved to a file named save2.data in the current directory. Note that the **Person** class implements **Serializable**.

```java
package serial;

import java.awt.*;
import java.io.*;
import java.util.*;

public class Save2 {
  public static void main(String args[]) {
    try {
      Vector v = new Vector();
      v.addElement(new Person("Joe", "7834"));
      v.addElement(new Person("Claire", "6550"));
      v.addElement(new Person("Viviane", "2323"));
      System.out.println(v);
      FileOutputStream fos;
      fos = new FileOutputStream("save2.data");
      ObjectOutputStream oos;
      oos = new ObjectOutputStream(fos);
      oos.writeObject(v);
      oos.flush();
      fos.close();
    }
    catch(Exception ex) {
      System.out.println("Exception: " + ex);
    }
  }
}
```

```
class Person implements Serializable {
  private String name, phone;
  public Person(String name, String phone) {
    this.name = name;
    this.phone = phone;
  }
  public String toString() {
    return "[" + name + "," + phone + "]";
  }
}
```

To test this program, type the following on the command line:

> java serial.Save2

The output from this program is shown here:

```
[[Joe,7834], [Claire,6550], [Viviane,2323]]
```

The **Restore** program from the previous example can also be used to read save2.data. Simply type the following on the command line:

> java serial.Restore save2.data

Observe that the output is identical to that of **Save2**.

You may wish to experiment with the **Save2** program by temporarily deleting the "implements Serializable" designation for the **Person** class. Compile the program and then attempt to execute it. You will observe the following output from **Save2**:

```
[[Joe,7834], [Claire,6550], [Viviane,2323]]
Exception: java.io.NotSerializableException: serial.Person
```

Serializing Simple Types and Objects

The following listing shows an application that uses several of the **ObjectOutputStream** methods to serialize simple types and an object. The data is saved to a file named save3.data in the current directory.

```
package serial;
import java.awt.*;
import java.io.*;
```

```
public class Save3 {
  public static void main(String args[]) {
    try {
      FileOutputStream fos;
      fos = new FileOutputStream("save3.data");
      ObjectOutputStream oos;
      oos = new ObjectOutputStream(fos);
      oos.writeInt(5);
      oos.writeDouble(Math.PI);
      oos.writeBoolean(true);
      oos.writeObject(Color.blue);
      oos.writeChar('a');
      oos.flush();
      fos.close();
    }
    catch(Exception ex) {
      System.out.println("Exception: " + ex);
    }
  }
}
```

To test this program, type the following on the command line:

    java serial.Save3

There is no output from the program.

The program to read save3.data is shown in the following listing. Note that you must read elements from the serial stream in the same sequence that they were written.

```
package serial;
import java.io.*;

public class Restore3 {
  public static void main(String args[]) {
    try {
      FileInputStream fis = new FileInputStream("save3.data");
      ObjectInputStream ois = new ObjectInputStream(fis);
      System.out.println(ois.readInt());
      System.out.println(ois.readDouble());
      System.out.println(ois.readBoolean());
      System.out.println(ois.readObject());
```

```
        System.out.println(ois.readChar());
        fis.close();
      }
    catch(Exception ex) {
      System.out.println("Exception: " + ex);
      }
    }
  }
}
```

To test this program, type the following on the command line:

    java serial.Restore3

The output from this program is shown next:

```
5
3.141592653589793
true
java.awt.Color[r=0,g=0,b=255]
a
```

Exceptions

There are various types of exceptions that can occur during the serialization/deserialization process. They are defined in the **java.io** package and are briefly summarized in Table 4-3. Watch for these when you're creating real-world programs. They can be valuable because you can provide a specific error message for the user. Each of these classes extends **ObjectStreamException**, which extends **IOException**.

Custom Serialization

The examples in the previous section used the default serialization mechanisms to save and restore the state of an object. However, there are situations when you need to customize this behavior.

To customize the serialization behavior for a class, you must provide this method:

    private void writeObject(ObjectOutputStream *oos*) throws IOException

Here, *oos* is an **ObjectOutputStream** to which the current object is serialized.

Exception	Meaning
InvalidClassException	There is a problem with a class (for example, it contains unknown data types, is not public, does not have a zero-arg constructor).
InvalidObjectException	An object failed validation tests after deserialization.
NotActiveException	Serialization or deserialization is not active.
NotSerializableException	An object's class does not implement **Serializable**.
OptionalDataException	The stream contains a simple data type rather than an object.
StreamCorruptedException	The stream is corrupted.
WriteAbortedException	This is thrown during deserialization to indicate that an **ObjectStreamException** occurred during serialization.

Serialization/
Deserialization
Exceptions
Table 4-3.

To customize the deserialization behavior for a class, you must provide this method:

> private void readObject(ObjectInputStream *ois*) throws IOException

Here, *ois* is an **ObjectInputStream** from which the current object is deserialized.

The serialization mechanisms are designed to invoke these methods if they exist. Otherwise, default processing is performed.

Notice that these methods are **private**. This prevents an object from having its data serialized on command from another object. However, the serialization mechanisms can still invoke the methods.

Custom Serialization Examples

The examples in the previous sections illustrated how Java makes it very easy to serialize and deserialize an object. The only effort required on the part of the programmer was to designate a class as **Serializable**. Unfortunately, things are not always this easy. This section develops examples to illustrate how to handle some special cases.

Threads

Consider a Bean that displays the current time in hours, minutes, and seconds. Figure 4-3 shows how this Bean appears in BeanBox.

Internally, it uses a thread to update the display every second. However, the **Thread** class is not serializable. How can you save and restore the state of this component?

The following listing shows a solution. An instance variable **thread** is designated as **transient**. Therefore, the serialization mechanisms ignore it. If the variable is not tagged in this manner, an attempt to serialize the **Clock** object generates a **java.io.NotSerializableException**. Next, the constructor creates a **TextField** object in which the time information is displayed and adds it to the container. The **startThread( )** method is then invoked to create and start the thread.

The **run( )** method defines an infinite loop in which the current time is updated every second. A **SimpleDateFormat** object is created. The argument to the constructor specifies that the date and time information is to be formatted with hours, minutes, and seconds. Inside the loop, the thread sleeps for 1,000 milliseconds. The current date and time information is then obtained by instantiating a **Date** object. This is passed as an argument to **format( )** of the **SimpleDateFormat** object. That method returns a **String** object containing the formatted information. The **setText( )** method of the **TextField** object updates that field.

The **readObject( )** method provides custom deserialization of this object. It first invokes the **defaultReadObject( )** method of **ObjectInputStream**

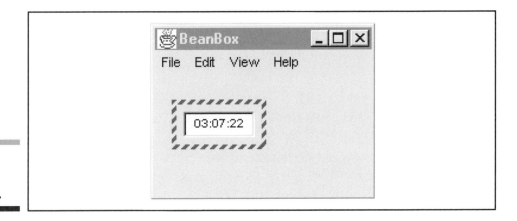

The **Clock**
Bean
Figure 4-3.

to restore the nonstatic and nontransient fields. Then it invokes the **startThread( )** method to create and start a thread to run the clock.

```java
package clock;
import java.awt.*;
import java.io.*;
import java.text.*;
import java.util.*;

public class Clock extends Panel implements Runnable {
  private TextField tf;
  private transient Thread thread;

  public Clock() {
    tf = new TextField("", 6);
    add(tf);
    startThread();
  }

  private void startThread() {
    thread = new Thread(this);
    thread.start();
  }

  public void run() {
    try {
      SimpleDateFormat sdf;
      sdf = new SimpleDateFormat("HH:mm:ss");
      while(true) {
        Thread.sleep(1000);
        tf.setText(sdf.format(new Date()));
      }
    }
    catch(Exception ex) {
      ex.printStackTrace();
    }
  }

  private void readObject(ObjectInputStream ois)
  throws IOException, ClassNotFoundException {
    try {
      ois.defaultReadObject();
      startThread();
    }
    catch(Exception ex) {
```

```
            ex.printStackTrace();
        }
    }
}
```

Static Variables

When making a Bean persistent, you must also consider its static variables. These are not handled by the default serialization mechanisms. Recall that a static variable is shared by all instances of a class. This presents a special challenge when serializing and deserializing Beans.

The **Widget** Bean in the next example appears as either a square or a circle filled with the foreground color. This is controlled by a static **boolean** property named **square**. If **square** is **true**, the component appears as a square. Otherwise, it appears as a circle. You may create several instances of **Widget** in BeanBox. If you change the **square** property for any one of these, the appearance of all **Widget** objects changes immediately. Figure 4-4 shows how instances of this Bean appear in BeanBox.

There are two static variables in the **Widget** class. The **widgets** variable is a vector that holds references to all of the **Widget** objects. The **square** variable is a **boolean** that determines the shape of the component. Both of these variables are initialized when the **Widget** class is loaded.

The constructor begins by adding the current object to the vector referenced by the **widgets** variable. It sets the size of the component to 40x40 pixels.

4

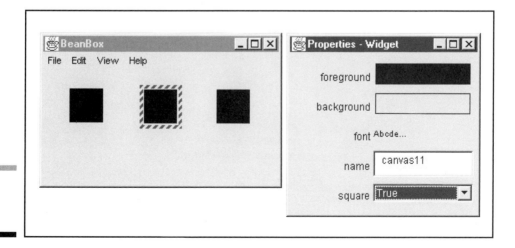

The **Widget**
Bean
Figure 4-4.

The access methods for the **square** property follow the constructor. Note that when the property is written, the **repaint( )** method is called for all **Widget** objects referenced by the **widgets** variable.

The **paint( )** method is straightforward. Its behavior is affected by the static variable **square**.

The **writeObject( )** method provides custom serialization for this object. It first invokes the **defaultWriteObject( )** method of the **ObjectOutputStream** to save the nonstatic variables. If the object being saved is the first element in the **widgets** vector, the **writeBoolean( )** method is also called to save the state of the **square** variable to the output stream. This design ensures that the static variable is saved only once in the stream.

The **readObject( )** method provides custom deserialization for this object. It first invokes the **defaultReadObject( )** method of the **ObjectInputStream** to restore the nonstatic variables. It then saves that object in the **widgets** vector. If the object being restored is the first element in the **widgets** vector, the **readBoolean( )** method is also called to restore the state of the **square** variable from the input stream.

```java
package widgets;
import java.awt.*;
import java.io.*;
import java.util.*;

public class Widget extends Canvas {
  private static Vector widgets = new Vector();
  private static boolean square = false;

  public Widget() {
    widgets.addElement(this);
    setSize(40, 40);
  }

  public boolean getSquare() {
    return square;
  }

  public void setSquare(boolean square) {
    this.square = square;
    Enumeration e = widgets.elements();
```

```java
    while(e.hasMoreElements()) {
      Widget w = (Widget)e.nextElement();
      w.repaint();
    }
  }

  public void paint(Graphics g) {
    Dimension d = getSize();
    if(square) {
      g.fillRect(0, 0, d.width - 1, d.height - 1);
    }
    else {
      g.fillOval(0, 0, d.width - 1, d.height - 1);
    }
  }

  private void writeObject(ObjectOutputStream oos)
  throws IOException {
    try {
      oos.defaultWriteObject();
      if(widgets.elementAt(0) == this) {
        oos.writeBoolean(square);
      }
    }
    catch(Exception ex) {
      ex.printStackTrace();
    }
  }

  private void readObject(ObjectInputStream ois)
  throws IOException, ClassNotFoundException {
    try {
      ois.defaultReadObject();
      widgets.addElement(this);
      if(widgets.elementAt(0) == this) {
        square = ois.readBoolean();
      }
    }
    catch(Exception ex) {
      ex.printStackTrace();
    }
  }
}
```

Version Control

Handling new versions of a class is an important part of your program's persistence mechanism.

It is common for developers to change class definitions as fixes and new functionality are added to an existing system. This raises the question: Can version N+1 of a class read serialized objects that were generated with version N (or earlier)?

The answer to this question depends on the nature of the change. Some changes do not invalidate older, serialized objects—for example, adding an instance variable, modifying its access permissions, or adding/removing subclasses.

Other changes cause incompatibilities between a class and older, serialized versions—for example, deleting an instance variable, modifying its type, or moving the class in the class hierarchy.

This section shows how to write code so that serialized objects written by older versions can be used.

A Version Control Example

This section leads you step-by-step through an example that illustrates how to manage the issues associated with serialized versions of older releases.

Create and Compile Source Files

There are three source files for this example. The object to be serialized is defined in the following listing. A **Box** object has three instance variables and a **toString( )** method that returns a string equivalent of the object.

```
package version;
import java.awt.*;
import java.io.*;

class Box implements Serializable {
  private int width, height, depth;

  public Box(int width, int height, int depth) {
    this.width = width;
    this.height = height;
    this.depth = depth;
  }

  public String toString() {
    return "[" + width + "," + height + "," + depth + "]";
```

```
      }
    }
```

The file Save.java contains a simple program to create a **Box** object and serialize it to a file box.data in the current directory. It is shown in the following listing:

```
package version;
import java.io.*;

public class Save {
  public static void main(String args[]) {
    try {
      Box box = new Box(3, 4, 5);
      System.out.println(box);
      FileOutputStream fos = new FileOutputStream("box.data");
      ObjectOutputStream oos = new ObjectOutputStream(fos);
      oos.writeObject(box);
      oos.flush();
      fos.close();
    }
    catch(Exception ex) {
      System.out.println("Exception: " + ex);
    }
  }
}
```

The file Restore.java contains a simple program that reads the serialized object from box.data and displays its string equivalent.

```
package version;
import java.io.*;

public class Restore {
  public static void main(String args[]) {
    try {
      FileInputStream fis = new FileInputStream(args[0]);
      ObjectInputStream ois = new ObjectInputStream(fis);
      Object obj = ois.readObject();
      fis.close();
      System.out.println(obj);
    }
    catch(Exception ex) {
      System.out.println("Exception: " + ex);
```

```
        }
    }
}
```

Compile these three files.

Determine the Stream Unique Identifier (SUID) for the Class

SUID stands for stream unique identifier.

When an object is serialized, the non-static and non-transient parts of its state are written to the stream. In addition, some information about its type must also be saved so that the correct object can be re-created as part of the deserialization process.

The serialization mechanisms in Java save the required type information by creating an **ObjectStreamClass** object and also saving it in the stream. One of the important pieces of information in this object is a *stream unique identifier* (SUID). This is a **long** value that uniquely identifies the version of the class being serialized. The calculation of the SUID includes the class name and its members. Therefore, changes to these cause the SUID to change. The SUID is calculated for you automatically by the serialization mechanisms.

The JDK also includes a command-line tool called **serialver** that calculates the SUID for a class. Enter this string at the command line:

```
serialver version.Box
```

You should see output similar to the following:

```
version.Box:  static final long serialVersionUID =
  -7948265217544761073L;
```

This is the SUID for the **Box** class. This value is included in the **ObjectStreamClass** object that was generated for the **Box** object.

Serialize the Object

Enter the following at the command line to create and serialize a **Box** object:

```
java version.Save
```

You should see the following output:

```
[3,4,5]
```

This is the string equivalent of the **Box** object that was returned by its **toString( )** method.

Deserialize the Object
Enter the following at the command line to read the serialized object from box.data:

>   java version.Restore box.data

You should see the following output:

```
[3,4,5]
```

This is exactly as expected and is identical to that obtained in the previous step.

Update and Recompile Source Files
Now modify the **Box** class by adding another instance variable to record the color of the box. The modified program should appear as shown here:

```
package version;
import java.awt.*;
import java.io.*;

class Box implements Serializable {
  private int width, height, depth;
  private Color color;

  public Box(int width, int height, int depth, Color color) {
    this.width = width;
    this.height = height;
    this.depth = depth;
    this.color = color;
  }

  public String toString() {
    String str = "[" + width + ",";
    str += height + ",";
    str += depth + ",";
    str += color + "]";
    return str;
  }
}
```

Now recompile Box.java.

Determine the SUID for the Updated Class

Since a new member has been added to the **Box** class, you should not be surprised to find that its SUID has also changed.

Enter the following at the command line:

```
serialver version.Box
```

Observe that the output shown next is different from its original value:

```
version.Box:  static final long serialVersionUID =
  -4258491325234241767L;
```

Deserialize the Object

Now try to read the older, serialized version of the object by entering the following at the command line:

```
java version.Restore box.data
```

The output is

```
Exception: java.io.InvalidClassException: version.Box;
  Local class not compatible
```

The SUID of the serialized object is not compatible with the current SUID of the **Box** class.

Define serialVersionUID in the Class

The new version of the **Box** class can accept serialized objects of the older version if you make one small change. Define the variable **serialVersionUID** as shown in the following listing. Note that its value is equal to the SUID of the original version of **Box**.

```
package version;
import java.awt.*;
import java.io.*;

class Box implements Serializable {
  static final long serialVersionUID = -7948265217544761073L;
  private int width, height, depth;
```

4

```java
    private Color color;

    public Box(int width, int height, int depth, Color color) {
        this.width = width;
        this.height = height;
        this.depth = depth;
        this.color = color;
    }

public String toString() {
    String str = "[" + width + ",";
    str += height + ",";
    str += depth + ",";
    str += color + "]";
    return str;
    }
}
```

Recompile Source File
Recompile the file Box.java.

Deserialize the Object
Enter the following at the command line to deserialize the contents of box.data:

> java version.Restore box.data

Now you should see the following output:

```
[3,4,5,null]
```

The older serialized version of the object has been accepted by the new version of the **Box** class. The two versions are serial compatible.

If you wish to supply a default color for older serialized objects, this can be done as shown in the following listing. The **readObject( )** method initializes the **color** variable if it is **null**.

```java
package version;
import java.awt.*;
import java.io.*;

class Box implements Serializable {
```

```
static final long serialVersionUID = -7948265217544761073L;
private int width, height, depth;
private Color color;

public Box(int width, int height, int depth, Color color) {
  this.width = width;
  this.height = height;
  this.depth = depth;
  this.color = color;
}

public String toString() {
  String str = "[" + width + ",";
  str += height + ",";
  str += depth + ",";
  str += color + "]";
  return str;
}

private void readObject(ObjectInputStream ois)
throws IOException, ClassNotFoundException {
  try {
    ois.defaultReadObject();
    if(color == null) {
      color = Color.blue;
    }
  }
  catch(Exception ex) {
    ex.printStackTrace();
  }
}
}
```

If you recompile Box.java and deserialize box.data, you should now see the following output:

```
[3,4,5,java.awt.Color[r=0,g=0,b=255]]
```

Externalization

The previous section described how to customize the serialization process. However, it is sometimes necessary to have more control over the content and format of data sent to the stream. In those situations, a class can implement the **Externalizable** interface defined by the **java.io** package.

Externalizable
is the interface
that you must
implement to
create your own
serialization
methods.

That interface extends **Serializable** and defines the two methods shown next:

> void readExternal(ObjectInput *oi*) throws IOException,
>   ClassNotFoundException
>
> void writeExternal(ObjectOutput *oo*) throws IOException

Here, *oi* is the **ObjectInput** from which the object is restored, and *oo* is the **ObjectOutput** to which the object is saved. Your implementation of these methods must save and restore the state of the object.

NOTE: The **writeExternal( )** method is **public** and can be invoked by any other object. Therefore, an **Externalizable** object can be issued a command to write itself to a stream. You must carefully consider the consequences of this. An object may have sensitive information (for example, bank account numbers, salaries, login and password data) that you do not want to be serialized in this manner. Once a set of objects has been serialized to a file, that file can then be examined by hackers to obtain this data.

An Externalization Example

This section provides an example of externalization by revising the **Graph** Bean that was presented earlier in this chapter.

The following listing shows the modified version of the **Graph** class. It is very similar to the version seen earlier in this chapter, except for three changes. First, the class is defined to implement the **Externalizable** interface. Second, it provides a **readExternal( )** method that restores the object. Third, it provides a **writeExternal( )** method that saves the object.

The goal of this program is to store this object in a more compact format than that used by the default serialization mechanism. Only two bytes are used to store the topology of the graph. These two bytes comprise a set of bits. There is one bit for each possible link in the graph. If the bit is set, the user defined a link between these two nodes. Otherwise, there is no such link.

The **readExternal( )** method begins by reading the two bytes from the **ObjectInput** stream, storing these in **h** and **l**. Two nested loops are used to test each bit in these bytes. If a bit is set, the **makeLink( )** method is invoked to create a **Link** object and add it to the **links** vector.

4

The **writeExternal( )** method uses the **linkExists( )** method to check for the existence of all possible links in the graph. A bit in the **int** variable **i** is set for each link that exists. The **write( )** method is used to output the two bytes.

```java
package graphe;
import java.awt.*;
import java.awt.event.*;
import java.io.*;
import java.util.*;

public class Graph extends Canvas implements Externalizable,
MouseListener, MouseMotionListener {
  private final static int NNODES = 6;
  private Vector nodes;
  private Vector links;
  private Node node1, node2;
  private int x, y;

  public Graph() {
    setSize(200, 200);
    nodes = new Vector();
    links = new Vector();
    addMouseListener(this);
    addMouseMotionListener(this);
    makeNodes();
  }

  public void mouseClicked(MouseEvent me) {
  }

  public void mouseEntered(MouseEvent me) {
  }

  public void mouseExited(MouseEvent me) {
  }

  public void mousePressed(MouseEvent me) {
    doMousePressed(me);
  }

  public void mouseReleased(MouseEvent me) {
    doMouseReleased(me);
  }
```

```java
public void mouseDragged(MouseEvent me) {
  doMouseDragged(me);
}

public void mouseMoved(MouseEvent me) {
}

public void doMousePressed(MouseEvent me) {
  // Check if node1 should be initialized
  x = me.getX();
  y = me.getY();
  Enumeration e = nodes.elements();
  while(e.hasMoreElements()) {
    node1 = (Node)e.nextElement();
    if(node1.contains(x, y)) {
      return;
    }
  }
  node1 = null;
}

public void doMouseDragged(MouseEvent me) {
  x = me.getX();
  y = me.getY();
  repaint();
}

public void doMouseReleased(MouseEvent me) {
  // Make a link between node1 and node2
  x = me.getX();
  y = me.getY();
  if(node1 != null) {
    Enumeration e = nodes.elements();
    while(e.hasMoreElements()) {
      node2 = (Node)e.nextElement();
      if(node2.contains(x, y)) {
        makeLink(node1.getId(), node2.getId());
        break;
      }
    }
    node1 = node2 = null;
    repaint();
  }
}
```

```
public void paint(Graphics g) {
  // Draw nodes
  Enumeration e = nodes.elements();
  while(e.hasMoreElements()) {
    ((Node)e.nextElement()).draw(g);
  }
  // Draw links
  e = links.elements();
  while(e.hasMoreElements()) {
    ((Link)e.nextElement()).draw(g);
  }
  // Draw rubber band line (if any)
  if(node1 != null) {
    g.drawLine(node1.getX(), node1.getY(), x, y);
  }
}

private void makeNodes() {
  // Initialize nodes variable
  Dimension d = getSize();
  int width = d.width;
  int height = d.height;
  int centerx = width/2;
  int centery = height/2;
  double radius =
    (width < height) ? 0.4 * width : 0.4 * height;
  for(int i = 0; i < NNODES; i++) {
    double theta = i*2*Math.PI/NNODES;
    int x = (int)(centerx + radius * Math.cos(theta));
    int y = (int)(centery - radius * Math.sin(theta));
    nodes.addElement(new Node(x, y));
  }
}

private void makeLink(int id1, int id2) {
  // Return if a link already exists between these nodes
  if(linkExists(id1, id2)) {
    return;
  }
  // Otherwise, create a new link
  Node n1 = (Node)nodes.elementAt(id1);
  Node n2 = (Node)nodes.elementAt(id2);
  links.addElement(new Link(n1, n2));
}
```

```
private boolean linkExists(int i, int j) {
  // Check if a link exists between nodes i and j
  Enumeration e = links.elements();
  while(e.hasMoreElements()) {
    Link link = (Link)e.nextElement();
    int id1 = link.getNode1().getId();
    int id2 = link.getNode2().getId();
    if((id1 == i && id2 == j) || (id1 == j && id2 == i)) {
      return true;
    }
  }
  return false;
}

public void readExternal(ObjectInput oi)
throws IOException, ClassNotFoundException {
  makeNodes();
  int i, h, l;
  try {
    h = oi.read(); // Read high-order byte
    l = oi.read(); // Read low-order byte
    i = (h << 8) | l;
    for(int j = 0; j < NNODES; j++) {
      for(int k = j + 1; k < NNODES; k++) {
        if((i & 0x4000) == 0x4000) {
          makeLink(j, k);
        }
        i <<= 1;
      }
    }
  }
  catch(Exception ex) {
    ex.printStackTrace();
  }
}

public void writeExternal(ObjectOutput oo)
throws IOException {
  int i = 0;
  for(int j = 0; j < NNODES; j++) {
    for(int k = j + 1; k < NNODES; k++) {
      i <<= 1;
      if(linkExists(j, k)) {
        i |= 1;
      }
```

```
      }
    }
    try {
      int h = (i >> 8) & 0xff;
      int l = i & 0xff;
      oo.write(h); // Write high-order byte
      oo.write(l); // Write low-order byte
    }
    catch(Exception ex) {
      ex.printStackTrace();
    }
  }
}
```

The following listing shows the source code for the **Node** class. It is identical to the previous version, except that the class no longer implements the **Serializable** interface. This is because the **writeExternal( )** and **readExternal( )** methods of **Graph** perform all of the processing for saving and restoring such an object.

```
package graphe;
import java.awt.*;
import java.io.*;

public class Node {
  private final static int NODERADIUS = 10;
  private static int count = 0;
  private int x, y, id;

  public Node(int x, int y) {
    this.x = x;
    this.y = y;
    id = count++;
  }

  public int getX() {
    return x;
  }

  public int getY() {
    return y;
  }

  public int getId() {
    return id;
```

```
        }

        public boolean contains(int x, int y) {
          int deltax = this.x - x;
          int deltay = this.y - y;
          int a = deltax * deltax + deltay * deltay;
          int b = NODERADIUS * NODERADIUS;
          return (a <= b);
        }

        public void draw(Graphics g) {
          int w = 2 * NODERADIUS;
          int h = w;
          g.fillOval(x - NODERADIUS, y - NODERADIUS, w, h);
        }
      }
```

The following listing shows the source code for the **Link** class. It is identical to the previous version, except that the class no longer implements the **Serializable** interface. This is because the **writeExternal( )** and **readExternal( )** methods of **Graph** perform all of the processing for saving and restoring such an object.

```
package graphe;
import java.awt.*;
import java.io.*;

public class Link {
  private Node node1, node2;

  public Link(Node node1, Node node2) {
    this.node1 = node1;
    this.node2 = node2;
  }

  public Node getNode1() {
    return node1;
  }

  public Node getNode2() {
    return node2;
  }

  public void draw(Graphics g) {
    int x1 = node1.getX();
```

```
    int y1 = node1.getY();
    int x2 = node2.getX();
    int y2 = node2.getY();
    g.drawLine(x1, y1, x2, y2);
  }
}
```

More discussion of externalization is beyond the scope of this book. You can consult the online Sun documentation if you need to use this advanced capability.

The Serialization Sequence

Since there are various ways in which object persistence can be achieved—the default methods, by implementing **writeObject( )** and **readObject( )**, or by implementing **Externalizable**—it is important to understand the relative priority of each.

These steps are followed to serialize an object:

1. If the class implements the **Externalizable** interface, the **writeExternal( )** method is called.
2. If the class does not implement the **Serializable** interface, a **java.io.NotSerializableException** is thrown.
3. If the class implements the **writeObject( )** method, that code is invoked.
4. Otherwise, the default serialization mechanisms are used.

These steps are followed to deserialize an object:

1. If the class implements the **Externalizable** interface, the **readExternal( )** method is called.
2. If the class does not implement the **Serializable** interface, a **java.io.NotSerializableException** is thrown.
3. If the class implements the **readObject( )** method, that code is invoked.
4. Otherwise, the default deserialization mechanisms are used.

A Note About Adapter Classes

Chapter 3 discussed how adapter classes could be used to streamline event handling code. However, the adapter classes in the **java.awt.event** package do not implement the **Serializable** interface. Therefore, if you attempt to save/restore an object that uses these classes, it will not work correctly when it is restored. Fortunately, there is an easy way around this.

Let's begin with an example. Chapter 3 showed you a package named **inner** that contained a **Dot2** class. Try this experiment to convince yourself that there is an issue:

1. Create an instance of **Dot2** in BeanBox. Click the mouse at a different position to move the dot.
2. Save the contents of BeanBox to a file.
3. Exit from BeanBox.
4. Restart the BDK.
5. Load the contents of the file. Observe that the Bean is re-created, and the dot is positioned where you left it. However, any mouse operations are ignored.

4

Now consider the version of the program shown in the following listing. It is very similar to the **Dot2** class taken from Chapter 3. However, the **MyMouseAdapter** class extends **MouseAdapter** and also implements the **Serializable** interface. Therefore, you may save/restore this Bean, and it will continue to operate correctly.

```
package innerserial;
import java.awt.*;
import java.awt.event.*;
import java.io.*;

public class Dot2S extends Canvas {
  private Point p;

  public Dot2S() {
    setSize(200, 200);
    p = new Point(100, 100);
    addMouseListener(new MyMouseAdapter());
  }

  public void changePoint(MouseEvent me) {
    p = new Point(me.getX(), me.getY());
    repaint();
  }

  public void paint(Graphics g) {
```

```
  Dimension d = getSize();
  g.drawRect(0, 0, d.width - 1, d.height - 1);
  g.fillRect(p.x - 2, p.y - 2, 4, 4);
}

class MyMouseAdapter extends MouseAdapter
implements Serializable {
  public void mouseClicked(MouseEvent me) {
    changePoint(me);
  }
}
}
```

This same general approach used to serialize **MouseAdapter** can be used to serialize any adapter class. Just extend it so that it implements **Serializable**.

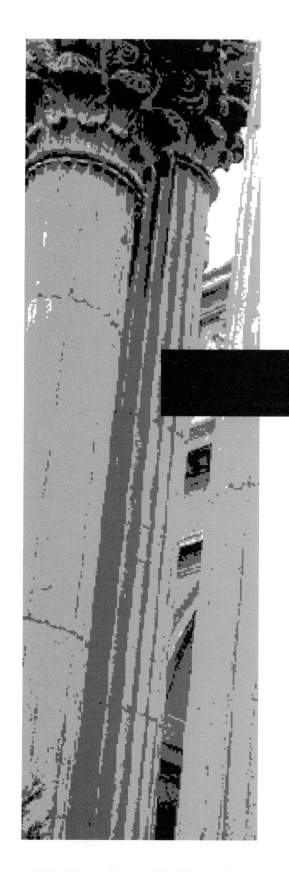

CHAPTER 5

Reflection and Introspection

A builder tool must dynamically examine a Bean and determine its properties, events, and methods. This information is required so a developer may configure and connect any set of components. The mechanisms that provide this data are called reflection and introspection.

Reflection is the ability to obtain information about the fields, constructors, and methods of any class. *Introspection* is the ability to obtain information about the properties, events, and methods of a Bean. You will see in this chapter how these two features are related to each other.

In previous chapters of this book, you saw how the introspection mechanisms automatically infer information about a Bean. You may also explicitly designate which properties, events, and methods of a component are presented by a builder tool. Several examples are developed to illustrate how this is done.

Reflection

Reflection is the ability to obtain information about the fields, constructors, and methods of any class at run time.

Reflection is the ability to obtain information about the fields, constructors, and methods of any class at run time. The typical Bean developer does not write code that uses reflection directly. However, it is necessary to understand reflection in order to understand introspection. In fact, introspection uses reflection to obtain information about a Bean. Therefore, it is recommended that you become comfortable with the concepts described here.

The following sections provide an overview of the classes and interfaces that provide this functionality.

Class

*There is an instance of **Class** for each type.*

The Java Virtual Machine creates an instance of the class **Class** for each type, including classes, interfaces, arrays, and simple types. **Class** provides various instance methods that allow you to get information about that type. These are the starting point for our discussion about reflection.

The class **Class** in the **java.lang** package provides more than 30 different instance methods. Table 5-1 lists only those methods that are relevant to our discussion about reflection.

The next listing contains a simple application that reports whether a class represents a class or interface. The class name is supplied to the application as a command-line argument. The program uses the **forName( )** and **isInterface( )** methods of **Class**.

Method	Description
static Class forName(String *clsName*) throws ClassNotFoundException	Returns a **Class** object for the class named *clsName*.
Constructor getConstructor(Class *ptypes*[ ]) throws NoSuchMethodException, SecurityException	Returns a **Constructor** object for the constructor whose parameters have types *ptypes*.
Constructor[ ] getConstructors( ) throws SecurityException	Returns an array of **Constructor** objects for the constructors for this class.
Class[ ] getDeclaredClasses( ) throws SecurityException	Returns an array of **Class** objects for the classes used as members of this class.
Constructor getDeclaredConstructor (Class *ptypes*[ ]) throws NoSuchMethodException, SecurityException	Returns a **Constructor** object for the constructor declared in this class whose parameters have types *ptypes*.
Constructor[ ] getDeclaredConstructors( ) throws SecurityException	Returns an array of **Constructor** objects for the constructors declared by this class.
Field getDeclaredField(String *fldName*) throws NoSuchFieldException, SecurityException	Returns a **Field** object for a field named *fldName* that is declared by this class.
Field[ ] getDeclaredFields( ) throws SecurityException	Returns an array of **Field** objects for the fields declared by this class.
Method getDeclaredMethod(String *mthName*, Class *ptypes*[ ]) throws NoSuchMethodException, SecurityException	Returns a **Method** object for a method named *mthName* with parameter types *ptypes* that is declared by this class.
Method[ ] getDeclaredMethods( ) throws SecurityException	Returns an array of **Method** objects for the methods declared by this class.

Some Methods Defined by
Class
Table 5-1.

5

Method	Description
Class getDeclaringClass( )	Returns a **Class** object for the class that declares this class or interface as a member. Returns **null** if this class or interface is not a member of another class.
Field getField(String *fldName*) throws NoSuchFieldException, SecurityException	Returns a **Field** object for the public field named *fldName*.
Field[ ] getFields( ) throws SecurityException	Returns an array of **Field** objects for the public fields of this class.
Class[ ] getInterfaces( )	Returns an array of **Class** objects for the interfaces implemented by this class. If this class represents an interface, the returned array describes the interfaces it extends.
Method getMethod(String *mthName*, Class[ ] *ptypes*) throws NoSuchMethodException, SecurityException	Returns a **Method** object for the method named *mthName* with parameter types *ptypes*.
Method[ ] getMethods( ) throws SecurityException	Returns an array of **Method** objects for the methods of this class.
int getModifiers( )	Returns an **int** describing the modifiers for this class.
String getName( )	Returns a **String** object for the name of this class.
Class getSuperclass( )	Returns a **Class** object for the superclass of this class.
boolean isArray( )	Returns **true** if this class represents an array. Otherwise, returns **false**.
boolean isInterface( )	Returns **true** if this class represents an interface. Otherwise, returns **false**.
Object newInstance( ) throws InstantiationException, IllegalAccessException	Returns an instance of this class.

Some Methods Defined by **Class** (*continued*)
Table 5-1.

```
package reflect;

public class IsInterfaceDemo {
  public static void main(String args[]) {
    try {

      // Get the class object
      Class c = Class.forName(args[0]);

      // Determine if it represents a class or interface
      if(c.isInterface()) {
        System.out.println(args[0] + " is an interface");
      }
      else {
        System.out.println(args[0] + " is not an interface");
      }
    }
    catch(Exception ex) {
      ex.printStackTrace();
    }
  }
}
```

5

Invoke this application by typing the following on the command line:

java reflect.IsInterfaceDemo java.lang.Runnable

Observe the following output:

```
java.lang.Runnable is an interface
```

Try experimenting with other classes and interfaces.

Member

The interface **Member** in the **java.lang.reflect** package defines methods that are common to the fields, constructors, and methods of a class. These are listed here:

Class getDeclaringClass( )

int getModifiers( )

String getName( )

The **getDeclaringClass( )** method returns the **Class** object for the class that declares this member. The **getModifiers( )** method returns an **int** representing the modifiers for this member. A string equivalent of the member name is returned by **getName( )**.

The **Member** interface is implemented by the **Field**, **Constructor**, and **Method** classes that are discussed in the next three sections.

Field

The class **Field** in the **java.lang.reflect** package contains methods that allow you to read and write the value of a field within another object. In addition, the class implements the **Member** interface.

One of the methods provided by **Field** is **getType( )**. Its signature is shown here:

```
Class getType( )
```

The return value is the **Class** object for the type of that field.

The methods that get and set the value of a field are summarized in Table 5-2. Each of these methods can throw an **IllegalArgumentException** or **IllegalAccessException**.

A simple application that displays all public fields for a class is shown in the following listing. The class name is supplied to the application

Method	Description
Object get(Object *obj*)	Returns the value of the field in object *obj*
boolean getBoolean(Object *obj*)	Returns the **boolean** value of the field in *obj*
byte getByte(Object *obj*)	Returns the **byte** value of the field in *obj*
char getChar(Object *obj*)	Returns the **char** value of the field in *obj*
double getDouble(Object *obj*)	Returns the **double** value of the field in *obj*
float getFloat(Object *obj*)	Returns the **float** value of the field in *obj*
int getInt(Object *obj*)	Returns the **int** value of the field in *obj*
long getLong(Object *obj*)	Returns the **long** value of the field in *obj*
short getShort(Object *obj*)	Returns the **short** value of the field in *obj*

Table 5-2. Some Methods Defined by **Field**

Method	Description
void set(Object *obj*, Object *value*)	Sets the field in *obj* to *value*
void setBoolean(Object *obj*, boolean *b*)	Sets the field in *obj* to *b*
void setByte(Object *obj*, byte *b*)	Sets the field in *obj* to *b*
void setChar(Object *obj*, char *ch*)	Sets the field in *obj* to *ch*
void setDouble(Object *obj*, double *d*)	Sets the field in *obj* to *d*
void setFloat(Object *obj*, float *f*)	Sets the field in *obj* to *f*
void setInt(Object *obj*, int *i*)	Sets the field in *obj* to *i*
void setLong(Object *obj*, long *l*)	Sets the field in *obj* to *l*
void setShort(Object *obj*, short *s*)	Sets the field in *obj* to *s*

5

Some Methods Defined by **Field** (*continued*) **Table 5-2.**

as a command-line argument. The program uses the **forName( )** and **getFields( )** methods of **Class** and the **getName( )** method of **Field**.

```
package reflect;
import java.lang.reflect.*;

public class GetFieldsDemo {

  public static void main(String args[]) {
    try {

      // Get the class object
      Class c = Class.forName(args[0]);

      // Display the fields
      Field fields[] = c.getFields();
      for(int i = 0; i < fields.length; i++) {
        System.out.println(fields[i].getName());
      }
    }
    catch(Exception ex) {
```

```
      ex.printStackTrace();
    }
  }
}
```

Invoke this application by typing the following on the command line:

    java reflect.GetFieldsDemo java.lang.Math

Observe the following output:

```
E
PI
```

Try experimenting with other classes and interfaces.

A simple application that displays the fields declared by a class is shown in the following listing. The class name is supplied to the application as a command-line argument. The program uses the **forName( )** and **getDeclaredFields( )** methods of **Class** and the **getName( )** method of **Field**.

```
package reflect;
import java.lang.reflect.*;

public class GetDeclaredFieldsDemo {
  public static void main(String args[]) {
    try {

      // Get the class object
      Class c = Class.forName(args[0]);

      // Display the declared fields
      Field fields[] = c.getDeclaredFields();
      for(int i = 0; i < fields.length; i++) {
        System.out.println(fields[i].getName());
      }
    }
    catch(Exception ex) {
      ex.printStackTrace();
    }
  }
}
```

Invoke this application by typing the following on the command line:

    java reflect.GetDeclaredFieldsDemo java.lang.Math

Observe the following output:

```
E
PI
randomNumberGenerator
negativeZeroFloatBits
negativeZeroDoubleBits
```

Compare this output with that of the previous program. Observe that the **getDeclaredFields( )** method returns an array of **Field** objects for all of the fields declared by that class, even if some of them are not publicly accessible. Note that although you can obtain a **Field** object for a field that is not publicly accessible, this does not mean that you can read or write its value by using the methods provided by **Field**. An **IllegalAccessException** is thrown in this situation.

5

Constructor

The class **Constructor** in the **java.lang.reflect** package contains methods that allow you to get information about a constructor. In addition, the class implements the **Member** interface.

Some of the additional methods provided by **Constructor** are shown here:

    Class[ ] getExceptionTypes( )

    Class[ ] getParameterTypes( )

    Object newInstance(Object[ ] *args*)

The **getExceptionTypes( )** method returns an array of **Class** objects for the exceptions that can be generated. An array of **Class** objects for the parameter types is returned by **getParameterTypes( )**. The **newInstance( )** method invokes the constructor with *args* and returns the created object. It can generate an **InstantiationException, IllegalAccessException, IllegalArgumentException**, or **InvocationTargetException**.

A simple application that displays information about each of the constructors for a class including the types of its parameters is shown in the following listing. The class name is supplied to the application as a command-line argument. The program uses the **forName( )** and **getConstructors( )** methods of **Class** and the **getName( )** and **getParameterTypes( )** methods of **Constructor**.

```
package reflect;
import java.lang.reflect.*;

public class GetConstructorsDemo {

  public static void main(String args[]) {
    try {

      // Get the class object
      Class c = Class.forName(args[0]);

      // Display the constructors and their parameters
      Constructor constructors[] = c.getConstructors();
      for(int i = 0; i < constructors.length; i++) {
        System.out.print(constructors[i].getName() + ": ");
        Class parameters[];
        parameters = constructors[i].getParameterTypes();
        for(int j = 0; j < parameters.length; j++) {
          String s = parameters[j].getName();
          s = s.substring(s.lastIndexOf(".") + 1, s.length());
          System.out.print(s + " ");
        }
        System.out.println("");
      }
    }
    catch(Exception ex) {
      ex.printStackTrace();
    }
  }
}
```

Invoke this application by typing the following on the command line:

java reflect.GetConstructorsDemo java.io.FileWriter

Observe the following output:

```
java.io.FileWriter: String
java.io.FileWriter: String boolean
java.io.FileWriter: File
java.io.FileWriter: FileDescriptor
```

Try experimenting with other classes.

Method

The class **Method** in the **java.lang.reflect** package allows you to get information about a method. In addition, the class implements the **Member** interface.

Table 5-3 summarizes some of the additional methods provided by **Method**.

A simple application that displays the names of all public methods of a class is shown in the following listing. The class name is supplied to the application as a command-line argument. The program uses the **forName( )** and **getMethods( )** methods of **Class** and the **getName( )** method of **Method**.

```
package reflect;
import java.lang.reflect.*;

public class GetMethodsDemo {
```

Some Methods
Defined by
Method
Table 5-3.

Method	Description
Class[ ] getExceptionTypes( )	Returns an array of **Class** objects for the types of exceptions that can be generated
Class[ ] getParameterTypes( )	Returns an array of **Class** objects for the parameters to the method
Class getReturnType( )	Returns the type of the return value
Object invoke(Object *obj*, Object *args*[ ])	Invokes the method on *obj* with arguments *args*

```
public static void main(String args[]) {
  try {

    // Get the class object
    Class c = Class.forName(args[0]);

    // Display the methods
    Method methods[] = c.getMethods();
    for(int i = 0; i < methods.length; i++) {
      System.out.println(methods[i].getName());
    }
  }
  catch(Exception ex) {
    ex.printStackTrace();
  }
}
}
```

Invoke this application by typing the following on the command line:

java reflect.GetMethodsDemo java.awt.AWTEvent

Observe the following output:

```
getClass
hashCode
equals
toString
notify
notifyAll
wait
wait
getSource
getID
paramString
```

A simple application that displays the names of all methods declared by a class is shown in the following listing. The class name is supplied to the application as a command-line argument. The program uses the **forName( )** and **getDeclaredMethods( )** methods of **Class** and the **getName( )** method of **Method**.

```
package reflect;
import java.lang.reflect.*;

public class GetDeclaredMethodsDemo {
  public static void main(String args[]) {
    try {

      // Get the class object
      Class c = Class.forName(args[0]);

      // Display the declared methods
      Method methods[] = c.getDeclaredMethods();
      for(int i = 0; i < methods.length; i++) {
        System.out.println(methods[i].getName());
      }
    }
    catch(Exception ex) {
      ex.printStackTrace();
    }
  }
}
```

5

Invoke this application by typing the following on the command line:

> java reflect.GetDeclaredMethodsDemo java.awt.AWTEvent

Observe the following output:

```
getID
toString
paramString
consume
isConsumed
convertToOld
setSource
```

Compare this output with that of the previous program. Note that **getDeclaredMethods( )** returns all methods declared by a class, even those that are not publicly accessible. In contrast, **getMethods( )** returns only publicly accessible methods, including those contributed by any superclasses.

The **invoke()** method of **Method** dynamically invokes a method of a Bean.

The invoke( ) Method

One of the members of the **Method** class is **invoke( )**. Its importance cannot be overstated. It allows a builder tool to dynamically invoke a method of a Bean, even if that component had not yet been developed when the builder tool was compiled. This is precisely what is needed to customize a Bean by accessing its properties and to connect several Beans!

The following listing shows a program that illustrates the concept. Several command-line arguments are accepted. The first is the name of a class, and the second is the name of a method in that class. The remaining arguments are parameters to that method.

The program begins by using the **forName( )** method of **Class** to obtain a reference to the appropriate **Class** object. Notice that the first command-line argument is the argument to this method.

An array of **double** types is created. These represent the types of the parameters for the method to be invoked. The **getMethod( )** method of **Class** is used to obtain the **Method** object for this method. Notice that the second command-line argument and the array are passed to **getMethod( )**. (For simplicity in this program, it is assumed that all target method arguments are **double** types.)

Next, an array of **Double** objects is created. The values passed to the **Double** constructor are those provided by the user on the command line.

The **isStatic( )** method is used to determine if the target method is a static or an instance method. In the former case, the **invoke( )** method is called with **null** as its first argument and the **parameters** array as its second argument. In the latter case, an instance of the target class must be created and supplied as the first argument to **invoke( )**. The result from the **invoke( )** method is then printed.

```
package reflect;
import java.lang.reflect.*;

public class InvokeDemo {

  public static void main(String args[]) {
    try {

      // Get the class object
      Class c = Class.forName(args[0]);

      // Get reference to Method object
```

```
     int nparameters = args.length - 2;
     Class parameterTypes[] = new Class[nparameters];
     for(int i = 0; i < nparameters; i++) {
       parameterTypes[i] = double.class;
     }
     Method m = c.getMethod(args[1], parameterTypes);

     // Generate parameters array
     Object parameters[] = new Double[nparameters];
     for(int i = 0; i < nparameters; i++) {
       parameters[i] = new Double(args[i + 2]);
     }

     // Invoke method
     Object r;
     if(Modifier.isStatic(m.getModifiers())) {
       r = m.invoke(null, parameters);
     }
     else {
       r = m.invoke(c.newInstance(), parameters);
     }

     // Display results
     System.out.println(r);
   }
   catch(Exception ex) {
     ex.printStackTrace();
   }
 }
}
```

Try using this application by typing the following at the command line:

    java reflect.InvokeDemo java.lang.Math cos 3.1415

The output is

```
-0.9999999957076562
```

The static method **cos( )** of the **Math** class was invoked.

You may also write your own classes and invoke them in this manner. Consider the **Circle** class defined in the following listing:

```
package reflect;

public class Circle {
  private double radius;

  public Circle() {
    radius = 1;
  }

  public double getArea() {
    return Math.PI * radius * radius;
  }

  public double getCircumference() {
    return 2 * Math.PI * radius;
  }

  public double getRadius() {
    return radius;
  }

  public void setRadius(double radius) {
    this.radius = radius;
  }
}
```

Try using this application by typing the following at the command line:

    java reflect.InvokeDemo reflect.Circle getArea

The output is

```
3.141592653589793
```

An instance of the **Circle** class was created, and its **getArea( )** method was invoked.

Modifier

The class **Modifier** in the **java.lang.reflect** package contains **int** constants and static methods that allow you to interpret the value returned by the **getModifiers( )** method of the **Member** interface.

Method	Description
static boolean isAbstract( )	Returns **true** if the member is abstract
static boolean isFinal( )	Returns **true** if the member is final
static boolean isInterface( )	Returns **true** if the member is an interface
static boolean isNative( )	Returns **true** if the member is native
static boolean isPrivate( )	Returns **true** if the member is private
static boolean isProtected( )	Returns **true** if the member is protected
static boolean isPublic( )	Returns **true** if the member is public
static boolean isStatic( )	Returns **true** if the member is static
static boolean isSynchronized( )	Returns **true** if the member is synchronized
static boolean isTransient( )	Returns **true** if the member is transient
static boolean isVolatile( )	Returns **true** if the member is volatile
static String toString( )	Returns a string equivalent of the modifiers

5

Methods
Defined by
Modifier
Table 5-4.

The **int** constants defined by **Modifier** are **ABSTRACT**, **FINAL**, **INTERFACE**, **NATIVE**, **PRIVATE**, **PROTECTED**, **PUBLIC**, **STATIC**, **SYNCHRONIZED**, **TRANSIENT**, and **VOLATILE**. The methods provided by **Modifier** are summarized in Table 5-4.

A simple application that displays the modifiers of all public methods of a class is shown in the following listing. The class name is supplied to the application as a command-line argument. An instance of the class is created from the information in the first command-line argument. An array of the public methods for that class is then obtained.

Each entry in that array is then processed. The name of the method is displayed. The **getModifiers( )** method of **Method** returns an **int** with the encoded modifiers information. The static **toString( )** method returns the string equivalent of the modifiers information that is then displayed.

```
package reflect;
import java.lang.reflect.*;

public class ModifierDemo {

  public static void main(String args[]) {
    try {

      // Get the class object
      Class c = Class.forName(args[0]);

      // Display each method name and its modifiers
      Method methods[] = c.getMethods();
      for(int i = 0; i < methods.length; i++) {
        System.out.print(methods[i].getName() + ": ");
        System.out.print(Modifier.toString(methods[i].getModifi-
ers()));
        System.out.println();
      }
    }
    catch(Exception ex) {
      ex.printStackTrace();
    }
  }
}
```

Try using this application by typing the following at the command line:

  java reflect.ModifierDemo java.awt.Dimension

The output is

```
getClass: public final native
hashCode: public native
equals: public
toString: public
notify: public final native
notifyAll: public final native
wait: public final native
wait: public final
wait: public final
getSize: public
setSize: public
setSize: public
```

Array

The class **Array** in the **java.lang.reflect** package allows you to build an array at run time. Both the type of the array elements and the size of the array can be determined at run time. This capability can be useful for a builder tool that is designed to work with indexed properties. It is not typically used by Bean developers.

Table 5-5 summarizes some of the methods of **Array**.

The following listing shows a program that illustrates building an array at run time. Its first command-line argument is the name of a class. This determines the type of the array elements. The remaining arguments are strings that are used to initialize the array elements.

The program begins by getting the **Class** object for the class named by the first command-line argument. This is done by calling the **forName( )** static method of **Class**.

Next, a reference to the constructor that accepts one **String** object is obtained. This is done by using the **getConstructor( )** instance method of **Class**. The argument to **getConstructor( )** is an array of **Class** objects representing the parameters to that constructor. In this program, the array has only one element.

The array can be created by the **newInstance( )** method of **Array**. The first argument to this method is the **Class** object, and the second is the size of the array.

5

Method	Description
static Object get(Object *array*, int *index*)	Returns the element from *array* at *index*.
static int getLength(Object *array*)	Returns the length of *array*.
static Object newInstance(Class *cls*, int *size*)	Returns an array of *size* entries. The type of each entry is *cls*.
static void set(Object *array*, int *index*, Object *value*)	Sets the element in *array* at *index* to *value*.

Some Methods
Defined by
Array
Table 5-5.

The elements of the array are initialized in a loop by calling the **set( )** method of **Array**. The arguments to this method are the array, an index to one of its entries, and the object used to initialize that array element. The object is created by use of the **newInstance( )** method of **Constructor**. The argument to the constructor is the next command-line argument.

The elements in the array are then displayed by use of the **getLength( )** and **get( )** methods of **Array**.

```
package reflect;
import java.lang.reflect.*;

public class ArrayDemo {

  public static void main(String args[]) {
    try {

      // Get the Class object
      Class c = Class.forName(args[0]);

      // Get the constructor that accepts String objects
      Class parameterTypes[] = new Class[1];
      parameterTypes[0] = String.class;
      Constructor constructor;
      constructor = c.getConstructor(parameterTypes);

      // Create the array
      Object a = Array.newInstance(c, args.length - 1);

      // initialize the elements of the array
      Object cargs[] = new Object[1];
      for(int i = 1; i < args.length; i++) {
        cargs[0] = args[i];
        Object object = constructor.newInstance(cargs);
        Array.set(a, i - 1, object);
      }

      // Get and display the elements of the array
      int length = Array.getLength(a);
      System.out.println("The array length is " + length);
      for(int i = 0; i < length; i++) {
        Object object = Array.get(a, i);
        System.out.println("Entry " + i + "=" + object);
      }
    }
```

```
      catch(Exception ex) {
        ex.printStackTrace();
      }
    }
}
```

Try using this application by typing the following at the command line:

> java reflect.ArrayDemo java.lang.Integer 3 4 5 6 7 8

This creates an integer array that is six elements long. The output is

```
The array length is 6
Entry 0=3
Entry 1=4
Entry 2=5
Entry 3=6
Entry 4=7
Entry 5=8
```

5

Introspection

Introspection is the ability to obtain information about the properties, events, and methods of a Bean. This feature is used by builder tools. It provides the data that is needed so developers who are using Beans can configure and connect components.

Chapter 2 introduced naming patterns for properties. Chapter 3 discussed how the methods used to handle events are named. You saw that the introspection mechanism automatically infers information about the properties and events of a Bean if these conventions are followed.

It is also possible for you to explicitly designate which properties, events, and methods are displayed to a user by a builder tool. This section describes how this can be accomplished. This is very important material and is necessary for building production quality Beans.

 NOTE: The reflection mechanisms work at a low level and deal only with the fields, constructors, and methods of a class. The introspection mechanisms work at a higher level and deal with the properties, events, and methods of a Bean.

The following sections present an overview of the classes and interfaces that provide this functionality. Some details have been deliberately omitted from this discussion in order to make it easier for you to see the manner in which these parts interact with one another.

Introspector

The **Introspector** class in the **java.beans** package provides static methods that allow you to obtain information about the properties, events, and methods of a Bean.

One of the most commonly used methods of **Introspector** is **getBeanInfo( )**. It has the two forms shown here:

static BeanInfo getBeanInfo(Class *beanCls*)

static BeanInfo getBeanInfo(Class *beanCls*, Class *ignoreCls*)

The first form returns an object that implements the **BeanInfo** interface. That object describes the properties, events, and methods of *beanCls* and all of its superclasses. The second form returns an object that implements the **BeanInfo** interface. That object describes the properties, events, and methods of *beanCls* and its superclasses up to but not including *ignoreCls*.

Each of these methods can throw an **IntrospectionException**.

 NOTE: When a Bean named **Xyz** is encountered, the introspection mechanisms look for a class named **XyzBeanInfo**. If such a class exists, it is used to provide information about the properties, events, and methods of that component. You will see later in this chapter how to write the **BeanInfo** methods to explicitly define what information is provided to a user. If such a class does not exist, the default introspection mechanisms are used to construct a **BeanInfo** object.

There are additional details that determine where the introspection mechanisms look for this data. These are not covered here.

BeanInfo

The **BeanInfo** interface in the **java.beans** package defines a set of constants and methods that are central to the process of introspection.

The **int** constants defined by **BeanInfo** are **ICON_COLOR_16x16**, **ICON_COLOR_32x32**, **ICON_MONO_16x16**, and **ICON_MONO_32x32**. These values are used to identify icons of different sizes that you can provide for a component. The builder tool can use these icons to provide a visual representation of a Bean.

Table 5-6 summarizes the most commonly used methods defined by this interface.

SimpleBeanInfo

You extend **SimpleBeanInfo** to control the information about a Bean that is presented by a builder tool.

The **SimpleBeanInfo** class in the **java.beans** package provides a default implementation of the **BeanInfo** interface. To provide information about a Bean, a developer extends this class and overrides the implementations of some of its methods. This technique is shown in the code examples later in this chapter.

FeatureDescriptor

The **FeatureDescriptor** class in the **java.beans** package is the immediate superclass of the **BeanDescriptor**, **EventSetDescriptor**, **MethodDescriptor**, **ParameterDescriptor**, and **PropertyDescriptor** classes that are discussed in the following sections. Table 5-7 summarizes the methods that read and write data associated with any of these features.

Method	Description
BeanDescriptor getBeanDescriptor( )	Returns a **BeanDescriptor** object for a Bean.
EventSetDescriptor[ ] getEventSetDescriptors( )	Returns an array of **EventSetDescriptor** objects for the events generated by a Bean.
Image getIcon(int *iconSize*)	Returns an icon that can be displayed to represent a Bean.
MethodDescriptor[ ] getMethodDescriptors( )	Returns an array of **MethodDescriptor** objects for the methods of a Bean.
PropertyDescriptor[ ] getPropertyDescriptors( )	Returns an array of **PropertyDescriptor** objects for the properties of a Bean.

Some Methods Defined by **BeanInfo**

Table 5-6.

Method	Description
Enumeration attributeNames( )	Returns an enumeration of the attribute names.
String getDisplayName( )	Returns the display name.
String getName( )	Returns the programmatic name.
String getShortDescription( )	Returns a short description.
Object getValue(String *attribute*)	Returns the value of *attribute*.
boolean isExpert( )	Returns **true** if the feature is for experts only. Otherwise, returns **false**.
boolean isHidden( )	Returns **true** if the feature should be hidden by a builder tool. Otherwise, returns **false**.
void setDisplayName(String *name*)	Sets the display name to *name*.
void setExpert(boolean *flag*)	If *flag* is **true**, the feature is for experts only.
void setHidden(boolean *flag*)	If *flag* is **true**, the feature is hidden.
void setName(String *name*)	Sets the programmatic name to *name*.
void setShortDescription(String *desc*)	Sets the short description to *desc*.
void setValue(String *attribute*, Object *value*)	Sets *attribute* to *value*.

Methods
Defined by
**Feature-
Descriptor
Table 5-7.**

BeanDescriptor

The **BeanDescriptor** class in the **java.beans** package associates a
customizer with a Bean. A customizer provides a graphical user interface
through which a user may modify the properties of a Bean. That topic is
covered later in this book.

Its most commonly used constructor is

BeanDescriptor(Class *beanCls*, Class *customizerCls*)

The two methods provided by this class are shown here:

Class getBeanClass( )

Class getCustomizerClass( )

The **getBeanClass( )** method returns the **Class** object for a Bean, and the **getCustomizerClass( )** method returns the **Class** object for a Bean customizer.

EventSetDescriptor

The **EventSetDescriptor** class in the **java.beans** package describes a set of events generated by a Bean. These are one or more events that are processed by an **EventListener** interface.

The class supports the constructors shown next:

5

EventSetDescriptor(Class *src*, String *esName*, Class *listener*,
  String *listenerMethName*)

EventSetDescriptor(Class *src*, String *esName*, Class *listener*,
  String[ ] *listenerMethNames*,
  String *addListenerMethName*,
  String *removeListenerMethName*)

EventSetDescriptor(String *esName*, Class *listener*,
  Method[ ] *listenerMeths*, Method *addListenerMeth*,
  Method *removeListenerMeth*)

EventSetDescriptor(String *esName*, Class *listener*,
  MethodDescriptor[ ] *listenerMethDescs*,
  Method *addListenerMeth*,
  Method *removeListenerMeth*)

The arguments to these constructors have the following meanings: *src* is the class of the Bean that generates the event set, *esName* is the name of the event set, *listener* is the class of the listener interface, *listenerMethName* is the name of the listener method, *listenerMethNames* are the names of the listener methods, *addListenerMethName* is the name of the method used to register a listener, *removeListenerMethName* is the name of the method used to unregister a listener, *listenerMeths* is an array of **Method** objects describing the listener methods, *listenerMethDescs* is an array of **MethodDescriptor** objects describing the methods in the listener interface, *addListenerMeth* is a **Method** object describing the method used to register a listener, and *removeListenerMeth* is a **Method** object describing the method used to unregister a listener.

Each of these constructors can generate an **IntrospectionException**.

Table 5-8 summarizes the methods provided by this class.

MethodDescriptor

The **MethodDescriptor** class in the **java.beans** package describes a
method of a Bean. The class supports the constructors shown next:

MethodDescriptor(Method *meth*)

Method	Descriptor
Method getAddListenerMethod( )	Returns a **Method** object for the registration method.
MethodDescriptor[ ] getListenerMethodDescriptors( )	Returns an array of **MethodDescriptor** objects for the methods in the listener interface.
Method[ ] getListenerMethods( )	Returns an array of **Method** objects for the methods in the listener interface.
Class getListenerType( )	Returns a **Class** object for the listener interface.
Method getRemoveListenerMethod( )	Returns a **Method** object for the unregistration method.
boolean isInDefaultEventSet( )	Returns **true** if the event set is in the "default set." Otherwise, returns **false**.
boolean isUnicast( )	Returns **true** if the event set is unicast. Otherwise, returns **false**.
void setInDefaultEventSet(boolean *flag*)	If *flag* is **true**, the event set is part of the "default set." Otherwise, it is not.
void setUnicast(boolean *flag*)	If *flag* is **true**, the event set is unicast. Otherwise, it is multicast.

Methods
Defined by
**EventSet-
Descriptor
Table 5-8.**

MethodDescriptor(Method *meth*, ParameterDescriptor[ ] *pds*)

Here, *meth* is the **Method** object for this method, and *pds* is an array of **ParameterDescriptor** objects that describe the parameters to this method.

The methods defined by **MethodDescriptor** are shown here:

Method getMethod( )

ParameterDescriptor[ ] getParameterDescriptors( )

The **getMethod( )** method returns a **Method** object for the associated method, and **getParameterDescriptors( )** returns an array of **ParameterDescriptor** objects for the parameters of this method.

ParameterDescriptor

The **ParameterDescriptor** class in the **java.beans** package describes the parameters of a method. The class does not provide any additional fields or methods beyond those of its **FeatureDescriptor** superclass.

PropertyDescriptor

The **PropertyDescriptor** class in the **java.beans** package describes a property of a Bean. It supports the constructors shown next:

PropertyDescriptor(String *pname*, Class *cls*)

PropertyDescriptor(String *pname*, Class *cls*, String *getMethName*,
    String *setMethName*)

PropertyDescriptor(String *pname*, Method *getMeth*, Method *setMeth*)

Here, *pname* is the name of the property, and *cls* is the class of the Bean. The names of the access methods for this property are *getMethName* and *setMethName*. The arguments *getMeth* and *setMeth* are **Method** objects for these access methods. These constructors can throw an **IntrospectionException**.

Table 5-9 summarizes some of the methods provided by this class.

5

Method	Description
Class getPropertyEditorClass( )	Returns a **Class** object for the associated property editor. If a property editor has not been defined for this property, **null** is returned. In that case, the **PropertyEditorManager** is used to obtain a property editor.
Class getPropertyType( )	Returns the **Class** object for the property.
Method getReadMethod( )	Returns a **Method** object for the reader.
Method getWriteMethod( )	Returns a **Method** object for the writer.
void setPropertyEditorClass(Class *pEdCls*)	Sets the property editor for this property to *pEdCls*.

Some Methods of **Property-Descriptor**
Table 5-9.

IndexedPropertyDescriptor

The **IndexedPropertyDescriptor** class in the **java.beans** package describes an indexed property of a Bean. It extends the **PropertyDescriptor** class and supports the constructors shown next:

IndexedPropertyDescriptor(String *pname*, Class *cls*)

IndexedPropertyDescriptor(String *pname*, Class *cls*, String *getMethName*, String *setMethName*, String *getIndexedMethName*, String *setIndexedMethName*)

IndexedPropertyDescriptor(String *pname*, Method *getMeth*, Method *setMeth*, Method *getIndexedMeth*, String *setIndexedMeth*)

Here, *pname* is the name of the property, and *cls* is the class of the Bean. Access methods for this property are *getMethName*, *setMethName*, *getIndexedMethName*, and *setIndexedMethName*. The arguments *getMeth*, *setMeth*, *getIndexedMeth*, and *setIndexedMeth* are **Method** objects for these access methods. These constructors can throw an **IntrospectionException**.

Some of the methods provided by **IndexedPropertyDescriptor** are shown here:

Class getIndexedPropertyType( )

Method getIndexedReadMethod( )

Method getIndexedWriteMethod( )

The **getIndexedPropertyType( )** method returns a **Class** object for the indexed property. The **getIndexedReadMethod( )** and **getIndexedWriteMethod( )** methods return the **Method** object for the indexed read and write methods, respectively.

Introspection Examples

5

This section describes how a Bean developer can explicitly control the properties, events, and methods that are presented to a user by a builder tool.

Designating Bean Properties

This example presents an enhanced version of the **Spectrum** Bean that was seen in Chapter 2. The Bean here is named **Spectrum2**. Its source code is identical to that seen previously except for the name change. It is reproduced in the following listing for your convenience.

```
package spectrum2;
import java.awt.*;

public class Spectrum2 extends Canvas {
  private boolean vertical;

  public Spectrum2() {
    vertical = true;
    setSize(100, 100);
  }

  public boolean getVertical() {
    return vertical;
  }
```

```
public void setVertical(boolean vertical) {
  this.vertical = vertical;
  repaint();
}

public void paint(Graphics g) {
  Color c;
  float saturation = 1.0f;
  float brightness = 1.0f;
  Dimension d = getSize();
  if(vertical) {
    for(int y = 0; y < d.height; y++) {
      float hue = (float)y/(d.height - 1);
      c = Color.getHSBColor(hue, saturation, brightness);
      g.setColor(c);
      g.drawLine(0, y, d.width - 1, y);
    }
  }
  else {
    for(int x = 0; x < d.width; x++) {
      float hue = (float)x/(d.width - 1);
      c = Color.getHSBColor(hue, saturation, brightness);
      g.setColor(c);
      g.drawLine(x, 0, x, d.height - 1);
    }
  }
}
}
```

A **Spectrum2BeanInfo** class is developed for this Bean. It extends **SimpleBeanInfo** and overrides the **getPropertyDescriptors( )**, **getEventSetDescriptors( )**, and **getMethodDescriptors( )** methods. This is the manner in which the Bean developer explicitly designates what is presented to a user of a builder tool.

The **getPropertyDescriptors( )** method returns an array of **PropertyDescriptor** objects. There is only one element in this array. It is the descriptor for the **vertical** property in the **Spectrum2** class.

The Bean does not generate or receive any events. Therefore, the **getEventSetDescriptors( )** and **getMethodDescriptors( )** methods return an empty array of **EventSetDescriptor** and **MethodDescriptor** objects, respectively.

```
package spectrum2;
import java.beans.*;
import java.awt.event.*;
import java.lang.reflect.*;

public class Spectrum2BeanInfo extends SimpleBeanInfo {

  public PropertyDescriptor[] getPropertyDescriptors() {
    try {
      Class cls = Spectrum2.class;
      PropertyDescriptor pd;
      pd = new PropertyDescriptor("vertical", cls);
      PropertyDescriptor pds[] = { pd };
      return pds;
    }
    catch(Exception ex) {
    }
    return null;
  }

  public EventSetDescriptor[] getEventSetDescriptors() {
    EventSetDescriptor esds[] = {  };
    return esds;
  }

  public MethodDescriptor[] getMethodDescriptors() {
    MethodDescriptor mds[] = {  };
    return mds;
  }
}
```

5

Figure 5-1 shows how **Spectrum2** appears in the BeanBox. Observe that the Properties window contains only one property. Also, if you pull down the Edit menu of BeanBox, you can see that this component generates no events. Finally, if you attempt to map an event generated by another Bean to a method of the **Spectrum2** Bean, the BeanBox provides a message box stating that there is no suitable target method.

Designating Bean Events and Methods

This example presents an enhanced version of the **MouseSource** and **MouseReceiver** Beans that were seen in Chapter 3. The Beans here are

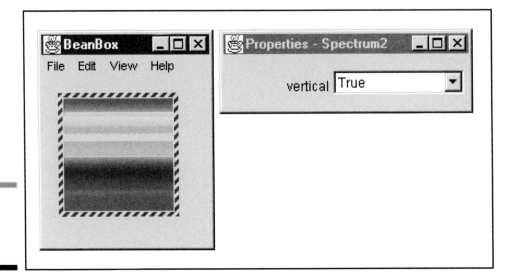

The
Spectrum2
Bean
Figure 5-1.

named **MouseSource2** and **MouseReceiver2**. Their source code is identical to that seen previously, except for the name changes.

The source code for **MouseSource2** is shown in the following listing:

```
package mouseevents2;
import java.awt.*;

public class MouseSource2 extends Canvas {
  public MouseSource2() {
    setSize(100, 100);
  }

  public void paint(Graphics g) {
    Dimension d = getSize();
    g.drawRect(0, 0, d.width - 1, d.height - 1);
  }
}
```

The source code for **MouseSource2BeanInfo** is shown in the following listing. The **MouseSource2** Bean has no properties or methods. It only generates events. Two **EventSetDescriptor** objects are created for the "mouse" and "mouseMotion" event sets. The names of the listener methods and the registration and unregistration methods are passed as arguments to the constructors.

```java
package mouseevents2;
import java.beans.*;
import java.awt.event.*;
import java.lang.reflect.*;

public class MouseSource2BeanInfo extends SimpleBeanInfo {

  public PropertyDescriptor[] getPropertyDescriptors() {
    PropertyDescriptor pds[] = {  };
    return pds;
  }

  public EventSetDescriptor[] getEventSetDescriptors() {
    try {
      EventSetDescriptor esd1, esd2;
      String mnames[] = { "mouseClicked", "mouseEntered",
        "mouseExited", "mousePressed", "mouseReleased" };
      esd1 = new EventSetDescriptor(MouseSource2.class,
        "mouse", MouseListener.class, mnames,
        "addMouseListener", "removeMouseListener");
      String mmnames[] = { "mouseDragged", "mouseMoved" };
      esd2 = new EventSetDescriptor(MouseSource2.class,
        "mouseMotion", MouseMotionListener.class, mmnames,
        "addMouseMotionListener", "removeMouseMotionListener");
      EventSetDescriptor esd[] = { esd1, esd2 };
      return esd;
    }
    catch(Exception ex) {
      ex.printStackTrace();
    }
    return null;
  }

  public MethodDescriptor[] getMethodDescriptors() {
    MethodDescriptor mds[] = {  };
    return mds;
  }
}
```

5

The source code for **MouseReceiver2** is shown in the following listing. Except for the name change, it is identical to **MouseReceiver**, which was seen in Chapter 3.

```java
package mouseevents2;
import java.awt.*;
import java.awt.event.*;

public class MouseReceiver2 extends Panel
implements MouseListener, MouseMotionListener {
  private TextArea ta;

  public MouseReceiver2() {
    setLayout(null);
    ta = new TextArea();
    ta.setBounds(0, 0, 150, 300);
    add(ta);
    setSize(150, 300);
  }

  public void mouseClicked(MouseEvent me) {
    ta.append("mouse clicked\n");
  }

  public void mouseEntered(MouseEvent me) {
    ta.append("mouse entered\n");
  }

  public void mouseExited(MouseEvent me) {
    ta.append("mouse exited\n");
  }

  public void mousePressed(MouseEvent me) {
    ta.append("mouse pressed\n");
  }

  public void mouseReleased(MouseEvent me) {
    ta.append("mouse released\n");
  }

  public void mouseDragged(MouseEvent me) {
    ta.append("mouse dragged\n");
  }
```

```
    public void mouseMoved(MouseEvent me) {
      ta.append("mouse moved\n");
    }
}
```

The source code for **MouseReceiver2BeanInfo** is shown in the following listing. The **MouseReceiver2** Bean has no properties and generates no events. It only receives events. Therefore, the **getPropertyDescriptors( )** and **getEventSetDescriptors( )** methods return an empty array of **PropertyDescriptor** and **EventSetDescriptor** objects, respectively.

The **getMethodDescriptors( )** method returns an array of seven **MethodDescriptor** objects. These describe the methods to receive mouse events.

The **Class** object for **MouseReceiver2** is obtained first. Then an array of **Class** objects representing the types of the method parameters is created. In this program, each of the seven methods accepts one **MouseEvent** parameter. The **getMethod( )** method of **Class** is used to obtain a **Method** object for each routine.

Finally, the **MethodDescriptor** constructor requires both a reference to the **Method** object and a reference to an array of **ParameterDescriptor** objects that describe the parameters of that method. In this case, no special information is provided for the parameter.

```
package mouseevents2;
import java.beans.*;
import java.awt.event.*;
import java.lang.reflect.*;

public class MouseReceiver2BeanInfo extends SimpleBeanInfo {

  public PropertyDescriptor[] getPropertyDescriptors() {
    PropertyDescriptor pds[] = {   };
    return pds;
  }

  public EventSetDescriptor[] getEventSetDescriptors() {
    EventSetDescriptor esds[] = {   };
    return esds;
  }

  public MethodDescriptor[] getMethodDescriptors() {
```

5

```
try {
  Class c = MouseReceiver2.class;
  Class pTypes[] = new Class[1];
  pTypes[0] = MouseEvent.class;
  Method method1 = c.getMethod("mouseClicked", pTypes);
  Method method2 = c.getMethod("mouseEntered", pTypes);
  Method method3 = c.getMethod("mouseExited", pTypes);
  Method method4 = c.getMethod("mousePressed", pTypes);
  Method method5 = c.getMethod("mouseReleased", pTypes);
  Method method6 = c.getMethod("mouseDragged", pTypes);
  Method method7 = c.getMethod("mouseMoved", pTypes);
  ParameterDescriptor pds[] = new ParameterDescriptor[1];
  pds[0] = new ParameterDescriptor();
  MethodDescriptor md1 = new MethodDescriptor(method1, pds);
  MethodDescriptor md2 = new MethodDescriptor(method2, pds);
  MethodDescriptor md3 = new MethodDescriptor(method3, pds);
  MethodDescriptor md4 = new MethodDescriptor(method4, pds);
  MethodDescriptor md5 = new MethodDescriptor(method5, pds);
  MethodDescriptor md6 = new MethodDescriptor(method6, pds);
  MethodDescriptor md7 = new MethodDescriptor(method7, pds);
  MethodDescriptor mds[] = { md1, md2, md3, md4,
    md5, md6, md7 };
  return mds;
}
catch(Exception ex) {
  ex.printStackTrace();
}
return null;
}
}
```

Figure 5-2 shows how these Beans appear in BeanBox. Notice that the only events listed for the source are those designated in **MouseSource2BeanInfo**.

Concluding Comments

This chapter presents an overview of reflection and introspection. It shows how Java provides capabilities that make it straightforward to develop reusable components and builder tools.

You now know how to explicitly control the information a builder tool presents about a Bean. The classes to accomplish this are frequently used in

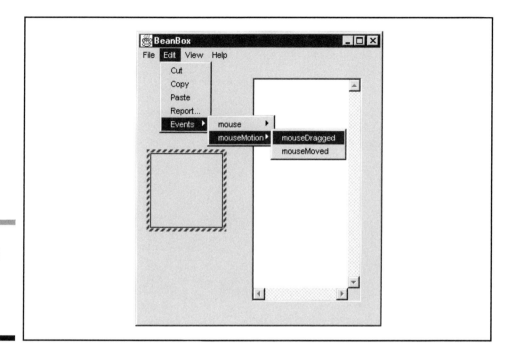

The **Mouse-Source2** and **Mouse-Receiver2** Beans

Figure 5-2.

5

the remainder of this book and are important when building production quality components.

Finally, Chapter 14 develops a very simple tool that can add Beans to a layout area and connect them. It illustrates how the material presented here can be applied in a very practical way.

CHAPTER 6

Bean Examples

The preceding chapters described some essential concepts of JavaBeans. Before proceeding, let's see how this knowledge can be applied. This chapter presents three examples to integrate what has been described so far in the book. First, a component is built to display a sequence of images. The images are packaged in the same JAR file with the Bean. Second, a set of components is built to simulate the operation of instruments you would find in an electronics laboratory. These use custom events to work together. Finally, a Bean is built to display a moving 3-D surface. This provides a computer-generated animation and illustrates how to apply custom deserialization.

The Slide Show Bean

The **Slides** Bean illustrates how to use images from a JAR file.

This section develops a Bean named **Slides** that displays a sequence of images. Its **interval** property determines the time in milliseconds that each image appears.

The images are packaged in the same JAR file that contains the Bean. There is also a file named slides.txt in the JAR file. This contains the names of the image files. The images are presented according to the order they are listed in this file. When all images have been displayed, the cycle repeats.

Figure 6-1 shows how the Bean appears in BeanBox.

The source code for the **Slides** class is shown in the following listing. It extends **Canvas** and implements **Runnable**. The **interval** variable defines the number of milliseconds between images and is the one property of this Bean. The **images** variable holds references to **Image** objects that are created from the JPG files contained in the JAR file. The **thread** variable holds a reference to the **Thread** object that runs the animation. Both variables are **transient** because **Image** and **Thread** objects cannot be serialized. The **index** variable keeps track of the slide that is currently being displayed. The **numimages** variable equals the total number of images. Both variables are **transient** because it is not necessary to store them in the serial stream.

The constructor begins by initializing the property and the **images** variable. The **loadImages( )** method is then invoked to read the images from the JAR file, create **Image** objects, and store these in the **images** vector. A thread is started and the dimensions of the Bean are set. The access methods for the property follow the constructor.

The **loadImages( )** method begins by using the **getClass( )** method to obtain the class of the current object. The **getResourceAsStream( )**

The **Slides**
Bean
Figure 6-1.

6

method returns an **InputStream** object for the slides.txt file that is located in the JAR file. Next, a **BufferedReader** object is created for this stream. A loop then reads each line from slides.txt. A line contains the name of an image file. This name is used as an argument to the **getResource( )** method to obtain a **URL** for that resource. The **getContent( )** method of **URL** reads the data from the image file, and the **createImage( )** method converts this to an **Image** object. The new object is added to the **images** vector, and the **numimages** counter is incremented.

The **paint( )** method displays the current image. The logic for the thread is in the **run( )** method. Its effect is to call **repaint( )** every **interval** millisecond and update **index** to identify the current image.

The **readObject( )** method is called when the object is restored from the serial stream. The **defaultReadObject( )** method restores its nontransient data. The **images** vector is initialized by calling **loadImages( )**, and the animation thread is started.

```
package slides;
import java.awt.*;
import java.awt.image.*;
```

```
import java.io.*;
import java.net.*;
import java.util.*;

public class Slides extends Canvas implements Runnable {
  private int interval;
  private transient Vector images;
  private transient Thread thread;
  private transient int index;
  private transient int numimages;

  public Slides() {
    interval = 1000;
    images = new Vector();
    loadImages();
    thread = new Thread(this);
    thread.start();
    setSize(300, 300);
  }

  public int getInterval() {
    return interval;
  }

  public void setInterval(int interval) {
    this.interval = interval;
  }

  private void loadImages() {
    try {
      InputStream is;
      is = getClass().getResourceAsStream("slides.txt");
      BufferedReader br;
      br = new BufferedReader(new InputStreamReader(is));
      String line;
      while((line = br.readLine()) != null) {
        URL url = getClass().getResource(line);
        ImageProducer ip = (ImageProducer)url.getContent();
        Image image = createImage(ip);
        images.addElement(image);
        ++numimages;
      }
    }
    catch(Exception ex) {
      ex.printStackTrace();
```

```
      }
    }

    public void paint(Graphics g) {
      g.drawImage((Image)images.elementAt(index), 0, 0, this);
    }

    public void run() {
      try {
        while(true) {
          repaint();
          index = (index + 1) % numimages;
          Thread.sleep(interval);
        }
      }
      catch(Exception ex) {
        ex.printStackTrace();
      }
    }

    private void readObject(ObjectInputStream ois)
    throws IOException, ClassNotFoundException {
      try {
        ois.defaultReadObject();
        images = new Vector();
        loadImages();
        thread = new Thread(this);
        thread.start();
      }
      catch(Exception ex) {
        ex.printStackTrace();
      }
    }
  }
}
```

The following listing shows the source code for the **SlidesBeanInfo** class.
It extends **SimpleBeanInfo** and overrides **getPropertyDescriptors( )**,
getEventSetDescriptors( ), and **getMethodDescriptors( )** to indicate
that this Bean has only one property.

```
package slides;
import java.beans.*;

public class SlidesBeanInfo extends SimpleBeanInfo {
```

```
public PropertyDescriptor[] getPropertyDescriptors() {
  try {
    PropertyDescriptor pd1;
    pd1 = new PropertyDescriptor("interval", Slides.class);
    PropertyDescriptor pds[] = { pd1 };
    return pds;
  }
  catch(Exception ex) {
    ex.printStackTrace();
  }
  return null;
}

public EventSetDescriptor[] getEventSetDescriptors() {
  EventSetDescriptor esds[] = { };
  return esds;
}

public MethodDescriptor[] getMethodDescriptors() {
  MethodDescriptor mds[] = { };
  return mds;
}
}
```

The following listing illustrates the format of slides.txt. (Although all of these entries are JPG files, the Bean also works with GIF files.)

```
slide1.jpg
slide2.jpg
slide3.jpg
slide4.jpg
```

To create a JAR file containing the Bean and all associated files, you may use this command:

> jar cfm c:\bdk\jars\slides.jar slides*.mft slides*.class slides\ *.txt slides*.jpg

Remember that all of these files may be downloaded from the Osborne web site at **http://www.osborne.com**.

The Circuit Beans

This section develops five Beans that might be interesting to someone who works with electrical circuits.

The **Generator** Bean simulates the action of a sine wave generator. It has three properties, **amplitude**, **frequency**, and **phase**, that control the appearance of the signal. This component sends **WaveformEvent** objects to registered listeners. These objects are custom events and contain the current value of the signal. One hundred event notifications are sent for every cycle of the waveform. As the frequency of the signal is increased, the notifications are generated more frequently. The **Generator** Bean is an invisible component.

The **Meter** and **Plotter** Beans simulate the action of an analog meter and plotter, respectively. Each component has two properties, **min** and **max**, that determine the minimum and maximum values it can display. They implement the **WaveformListener** interface to receive **WaveformEvent** notifications.

6

The **Rectifier** Bean simulates the action of a circuit that converts a negative signal into a positive signal of the same magnitude. The **Clamp** Bean simulates the action of a circuit that prevents a signal from going above a maximum value or below a minimum value. These thresholds are determined by two properties, **min** and **max**. Both components implement the **WaveformListener** interface to receive **WaveformEvent** notifications. The received events are processed and forwarded to any listeners who register with the Beans. Both the **Rectifier** and **Clamp** Beans are invisible components.

Figure 6-2 shows how these components appear in BeanBox.

The classes and interfaces used in this example are summarized in the following table:

WaveformEvent	Contains the current signal value
WaveformListener	Receives **WaveformEvent** objects
Generator	Generates the signal

GeneratorBeanInfo	Designates the properties, events, and methods of **Generator**
Meter	Displays an analog meter
MeterBeanInfo	Designates the properties, events, and methods of **Meter**
Plotter	Displays a plotter
PlotterBeanInfo	Designates the properties, events, and methods of **Plotter**
Rectifier	Rectifies the signal
RectifierBeanInfo	Designates the properties, events, and methods of **Rectifier**
Clamp	Clamps the signal between a maximum and minimum value
ClampBeanInfo	Designates the properties, events, and methods of **Clamp**

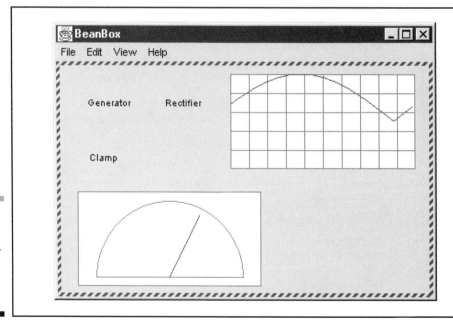

The
Generator,
Meter, **Plotter**,
Rectifier, and
Clamp Beans

Figure 6-2.

WaveformEvent

The source code for **WaveformEvent** is shown in the following listing. It extends **EventObject** and encapsulates the current value of the signal. The first argument to the constructor is a reference to the source of the event. Notice that this value is provided to the superclass constructor via the call to **super**. The second argument to the constructor is the current value of the signal.

```
package ee;
import java.util.*;

public class WaveformEvent extends EventObject {
  private double value;

  public WaveformEvent(Object source, double value) {
    super(source);
    this.value = value;
  }

  public double getValue() {
    return value;
  }

  public void setValue(double value) {
    this.value = value;
  }
}
```

WaveformListener

The source code for **WaveformListener** is shown in the following listing. This interface extends **EventListener** and defines one method, **waveformValueChanged( )**, to receive **WaveformEvent** notifications.

```
package ee;
import java.util.*;

public interface WaveformListener extends EventListener {

  public abstract void waveformValueChanged(WaveformEvent we);
}
```

6

Generator

The source code for the **Generator** Bean is shown in the next listing. The class implements **Serializable** so it can be saved by the serialization mechanisms and implements **Runnable** so it can run as a separate thread. There are three **double** properties that define the amplitude, frequency (in cycles/sec), and phase (in radians) of the generated signal. The **listeners** variable is a **Vector** object that holds references to all of the registered listeners. The current time in milliseconds is stored in a **double** instance variable named **time**, and the current value of the sine wave is stored in a **double** instance variable named **value**. These variables are **transient** because we do not want to save them in the serialization process. Finally, the variable **t** holds a reference to the **Thread** object that generates the event notifications. This variable must be **transient** because **Thread** objects cannot be serialized.

The constructor begins by initializing some of the instance variables and calling the **startThread( )** method to run the current object. The access methods for the properties are next in the listing.

The **run( )** method has an infinite loop to generate the event notifications. It first checks if **frequency** is zero. If so, it sleeps for one second before checking the value again. This is done to avoid dividing by zero later in the loop. If **frequency** is nonzero, the current value of the sine wave is calculated and stored in **value**. The number of milliseconds before the next sample value is computed by dividing the period of the waveform in milliseconds by 100. (Recall that the frequency is specified in cycles/sec.) The value in **interval** is added to **time**. The **fireWaveformEvent( )** method is called to generate and multicast a **WaveformEvent** object. Then the **sleep( )** method is called to insert a delay before the next sample is calculated.

The registration and unregistration functionality is provided by the **addWaveformListener( )** and **removeWaveformListener( )** methods.

The **fireWaveformEvent( )** method creates and multicasts a **WaveformEvent** object. The code is similar to what has been seen in previous chapters.

Finally, the **readObject( )** method invokes the **defaultReadObject( )** method of **ObjectInputStream** to restore the nontransient instance variables of this object. It then invokes the **startThread( )** method to initiate the thread.

```
package ee;
import java.io.*;
import java.util.*;

public class Generator implements Runnable, Serializable {
  private double amplitude;
  private double frequency;
  private double phase;
  private Vector listeners;
  private transient double time;
  private transient double value;
  private transient Thread t;

  public Generator() {
    amplitude = 1;
    frequency = 0.2;   //  cycles/sec
    phase = 0;
    listeners = new Vector();
    time = 0;
    startThread();
  }

  private void startThread() {
    t = new Thread(this);
    t.start();
  }

  public double getAmplitude() {
    return amplitude;
  }

  public void setAmplitude(double amplitude) {
    this.amplitude = amplitude;
  }

  public double getFrequency() {
    return frequency;
  }

  public void setFrequency(double frequency) {
    this.frequency = frequency;
  }
```

6

```
public double getPhase() {
  return phase;
}

public void setPhase(double phase) {
  this.phase = phase;
}

public void run() {
  try {
    while(true) {
      double f = frequency;
      if(f == 0) {
        Thread.sleep(1000);
        continue;
      }
      double radians = 2 * Math.PI * f * time/1000 + phase;
      value = amplitude * Math.sin(radians);
      long interval = (long)(10/f);
      time += interval;
      fireWaveformEvent();
      Thread.sleep(interval);
    }
  }
  catch(Exception ex) {
    ex.printStackTrace();
  }
}

public void addWaveformListener(WaveformListener wl) {
  listeners.addElement(wl);
}

public void removeWaveformListener(WaveformListener wl) {
  listeners.removeElement(wl);
}

protected synchronized void fireWaveformEvent() {
  Vector v;
  synchronized(this) {
    v = (Vector)listeners.clone();
  }
  WaveformEvent we = new WaveformEvent(this, value);
  for(int i = 0; i < v.size(); i++) {
    WaveformListener wl = (WaveformListener)v.elementAt(i);
```

```
        wl.waveformValueChanged(we);
      }
    }

    private void readObject(ObjectInputStream ois) {
      try {
        ois.defaultReadObject();
        startThread();
      }
      catch(Exception ex) {
        ex.printStackTrace();
      }
    }
  }
}
```

GeneratorBeanInfo

The source code for **GeneratorBeanInfo** is shown in the following listing.
The class extends **SimpleBeanInfo** and overrides three methods to
explicitly designate the properties, events, and methods that should be
shown to a user by a builder tool.

The **getPropertyDescriptors( )** method returns an array of
three **PropertyDescriptor** objects for the three properties. The
getEventSetDescriptors( ) method returns an array with one
EventSetDescriptor object. The arguments to the **EventSetDescriptor**
constructor are the class of the source, the name of the event set, the type
of the listener interface, the names of the listener methods, the name
of the registration method, and the name of the unregistration
method. The **Generator** Bean does not receive any events, so the
getMethodDescriptors( ) method returns an empty array of
MethodDescriptor objects.

6

```
package ee;
import java.beans.*;
import java.lang.reflect.*;

public class GeneratorBeanInfo extends SimpleBeanInfo {

  public PropertyDescriptor[] getPropertyDescriptors() {
    try {
      PropertyDescriptor a, f, p;
      Class cls = Generator.class;
      a = new PropertyDescriptor("amplitude", cls);
```

```
      f = new PropertyDescriptor("frequency", cls);
      p = new PropertyDescriptor("phase", cls);
      PropertyDescriptor pds[] = { a, f, p };
      return pds;
    }
    catch(Exception ex) {
      ex.printStackTrace();
    }
    return null;
  }

  public EventSetDescriptor[] getEventSetDescriptors() {
    try {
      EventSetDescriptor esd1;
      Class c = Generator.class;
      String es = "waveform";
      Class lc = WaveformListener.class;
      String names[] = { "waveformValueChanged" };
      String al = "addWaveformListener";
      String rl = "removeWaveformListener";
      esd1 = new EventSetDescriptor(c, es, lc, names, al, rl);
      EventSetDescriptor esd[] = { esd1 };
      return esd;
    }
    catch(Exception ex) {
      ex.printStackTrace();
    }
    return null;
  }

  public MethodDescriptor[] getMethodDescriptors() {
    MethodDescriptor mds[] = { };
    return mds;
  }
}
```

Meter

The source code for the **Meter** Bean is shown in the next listing. The class extends **Canvas** and implements **WaveformListener** so it can receive **WaveformEvent** notifications. It can be serialized because it indirectly inherits from **Component** and that class implements **Serializable**. There are two properties that define the minimum and maximum values of the range. In addition, the background color of the meter is an inherited property. The current value of the sine wave is stored in a **double** instance variable named **value**. This variable is **transient** because we do not want to save it in the serialization process.

The constructor begins by initializing the instance variables and calling the **setSize( )** method to define the dimensions of the Bean. The access methods for the properties are next in the listing.

The **waveformValueChanged( )** method is called when an event notification is received. The value of the signal is read from the event object and saved in **value**, and the **repaint( )** method is called to update the display.

The **paint( )** method draws a display with the analog meter. The needle position is calculated as a function of the variable **value**.

```java
package ee;
import java.awt.*;

public class Meter extends Canvas
implements WaveformListener {
  private final static int NDEGREES = 180;
  public double min;
  public double max;
  public transient double value;

  public Meter() {
    min = -1;
    max = 1;
    value = 0;
    setSize(200, 100);
  }

  public double getMin() {
    return min;
  }

  public void setMin(double min) {
    this.min = min;
    repaint();
  }

  public double getMax() {
    return max;
  }
}
```

6

```
public void setMax(double max) {
  this.max = max;
  repaint();
}

public void waveformValueChanged(WaveformEvent we) {
  value = we.getValue();
  repaint();
}

public void paint(Graphics g) {

  // Draw rectangle around the display area
  Dimension d = getSize();
  int h = d.height;
  int w = d.width;
  g.setColor(Color.gray);
  g.drawRect(0, 0, w - 1, h - 1);

  // Draw arc representing the dial
  int centerx = (int)(w * 0.5);
  int centery = (int)(h * 0.9);
  int radius = (int)(w * 0.4);
  int xa = (int)(w * 0.1);
  int ya = (int)(h * 0.1);
  int wa = 2 * radius;
  int ha = 2 * radius;
  g.drawArc(xa, ya, wa, ha, 0, 180);

  // Draw line representing the base of the meter
  g.drawLine(centerx - radius, centery,
    centerx + radius, centery);

  // Compute position of needle
  double angle;
  if(value > max) {
    angle = 180;
  }
  else if(value < min) {
    angle = 0;
  }
  else {
    angle = (int)(180 * (value - min)/(max - min));
  }
```

```
      // Draw line representing the needle
      double radians = angle * Math.PI/180;
      int x = (int)(centerx - radius * 0.9 * Math.cos(radians));
      int y = (int)(centery - radius * 0.9 * Math.sin(radians));
      g.setColor(Color.blue);
      g.drawLine(centerx, centery, x, y);
  }
}
```

MeterBeanInfo

The source code for **MeterBeanInfo** is shown in the next listing. The class
extends **SimpleBeanInfo** and overrides three methods to explicitly
designate the properties, events, and methods that should be shown to a user
by a builder tool.

The **getPropertyDescriptors( )** method returns an array of
PropertyDescriptor objects for the three properties. The **Meter** Bean does
not generate any events, so **getEventSetDescriptors( )** returns an empty
array of **EventSetDescriptor** objects.

The **getMethodDescriptors( )** method returns an array with one
MethodDescriptor object. The **Class** object for **Meter** is obtained first.
Then an array of **Class** objects representing the types of the method
parameters is created. In this program, the method accepts one
WaveformEvent parameter. The **getMethod( )** method of **Class** is used to
obtain a **Method** object for that routine. Finally, the **MethodDescriptor**
constructor requires both a reference to the **Method** object and a reference
to an array of **ParameterDescriptor** objects that describe the parameters
of that method. In this case, no special information is provided for
the parameter.

```
package ee;
import java.beans.*;
import java.lang.reflect.*;

public class MeterBeanInfo extends SimpleBeanInfo {

  public PropertyDescriptor[] getPropertyDescriptors() {
    try {
      PropertyDescriptor min, max, background;
      Class cls = Meter.class;
      min = new PropertyDescriptor("min", cls);
```

```
      max = new PropertyDescriptor("max", cls);
      background = new PropertyDescriptor("background", cls);
      PropertyDescriptor pd[] = { min, max, background };
      return pd;
    }
  catch(Exception ex) {
    ex.printStackTrace();
  }
  return null;
}

public EventSetDescriptor[] getEventSetDescriptors() {
  EventSetDescriptor esds[] = { };
  return esds;
}

public MethodDescriptor[] getMethodDescriptors() {
  try {
    Class c = Meter.class;
    Class parameterTypes[] = new Class[1];
    parameterTypes[0] = WaveformEvent.class;
    String name = "waveformValueChanged";
    Method method1 = c.getMethod(name, parameterTypes);
    ParameterDescriptor pds[] = new ParameterDescriptor[1];
    pds[0] = new ParameterDescriptor();
    MethodDescriptor md1;
    md1 = new MethodDescriptor(method1, pds);
    MethodDescriptor mds[] = { md1 };
    return mds;
  }
  catch(Exception ex) {
    ex.printStackTrace();
  }
  return null;
  }
}
```

Plotter

The source code for the **Plotter** Bean is shown in the next listing. The class extends **Canvas** and implements **WaveformListener** so it can receive **WaveformEvent** notifications. It can be serialized because it indirectly inherits from **Component** and that class implements **Serializable**. The **int** constant **NVALUES** defines the number of data points that are displayed by the Bean. There are two properties that define the minimum and maximum values of the range. The current set of data values is stored in a **double** array named **data**. The number of valid entries in data is recorded in **validEntries**. The index of the next entry to be updated is maintained in **writeIndex**. The position of the chart grid is maintained in **gridOffset**. These variables are **transient** because we do not want to save them in the serialization process.

The constructor begins by initializing the instance variables and calling the **setSize( )** method to define the dimensions of the Bean. The access methods for the properties are next in the listing.

The **waveformValueChanged( )** method is called when an event notification is received. The value of the signal is read from the event object and is scaled to the height of the Bean. The **validEntries** and **writeIndex** variables are updated. The **repaint( )** method is called to update the display.

The **scale( )** method accepts the **double** value of the signal and the height of the display area. It returns an **int** that is the y coordinate of that point in the display area. Note that the maximum value of the signal has a y coordinate of zero. The minimum value of the signal has a y coordinate equal to the height of the Bean.

The **paint( )** method draws the plotter grid and the signal.

The **readObject( )** method is needed so that space can be allocated for the **int** array **data** during the deserialization process.

6

```
package ee;
import java.awt.*;
import java.io.*;

public class Plotter extends Canvas
implements WaveformListener {
  private final static int NVALUES = 51;
  private double min;
  private double max;
  private transient int data[];
  private transient int validEntries;
  private transient int writeIndex;
  private transient int gridOffset;

  public Plotter() {
    min = -1;
    max = 1;
    data = new int[NVALUES];
```

```
  validEntries = 0;
  writeIndex = 0;
  gridOffset = 0;
  setSize(200, 100);
}

public double getMax() {
  return max;
}

public void setMax(double max) {
  this.max = max;
  repaint();
}

public double getMin() {
  return min;
}

public void setMin(double min) {
  this.min = min;
  repaint();
}

public void waveformValueChanged(WaveformEvent we) {
  Dimension d = getSize();
  int h = d.height;
  data[writeIndex] = scale(we.getValue(), h);
  if(validEntries < NVALUES) {
    ++validEntries;
  }
  if(++writeIndex >= NVALUES) {
    writeIndex = 0;
  }
  repaint();
}

private int scale(double value, int h) {
  if(value > max) {
    return 0;
  }
  else if(value < min) {
    return h;
  }
  else {
```

```java
      double k = (value-min)/(max-min);
      return (int)(h * (1 - k));
  }
}

public void paint(Graphics g) {

  // Draw rectangle around the display area
  Dimension d = getSize();
  int h = d.height;
  int w = d.width;
  g.setColor(Color.gray);
  g.drawRect(0, 0, w - 1, h - 1);

  // Draw vertical lines
  double deltax = w/(NVALUES - 1);
  int x;
  for(int i = 0; i <= 10; i++) {
    x = i * w/10 - gridOffset;
    if(x < 0) {
      continue;
    }
    g.drawLine(x, 0, x, h);
  }
  gridOffset += deltax;
  if(gridOffset >= w/10) {
    gridOffset = 0;
  }

  // Draw horizontal lines
  int y;
  for(int i = 1; i < 5; i++) {
    y = i * h/5;
    g.drawLine(0, y, w, y);
  }

  // Prepare to plot the WaveformEvent objects
  g.setColor(Color.blue);
  int readIndex = 0;
  if(validEntries == NVALUES) {
    readIndex = writeIndex + 1;
    if(readIndex == NVALUES) {
      readIndex = 0;
    }
  }
```

```
    // Return if there are not at least two points
    if(validEntries < 2) {
      return;
    }

    // Draw the plot
    for(int i = 0; i < validEntries - 2; i++) {
      int x1, y1, x2, i2, y2;
      x1 = (int)(i * deltax);
      y1 = data[readIndex];
      x2 = (int)((i + 1) * deltax);
      i2 = (readIndex+1 == NVALUES) ? 0 : readIndex+1;
      y2 = data[i2];
      g.drawLine(x1, y1, x2, y2);
      ++readIndex;
      if(readIndex == NVALUES) {
        readIndex = 0;
      }
    }
  }

  private void readObject(ObjectInputStream ois) {
    try {
      ois.defaultReadObject();
      data = new int[NVALUES];
    }
    catch(Exception ex) {
      ex.printStackTrace();
    }
  }
}
```

PlotterBeanInfo

The source code for **PlotterBeanInfo** is shown in the following listing. It is identical to **MeterBeanInfo**, except for the obvious change in the name of the Bean.

```
package ee;
import java.beans.*;
import java.lang.reflect.*;

public class PlotterBeanInfo extends SimpleBeanInfo {
```

```
public PropertyDescriptor[] getPropertyDescriptors() {
  try {
    PropertyDescriptor min, max, background;
    Class cls = Plotter.class;
    min = new PropertyDescriptor("min", cls);
    max = new PropertyDescriptor("max", cls);
    background = new PropertyDescriptor("background", cls);
    PropertyDescriptor pd[] = { min, max, background };
    return pd;
  }
  catch(Exception ex) {
    ex.printStackTrace();
  }
  return null;
}

public EventSetDescriptor[] getEventSetDescriptors() {
  EventSetDescriptor esds[] = { };
  return esds;
}

public MethodDescriptor[] getMethodDescriptors() {
  try {
    Class c = Plotter.class;
    Class parameterTypes[] = new Class[1];
    parameterTypes[0] = WaveformEvent.class;
    String name = "waveformValueChanged";
    Method method1 = c.getMethod(name, parameterTypes);
    ParameterDescriptor pds[] = new ParameterDescriptor[1];
    pds[0] = new ParameterDescriptor();
    MethodDescriptor md1 = new MethodDescriptor(method1, pds);
    MethodDescriptor mds[] = { md1 };
    return mds;
  }
  catch(Exception ex) {
    ex.printStackTrace();
  }
  return null;
}
}
```

6

Rectifier

The source code for the **Rectifier** Bean is shown in the next listing. (A *rectifier* is an electrical circuit or device whose output is always positive and equal in magnitude to its input.) The class implements **Serializable** so it can be saved by the serialization mechanisms. It implements **WaveformListener** so it can receive **WaveformEvent** objects. The **listeners** variable is a **Vector** object that holds references to all of the registered listeners. This variable is not **transient** because we do want to record the connectivity among the Beans in the serial stream.

The constructor initializes the **listeners** variable. The registration and unregistration functionality is provided by the **addWaveformListener( )** and **removeWaveformListener( )** methods.

The **waveformValueChanged( )** method is called when an event notification is received. It creates a new **WaveformEvent** object whose value is always positive and equal in magnitude to the original value. This new object is multicast to all registered listeners.

```java
package ee;
import java.io.*;
import java.util.*;

public class Rectifier
implements Serializable, WaveformListener {
  private Vector listeners;

  public Rectifier() {
    listeners = new Vector();
  }

  public void addWaveformListener(WaveformListener wl) {
    listeners.addElement(wl);
  }

  public void removeWaveformListener(WaveformListener wl) {
    listeners.removeElement(wl);
  }

  public void waveformValueChanged(WaveformEvent we) {
    WaveformEvent we2;
    we2 = new WaveformEvent(we.getSource(), we.getValue());
    double value = we2.getValue();
    if(value < 0) {
      we2.setValue(-value);
    }
    Vector v;
    synchronized(this) {
```

```
      v = (Vector)listeners.clone();
    }
    for(int i = 0; i < v.size(); i++) {
      WaveformListener wl = (WaveformListener)v.elementAt(i);
      wl.waveformValueChanged(we2);
    }
  }
}
```

RectifierBeanInfo

The source code for **RectifierBeanInfo** is shown in the following listing. It has no properties, but can both receive and generate events. The **getEventSetDescriptors( )** method returns an array with one **EventSetDescriptor** object. That array element describes the "waveform" event set. The **getMethodDescriptors( )** method returns an array with one **MethodDescriptor** object. That array element describes the **waveformValueChanged( )** method.

6

```
package ee;
import java.beans.*;
import java.lang.reflect.*;

public class RectifierBeanInfo extends SimpleBeanInfo {

  public PropertyDescriptor[] getPropertyDescriptors() {
    PropertyDescriptor pds[] = { };
    return pds;
  }

  public EventSetDescriptor[] getEventSetDescriptors() {
    try {
      EventSetDescriptor esd1;
      Class c = Rectifier.class;
      String es = "waveform";
      Class lc = WaveformListener.class;
      String names[] = { "waveformValueChanged" };
      String al = "addWaveformListener";
      String rl  = "removeWaveformListener";
      esd1 = new EventSetDescriptor(c, es, lc, names, al, rl);
      EventSetDescriptor esd[] = { esd1 };
      return esd;
    }
    catch(Exception ex) {
```

```
      ex.printStackTrace();
    }
    return null;
  }

  public MethodDescriptor[] getMethodDescriptors() {
    try {
      Class c = Rectifier.class;
      Class parameterTypes[] = new Class[1];
      parameterTypes[0] = WaveformEvent.class;
      String name = "waveformValueChanged";
      Method method1 = c.getMethod(name, parameterTypes);
      ParameterDescriptor pds[] = new ParameterDescriptor[1];
      pds[0] = new ParameterDescriptor();
      MethodDescriptor md1 = new MethodDescriptor(method1, pds);
      MethodDescriptor mds[] = { md1 };
      return mds;
    }
    catch(Exception ex) {
      ex.printStackTrace();
    }
    return null;
  }
}
```

Clamp

The source code for the **Clamp** Bean is shown in the next listing.
(A *clamp* is an electrical circuit or device whose output is prevented from
exceeding a threshold.) The class implements **Serializable** so it can be saved
by the serialization mechanisms. It implements **WaveformListener** so it
can receive **WaveformEvent** objects. There are two **double** properties that
define the maximum and minimum limits for the clamp. All values are
forced to remain within this range. The **listeners** variable is a **Vector** object
that holds references to all of the registered listeners. This variable is not
transient because we do want to record the connectivity among the
Beans in the serial stream.

The constructor begins by initializing the instance variables. The access
methods for the properties are next in the listing.

The registration and unregistration functionality is provided by the
addWaveformListener( ) and **removeWaveformListener( )** methods.

The **waveformValueChanged( )** method is called when an event notification is received. It creates a new **WaveformEvent** object whose value is always limited to the range defined by the **min** and **max** variables. This new object is multicast to all registered listeners.

```java
package ee;
import java.io.*;
import java.util.*;

public class Clamp implements Serializable, WaveformListener {
  private double max;
  private double min;
  private Vector listeners;

  public Clamp() {
    max = 0.5;
    min = -0.5;
    listeners = new Vector();
  }

  public double getMax() {
    return max;
  }

  public double getMin() {
    return min;
  }

  public void setMax(double max) {
    this.max = max;
  }

  public void setMin(double min) {
    this.min = min;
  }

  public void addWaveformListener(WaveformListener wl) {
    listeners.addElement(wl);
  }

  public void removeWaveformListener(WaveformListener wl) {
    listeners.removeElement(wl);
  }
```

```
public void waveformValueChanged(WaveformEvent we) {
  WaveformEvent we2;
  we2 = new WaveformEvent(we.getSource(), we.getValue());
  double value = we2.getValue();
  if(value < min) {
    we2.setValue(min);
  }
  else if(value > max) {
    we2.setValue(max);
  }
  Vector v;
  synchronized(this) {
    v = (Vector)listeners.clone();
  }
  for(int i = 0; i < v.size(); i++) {
    WaveformListener wl = (WaveformListener)v.elementAt(i);
    wl.waveformValueChanged(we2);
  }
}
}
```

ClampBeanInfo

The source code for the **ClampBeanInfo** class is shown in the
following listing. The logic is very similar to that seen for the other
Beans. Notice that this Bean can both receive and generate events. The
getEventSetDescriptors( ) and **getMethodDescriptors( )** methods
are identical to those seen for **RectifierBeanInfo**.

```
package ee;
import java.beans.*;
import java.lang.reflect.*;

public class ClampBeanInfo extends SimpleBeanInfo {

  public PropertyDescriptor[] getPropertyDescriptors() {
    try {
      PropertyDescriptor min, max;
      min = new PropertyDescriptor("min", Clamp.class);
      max = new PropertyDescriptor("max", Clamp.class);
      PropertyDescriptor pd[] = { min, max };
      return pd;
    }
```

```
      catch(Exception ex) {
        ex.printStackTrace();
      }
      return null;
    }

    public EventSetDescriptor[] getEventSetDescriptors() {
      try {
        EventSetDescriptor esd1;
        Class c = Clamp.class;
        String es = "waveform";
        Class lc = WaveformListener.class;
        String names[] = { "waveformValueChanged" };
        String al = "addWaveformListener";
        String rl  = "removeWaveformListener";
        esd1 = new EventSetDescriptor(c, es, lc, names, al, rl);
        EventSetDescriptor esd[] = { esd1 };
        return esd;
      }
      catch(Exception ex) {
        ex.printStackTrace();
      }
      return null;
    }

    public MethodDescriptor[] getMethodDescriptors() {
      try {
        Class c = Clamp.class;
        Class parameterTypes[] = new Class[1];
        parameterTypes[0] = WaveformEvent.class;
        String name = "waveformValueChanged";
        Method method1 = c.getMethod(name, parameterTypes);
        ParameterDescriptor pds[] = new ParameterDescriptor[1];
        pds[0] = new ParameterDescriptor();
        MethodDescriptor md1 = new MethodDescriptor(method1, pds);
        MethodDescriptor mds[] = { md1 };
        return mds;
      }
      catch(Exception ex) {
        ex.printStackTrace();
      }
      return null;
    }
}
```

6

A 3-D Graph Bean

This section develops a Bean that displays a 3-D plot of the following function:

$$z = f(x, y) = 0.01 \times (x^2 - y^2)$$

The **Plot3D** Bean provides a simple computer-generated animation and illustrates the use of custom deserialization.

An animation thread rotates this surface around the Z axis.

Figure 6-3 shows how the Bean appears in BeanBox. You can see that it is shaped like a horse saddle.

The center of your monitor screen is at position (0, –150, 0). The X axis is located in the middle of the screen and increases as you move to the right. The x = 0 position is at the middle of the screen. The Y axis increases as you move directly into the screen. The Z axis increases as you move toward the top of the screen. The surface covers the area where x varies from –100 to +100, and y varies from –100 to +100.

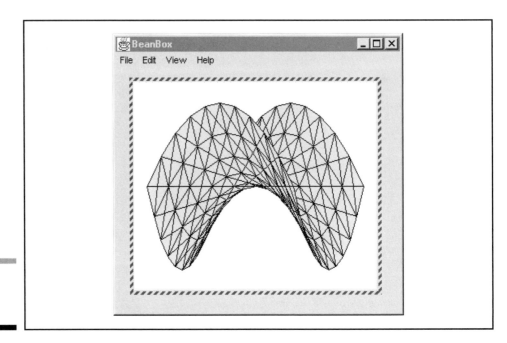

The **Plot3D** Bean

Figure 6-3.

Design Overview

Before looking at the source code, let's first outline the general strategy to generate and display this 3-D surface. The surface itself is composed of many small triangles. This is done because the three points of a triangle uniquely determine a plane in space.

The entire surface rotates around the Z axis. This is done by using a thread to compute and display a new view of the surface every 150 milliseconds. A mathematical transformation is used to rotate each triangle.

After all of the triangles have been generated, they must be sorted according to their distance from the viewer. This is necessary because triangles closer to the viewer may partly or completely obscure those more distant from the viewer.

Finally, the triangles are displayed. Those most distant from the viewer are drawn first. Those closest to the viewer are drawn last.

Source Code Listings

The source code for the Bean is shown in the next listing. It extends **Canvas** and implements **Runnable**.

The overall width and height of the component are determined by **int** constants named **WIDTH** and **HEIGHT**, respectively. The x values range from +**XMAX** to –**XMAX**, and the y values range from +**YMAX** to –**YMAX**. The size of the triangles is determined by the **int** constants **DELTAX** and **DELTAY**. The maximum value of the surface is **ZMAX**. The total number of triangles is computed as the **int** constant **NTRIANGLES**. The current rotation (in radians) of the surface is maintained in **theta**. This variable is **transient** because we do not want to store it in the stream. A reference to the thread that causes the surface to rotate is held in **thread**. This variable must be **transient** because a **Thread** object cannot be serialized.

The constructor sets the size of the Bean, initializes **theta**, and starts the thread.

The **run( )** method sits in an infinite loop. It sleeps for 150 milliseconds, increments **theta** by 1 degree, and regenerates the display.

The **update( )** method is overridden to avoid display flicker. The **paint( )** method generates the triangles. It begins by creating and allocating space for a set of **Triangle** objects. There are two nested loops that vary the values of x and y. In each pass through the inner loop, five **Point3D** objects are generated. These are rotated by the value of **theta**. Then four **Triangle** objects are created and added to the **triangles** array. After all triangles have been created, the **sortTriangles( )** method is called to sort these according to their distance from **viewPoint** (that is, the center of the monitor screen). A background buffer is then created in which to initially draw the triangles via the **drawTriangles( )** method. The background buffer is then drawn on the current graphics context.

The method **f( )** computes the z value of the surface at a given x, y coordinate.

The triangles are sorted as previously described by **sortTriangles( )**. Note that it uses the **computeDistance( )** method to do its work. That method begins by calculating the center of a triangle by averaging the x, y, and z coordinates of its corners and then computing the distance between the center and the **viewPoint**.

The surface is displayed by the **drawTriangles( )** method. The triangles are drawn in sorted order. The **fillPolygon( )** and **drawPolygon( )** methods are used to draw each triangle.

Finally, the **readObject( )** method is needed so that the thread can be started when this object is deserialized.

```java
package plot3d;
import java.awt.*;
import java.io.*;
import java.util.*;

public class Plot3D extends Canvas implements Runnable {
  private final static int WIDTH = 300;
  private final static int HEIGHT = 250;
  private final static double XMAX = 100;
  private final static double DELTAX = 20;
  private final static double YMAX = 100;
  private final static double DELTAY = 20;
  private final static double ZMAX = 100;
  private final static int NTRIANGLES =
    (int)(4 * (2 * XMAX/DELTAX) * (2 * YMAX/DELTAY));
  private transient double theta;
  private transient Thread thread;

  public Plot3D() {
```

```
    setSize(WIDTH, HEIGHT);
    theta = 0;
    thread = new Thread(this);
    thread.start();
}

public void run() {
  try {
    while(true) {
      Thread.sleep(150);
      theta += Math.PI/180;
      repaint();
    }
  }
  catch(Exception ex) {
    ex.printStackTrace();
  }
}

public void update(Graphics g) {
  paint(g);
}

public void paint(Graphics g) {

  // Generate triangles
  Triangle triangles[] = new Triangle[NTRIANGLES];
  Triangle t;
  int index = 0;
  for(double y = YMAX; y > -YMAX; y -= DELTAY) {
    for(double x = XMAX; x > -XMAX; x -= DELTAX) {
      Point3D p1, p2, p3, p4, p5;
      double z;
      z = f(x, y);
      p1 = new Point3D(x, y, z);
      z = f(x - DELTAX, y);
      p2 = new Point3D(x - DELTAX, y, z);
      z = f(x - DELTAX/2, y - DELTAY/2);
      p3 = new Point3D(x - DELTAX/2, y - DELTAY/2, z);
      z = f(x - DELTAX, y - DELTAY);
      p4 = new Point3D(x - DELTAX, y - DELTAY, z);
      z = f(x, y - DELTAY);
      p5 = new Point3D(x, y - DELTAY, z);
      p1.rotateZ(theta);
      p2.rotateZ(theta);
```

6

```
      p3.rotateZ(theta);
      p4.rotateZ(theta);
      p5.rotateZ(theta);
      t = new Triangle(p1, p2, p3);
      triangles[index++] = t;
      t = new Triangle(p2, p4, p3);
      triangles[index++] = t;
      t = new Triangle(p3, p4, p5);
      triangles[index++] = t;
      t = new Triangle(p1, p3, p5);
      triangles[index++] = t;
    }
  }

  // Sort triangles according to distance from
  // viewPoint center
  Point3D vc = new Point3D(0, -150, 0);
  Triangle sortedTriangles[];
  sortedTriangles = sortTriangles(triangles, vc);

  // Draw triangles in background buffer
  Image buffer = createImage(WIDTH, HEIGHT);
  Graphics bufferg = buffer.getGraphics();

  // Create white background
  bufferg.setColor(Color.white);
  bufferg.fillRect(0, 0, WIDTH - 1, HEIGHT - 1);

  // Draw triangles in background buffer
  Point3D viewPoint = new Point3D(0, -150, 0);
  drawTriangles(bufferg, sortedTriangles, viewPoint);

  // Copy background buffer to foreground
  g.drawImage(buffer, 0, 0, null);
}

private double f(double x, double y) {
  return 0.01 * (x * x - y * y);
}

private Triangle[] sortTriangles(Triangle triangles[],
Point3D vc) {
  double distance[] = new double[NTRIANGLES];
  for(int i = 0; i < NTRIANGLES; i++) {
    distance[i] = computeDistance(triangles[i], vc);
```

```
      }
      Triangle sortedTriangles[] = new Triangle[NTRIANGLES];
      for(int i = 0; i < NTRIANGLES; i++) {
        double d = -1;
        int k = 0;
        for(int j = 0; j < NTRIANGLES; j++) {
          if(distance[j] > d) {
            d = distance[j];
            k = j;
          }
        }
        sortedTriangles[i] = triangles[k];
        distance[k] = -1;
      }
      return sortedTriangles;
    }

    private double computeDistance(Triangle t, Point3D p) {
      double xc = (t.p1.x + t.p2.x + t.p3.x)/3;
      double yc = (t.p1.y + t.p2.y + t.p3.y)/3;
      double zc = (t.p1.z + t.p2.z + t.p3.z)/3;
      double xp = p.x;
      double yp = p.y;
      double zp = p.z;
      double dx = xc - xp;
      double dy = yc - yp;
      double dz = zc - zp;
      return Math.sqrt(dx * dx + dy * dy + dz * dz);
    }

    private void drawTriangles(Graphics g,
    Triangle sortedTriangles[], Point3D viewPoint) {
      Dimension d = getSize();
      int w = d.width;
      int h = d.height;
      int xpoints[] = new int[3];
      int ypoints[] = new int[3];
      for(int i = 0; i < NTRIANGLES; i++) {
        Triangle t = sortedTriangles[i];
        xpoints[0] = (int)(w/2 + t.p1.x);
        ypoints[0] = (int)(h/2 - t.p1.z);
        xpoints[1] = (int)(w/2 + t.p2.x);
        ypoints[1] = (int)(h/2 - t.p2.z);
        xpoints[2] = (int)(w/2 + t.p3.x);
        ypoints[2] = (int)(h/2 - t.p3.z);
```

6

```
      g.setColor(Color.yellow);
      g.fillPolygon(xpoints, ypoints, 3);
      g.setColor(Color.black);
      g.drawPolygon(xpoints, ypoints, 3);
    }
  }

  private void readObject(ObjectInputStream ois)
  throws IOException, ClassNotFoundException {
    try {
      ois.defaultReadObject();
      thread = new Thread(this);
      thread.start();
    }
    catch(Exception ex) {
      ex.printStackTrace();
    }
  }
}
```

The source code for **Point3D** is shown in the next listing. Objects of this type hold information about a point.

The **rotateZ( )** method rotates that point around the Z axis by **theta** radians.

If you are wondering about the transforms, here is how they are derived. Begin with a point (x1, y1) that can be expressed in polar coordinates as (r, a) where r is the direct distance from the origin and a is the angle from the X axis. Now rotate the point by b radians. The position of the new point (x2, y2) can be expressed in polar coordinates as (r, a + b). From this, compute x2 as $r \times \cos(a + b)$. However, $\cos(a + b)$ is equal to $\cos(a) \times \cos(b) - \sin(a) \times \sin(b)$. That is the key! Therefore, we get $x2 = r \times \cos(a) \times \cos(b) - r \times \sin(a) \times \sin(b)$. However, $r \times \cos(a)$ is x1 and $r \times \sin(a)$ is y1. The derivation of y2 is similar. The key there is that $\sin(a + b) = \sin(a) \times \cos(b) + \cos(a) \times \sin(b)$.

Note that this class does not implement the **Serializable** interface. This is unnecessary because **Point3D** objects are not saved to the serial stream when a **Plot3D** object is saved. Instead, all of the **Point3D** and **Triangle** objects are dynamically computed as the **Plot3D** thread executes.

```
package plot3d;

public class Point3D {
```

```
public double x, y, z;

public Point3D(double x, double y, double z) {
   this.x = x;
   this.y = y;
   this.z = z;
}

public void rotateZ(double theta) {
   double newx = x * Math.cos(theta) - y * Math.sin(theta);
   double newy = x * Math.sin(theta) + y * Math.cos(theta);
   x = newx;
   y = newy;
}
}
```

Finally, the source code for the **Triangle** class is shown in the following listing. Objects of this type hold references to the three corners of a triangle.

6

```
package plot3d;
import java.awt.*;

public class Triangle {
   public Point3D p1, p2, p3;

   public Triangle(Point3D p1, Point3D p2, Point3D p3) {
      this.p1 = p1;
      this.p2 = p2;
      this.p3 = p3;
   }
}
```

This simple component certainly does not do justice to the full power of computer graphics. Nonetheless, it is an interesting example of a Bean, and you see that we need to provide custom deserialization for it to work correctly. It also demonstrates that not all of the classes associated with a Bean need to be serializable. Specifically, the **Point3D** and **Triangle** objects are dynamically generated and are not saved to the serial stream.

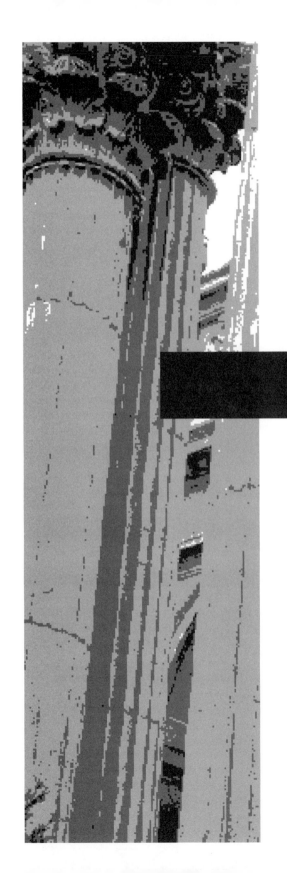

CHAPTER 7

Bound and Constrained Properties

Chapter 2 defined a property as a subset of a Bean's state and demonstrated that the behavior of a component can be affected by changing its value. It also distinguished among simple, boolean, and indexed properties.

This chapter discusses bound and constrained properties. These provide mechanisms so that other components may be informed when a Bean property is updated. In addition, when a constrained property is updated, other Beans can veto the proposed change. The advantages of this feature are discussed.

Finally, a brief overview of the HotJava™ Browser Beans is provided. These components encapsulate some of the major functions of that application. They can be downloaded without charge from the Sun Microsystems web site and are discussed here because they provide an excellent example of how to use bound properties.

Bound Properties

When a *bound property* is changed, a property change event is multicast to other Beans to inform them of this update. This provides a convenient mechanism to communicate a change in a property among a set of components. To understand why this is important, consider the following scenario.

Assume you have built an application by using one Bean that displays a set of data as a pie chart and another Bean that displays that same data as a bar chart. A third component is the source of the information. When the data in the third Bean changes, you want the two chart Beans to be notified and update their displays. In addition, you want the same colors to be used by the two chart Beans so it is easy for an end user to understand the relationships among them. Specifically, an arc of the pie chart that represents some value should be displayed in the same color as a rectangle of the bar chart that represents the same value. Bound properties are useful for this application because they allow one Bean to notify other components about relevant changes to its properties.

Let's begin by looking at an example Bean provided with the BDK. The **color** property of **JellyBean** is a bound property. Therefore, a property change event is generated whenever that property changes, and it is multicast to any listeners who previously registered to receive such notifications.

Follow these steps to experiment with bound properties in the BDK:

1. Start the BDK and create an instance of **JellyBean**. It appears as a rectangle with rounded corners and has several properties. The **color** property determines its color. Change this property and observe that the appearance of **JellyBean** immediately reflects the update.

2. Create a second instance of **JellyBean**. Set its **color** property to a different value from the first object.

3. Select your first **JellyBean** by clicking the mouse button on it.

4. Select the Edit | Bind Property options from the BeanBox menu bar. Observe that a dialog box titled PropertyNameDialog appears, as shown in Figure 7-1. This allows you to select a source property.

5. Select the **color** property from this dialog box and press the OK button. Observe that a red line extends from the **JellyBean** component to the cursor position.

6. Position the mouse inside your second **JellyBean** and click the left mouse button. Observe that a dialog box titled PropertyNameDialog appears, as shown in Figure 7-2. This allows you to select a target property.

7

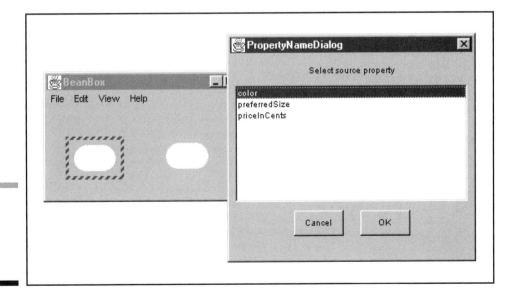

Selecting a source property of **JellyBean**

Figure 7-1.

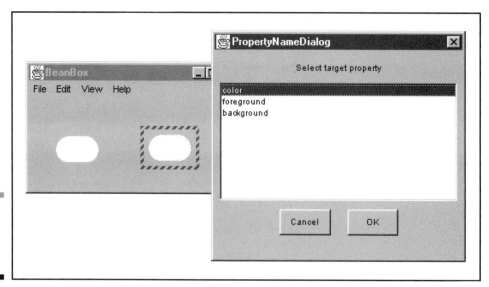

Selecting a
target property
of **JellyBean**
Figure 7-2.

7. Select the **color** property from this dialog box and press the OK button. Observe that the color of the second **JellyBean** immediately changes to that of the first **JellyBean**.

8. Change the color of the first **JellyBean**, and observe that the color of the second **JellyBean** also changes to that value.

9. Change the color of the second **JellyBean**, and observe that the color of the first **JellyBean** does not change to that same value.

You may also bind the **color** property of the first **JellyBean** to the **color** property of the second **JellyBean**. In that case, the colors of both components will always be the same. You may change the **color** property of either the first or second Bean, and the appearance of both components changes immediately.

NOTE: The Edit I Bind Property option is available from the BeanBox menu bar only if the selected Bean has one or more bound properties.

Now let's look at the classes and interfaces that provide this functionality.

PropertyChangeEvent

The **PropertyChangeEvent** class in the **java.beans** package defines the event notifications that are multicast by a Bean when one of its bound properties is changed. Its constructor has the form shown next:

PropertyChangeEvent(Object *src*, String *pname*, Object *oValue*, Object *nValue*)

Here, *src* is the Bean whose property has changed, and *pname* is the name of that property. The old and new values of the property are *oValue* and *nValue*.

If a property is a simple type, the constructor requires that a wrapper object be created to encapsulate such a value. There are wrapper classes in **java.lang** for all of the simple types. For example, **Integer** objects encapsulate **int** values. You may use **null** for *oValue* or *nValue* if the actual values are not known. The value of *pname* may also be **null** to notify the listeners that some or all of the properties have changed. (In that case, *oValue* and *nValue* should also be **null**.)

The methods provided by **PropertyChangeEvent** are summarized in Table 7-1.

7

NOTE: The propagation ID referred to in Table 7-1 is reserved for future use. However, in Beans 1.0, if a listener receives a property change event and wishes to forward it to another listener, it should use the same propagation ID in the second notification.

Method	Description
Object getNewValue( )	Returns an **Object** with the new value of the property.
Object getOldValue( )	Returns an **Object** with the old value of the property.
Object getPropagationId( )	Returns the propagation ID.
String getPropertyName( )	Returns the string equivalent of the property name.
void setPropagationId(Object *propId*)	Sets the propagation ID.

The Methods Defined by **PropertyChangeEvent**
Table 7-1.

PropertyChangeListener

The **PropertyChangeListener** interface in the **java.beans** package is used to receive **PropertyChangeEvent** notifications. It defines one method shown next:

> void propertyChange(PropertyChangeEvent *pce*)

Here, *pce* is the **PropertyChangeEvent** object.

PropertyChangeSupport

A Property-ChangeSupport object does much of the work to provide bound properties.

The **PropertyChangeSupport** class in the **java.beans** package can be used to perform much of the work associated with bound properties. It has the following constructor:

> PropertyChangeSupport(Object *src*)

Here, *src* is the Bean whose bound property is changed.

There are three methods whose forms are shown next:

> synchronized void addPropertyChangeListener(PropertyChangeListener *pcl*)

> synchronized void removePropertyChangeListener(PropertyChangeListener *pcl*)

> void firePropertyChange(String *pname*, Object *oldValue*, Object *newValue*)

The **addPropertyChangeListener( )** and **removePropertyChange-Listener( )** methods register and unregister listeners for property change events. The argument *pcl* is a reference to a listener. A property change notification is multicast to the listeners via **firePropertyChange( )**. In that method, *pname* is the name of the property, and *oldValue* and *newValue* are the old and new values of the property.

A Simple Example of Bound Properties

This section develops an example to illustrate how you can use bound properties. It involves three components. The **Circle** Bean appears as a filled circle. Its **color** property determines the color used to paint the component. This is a bound property because a property change event is fired when its value is changed. The **Square** and **Triangle** Beans appear as a filled square or triangle, respectively. They also have a **color** property. However, these are not bound properties because they do not cause property change events to be fired.

Follow these steps to experiment with your Beans:

1. Start the BDK and create an instance of the **Circle**, **Square**, and **Triangle** Beans.

2. Select the **Circle** component.

3. Select the Edit | Bind Property options from the BeanBox menu bar. Observe that a dialog box titled PropertyNameDialog appears, as shown in Figure 7-3. This allows you to select a source property.

4. Select the **color** property from this dialog box and press the OK button. A red line extends from the **Circle** component to the cursor position.

5. Position the mouse inside the **Square** component and click the left mouse button. Observe that a dialog box titled PropertyNameDialog appears, as shown in Figure 7-4. This allows you to select a target property.

7

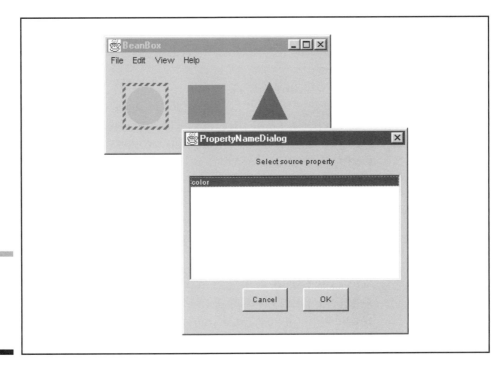

Selecting
a source
property
of **Circle**

Figure 7-3.

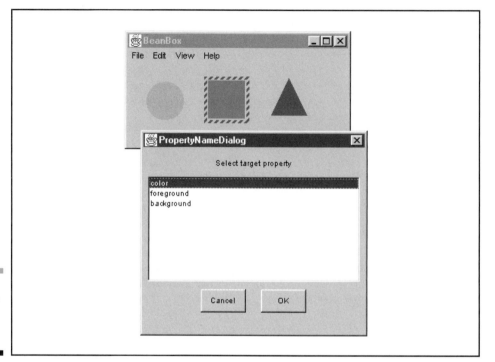

Selecting a
target property
of **Square**

Figure 7-4.

6. Select the **color** property from the dialog box and press the OK button. Observe that the color of **Square** changes to that of **Circle**.

7. Change the color of **Circle**, and observe that the color of **Square** also changes. This is because the **color** property of **Square** is bound to the **color** property of **Circle**.

The previous examples in this chapter illustrate how to use the Edit | Bind Property options on the BeanBox menu bar. This causes the property change events generated by one Bean to change a property of another Bean. It is also possible to use another menu sequence in the BeanBox. This is illustrated in the following steps:

1. Select the **Circle** component.

2. Select the Edit | Events | propertyChange | propertyChange options from the BeanBox menu bar. Observe that a red line extends from **Circle** to the cursor position.

3. Position the mouse inside the **Triangle** component and click the left mouse button. Observe that a dialog box titled EventTargetDialog appears. This allows you to select a target method.

4. Select the **propertyChange** method from this dialog box and press the OK button. Observe that a dialog box appears momentarily to report that an adapter class is being generated.

5. Change the color property of **Circle**. Observe that both **Square** and **Triangle** also change color.

The source code for the **Circle** Bean is shown in the next listing. It extends **Canvas**. The **color** variable is one of its properties and **pcs** is a **PropertyChangeSupport** object.

The constructor initializes the **color** property, sets the size of the Bean, and creates a **PropertyChangeSupport** object to perform some of the tasks associated with managing the bound property.

Access methods for the property follow the constructor. The **setColor( )** method invokes the **firePropertyChange( )** method of the **PropertyChangeSupport** object to multicast a property change event to any listeners that registered for these notifications. The **repaint( )** method is called to update the display.

The **paint( )** method displays a colored circle. Notice that the **color** property is used as an argument to the **setColor( )** method of the **Graphics** object.

Listeners register and unregister for property change events via **addPropertyChangeListener( )** and **removePropertyChange Listener( )**. Note that the corresponding methods of the **Property ChangeSupport** object are used to handle the details. They make your job considerably easier because they keep track of the set of registered listeners and multicast property change events to them.

```
package binding;
import java.awt.*;
import java.beans.*;

public class Circle extends Canvas {
  private Color color;
  private PropertyChangeSupport pcs;

  public Circle() {
```

```
    color = Color.green;
    setSize(50, 50);
    pcs = new PropertyChangeSupport(this);
  }

  public Color getColor() {
    return color;
  }

  public void setColor(Color newColor) {
    Color oldColor = color;
    this.color = newColor;
    pcs.firePropertyChange("color", oldColor, newColor);
    repaint();
  }

  public void paint(Graphics g) {
    Dimension d = getSize();
    g.setColor(color);
    g.fillOval(0, 0, d.width - 1, d.height - 1);
  }

  public void
  addPropertyChangeListener(PropertyChangeListener pcl) {
    pcs.addPropertyChangeListener(pcl);
  }

  public void
  removePropertyChangeListener(PropertyChangeListener pcl) {
    pcs.removePropertyChangeListener(pcl);
  }
}
```

The source code for the **Square** Bean is shown in the following listing. This
component implements the **PropertyChangeListener** interface. The
propertyChange( ) method is invoked when a **PropertyChangeEvent**
object is received. It uses **newValue( )** to obtain the new value of the **color**
property. This value is passed as an argument to the **setColor( )** method of
Square.

```
package binding;
import java.awt.*;
import java.beans.*;

public class Square extends Canvas
```

```
implements PropertyChangeListener {
  private Color color;

  public Square() {
    color = Color.red;
    setSize(50, 50);
  }

  public Color getColor() {
    return color;
  }

  public void setColor(Color newColor) {
    this.color = newColor;
    repaint();
  }

  public void propertyChange(PropertyChangeEvent pce) {
    setColor((Color)pce.getNewValue());
  }

  public void paint(Graphics g) {
    Dimension d = getSize();
    g.setColor(color);
    g.fillRect(0, 0, d.width - 1, d.height - 1);
  }
}
```

The source code for the **Triangle** Bean is shown in the following listing. This component implements the **PropertyChangeListener** interface. The **propertyChange( )** method is invoked when a **PropertyChangeEvent** object is received. It uses **newValue( )** to obtain the new value of the **color** property. This value is passed as an argument to the **setColor( )** method of **Triangle**.

```
package binding;
import java.awt.*;
import java.beans.*;

public class Triangle extends Canvas
implements PropertyChangeListener {
  private Color color;

  public Triangle() {
    color = Color.blue;
```

```
    setSize(50, 50);
  }

  public Color getColor() {
    return color;
  }

  public void setColor(Color newColor) {
    this.color = newColor;
    repaint();
  }

  public void propertyChange(PropertyChangeEvent pce) {
    setColor((Color)pce.getNewValue());
  }

  public void paint(Graphics g) {
    Dimension d = getSize();
    g.setColor(color);
    int xpoints[] = new int[3];
    int ypoints[] = new int[3];
    xpoints[0] = 0;
    ypoints[0] = d.height - 1;
    xpoints[1] = d.width/2;
    ypoints[1] = 0;
    xpoints[2] = d.width - 1;
    ypoints[2] = d.height - 1;
    g.fillPolygon(xpoints, ypoints, 3);
  }
}
```

This example shows how properties used by several Beans can be coordinated.

Another Example of Bound Properties

This example involves two components. The **Needle** Bean appears as a circle. A line beginning at its center extends to the perimeter of the circle and rotates in a counterclockwise direction. A **boolean** variable named **operate** is one of the properties of this Bean. When it is set to **true**, the needle rotates. Otherwise, the needle stops.

The **ToggleButton** Bean appears as a 3-D button. Each time the button is pressed, its label toggles between two values. The **label1** and **label2** properties determine the strings used to create these values. The **state** property is a **boolean** value that is also toggled by pressing the button. This is a bound property.

Follow these steps to experiment with these two Beans:

1. Start the BDK and create an instance of the **Needle** and **ToggleButton** Beans.
2. Select **ToggleButton**.
3. Select the Edit | Bind Property options from the BeanBox menu bar. Observe that a dialog box titled PropertyNameDialog appears, as shown in Figure 7-5. This allows you to select a source property.

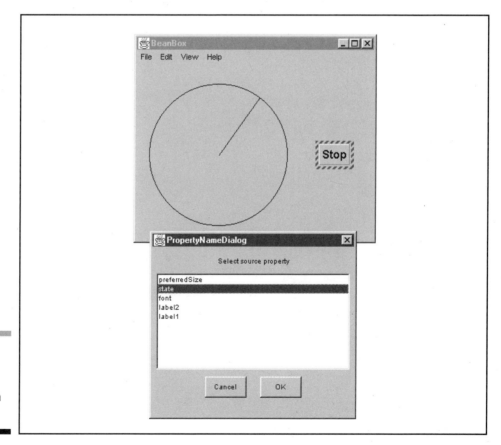

7

Selecting
a source
property of
ToggleButton
Figure 7-5.

4. Select the **state** property of the source from this dialog box and press the OK button. Observe that a red line extends from **ToggleButton** to the cursor position.

5. Position the mouse inside **Needle** and click the left mouse button.

6. Observe that a dialog box titled PropertyNameDialog appears, as shown in Figure 7-6. This allows you to select a target property.

7. Select the **operate** property of the target from the list and press the OK button.

8. Press the button. Observe that the needle stops moving and the button label changes from Stop to Run.

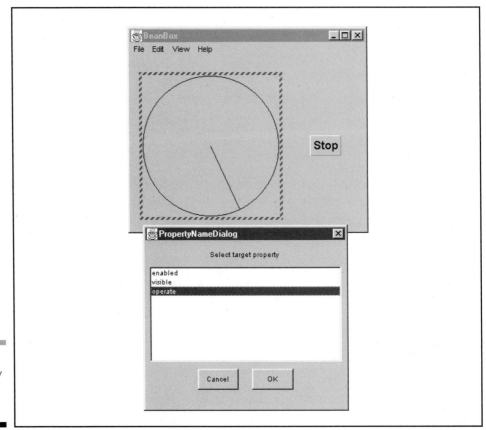

Selecting a
target property
of **Needle**
Figure 7-6.

9. Press the button. Observe that the needle starts moving and the button label changes from Run to Stop.

The source code for the **ToggleButton** Bean is shown in the next listing. It extends **Canvas** and implements **MouseListener**. The **label1**, **label2**, and **state** variables contain three of the properties. The transient **boolean** variable **pressed** records whether the button is currently pressed. You will see that this determines its appearance. The transient **boolean** variable **inside** records whether the mouse is positioned inside the button. A reference to a **PropertyChangeSupport** object is held by the variable **pcs**.

The constructor initializes the instance variables, sets the font, and registers to receive mouse events.

Access methods for some properties follow the constructor. Notice that the **adjustSize( )** method is called if the **font**, **label1**, or **label2** properties are changed.

The **getPreferredSize( )** and **adjustSize( )** methods are similar to what has been seen previously in this book. In this example, the preferred size of the Bean is calculated by determining which of the two labels is larger.

7

The **paint( )** method generates the appearance of the button. A 3-D look for the button is produced by **fill3DRect( )**. The **fillRect( )** method is called to produce the interior of the button. An appropriate label is selected based on the **state** variable. The position of this string within the button is calculated by using the font metrics, and the **drawString( )** method displays the string.

Listeners are registered and unregistered for property change events via **addPropertyChangeListener( )** and **removePropertyChangeListener( )**.

The **mouseEntered( )** method sets **inside** to **true**. This indicates that the mouse is now positioned inside the button.

The **mouseExited( )** method sets **inside** to **false**. This indicates that the mouse is now positioned outside the button. In addition, if the button is pressed, the **doMouseReleased( )** method is also invoked. (The net effect is to cause the button to "spring back" if the user presses the mouse on it and then drags the mouse outside the bounds of the button.)

The **mousePressed( )** method calls **doMousePressed( )** if the mouse is positioned inside the button.

The **mouseReleased( )** method calls **doMouseReleased( )** if the mouse is positioned inside the button.

The **doMousePressed( )** method sets the **pressed** variable to **true** and calls **repaint( )** to update the display.

The **doMouseReleased( )** method fires the property change event, toggles the **state** variable, sets the **pressed** variable to **false**, and calls **repaint( )** to update the appearance of the Bean.

```java
package toggleb;
import java.awt.*;
import java.awt.event.*;
import java.beans.*;

public class ToggleButton extends Canvas
implements MouseListener {
  private final static int XPAD = 5;
  private final static int YPAD = 5;
  private String label1, label2;
  private boolean state;
  private transient boolean pressed;
  private transient boolean inside;
  private PropertyChangeSupport pcs;

  public ToggleButton() {
    label1 = "Stop";
    label2 = "Run";
    state = true;
    pressed = false;
    inside = false;
    pcs = new PropertyChangeSupport(this);
    setFont(new Font("SansSerif", Font.BOLD, 16));
    addMouseListener(this);
  }

  public String getLabel1() {
    return label1;
  }

  public String getLabel2() {
    return label2;
  }

  public boolean getState() {
    return state;
  }
```

```
public void setFont(Font font) {
  super.setFont(font);
  adjustSize();
}

public void setLabel1(String label1) {
  this.label1 = label1;
  adjustSize();
}

public void setLabel2(String label2) {
  this.label2 = label2;
  adjustSize();
}

public Dimension getPreferredSize() {
  FontMetrics fm = getFontMetrics(getFont());
  int w1 = fm.stringWidth(label1);
  int w2 = fm.stringWidth(label2);
  int w = (w1 > w2) ? w1 : w2;
  int width = w + 2 * XPAD;
  int height = fm.getHeight() + 2 * YPAD;
  return new Dimension(width, height);
}

public void adjustSize() {
  Dimension d = getPreferredSize();
  setSize(d.width, d.height);
  Component parent = getParent();
  if(parent != null) {
    parent.invalidate();
    parent.doLayout();
  }
}

public void paint(Graphics g) {
  Dimension d = getSize();
  g.setColor(getBackground());
  g.fill3DRect(0, 0, d.width - 1, d.height - 1, !pressed);
  g.fillRect(1, 1, d.width - 3, d.height - 3);
  g.setColor(getForeground());
  FontMetrics fm = g.getFontMetrics();
  String s = state ? label1 : label2;
  int x = (d.width - fm.stringWidth(s))/2;
  int y = (d.height + fm.getMaxAscent()
```

```
        - fm.getMaxDescent())/2;
    g.drawString(s, x, y);
}

public void
addPropertyChangeListener(PropertyChangeListener pcl) {
  pcs.addPropertyChangeListener(pcl);
}

public void
removePropertyChangeListener(PropertyChangeListener pcl) {
  pcs.removePropertyChangeListener(pcl);
}

public void mouseClicked(MouseEvent me) {
}

public void mouseEntered(MouseEvent me) {
  inside = true;
}

public void mouseExited(MouseEvent me) {
  inside = false;
  if(pressed) {
    doMouseReleased();
  }
}

public void mousePressed(MouseEvent me) {
  if(inside) {
    doMousePressed();
  }
}

public void mouseReleased(MouseEvent me) {
  if(inside) {
    doMouseReleased();
  }
}

public void doMousePressed() {
  pressed = true;
  repaint();
}
```

```
      public void doMouseReleased() {
        Boolean t = new Boolean(true);
        Boolean f = new Boolean(false);
        if(state) {
          pcs.firePropertyChange("state", t, f);
        }
        else {
          pcs.firePropertyChange("state", f, t);
        }
        state = !state;
        pressed = false;
        repaint();
      }
    }
```

The source code for the **Needle** Bean is shown in the next listing. It extends **Canvas** and implements the **PropertyChangeListener** and **Runnable** interfaces. The **int** property **interval** determines the number of milliseconds between updates of the display. If the **boolean** property **operate** is **true**, the needle rotates; otherwise, it remains stopped. The variable **angle** records the current position of the needle.

The constructor initializes the instance variables, sets the size of the component, and starts a thread to move the needle. Access methods for the **interval** and **operate** properties follow the constructor.

Control of the thread is provided by the **run( )** method. Every **interval** milliseconds, it checks if **operate** is **true**. If so, **angle** is incremented by one and **repaint( )** is called to update the display.

Both the needle and its enclosing circle are drawn by the **paint( )** method.

Finally, the **readObject( )** method is needed to perform custom deserialization. It calls the **defaultReadObject( )** method of the **ObjectInputStream** object to restore the nonstatic and nontransient variables for this object and then creates and starts a thread to rotate the needle.

```
package toggleb;
import java.awt.*;
import java.beans.*;
import java.io.*;

public class Needle extends Canvas
implements PropertyChangeListener, Runnable {
  private int interval;
```

7

```java
private boolean operate;
private int angle;

public Needle() {
  interval = 10;
  operate = true;
  angle = 0;
  setSize(200, 200);
  Thread t = new Thread(this);
  t.start();
}

public int getInterval() {
  return interval;
}

public boolean getOperate() {
  return operate;
}

public void setInterval(int interval) {
  this.interval = interval;
}

public void setOperate(boolean operate) {
  this.operate = operate;
}

public void run() {
  try {
    while(true) {
      Thread.sleep(interval);
      if(operate) {
        ++angle;
        repaint();
      }
    }
  }
  catch(Exception ex) {
    ex.printStackTrace();
  }
}

public void propertyChange(PropertyChangeEvent pce) {
  Boolean b = (Boolean)pce.getNewValue();
```

```
      setOperate(b.booleanValue());
   }

   public void paint(Graphics g) {
      Dimension d = getSize();
      g.drawOval(0, 0, d.width - 1, d.height - 1);
      int centerx = d.width/2;
      int centery = d.height/2;
      int radius = d.width/2;
      int x = (int)(radius * Math.sin(Math.PI * angle / 180));
      int y = (int)(radius * Math.cos(Math.PI * angle / 180));
      g.drawLine(centerx, centery, centerx + x, centery - y);
   }

   private void readObject(ObjectInputStream ois)
   throws IOException, ClassNotFoundException {
      try {
         ois.defaultReadObject();
         Thread t = new Thread(this);
         t.start();
      }
      catch(Exception ex) {
         ex.printStackTrace();
      }
   }
}
```

Constrained Properties

When a *constrained property* is changed, an event notification can be multicast to other Beans to inform them of the proposed modification. The listeners may accept the update. However, it is also possible for one or more listeners to veto the change. In that case, the source receives an exception and restores the property to its old value.

Assume that you are designing an application to control a set of electrical appliances such as air conditioners in a building. A separate Bean exists to control each device. In addition, there is a controller Bean to monitor total power consumption. Its goal is to keep this value under a certain threshold during periods of peak demand.

Constrained properties are useful for this application because they allow the controller Bean to veto property changes to individual device Beans that would cause the total power consumption threshold to be exceeded.

Let us begin by looking at some sample Beans provided with the BDK. The **JellyBean** has a constrained property named **priceInCents**. The **Voter** Bean can be configured to veto any property change event it receives.

Follow these steps to experiment with constrained properties in the BDK:

1. Start the BDK and create an instance of **Voter**. It initially appears as a rectangle that contains the string "No". Note that it has a **boolean** property named **vetoAll**, which is initially **true**. This means the Bean is set to veto any property change event it receives.

2. Create an instance of **JellyBean**. Note that it has a property named **priceInCents**.

3. Select **JellyBean** and choose the Edit | Events | vetoableChange | vetoableChange options from the BeanBox menu bar. Observe that a red line extends from **JellyBean** to the cursor position.

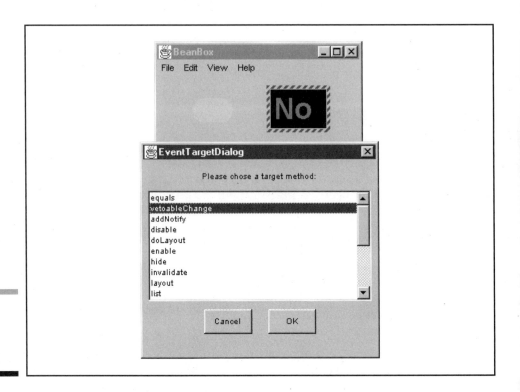

Selecting
an event of
JellyBean
Figure 7-7.

4. Position the cursor in **Voter** and press the mouse button. Observe that a dialog box titled EventTargetDialog appears, as shown in Figure 7-7. This allows you to select a target method.

5. Select the **vetoableChange** method from this dialog box and press the OK button. Observe that a message box appears momentarily, indicating that an adapter class is being generated.

6. Try to change the **priceInCents** property of **JellyBean**. Observe that the message box shown in Figure 7-8 appears. This reports that the proposed property change is vetoed.

7. Press the Continue button to dismiss the message box.

8. Change the **vetoAll** property of **Voter** to **false**. Observe that the string displayed by that Bean changes to "Yes".

9. Change the **priceInCents** property of **JellyBean**. Observe that you may now update that property without problems.

Now let's look at the classes and interfaces that provide this functionality.

VetoableChangeListener

The **VetoableChangeListener** interface in the **java.beans** package is used to receive **PropertyChangeEvent** notifications when constrained properties are changed. It defines one method shown next:

7

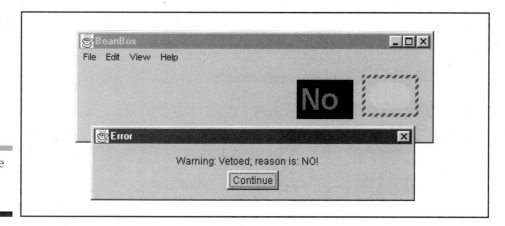

Figure 7-8.

void vetoableChange(PropertyChangeEvent *pce*) throws
PropertyVetoException

Here, *pce* is the **PropertyChangeEvent** object.

Your implementation of this method should throw a
PropertyVetoException if it wants to reject the property change.

PropertyVetoException

The **PropertyVetoException** class is defined in the **java.beans** package.
It has the following constructor:

PropertyVetoException(String *message*, PropertyChangeEvent *pce*)

Here, *message* is a string that is presented to the user if the property change is
rejected, and *pce* is a reference to the **PropertyChangeEvent** object.

A *Vetoable-ChangeSupport* object does much of the work to provide constrained properties.

VetoableChangeSupport

The **VetoableChangeSupport** class in the **java.beans** package can be
used to perform much of the work associated with constrained properties. It
has the following constructor:

VetoableChangeSupport(Object *src*)

Here, *src* is the Bean whose constrained property is changed.

There are three methods whose forms are shown next:

synchronized void addVetoableChangeListener(VetoableChangeListener *pcl*)

synchronized void
removeVetoableChangeListener(VetoableChangeListener *pcl*)

void fireVetoableChange(String *pname*, Object *oldValue*, Object *newValue*)
throws PropertyVetoException

Listeners register and unregister for property change events associated with
constrained properties via the **addPropertyChangeListener( )** and
removePropertyChangeListener( ) methods. The **firePropertyChange( )**
method multicasts a notification about a property change to the listeners. In

that method, *pname* is the name of the property, and *oldValue* and *newValue* are the old and new values of the property.

A Simple Example of Constrained Properties

This section develops an example to illustrate how you can use constrained properties. It involves two components. The **Auto** Bean has one **int** property named **speed**. This is a constrained property. Property change events are generated when this property is changed. The **Police** Bean is designed to veto any speed value outside the range 0 to 85.

Follow these steps to experiment with your Beans:

1. Start the BDK and create an instance of the **Police** and **Auto** Beans.
2. Select **Auto** and choose the Edit | Events | vetoableChange | vetoableChange options from the BeanBox menu bar. Observe that a red line extends from **Auto** to the cursor position.
3. Position the cursor in **Police** and press the mouse button. Observe that a dialog box titled EventTargetDialog appears. This allows you to select a target method.
4. Select the **vetoableChange** method from this dialog box and press the OK button. Observe that a message box appears momentarily to report that an adapter class is being generated.
5. Try to change the **speed** property of **Auto** to 200. Observe that a message box appears to report that the proposed change is vetoed.
6. Press the Continue button to dismiss the message box.

Now let's examine the code for these two classes.

The source code for the **Police** Bean is shown in the next listing. The static constants **MAXSPEED** and **MINSPEED** define the maximum and minimum speed limits.

The **vetoableChange( )** method receives a **PropertyChangeEvent** object as its argument. It obtains the name of the property via the **getPropertyName( )** method of **PropertyChangeEvent** and checks whether this is "speed". If so, the **getNewValue( )** method is used to obtain the new value for the property. If the speed is outside the allowed range, a **PropertyVetoException** object is created. The first argument to the constructor is a string that will be displayed in an error message dialog box, and the second argument is the **PropertyChangeEvent** object.

7

```
package veto;
import java.beans.*;

public class Police
implements VetoableChangeListener {
  private static final int MAXSPEED = 85;
  private static final int MINSPEED = 0;

  public Police() {
  }

  public void vetoableChange(PropertyChangeEvent pce)
  throws PropertyVetoException {
    if(pce.getPropertyName().equals("speed")) {
      Integer i = (Integer)pce.getNewValue();
      int speed = i.intValue();
      if(speed < MINSPEED || speed > MAXSPEED) {
        String msg = "Speed out of range";
        throw new PropertyVetoException(msg, pce);
      }
    }
  }
}
```

The source code for the **Auto** Bean is shown in the next listing. The **int** variable named **speed** is the constrained property. A **VetoableChangeSupport** object is created by the constructor, and the variable **vcs** is initialized to hold a reference to this object.

The **setSpeed( )** method is called to change the property, and the proposed value is passed as the argument. A **PropertyChange** object is generated and multicast to the listeners via the **fireVetoableChange( )** method of **VetoableChangeSupport**. If any listener objects, a **PropertyVetoException** is thrown by the **fireVetoableChange( )** method. This changes the control flow of the program, and the last statement in **setSpeed( )** is not executed.

The **PropertyVetoException** is caught by the BDK. That code displays a modal dialog box informing the user that the proposed change is rejected.

The last two methods in the **Auto** class register and unregister **VetoableChangeListener** objects.

```
package veto;
import java.beans.*;
```

```
public class Auto {
  private int speed;
  private VetoableChangeSupport vcs;

  public Auto() {
    speed = 0;
    vcs = new VetoableChangeSupport(this);
  }

  public int getSpeed() {
    return speed;
  }

  public void setSpeed(int value)
  throws PropertyVetoException {
    Integer oldSpeed = new Integer(speed);
    Integer newSpeed = new Integer(value);
    vcs.fireVetoableChange("speed", oldSpeed, newSpeed);
    speed = value;
  }

  public void
  addVetoableChangeListener(VetoableChangeListener vcl) {
    vcs.addVetoableChangeListener(vcl);
  }

  public void
  removeVetoableChangeListener(VetoableChangeListener vcl) {
    vcs.removeVetoableChangeListener(vcl);
  }
}
```

This example illustrates how to develop Beans that use constrained properties.

The HotJava™ Browser Beans

Chapter 1 of this book introduced the concept of a software component and described how this technology made it possible to achieve software reuse. A web browser was used as an example. In this section, you will see exactly how this can be done by using the HotJava™ Browser Beans from Sun Microsystems. This material is included here because it illustrates how bound properties can be used to build production software.

Component	Description
HotJavaBrowserBean	Parses and renders HTML.
HotJavaDocumentStack	Maintains a stack of the URLs that have been visited.
HotJavaSystemState	Allows configuration of the HotJavaBrowserBean.
AuthenticatorBean	Allows connections to secure sites.

The HotJava Browser Beans
Table 7-2.

These Beans encapsulate much of the functionality used to build the HotJava Browser. Four components are available. Their primary functions are summarized in Table 7-2 (above).

This book doesn't have sufficient space to discuss all of these components, but an example is presented that illustrates how to use the **HotJavaBrowserBean**. This component has numerous bound properties, some of which are listed and briefly described in Table 7-3.

As you can see, these bound properties allow other components to obtain valuable information about the activities of this Bean.

In this example, a Bean named **UrlTextField** is developed. It allows a user to enter a URL that should be retrieved and displayed by the **HotJavaBrowserBean**. Figure 7-9 shows how these two components appear in BeanBox.

The **UrlTextField** Bean has one bound property named **text**. When the ENTER key is pressed, a property change event is generated and sent to all registered listeners.

Name	Description
documentString	A String object representing the document URL.
documentURL	A URL object representing the document URL.
documentTitle	A String object representing the document title.
errorMessage	A String object representing the latest error message.
statusMessage	A String object representing the latest status message.

Some Bound Properties of HotJava-BrowserBean
Table 7-3.

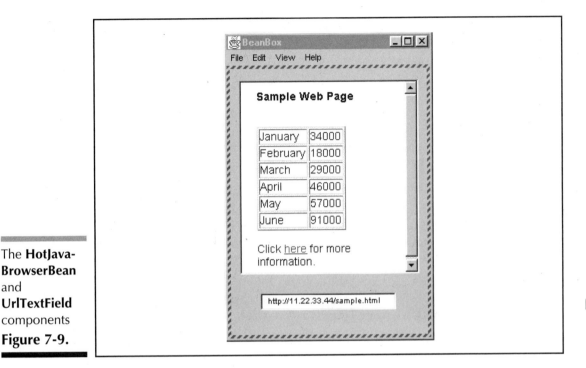

The **HotJava-BrowserBean** and **UrlTextField** components
Figure 7-9.

7

In this example, the **text** property of **UrlTextField** and the **documentString** property of the **HotJavaBrowserBean** are bound to each other. Therefore, when a user changes the string in the **UrlTextField** component and presses the ENTER key, the specified URL is retrieved, parsed, and displayed. In addition, when a user clicks on a hyperlink in an HTML page, the URL displayed by the **UrlTextField** is updated.

Follow these steps to experiment with these Beans:

1. Start the BDK and create an instance of **HotJavaBrowserBean** and **UrlTextField**.

2. Select **UrlTextField**.

3. Select the Edit | Bind Property options from the BeanBox menu bar. A dialog box appears. Select **text** as the source property.

4. Position the mouse inside **HotJavaBrowserBean** and click the left mouse button. Another dialog box appears. Select **documentString** as the target property.

5. Select **HotJavaBrowserBean**.

6. Select the Edit | Bind Property options from the BeanBox menu bar. A dialog box appears. Select **documentString** as the source property.

7. Position the mouse inside **UrlTextField** and click the left mouse button. Another dialog box appears. Select **text** as the target property.

The source code for **UrlTextField** is shown in the next listing. This class extends **TextField** and implements the **ActionListener** and **PropertyChangeListener** interfaces.

A reference to a **PropertyChangeSupport** object is held in the variable **pcs**.

The constructor begins by calling the superclass constructor to initialize its contents and width. The **UrlTextField** object is registered to receive action events, and **pcs** is initialized. Access methods for the **text** property follow the constructor.

When the user presses the ENTER key, the **actionPerformed( )** method is invoked. It invokes **firePropertyChange( )** to notify the **HotJavaBrowserBean** that the **text** property has changed.

Listeners register and unregister for property change events via the **addPropertyChangeListener( )** and **removePropertyChangeListener( )**.

```
package hotjava;
import java.awt.*;
import java.awt.event.*;
import java.beans.*;

public class UrlTextField extends TextField
implements ActionListener, PropertyChangeListener {
  private PropertyChangeSupport pcs;

  public UrlTextField() {
    super("", 25);
    addActionListener(this);
    pcs = new PropertyChangeSupport(this);
  }

  public String getText() {
    return super.getText();
  }
```

```
public void setText(String str) {
  super.setText(str);
}

public void actionPerformed(ActionEvent ae) {
  pcs.firePropertyChange("text", "", getText());
}

public void propertyChange(PropertyChangeEvent pce) {
  setText((String)pce.getNewValue());
}

public void
addPropertyChangeListener(PropertyChangeListener pcl) {
  pcs.addPropertyChangeListener(pcl);
}

public void
removePropertyChangeListener(PropertyChangeListener pcl) {
  pcs.removePropertyChangeListener(pcl);
}
}
```

7

This example illustrates how bound properties can be used to coordinate the activities of several Beans. The **UrlTextField** component informs the **HotJavaBrowserBean** when a user types a new URL and presses the ENTER key. The **HotJavaBrowserBean** informs the **UrlTextField** component when a user clicks on a hyperlink to request a new web page.

CHAPTER 8

Applets, Applications, and Beans

This chapter explains how Beans relate to applets and applications. You will see that components may be fully integrated into the overall Java programming environment.

None of the Beans presented so far in this book has been an applet. In other words, they have not extended the **java.applet.Applet** class. It is easy to create such components. However, you must be aware of some information presented in this chapter.

You may also build applications that directly instantiate, configure, and connect Beans. The technique needed to accomplish this is described along with instructions for working with serialized components. It is also possible to use Beans from a JAR file. In order to do this, a class loader is developed.

Applets

An applet executes within a specific context. The **AppletContext** interface defines a set of methods that allow an applet to interact with its context. This functionality is typically provided by a Web browser or a tool such as the applet viewer from the JDK. When the BDK instantiates any Bean that is an instance of the **Applet** class, it takes some special actions to provide that component with a default applet context. This context is a subset of the standard **AppletContext** functionality. Table 8-1 lists the methods of **AppletContext** and summarizes their current BDK implementation.

If you scan through this table, most of the information should be intuitive. Some of the most commonly used methods, such as **getImage( )**, have been provided for your convenience. In other cases, such as **showStatus( )**, it was not possible to provide the same functionality as an applet would have in a browser.

The BDK also provides some of the functionality defined by the **AppletStub** interface, so it is available for Beans that execute in the BeanBox. An applet stub provides an interface between the applet and its execution environment. Table 8-2 lists the methods of **AppletStub** and summarizes their current BDK implementation.

Beans that are applets begin execution at init( ).

One last point—any Bean that is an instance of **Applet** begins execution at its **init( )** method. Unlike all of the other Beans we have seen so far in this book, it does not use a zero argument constructor.

Method	Current BDK Implementation
Applet getApplet(String *aname*)	Returns null.
Enumeration getApplets( )	Returns an Enumeration of all executing Beans that are applets.
AudioClip getAudioClip(URL *url*)	Returns null unless an AudioClip can be generated from *url*.
Image getImage(URL *url*)	Returns an Image object obtained from *url*.
void showDocument(URL *url*)	Does nothing.
void showDocument(URL url, String *target*)	Does nothing.
void showStatus(String str)	Does nothing.

Methods
Defined by
AppletContext
Table 8-1.

The Applet Slide Show Bean

This section develops a Bean named **SlidesApplet** that displays a sequence of images. Its **interval** property determines the time in milliseconds that each image appears.

8

Method	Current BDK Implementation
void appletResize(int *w*, int *h*)	Does nothing.
AppletContext getAppletContext( )	Returns an AppletContext object for this applet.
URL getCodeBase( )	Returns the directory in which the class or serialized object was found.
URL getDocumentBase( )	Returns the root directory of the class loader for the applet.
String getParameter(String *pname*)	Returns null.
boolean isActive( )	Returns true if the applet is active. Otherwise, returns false.

Methods
Defined by
AppletStub
Table 8-2.

The images are packaged in the same JAR file that contains the Bean. They are named slide1.jpg, slide2.jpg, slide3.jpg, and slide4.jpg. When all of the images have been displayed, the cycle repeats.

Figure 8-1 shows how the Bean appears in BeanBox.

The manifest template file for this example is slidesapplet\slidesapplet.mft. Its contents are shown here:

```
Name: slidesapplet/SlidesApplet.class
Java-Bean: True
```

Follow these instructions to build and execute this software in the BDK:

1. Change to the parent directory of slidesapplet.
2. Type **javac slidesapplet*.java** at the command prompt.
3. Type **jar cfm c:\bdk\jars\slidesapplet.jar slidesapplet*.mft slidesapplet*.class slidesappletlet*.jpg** to build a JAR file.
4. Start the BDK and create an instance of **SlidesApplet**.

The
SlidesApplet
Bean
Figure 8-1.

This Bean is a fully functional applet. Therefore, it may also be executed by using the appletviewer. Follow these instructions:

1. Copy the JAR file you previously built to the slidesapplet directory.
2. Change to the slidesapplet directory.
3. Type **appletviewer slidesapplet.html**. Observe that the component operates as it did in the BDK.

The file slidesapplet.html is shown here:

```
<applet
  code="slidesapplet.SlidesApplet.class"
  archive="slidesapplet.jar"
  width=300 height=300>
</applet>
```

The source code for **SlidesApplet** is shown in the next listing. It extends **Canvas** and implements **Runnable**. The **interval** variable is a property of the Bean. References to **Image** objects that are created from the files contained in the JAR file are held in the **images** vector. A reference to the **Thread** object that runs the animation is held in the **thread** variable. Both of these variables are **transient** because **Image** and **Thread** objects cannot be serialized. The **index** variable is used to keep track of the slide that is currently being displayed. This variable is **transient** because it is not necessary to store it in the serial stream.

The **init( )** method begins by initializing the property and the **images** variable. The **loadImages** method is then invoked to read the images from the JAR file, create **Image** objects, and store these in the **images** vector. A thread is started and the dimensions of the Bean are set. Access methods for the property follow the **init( )** method.

The **loadImages( )** method creates a new **URL** object to identify the source of an image. Note that the **getCodeBase( )** method of **AppletStub** and **getImage( )** method of **AppletContext** are used in the steps to obtain an **Image** object. These steps are executed for each image file.

The **paint( )** method displays the current image. Logic for the thread is in the **run( )** method. Its effect is to call **repaint( )** every **interval** milliseconds and update **index** to identify the current image.

The **readObject( )** method is called when the object is restored from the serial stream. The **defaultReadObject( )** method restores the nonstatic and

8

nontransient variables. The **images** vector is initialized by calling
loadImages( ), and an animation thread is started.

```
package slidesapplet;
import java.applet.*;
import java.awt.*;
import java.io.*;
import java.net.*;
import java.util.*;

public class SlidesApplet
extends Applet implements Runnable {
  private final static int NUMIMAGES = 4;
  private int interval;
  private transient Vector images;
  private transient Thread thread;
  private transient int index;

  public void init() {
    interval = 1000;
    images = new Vector();
    loadImages();
    thread = new Thread(this);
    thread.start();
    setSize(300, 300);
  }

  public int getInterval() {
    return interval;
  }

  public void setInterval(int interval) {
    this.interval = interval;
  }

  private void loadImages() {
    try {
      for(int i = 1; i <= NUMIMAGES; i++) {
        String name = "slidesapplet/slide" + i + ".jpg";
        URL url = new URL(getCodeBase(), name);
        Image image = getImage(url);
        images.addElement(image);
      }
    }
    catch(Exception ex) {
      ex.printStackTrace();
```

```
      }
   }

   public void paint(Graphics g) {
      g.drawImage((Image)images.elementAt(index), 0, 0, this);
   }

   public void run() {
      try {
         while(true) {
            repaint();
            index = (index + 1) % NUMIMAGES;
            Thread.sleep(interval);
         }
      }
      catch(Exception ex) {
         ex.printStackTrace();
      }
   }

   private void readObject(ObjectInputStream ois)
   throws IOException, ClassNotFoundException {
      try {
         ois.defaultReadObject();
         images = new Vector();
         loadImages();
         thread = new Thread(this);
         thread.start();
      }
      catch(Exception ex) {
         ex.printStackTrace();
      }
   }
}
```

The following listing shows the source code for the **SlidesAppletBeanInfo** class. It extends **SimpleBeanInfo** and overrides **getPropertyDescriptors( )**, **getEventSetDescriptors( )**, and **getMethodDescriptors( )** to indicate that this Bean has only one property.

```
package slidesapplet;
import java.beans.*;

public class SlidesAppletBeanInfo extends SimpleBeanInfo {

   public PropertyDescriptor[] getPropertyDescriptors() {
```

8

```
try {
  PropertyDescriptor pd1 =
    new PropertyDescriptor("interval", SlidesApplet.class);
  PropertyDescriptor pds[] = { pd1 };
  return pds;
}
catch(Exception ex) {
  ex.printStackTrace();
}
return null;
}

public EventSetDescriptor[] getEventSetDescriptors() {
  EventSetDescriptor esds[] = { };
  return esds;
}

public MethodDescriptor[] getMethodDescriptors() {
  MethodDescriptor mds[] = { };
  return mds;
}
}
```

A Shaded 3-D Surface Bean

This section develops a Bean that displays a shaded 3-D plot of the
following function:

$$z = f(x, y) = 100 \times e^a$$

where

$$a = -(x^2 + y^2)/5000$$

The surface rotates around the Z axis.

Figure 8-2 shows how the Bean appears in BeanBox. You can see the surface is
shaped like a hill.

The center of your screen is at position (0, -150, 0). This is also the position of
a light shining into the scene. The X axis is located in the middle of the
screen and increases as you move to the right. The x = 0 position is at the
middle of the screen. The Y axis increases as you move directly into the

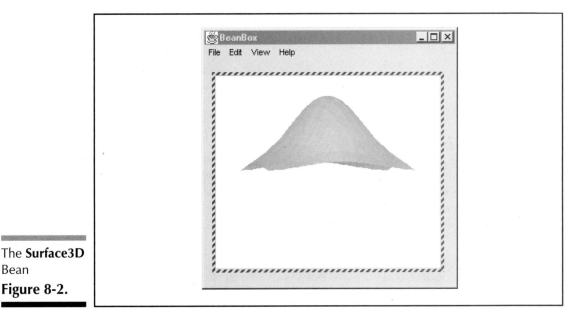

screen. The Z axis increases as you move toward the top of the screen. The surface covers the area where x varies from -100 to +100 and y varies from -100 to +100.

Follow these instructions to build and execute this software in the BDK:

1. Change to the parent directory of surface3d.
2. Type **javac surface3d*.java** at the command prompt.
3. Type **jar cfm c:\bdk\jars\surface3d.jar surface3d*.mft surface3d*.class** to build a JAR file.
4. Start the BDK and create an instance of **Surface3D**.

This Bean is a fully functional applet. Therefore, it may also be executed by using the appletviewer. Follow these instructions:

1. Copy the JAR file you previously built to the surface3d directory.
2. Change to the surface3d directory.
3. Type **appletviewer surface3d.html**. Observe that the component operates as it did in the BDK.

8

The file surface3d.html is shown here:

```
<applet
  code="surface3d.Surface3D.class"
  archive="surface3d.jar"
  width=300 height=300>
</applet>
```

Design Overview

The design and code used for this Bean is very similar to the **Plot3D** Bean from Chapter 6. In this example, however, the triangles are each colored a shade of gray. The exact color of a triangle is computed based on its orientation relative to the light source. This is how the shading effect is achieved.

Source Code Listings

The source code for the Bean is shown in the next listing. It is identical to that seen previously for **Plot3D** except for the following differences:

- The Bean extends **Applet**.

- There is no default constructor. Instead, an **init( )** method is supplied, which contains the same code.

- The method **f( )** is changed because a different surface is being graphed.

- The **drawTriangles( )** method is slightly different because the color of each triangle must be calculated by calling the **computeColor( )** method of **Triangle**.

```
package surface3d;
import java.awt.*;
import java.applet.*;
import java.io.*;
import java.util.*;

public class Surface3D extends Applet
implements Runnable {
  private final static int WIDTH = 300;
  private final static int HEIGHT = 250;
  private final static double XMAX = 100;
  private final static double DELTAX = 20;
  private final static double YMAX = 100;
  private final static double DELTAY = 20;
  private final static double ZMAX = 100;
  private final static int NTRIANGLES =
```

```
          (int)(4 * (2 * XMAX/DELTAX) * (2 * YMAX/DELTAY));
  private transient double theta;
  private transient Thread thread;

  public void init() {
    setSize(WIDTH, HEIGHT);
    theta = 0;
    thread = new Thread(this);
    thread.start();
  }

  public void run() {
    try {
      while(true) {
        Thread.sleep(200);
        theta += Math.PI/180;
        repaint();
      }
    }
    catch(Exception ex) {
      ex.printStackTrace();
    }
  }

  public void update(Graphics g) {
    paint(g);
  }

  public void paint(Graphics g) {

    // Generate triangles
    Triangle triangles[] = new Triangle[NTRIANGLES];
    Triangle t;
    int index = 0;
    for(double y = YMAX; y > -YMAX; y -= DELTAY) {
      for(double x = XMAX; x > -XMAX; x -= DELTAX) {
        Point3D p1, p2, p3, p4, p5;
        double z;
        z = f(x, y);
        p1 = new Point3D(x, y, z);
        z = f(x - DELTAX, y);
        p2 = new Point3D(x - DELTAX, y, z);
        z = f(x - DELTAX/2, y - DELTAY/2);
        p3 = new Point3D(x - DELTAX/2, y - DELTAY/2, z);
        z = f(x - DELTAX, y - DELTAY);
```

8

```
      p4 = new Point3D(x - DELTAX, y - DELTAY, z);
      z = f(x, y - DELTAY);
      p5 = new Point3D(x, y - DELTAY, z);
      p1.rotateZ(theta);
      p2.rotateZ(theta);
      p3.rotateZ(theta);
      p4.rotateZ(theta);
      p5.rotateZ(theta);
      t = new Triangle(p1, p2, p3);
      triangles[index++] = t;
      t = new Triangle(p2, p4, p3);
      triangles[index++] = t;
      t = new Triangle(p3, p4, p5);
      triangles[index++] = t;
      t = new Triangle(p1, p3, p5);
      triangles[index++] = t;
    }
  }

  // Sort triangles according to distance from
  // viewport center
  Point3D viewportCenter = new Point3D(0, -150, 0);
  Triangle sortedTriangles[] =
    sortTriangles(triangles, viewportCenter);

  // Draw triangles in background buffer
  Image buffer = createImage(WIDTH, HEIGHT);
  Graphics bufferg = buffer.getGraphics();

  // Create white background
  bufferg.setColor(Color.white);
  bufferg.fillRect(0, 0, WIDTH - 1, HEIGHT - 1);

  // Draw triangles in background buffer
  Point3D lightSource = new Point3D(0, -150, 0);
  drawTriangles(bufferg, sortedTriangles, lightSource);

  // Copy background buffer to foreground
  g.drawImage(buffer, 0, 0, null);
}

private double f(double x, double y) {
  double exponent = -(x * x + y * y)/5000;
  return 100 * Math.pow(Math.E, exponent);
}
```

```
private Triangle[] sortTriangles(Triangle triangles[],
Point3D viewportCenter) {
  double distance[] = new double[NTRIANGLES];
  for(int i = 0; i < NTRIANGLES; i++) {
    distance[i] =
      computeDistance(triangles[i], viewportCenter);
  }
  Triangle sortedTriangles[] = new Triangle[NTRIANGLES];
  for(int i = 0; i < NTRIANGLES; i++) {
    double d = -1;
    int k = 0;
    for(int j = 0; j < NTRIANGLES; j++) {
      if(distance[j] > d) {
        d = distance[j];
        k = j;
      }
    }
    sortedTriangles[i] = triangles[k];
    distance[k] = -1;
  }
  return sortedTriangles;
}

private double computeDistance(Triangle t, Point3D p) {
  double xc = (t.p1.x + t.p2.x + t.p3.x)/3;
  double yc = (t.p1.y + t.p2.y + t.p3.y)/3;
  double zc = (t.p1.z + t.p2.z + t.p3.z)/3;
  double xp = p.x;
  double yp = p.y;
  double zp = p.z;
  double dx = xc - xp;
  double dy = yc - yp;
  double dz = zc - zp;
  return Math.sqrt(dx * dx + dy * dy + dz * dz);
}

private void drawTriangles(Graphics g,
Triangle sortedTriangles[], Point3D lightSource) {
  Dimension d = getSize();
  int w = d.width;
  int h = d.height;
  int xpoints[] = new int[3];
  int ypoints[] = new int[3];
  for(int i = 0; i < NTRIANGLES; i++) {
```

8

```
      Triangle t = sortedTriangles[i];
      xpoints[0] = (int)(w/2 + t.p1.x);
      ypoints[0] = (int)(h/2 - t.p1.z);
      xpoints[1] = (int)(w/2 + t.p2.x);
      ypoints[1] = (int)(h/2 - t.p2.z);
      xpoints[2] = (int)(w/2 + t.p3.x);
      ypoints[2] = (int)(h/2 - t.p3.z);
      g.setColor(t.computeColor(lightSource));
      g.fillPolygon(xpoints, ypoints, 3);
    }
  }

  private void readObject(ObjectInputStream ois)
  throws IOException, ClassNotFoundException {
    try {
      ois.defaultReadObject();
      thread = new Thread(this);
      thread.start();
    }
    catch(Exception ex) {
      ex.printStackTrace();
    }
  }
}
```

The source code for the **Point3D** class is identical to that seen in Chapter 6. It is reproduced here for your convenience.

```
package surface3d;

public class Point3D {
  public double x, y, z;

  public Point3D(double x, double y, double z) {
    this.x = x;
    this.y = y;
    this.z = z;
  }

  public void rotateZ(double theta) {
    double newx = x * Math.cos(theta) - y * Math.sin(theta);
    double newy = x * Math.sin(theta) + y * Math.cos(theta);
    x = newx;
    y = newy;
  }
}
```

The source code for the **Triangle** class is shown in the next listing. Here, the color of a triangle is calculated by the **computeColor( )** method. It accepts a **Point3D** object, which is the position of the light source (the center of your screen). There are four primary steps to achieve this.

First, a vector is computed from **p1** to **p2**. Another vector is computed from **p1** to **p3**. The cross product of these vectors is calculated, and the result is scaled so that its overall size is one unit in length. These calculations provide a unit vector that is normal to the plane defined by the triangle.

Second, a unit vector from **p1** to the light source is computed.

Third, the dot product of these two unit vectors is computed. This yields a scalar value between -1 and +1 depending upon the angle between these vectors.

Finally, this value is used to generate a **Color** object representing a color between pure black and pure white. If the triangle directly faces the light source, it is colored pure white. If it faces directly away from the light source, it is colored pure black. Otherwise, it is some intermediate shade of gray.

```
package surface3d;
import java.awt.*;

public class Triangle {
  public Point3D p1, p2, p3;

  public Triangle(Point3D p1, Point3D p2, Point3D p3) {
    this.p1 = p1;
    this.p2 = p2;
    this.p3 = p3;
  }

  public Color computeColor(Point3D lightSource) {

    // Compute unit vector normal to triangle
    double x21 = p2.x - p1.x;
    double y21 = p2.y - p1.y;
    double z21 = p2.z - p1.z;
    double x31 = p3.x - p1.x;
    double y31 = p3.y - p1.y;
    double z31 = p3.z - p1.z;
    double xn = y21 * z31 - z21 * y31;
    double yn = z21 * x31 - x21 * z31;
    double zn = x21 * y31 - y21 * x31;
```

8

```
        double l = Math.sqrt(xn * xn + yn * yn + zn * zn);
        xn /= l;
        yn /= l;
        zn /= l;

        // Compute unit vector from p1 to the lightSource
        double xs = lightSource.x - p1.x;
        double ys = lightSource.y - p1.y;
        double zs = lightSource.z - p1.z;
        l = Math.sqrt(xs * xs + ys * ys + zs * zs);
        xs /= l;
        ys /= l;
        zs /= l;

        // Compute dot product of these two vectors
        double product = xn * xs + yn * ys + zn * zs;

        // Select color based on dot product
        int i = (int)(127 * ((product + 1)/2) + 128);
        return new Color(i, i, i);
    }
}
```

Applications

Part of the power of the Beans technology is that it allows an application to dynamically create instances of Beans. This is an important aspect of the component software philosophy. An application need not provide every part of its functionality. Instead, it can enlist the aid of various components as needed. This approach has several advantages. For example, it is possible to upgrade a component without changing the entire application. It also allows different users to have access to different features based upon their usage patterns. This section describes how to write Java applications that directly instantiate and connect Beans.

The Beans Class

The **Beans** class in the **java.beans** package has several static methods that instantiate a Bean or obtain information about its environment. These are summarized in Table 8-3.

Of these methods, the most relevant for our discussion in this chapter is the **instantiate( )** method. It is used in the following examples to create an instance of a Bean.

Method	Description
Object getInstanceOf(Object *bean*, Class *cls*)	Casts *bean* to type *cls* and returns an object of that type. (If *cls* is not available, *bean* is returned.)
Object instantiate(ClassLoader *clsLoader*, String *beanName*)	Uses *clsLoader* to instantiate the component named *beanName*. (If *clsLoader* is null, the System Class Loader is used.)
boolean isDesignTime( )	Returns true if the execution environment is provided by a builder tool. Otherwise, returns false.
boolean isGuiAvailable( )	Returns true if the execution environment supports an interactive GUI, otherwise, returns false.
boolean isInstanceOf(Object *bean*, Class *cls*)	Returns true if *bean* is an instance of *cls*, otherwise, returns false.
void setDesignTime(boolean *flag*) throws SecurityException	If *flag* is true, a builder tool is providing the execution environment.
void setGuiAvailable(boolean *flag*) throws SecurityException	If *flag* is true, an interactive GUI is available.

Methods Defined by **Beans**
Table 8-3.

8

Instantiating and Configuring a Bean

The next listing shows an application that uses the **Spectrum** Bean from Chapter 2. It creates a frame, instantiates the Bean, modifies its **vertical** property, adds the Bean to the frame, and makes the frame visible. Figure 8-3 shows how the application appears.

The **instantiate( )** method of **Beans** is used to create an instance of the Bean named **spectrum.Spectrum**. The first argument to this method is **null**. This indicates that the System Class Loader is used to load the component by searching for it in the directories and .zip files defined by

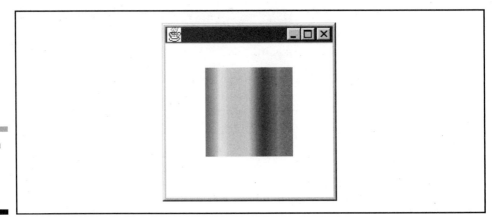

the CLASSPATH environment variable. The second argument is the name of the Bean.

```java
package applications;
import java.awt.*;
import java.awt.event.*;
import java.beans.*;
import spectrum.*;

public class SpectrumApplication {

  public static void main(String args[]) {
    new SpectrumApplication();
  }

  public SpectrumApplication() {
    Frame f = new Frame();
    f.setSize(200, 200);
    f.addWindowListener(new MyWindowAdapter());
    try {
      String name = "spectrum.Spectrum";
      Spectrum spectrum =
        (Spectrum)Beans.instantiate(null, name);
      spectrum.setVertical(false);
      f.setLayout(null);
      Dimension d = spectrum.getSize();
      spectrum.setBounds(50, 50, d.width, d.height);
      f.add(spectrum);
    }
```

```
      catch(Exception ex) {
        ex.printStackTrace();
      }
      f.setVisible(true);
    }

    class MyWindowAdapter extends WindowAdapter {
      public void windowClosing(WindowEvent we) {
        System.exit(0);
      }
    }
  }
```

Using Several Beans

The next listing shows an application that uses the **Selector** and **Painter**
Beans from Chapter 2. It creates a frame, instantiates the Beans, registers
Painter to receive **ColorEvent** notifications from **Selector**, adds the Beans
to the frame, and makes the frame visible. Figure 8-4 shows how the
application appears.

The **instantiate( )** method of **Beans** is again used to create the
components. The **addColorListener( )** method of **Selector** registers
Painter to receive **ColorEvent** notifications.

8

```
package applications;
import java.awt.*;
import java.awt.event.*;
import java.beans.*;
import cselector.*;

public class ColorSelectorApplication {

  public static void main(String args[]) {
    new ColorSelectorApplication();
  }

  public ColorSelectorApplication() {
    Frame f = new Frame();
    f.setSize(200, 200);
    f.addWindowListener(new MyWindowAdapter());
    try {
      String name = "cselector.Painter";
      Painter painter = (Painter)Beans.instantiate(null, name);
      name = "cselector.Selector";
```

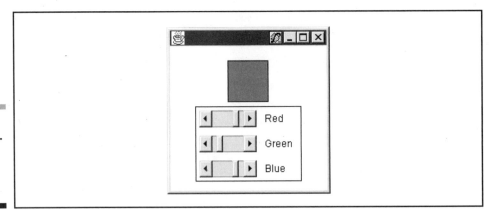

```
    Selector selector = (Selector)Beans.instantiate(null, name);
    selector.addColorListener(painter);
    f.setLayout(null);
    selector.setBounds(35, 95, 130, 90);
    f.add(selector);
    painter.setBounds(75, 40, 50, 50);
    f.add(painter);
  }
  catch(Exception ex) {
    ex.printStackTrace();
  }
  f.setVisible(true);
}

class MyWindowAdapter extends WindowAdapter {
  public void windowClosing(WindowEvent we) {
    System.exit(0);
  }
}
}
```

Instantiating Serialized Beans

In the previous two examples, the **instantiate( )** method was used to create an instance of a Bean. You may be wondering why the **new** operator was not used to accomplish this. One reason is that **instantiate( )** is designed so it can automatically load serialized Beans. This is an advantage because it allows you to build programs whose components begin execution by retrieving stored state information.

As previously noted, the first argument to **instantiate( )** is a class loader, and the second argument is the name of the Bean. The current Beans technology attempts to find a serialized object with the specified name. If this cannot be done, an attempt is made to find a class with the specified name. If this cannot be done, a **ClassNotFoundException** is thrown.

For example, if a Bean is named **graphs.Graph**, the **instantiate( )** method first tries to locate a file named graphs/Graph.ser. If such a file is not found, a search is made for a class named **graphs.Graph**. Both of these searches are done relative to the CLASSPATH environment variable.

The next listing shows an application that illustrates this concept. It instantiates the **Graph** Bean from the **graphs** package that was seen in Chapter 4. Users can press and drag the mouse to create links between nodes in the graph. Figure 8-5 shows how this application appears.

The application is designed so that when a user issues a request to close the window, the **Graph** object is serialized to a file named graphs/Graph.ser. Therefore, when the application is started again, the **instantiate( )** method

8

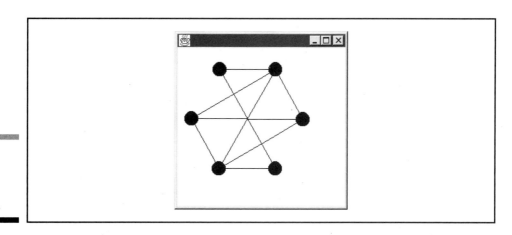

The **Graph Application** program
Figure 8-5.

will find the serialized object. Follow these steps to experiment with this application:

1. Start the application by typing **java applications.GraphApplication** on the command line.
2. Create some links.
3. Exit from the application by clicking the mouse button on the icon in the upper-right corner of the window.
4. Check that a file named Graph.ser has been created in the graphs subdirectory.
5. Restart the application. Observe that the links are visible because the **instantiate( )** method found the serialized object.

You may add some more links to the graph and again close the application. When it is restarted, the links are visible. This demonstrates that the **instantiate( )** method uses a serialized object if this file exists.

```
package applications;
import java.awt.*;
import java.awt.event.*;
import java.beans.*;
import java.io.*;
import graphs.*;

public class GraphApplication {
  Graph graph;

  public static void main(String args[]) {
    new GraphApplication();
  }

  public GraphApplication() {
    Frame f = new Frame();
    f.setSize(250, 250);
    f.addWindowListener(new MyWindowAdapter());
    try {
      graph = (Graph)Beans.instantiate(null, "graphs.Graph");
      f.add(graph);
    }
    catch(Exception ex) {
      ex.printStackTrace();
    }
    f.setVisible(true);
```

```
          }

          class MyWindowAdapter extends WindowAdapter {
            public void windowClosing(WindowEvent we) {
              try {
                FileOutputStream fos =
                  new FileOutputStream("graphs/Graph.ser");
                ObjectOutputStream oos =
                  new ObjectOutputStream(fos);
                oos.writeObject(graph);
                oos.flush();
                oos.close();
              }
              catch(Exception ex) {
                ex.printStackTrace();
              }
              System.exit(0);
            }
          }
        }
```

Using Beans from JAR Files

This section illustrates how to use Beans from JAR files. Because Beans are packaged in JAR files, this can be valuable information.

8

Figure 8-6 shows how this application appears. As you can see, the program creates instances of the **Plot3D** and **Spectrum** Beans in a frame. It begins by reading the .class files from the zip1\plot3d.jar and zip1\spectrum.jar archives. In order to read the entries from a .zip file, a special type of input stream is required. This functionality is provided by the class **java.util.zip.ZipInputStream**.

A class loader is also developed in this example. This is needed to convert a set of bytecodes to an instance of class **Class**. The Java Virtual Machine (JVM) contains a class loader that it uses to load .class files from the locations defined by the CLASSPATH environment variable. However, you may also write your own class loader to retrieve and process bytecodes from other sources, such as a network server or JAR file.

Finally, this example illustrates how to use the **instantiate( )** method of the **Beans** class with your own class loader.

The program consists of three source files. The Demo.java file contains the static **main( )** method for the application. Overall coordination of the

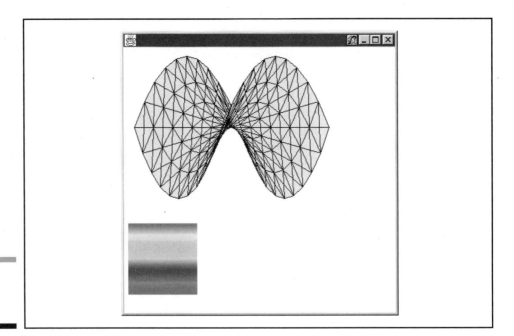

application is also provided in this file. The Jar.java file reads the entries from the JAR files in the directory named zip1\jars. The class loader is in JarClassLoader.java.

The source code for **Demo** is shown in the next listing. This class extends **Frame**. Its **main( )** method creates a **Demo** object.

The constructor begins by setting the overall dimensions of the frame. The static **process( )** method of **Jar** is called to process all of the JAR files located in the zip1\jars subdirectory. As you will see, the entries in each JAR file are read. All entries whose name ends with ".class" are saved in a data structure maintained by the **JarClassLoader** object. A reference to the one **JarClassLoader** object is saved in the variable **jcl**. The layout manager for this frame is set to **null** since the program does its own layout of the components.

The next few lines of the constructor use the **instantiate( )** method of the **Beans** class to create two Beans. The first argument to this method is a reference to the **JarClassLoader** object. The other argument is the fully qualified name of the component. As you can see, this program creates instances of the **plot3d.Plot3D** and **spectrum.Spectrum** Beans and adds these to the frame.

A **MyWindowAdapter** object is created and registered to process any window events generated by this frame. The **setVisible( )** method must be called to make the frame visible.

The **MyWindowAdapter** class overrides the **windowClosing( )** method so the program exits when the user closes the window.

```java
package zip1;
import java.awt.*;
import java.awt.event.*;
import java.beans.*;

public class Demo extends Frame {

  public static void main(String[] args) {
    new Demo();
  }

  public Demo() {

    // Set the overall dimensions of the frame
    setSize(400, 400);

    // Process the contents of all the JAR files
    Jar.process();

    // Get reference to the one instance of JarClassLoader
    JarClassLoader jcl = JarClassLoader.singleton;

    // Set the layout manager to null
    setLayout(null);

    try {
      // Instantiate two Beans and add these to the frame
      Component component;
      String name = "plot3d.Plot3D";
      component = (Component)Beans.instantiate(jcl, name);
      component.setBounds(10, 10, 300, 250);
      add(component);
      name = "spectrum.Spectrum";
      component = (Component)Beans.instantiate(jcl, name);
      component.setBounds(10, 270, 100, 100);
      add(component);
    }
    catch(Exception ex) {
```

8

```
      System.out.println(ex);
    }

    // Arrange to handle window events
    addWindowListener(new MyWindowAdapter());

    // make the frame visible
    setVisible(true);
  }

  class MyWindowAdapter extends WindowAdapter {
    public void windowClosing(WindowEvent we) {
      System.exit(0);
    }
  }
}
```

The source code for **Jar** is shown in the next listing. A static variable named **data** holds a reference to a hash table. This data structure contains the bytecodes that are read from all of the JAR files. The key to this hash table is the name of the class. An instance variable named **filename** holds the name of the JAR file.

The static **putData( )** method saves the bytecodes for a class in **data**. This information can be retrieved via the **getData( )** method.

The static **process( )** method creates a **Jar** object for each of the .jar files in the zip1\jars directory. (Any other files in that directory are ignored.)

The **Jar** constructor reads each of the entries in one JAR file. Because a JAR file is a ZIP file, the functionality provided by **ZipInputStream** must be used to read its contents. A **FileInputStream** object is first created for the file. Then a **ZipInputStream** object is created for this file input stream. The entries in the zip input stream can be obtained by calling the **getNextEntry( )** method in a loop. This method returns **null** when there are no remaining entries in the stream. Otherwise, it returns a **ZipEntry** object that encapsulates information about that item. The **getName( )** method returns a **String** object containing the name of that entry. If the name ends with a .class suffix, the **processClassFile( )** method is called to process those bytecodes. (Any entries in the JAR file that are not .class files are ignored.)

The **processClassFile( )** method processes the bytecodes for a .class entry in a JAR file. The first argument to this method is the name of the class file and the second argument is the **ZipInputStream** object. The name of the class is obtained by dropping the suffix from the name of the class file and replacing each forward slash by a period. The bytecodes are read from the zip input stream and are written to a **ByteArrayOutputStream** object. This is done because the **toByteArray( )** method of that class makes it very easy to obtain a byte array containing the bytecodes for the class. The bytecodes are then saved via the **putData( )** method. The name of the class is the first argument to this method, and the byte array with the associated bytecodes is the second argument.

```java
package zip1;
import java.io.*;
import java.util.*;
import java.util.zip.*;

public class Jar {
  private static Hashtable data = new Hashtable();
  private String filename;

  public static void putData(String clsName, byte[] buffer) {
    data.put(clsName, buffer);
  }

  public static Object getData(String clsName) {
    return data.get(clsName);
  }

  public static void process() {
    try {
      char c = File.separatorChar;
      File dir = new File("zip1" + c + "jars");
      String entries[] = dir.list();
      for(int i = 0; i < entries.length; i++) {
        if(entries[i].endsWith(".jar")) {
          new Jar("zip1" + c + "jars" + c + entries[i]);
        }
      }
    }
    catch(Exception ex) {
      ex.printStackTrace();
    }
  }

  public Jar(String filename) {
    // Read and process the .class entries in the JAR file
```

8

```
  this.filename = filename;
  try {
    FileInputStream fis = new FileInputStream(filename);
    ZipInputStream zis = new ZipInputStream(fis);
    ZipEntry ze = null;
    while((ze = zis.getNextEntry()) != null) {
      String name = ze.getName();
      if(name.endsWith(".class")) {
        processClassFile(name, zis);
      }
    }
    zis.close();
  }
  catch(Exception ex) {
    ex.printStackTrace();
  }
}

private void processClassFile(String name1,
ZipInputStream zis) {

  // Determine class name
  String name2 = name1.replace('/','.');
  int i = name2.indexOf(".class");
  if(i != -1) {
    name2 = name2.substring(0, i);
  }

  try {

    // Read bytecodes from the zip input stream
    ByteArrayOutputStream baos =
      new ByteArrayOutputStream();
    for(;;) {
      byte block[] = new byte[1024];
      int len = zis.read(block);
      if(len < 0) {
        break;
      }
      baos.write(block, 0, len);
    }
    byte buffer[] = baos.toByteArray();

    // Save these bytecodes
    putData(name2, buffer);
```

```
    }
    catch(Exception ex) {
      ex.printStackTrace();
    }
  }
}
```

The source code for **JarClassLoader** is shown in the next listing. This class extends the abstract **ClassLoader** class. Its static **singleton** variable holds a reference to the one instance of this class. Notice that a **JarClassLoader** object is created as part of the static initialization for this class.

To resolve a class means that the classes referenced by it are also loaded.

The **loadClass( )** method loads a class with a specific name. Its first argument is the name of the requested class, and its second argument is a **boolean** flag that indicates whether this class is to be resolved. A **Class** object is returned for that class. Every subclass of **ClassLoader** must override this method. In this example, it performs six different functions. First, the **findSystemClass( )** method of the superclass is called to determine whether a class by this name is already known to the System Class Loader. If so, the **Class** object is returned. Otherwise, a **ClassNotFoundException** or **NoClassDefFoundError** is thrown by **findSystemClass( )**, and processing continues. Second, the **findLoadedClass( )** method is used to determine whether a class by this name has previously been defined by this class loader. If so, the **Class** object is returned. Third, the static **getData( )** method of **Jar** is called to determine whether a set of bytecodes exists for this class name. If not, a **ClassNotFoundException** is thrown. Fourth, **defineClass( )** is invoked to convert the bytecodes into a **Class** object. This method takes the name of the new class as its first argument, the byte array containing the bytecodes as its second argument, the offset into that byte array as its third argument, and the number of bytecodes as its last argument. If a problem is encountered, a **ClassFormatError** is thrown. Fifth, if the second argument to **loadClass( )** is set, **resolveClass( )** is called. This is done so that any classes referenced by **cls** are also loaded. In this book, the second argument to **loadClass( )** will always be **true**. Finally, the **Class** object is returned.

8

```
package zip1;

public class JarClassLoader extends ClassLoader {
  public static JarClassLoader singleton =
    new JarClassLoader();
```

```
protected Class loadClass(String clsName, boolean resolve)
throws ClassNotFoundException {

  // Check the System class loader
  Class cls;
  try {
    cls = super.findSystemClass(clsName);
    return cls;
  }
  catch(ClassNotFoundException ex) {
  }
  catch(NoClassDefFoundError err) {
  }

  // Check if this class has already
  // been loaded
  cls = findLoadedClass(clsName);
  if(cls != null) {
    return cls;
  }

  // Get the bytecodes for this class
  byte buffer[] = (byte[])Jar.getData(clsName);
  if(buffer == null) {
    throw new ClassNotFoundException();
  }

  // Parse the data
  cls = defineClass(clsName, buffer, 0, buffer.length);
  if(cls == null) {
    throw new ClassFormatError();
  }

  // Resolve the class if necessary
  if(resolve) {
    resolveClass(cls);
  }

  // Return the class
  return cls;
  }
}
```

In this example, you have seen how to read a .class file from a JAR file, use a
class loader to define classes from those bytecodes, and create instances of

that new class. However, this simple program does not illustrate all of the capabilities of class loaders. For example, a class loader also allows you to get resources. In particular, **ClassLoader** defines the following two methods:

URL getResource(String *name*)

InputStream getResourceAsStream(String *name*)

Here, *name* is the name of the desired resource. These methods are used by Beans that have image files or other resources associated with them. Because **JarClassLoader** does not provide this functionality, such components won't work with the limited functionality shown in this example.

CHAPTER 9

Property Editors and Customizers

As you know, the behavior of a Bean is affected by the values of its properties. This chapter examines two features that allow a user to manage those properties: property editors and customizers. A property editor allows a developer to read and modify the value of one property. In previous chapters of this book, you have seen that the Properties window allows one to edit the various properties of a selected Bean. A customizer provides a graphical user interface that allows a user to edit multiple properties. Nearly all production quality components provide these features since they are the means by which a Bean is configured by a user.

A property may be represented on the Properties window in one of three ways. First, its value can be displayed in a text field. Second, it can be shown as a choice element. This is useful for a property that is limited to a set of fixed values. Third, an image representing the property value can be painted into a small rectangle on the Properties window. You have seen that the foreground and background color properties of the components are represented in this way. Similarly, the font is also represented as an image in a small rectangle. In these cases, when the developer clicks the mouse on that image, a new window for the property editor appears. It contains a graphical user interface that allows modification of the property value.

Since a customizer allows the user to edit two or more properties of a Bean, it can be extremely valuable for components that have complex functions. A customizer can lead a user step-by-step through the process of configuring a Bean and help differentiate your product from that of a competitor.

Property Editors

A property editor allows a user to edit the value of one property.

This section discusses how to build editors that allow a user to read and modify the value of a property. It begins by discussing the **PropertyEditor** interface and **PropertyEditorSupport** class. These provide support for property editors. Examples illustrate how properties can be represented as text fields, choices, or images in the Properties window. As you will see, the process of adding a property editor to a Bean is straightforward.

The PropertyEditor Interface

Table 9-1 summarizes the methods that are defined by the **PropertyEditor** interface in the **java.beans** package.

The examples in this chapter illustrate when and how to apply these methods.

Method	Description
void addPropertyChangeListener (PropertyChangeListener *pcl*)	Registers *pcl* to receive property change events from this property editor.
String getAsText( )	Returns a text representation of the property.
Component getCustomEditor( )	Returns a reference to the custom property editor. If there is no custom property editor, **null** is returned.
String getJavaInitializationString( )	Returns a string that is a fragment of Java source code that can be used to initialize a variable with the value of the property.
String[ ] getTags( )	Returns an array of strings that are the set of allowed values for this property.
Object getValue( )	Returns an **Object** that contains the value of the property.
boolean isPaintable( )	Returns **true** if the **paintValue( )** method can be used for this property.
void paintValue(Graphics *g*, Rectangle *r*)	Paints a representation of this property in the **Rectangle** *r* on **Graphics** *g*.
void removePropertyChangeListener (PropertyChangeListener *pcl*)	Unregisters *pcl* to receive property change events from this property editor.
void setAsText(String *str*) throws IllegalArgumentException	Uses *str* to set the property. An **IllegalArgumentException** is throw if *str* is not formatted correctly.
void setValue(Object *object*)	Uses *object* to set the value of the property.
boolean supportsCustomEditor( )	Returns **true** if a custom property editor is available to edit the property.

9

The
PropertyEditor
Interface
Table 9-1.

The PropertyEditorSupport Class

The **PropertyEditorSupport** class in the **java.beans** package provides a default implementation of the **PropertyEditor** interface. It is generally easier to extend this class and override a few methods, rather than implement the entire **PropertyEditor** interface.

This class has two protected constructors as shown here:

protected PropertyEditorSupport( )

protected PropertyEditorSupport(Object *source*)

Here, *source* is the object that generates the property event.

Table 9-2 summarizes the default implementations of the **PropertyEditor** methods that are provided by the **PropertyEditorSupport** class.

Method	Description
void addPropertyChangeListener (PropertyChangeListener *pcl*)	Registers *pcl* to receive property change events from this property editor.
String getAsText( )	Returns a text representation of the property.
Component getCustomEditor( )	Returns **null**.
String getJavaInitializationString( )	Returns question marks.
String[ ] getTags( )	Returns **null**.
Object getValue( )	Returns an **Object** that contains the value of the property.
boolean isPaintable( )	Returns **false**.
void paintValue(Graphics *g*, Rectangle *r*)	Does nothing.
void removePropertyChangeListener (PropertyChangeListener *pcl*)	Unregisters *pcl* to receive property change events from this property editor.

Methods of the
**PropertyEditor-
Support** Class
Table 9-2.

Method	Description
void setAsText(String *str*) throws IllegalArgumentException	Uses *str* to set the property. An **IllegalArgumentException** is thrown if *str* is not formatted correctly.
void setValue(Object *object*)	Uses *object* to set the value of the property.
boolean supportsCustomEditor( )	Returns **false**.

Methods of the
**PropertyEditor-
Support** Class
(*continued*)

Table 9-2.

In addition to these methods, **PropertyEditorSupport** also provides a **firePropertyChange( )** method whose signature is shown here:

    void firePropertyChange( )

This method sends a property change event to all registered listeners.

Representing Properties as Text Fields

This section illustrates how to represent a property as a text field element in the Properties window. There are three classes in this example. First, **PointViewer** is a Bean that displays a square in which a point is positioned. Second, **PointEditor** defines how the x and y coordinates of this point are represented. This is the property editor. Third, **PointViewerBeanInfo** associates **PointEditor** and **PointViewer**.

Figure 9-1 shows how the BeanBox and Properties windows appear when the **PointViewer** Bean is selected.

The following listing shows the code for the **PointViewer** Bean. It has one property called **point**. This is a **Point** object that contains the x and y coordinates of the point. The point is represented as a filled square that is 6×6 pixels in size and centered at (x, y). When the property is modified through its access method, the **repaint( )** method is also invoked to update the display. If either the x or y coordinate is negative, the point is not visible. Similarly, if either x or y exceeds the dimensions of the square, the point is not visible.

9

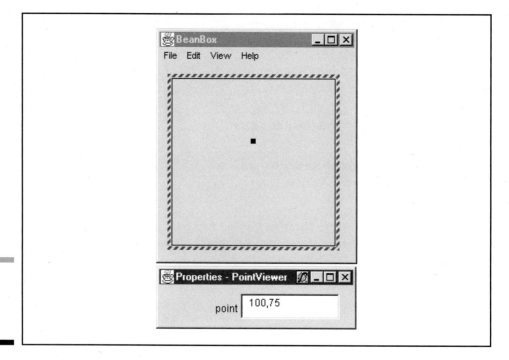

```
package point;
import java.awt.*;

public class PointViewer extends Canvas {
  private Point point;

  public PointViewer() {
    point = new Point(0, 0);
    setSize(200, 200);
  }

  public Point getPoint() {
    return point;
  }

  public void setPoint(Point point) {
    this.point = point;
    repaint();
  }

  public void paint(Graphics g) {
```

```
    Dimension d = getSize();
    g.drawRect(0, 0, d.width - 1, d.height - 1);
    g.fillRect(point.x - 3, point.y - 3, 6, 6);
  }
}
```

The following listing shows the code for **PointEditor**. Note that it extends **PropertyEditorSupport** and overrides the **getAsText( )** and **setAsText( )** methods.

The **getAsText( )** method invokes **getValue( )** to obtain the value of this property and casts its return value to a **Point** object. A string is created from the x and y coordinates obtained from the **Point** object. This string is then returned from the method.

The **setAsText( )** method processes the string that is supplied as an input parameter to create a new **Point** object. This object is then passed as an argument to the **setValue( )** method.

```
package point;
import java.awt.*;
import java.beans.*;

public class PointEditor extends PropertyEditorSupport {

  public String getAsText() {
    Point point = (Point)getValue();
    return "" + point.x + "," + point.y;
  }

  public void setAsText(String text)
  throws IllegalArgumentException {
    try {
      int index = text.indexOf(",");
      String sx = (index == -1) ? text :
        text.substring(0, index);
      String sy = (index == -1) ? "0" :
        text.substring(index + 1);
      int x = Integer.parseInt(sx.trim());
      int y = Integer.parseInt(sy.trim());
      setValue(new Point(x, y));
    }
    catch(Exception ex) {
      throw new IllegalArgumentException();
    }
```

9

```
}
}
```

PointViewerBeanInfo extends **SimpleBeanInfo** and overrides the
getPropertyDescriptors( ) method. You can see that a **PropertyDescriptor**
object is created. The arguments to the constructor are a **String** object
containing the name of the property and the **Class** object for the Bean. The
setPropertyEditorClass( ) method is called to associate an editor with that
property. In this case, **PointEditor** is used to edit the **point** property. The
following listing contains the code for **PointViewerBeanInfo**.

*The **set-PropertyEditor-Class( )** method of the **Property-Descriptor** object associates an editor with a property.*

```
package point;
import java.beans.*;

public class PointViewerBeanInfo extends SimpleBeanInfo {

  public PropertyDescriptor[] getPropertyDescriptors() {
    try {
      PropertyDescriptor p1;
      p1 = new PropertyDescriptor("point", PointViewer.class);
      p1.setPropertyEditorClass(PointEditor.class);
      PropertyDescriptor pds[] = { p1 };
      return pds;
    }
    catch(Exception ex) {
      ex.printStackTrace();
    }
    return null;
  }
}
```

Representing Properties as Choices

This section illustrates how to represent a property as a choice element in the
Properties window. The Bean presents a colored square that represents an ice
cream flavor. There are four possible flavors: vanilla, chocolate, strawberry,
and pistachio. When the user selects one of these entries in the choice
element, the color displayed by the Bean changes.

There are three classes in this example. First, **IceCream** is a Bean that
displays a square filled with the color of the selected flavor. Second,
FlavorEditor defines how this property is presented. Third,
IceCreamBeanInfo associates **FlavorEditor** and **IceCream**.

Figure 9-2 shows the BeanBox and Properties windows when the **IceCream** Bean is selected.

The following listing shows the code for the **IceCream** Bean. It has one property called **flavor**. This is a **String** object that indicates which entry has been selected in the choice element. When the property is changed by the **setFlavor( )** method, the **repaint( )** method is called to update Bean's appearance.

IceCream has a static hash table that is used to map these strings to a corresponding **Color** object. The **paint( )** method makes use of this information to select the color.

```
package icecream;
import java.awt.*;
import java.util.*;

public class IceCream extends Canvas {
  private static Hashtable flavorToColor;
  static {
    flavorToColor = new Hashtable();
    flavorToColor.put("Vanilla", new Color(255, 255, 255));
```

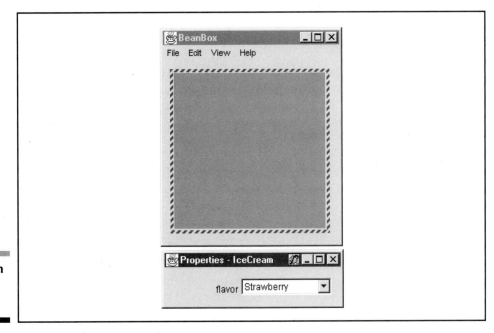

9

The **IceCream** Bean

Figure 9-2.

```
    flavorToColor.put("Chocolate", new Color(119, 66, 8));
    flavorToColor.put("Strawberry", new Color(236, 112, 132));
    flavorToColor.put("Pistachio", new Color(113, 249, 158));
  }
  private String flavor;

  public IceCream() {
    flavor = "Strawberry";
    setSize(200, 200);
  }

  public String getFlavor() {
    return flavor;
  }

  public void setFlavor(String flavor) {
    this.flavor = flavor;
    repaint();
  }

  public void paint(Graphics g) {
    Color color = (Color)flavorToColor.get(flavor);
    g.setColor(color);
    Dimension d = getSize();
    g.fillRect(0, 0, d.width - 1, d.height - 1);
  }
}
```

FlavorEditor extends **PropertyEditorSupport**. It overrides the **getTags( )**
method to define the strings that should be associated with the choice
element in the Properties window. The following listing shows the code
for **FlavorEditor**.

```
package icecream;
import java.beans.*;

public class FlavorEditor extends PropertyEditorSupport {

  public String[] getTags() {
    String flavors[] = { "Vanilla", "Chocolate",
      "Strawberry", "Pistachio" };
    return flavors;
  }
}
```

IceCreamBeanInfo extends **SimpleBeanInfo** and overrides
the **getPropertyDescriptors( )** method. You can see that a
PropertyDescriptor object is created. The arguments to the constructor
are a **String** object containing the name of the property and the **Class**
object for the Bean. The **setPropertyEditorClass( )** method is called to
associate an editor with that property. In this case, **FlavorEditor** is used
to edit the **flavor** property. The following listing contains the code for
IceCreamBeanInfo.

```
package icecream;
import java.beans.*;

public class IceCreamBeanInfo extends SimpleBeanInfo {

  public PropertyDescriptor[] getPropertyDescriptors() {
    try {
      PropertyDescriptor p1;
      p1 = new PropertyDescriptor("flavor", IceCream.class);
      p1.setPropertyEditorClass(FlavorEditor.class);
      PropertyDescriptor pds[] = { p1 };
      return pds;
    }
    catch(Exception ex) {
      ex.printStackTrace();
    }
    return null;
  }
}
```

Custom Property Editors

This section illustrates how to build a custom property editor. There are
three classes in this example. First, **ColorViewer** is a Bean that displays a
square filled with a selected color. Second, **ColorEditor** implements a
graphical user interface that allows the user to edit the color. Third,
ColorViewerBeanInfo associates **ColorEditor** and **ColorViewer**.

Figure 9-3 shows how the BeanBox and Properties window appear when the
ColorViewer Bean is selected.

The following listing shows the code for the **ColorViewer** Bean. It has one
property named **color** that indicates the color of the square drawn by the
paint( ) method.

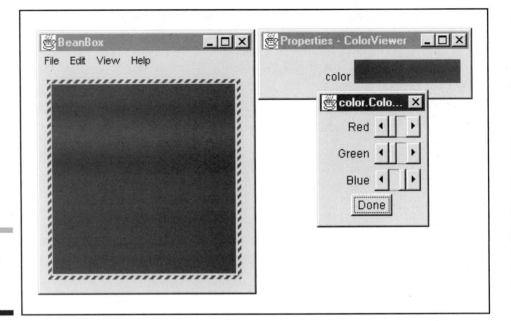

The
ColorViewer
Bean
Figure 9-3.

```
package color;
import java.awt.*;

public class ColorViewer extends Canvas {
  private Color color;

  public ColorViewer() {
    color = Color.blue;
    setSize(200, 200);
  }

  public Color getColor() {
    return color;
  }

  public void setColor(Color color) {
    this.color = color;
    repaint();
  }

  public void update(Graphics g) {
    paint(g);
```

```
  }

  public void paint(Graphics g) {
    g.setColor(color);
    Dimension d = getSize();
    g.fillRect(0, 0, d.width-1, d.height-1);
  }
}
```

ColorEditor presents the graphical user interface for the custom property editor. The constructor creates three scroll bars that can be manipulated to adjust the red, green, and blue components of the color. The **ColorEditor** object itself receives any adjustment events generated by the scroll bars. There are also three labels for these scroll bars.

When any of the scroll bars are changed, the **adjustmentValueChanged( )** method is invoked. This reads the settings of the scroll bars and fires a property change event.

The **setValue( )** method is called by the builder tool to provide a reference to the **Color** object to be changed. It determines the red, green, and blue components of this color and uses these to initialize the scroll bars. A property change event is then fired. The **getValue( )** method simply returns a reference to the **Color** object.

The **getJavaInitializationString( )** and **getAsText( )** methods return **null** because this property is not represented as a text field in the Properties window. The **setAsText( )** method throws an **IllegalArgumentException** for the same reason.

The **getTags( )** method returns **null** because this property is not represented as a choice element in the Properties window.

The **isPaintable( )** method returns **true** because this property is represented as a rectangular image in the Properties window. The **paintValue( )** method does the work required to create this representation of the property. Notice that the method accepts two arguments. The first is a **Graphics** object on which drawing is to be done. The second is a **Rectangle** object in which drawing is to be limited. For this custom property editor, the image is simply a rectangle filled with the chosen color.

The **supportsCustomEditor( )** method returns **true** and the **getCustomEditor( )** method returns a reference to the **ColorEditor** object.

The following listing contains the code for **ColorEditor**.

9

```
package color;
import java.awt.*;
import java.awt.event.*;
import java.beans.*;

public class ColorEditor extends Panel
implements AdjustmentListener, PropertyEditor {
  private PropertyChangeSupport support;
  private Color color;
  private Scrollbar sr, sg, sb;

  public ColorEditor() {

    // Create and arrange GUI elements
    setLayout(new GridLayout(3, 2, 5, 5));
    Label lr = new Label("Red");
    lr.setAlignment(Label.RIGHT);
    add(lr);
    sr = new Scrollbar(Scrollbar.HORIZONTAL, 0, 10, 0, 255);
    add(sr);
    sr.addAdjustmentListener(this);
    Label lg = new Label("Green");
    lg.setAlignment(Label.RIGHT);
    add(lg);
    sg = new Scrollbar(Scrollbar.HORIZONTAL, 0, 10, 0, 255);
    add(sg);
    sg.addAdjustmentListener(this);
    Label lb = new Label("Blue");
    lb.setAlignment(Label.RIGHT);
    add(lb);
    sb = new Scrollbar(Scrollbar.HORIZONTAL, 0, 10, 0, 255);
    add(sb);
    sb.addAdjustmentListener(this);

    // Create a PropertyChangeSupport object
    support = new PropertyChangeSupport(this);
  }

  public void adjustmentValueChanged(AdjustmentEvent ae) {
    int r = sr.getValue();
    sr.setValue(r);
    int g = sg.getValue();
    sg.setValue(g);
    int b = sb.getValue();
    sb.setValue(b);
```

```
      color = new Color(r, g, b);
      support.firePropertyChange("", null, null);
}

public void setValue(Object o) {
   color = (Color)o;
   sr.setValue(color.getRed());
   sg.setValue(color.getGreen());
   sb.setValue(color.getBlue());
   support.firePropertyChange("", null, null);
}

public Object getValue() {
   return color;
}

public String getJavaInitializationString() {
   return null;
}

public boolean isPaintable() {
   return true;
}

public void paintValue(Graphics g, Rectangle r) {
   g.setColor(color);
   g.fillRect(0, 0, r.width - 1, r.height - 1);
}

public String getAsText() {
   return null;
}

public void setAsText(String s)
throws IllegalArgumentException {
   throw new IllegalArgumentException(s);
}

public String[] getTags() {
   return null;
}

public boolean supportsCustomEditor() {
   return true;
}
```

9

```
public Component getCustomEditor() {
  return this;
}

public void
addPropertyChangeListener(PropertyChangeListener pcl) {
  support.addPropertyChangeListener(pcl);
}

public void
removePropertyChangeListener(PropertyChangeListener pcl) {
  support.removePropertyChangeListener(pcl);
}
}
```

ColorViewerBeanInfo extends **SimpleBeanInfo** and overrides the **getPropertyDescriptors( )** method. You can see that a **PropertyDescriptor** object is created. The arguments to the constructor are a **String** object containing the name of the property and the **Class** object for the Bean. The **setPropertyEditorClass( )** method is called to associate an editor with that property. In this case, **ColorEditor** is used to edit the **color** property. The following listing contains the code for **ColorViewerBeanInfo**.

```
package color;
import java.beans.*;

public class ColorViewerBeanInfo extends SimpleBeanInfo {

  public PropertyDescriptor[] getPropertyDescriptors() {
    try {
      PropertyDescriptor p1;
      p1 = new PropertyDescriptor("color", ColorViewer.class);
      p1.setPropertyEditorClass(ColorEditor.class);
      PropertyDescriptor pds[] = { p1 };
      return pds;
    }
    catch(Exception ex) {
      ex.printStackTrace();
    }
    return null;
  }
}
```

Customizers

This section discusses how to build a customizer that allows a user to read and write several properties of a Bean. As stated at the start of this chapter, a customizer can lead the user step by step through the process of configuring a complex Bean.

The Customizer Interface

The **Customizer** interface is defined in the **java.beans** package. It specifies the three methods shown here:

    void addPropertyChangeListener(PropertyChangeListener *pcl*)

    void removePropertyChangeListener(PropertyChangeListener *pcl*)

    void setObject(Object *bean*)

The first two methods allow listeners to register and unregister for **PropertyChangeEvent** objects from this customizer. The last method is called by the builder tool to give the customizer a reference to the Bean whose properties are to be modified.

A Simple Customizer Example

This section provides an example of a Bean customizer. The Bean displays a graph of an electrical waveform that is calculated by summing together several different sine waves. These individual sine waves are related because their frequencies are integral multiples of each other. In electrical engineering jargon, the signals are called *harmonics*.

9

You can test the example by creating an instance of the **Harmonics** Bean in the BeanBox. It initially appears as a rectangular region with a border and set of axes. To invoke the customizer, select Edit | Customize from the BeanBox menu. This causes the customizer to appear. Select some of the harmonics that are listed. As you select and deselect harmonics, the Bean appearance changes immediately. Figure 9-4 shows both the Bean and its customizer.

There are three classes in this example. First, **Harmonics** is a Bean that calculates and displays the total signal. Second, **HarmonicsCustomizer** presents a graphical user interface that allows one to select which harmonics are added together to calculate the total waveform. Third,

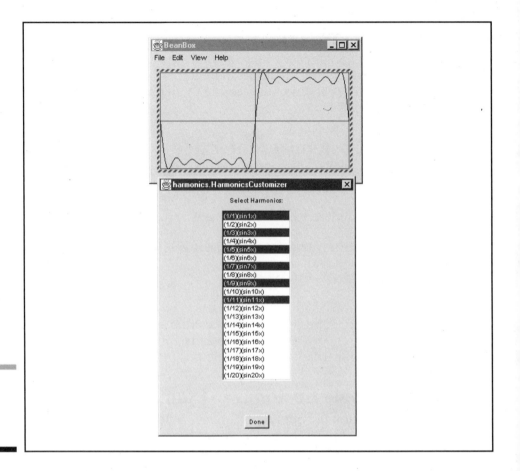

The
Harmonics
Bean
Figure 9-4.

HarmonicsBeanInfo associates **HarmonicsCustomizer** and
Harmonics.

The following listing shows the code for the **Harmonics** Bean. It has one
property called **frequencies**. This is a **BitSet** object that indicates if a
particular harmonic should be included when computing the total waveform.
A maximum of twenty different harmonics can be summed together. The
constructor initializes the property and sets the overall size of the Bean.
The **getFrequencies( )** and **setFrequencies( )** methods provide access
to the property.

The **paint( )** method draws a rectangle to enclose the display area, a set of
axes, and the waveform itself. The actual computation of the signal values is

done by the method **f( )**. Note that the **paint( )** method scales these values
so they fit within the available display region.

```java
package harmonics;
import java.awt.*;
import java.util.*;

public class Harmonics extends Canvas  {
  public final static int NFREQUENCIES = 20;
  private BitSet frequencies;

  public Harmonics() {
    frequencies = new BitSet(NFREQUENCIES);
    setSize(301, 150);
  }

  public BitSet getFrequencies() {
    return frequencies;
  }

  public void setFrequencies(BitSet frequencies) {
    this.frequencies = frequencies;
    repaint();
  }

  public void paint(Graphics g) {

    // Draw rectangle around the display area
    Dimension d = getSize();
    int width = d.width;
    int height = d.height;
    g.setColor(Color.blue);
    g.drawRect(0, 0, width - 1, height - 1);

    // Draw lines for x and y axes
    int y = height/2;
    g.drawLine(0, y, width, y);
    g.drawLine(width/2, 0, width/2, height);

    // Compute data values and remember
    // max and min values
    double max = 0;
    double min = 0;
    double deltax = 2 * Math.PI/(width - 1);
```

9

```
    double x = -Math.PI;
    double data[] = new double[width];
    for(int i = 0; i < width; i++) {
      double value = f(x);
      data[i] = value;
      min = (value < min) ? value : min;
      max = (value > max) ? value : max;
      x += deltax;
    }

    // Scale and translate data values
    double scale = height/(max - min);
    for(int i = 0; i < width; i++) {
      double value = data[i];
      double k = (value - min)/(max - min);
      data[i] = height * (1 - k);
    }

    // Draw curve for data values
    g.setColor(Color.black);
    for(int i = 1; i < width; i++) {
      g.drawLine(i - 1, (int)data[i - 1], i, (int)data[i]);
    }
  }

  private double f(double x) {
    double value = 0;
    for(int i = 0; i < NFREQUENCIES; i++) {
      if(frequencies.get(i)) {
        value += ((double)1/(i + 1)) * Math.sin((i+1) * x);
      }
    }
    return value;
  }
}
```

The following listing shows the code for **HarmonicsCustomizer**. It is a subclass of **Panel** that presents a **List** containing all of the possible harmonics that may be summed to produce the total waveform. The constructor initializes the list box with the available harmonics.

The **Customizer** interface consists of three methods that are implemented by the **HarmonicsCustomizer**. First, the **setObject( )** method is called by the builder tool when the customizer is started. A reference to the Bean to be customized is passed as an argument to this method. The **getFrequencies( )**

accessor method of the Bean is invoked so that the appropriate entries in the listbox can be set. Finally, the **addPropertyChangeListener( )** and **removePropertyChangeListener( )** methods are implemented.

Notice that the **itemStateChanged( )** method is invoked when the user selects or deselects an entry in the list box. It examines all of the entries to build a **BitSet** object and invokes **setFrequencies( )**.

```java
package harmonics;
import java.awt.*;
import java.awt.event.*;
import java.beans.*;
import java.util.*;

public class HarmonicsCustomizer extends Panel
implements Customizer, ItemListener {
  private PropertyChangeSupport pcsupport =
    new PropertyChangeSupport(this);
  private Harmonics harmonics;
  private java.awt.List list;
  private Panel p;

  public HarmonicsCustomizer() {
    setLayout(new BorderLayout());
    Label label =
      new Label("Select Harmonics:", Label.CENTER);
    add("North", label);
    list = new java.awt.List(Harmonics.NFREQUENCIES, true);
    for(int i = 1; i <= Harmonics.NFREQUENCIES; i++) {
      String s = "(1/" + i + ")(sin" + i + "x)";
      list.addItem(s);
    }
    list.addItemListener(this);
    p = new Panel();
    p.add(list);
    add("Center", p);
  }

  public Dimension getPreferredSize() {
    return new Dimension(300, 340);
  }

  public void setObject(Object object) {

    // Save reference to the Harmonics object
```

9

```
    harmonics = (Harmonics)object;

    // Get data from the harmonics object
    BitSet frequencies = harmonics.getFrequencies();
    for(int i = 0; i < Harmonics.NFREQUENCIES; i++) {
      if(frequencies.get(i)) {
        list.select(i);
      }
    }
  }

  public void
  addPropertyChangeListener(PropertyChangeListener pcl) {
    pcsupport.addPropertyChangeListener(pcl);
  }

  public void
  removePropertyChangeListener(PropertyChangeListener pcl) {
    pcsupport.removePropertyChangeListener(pcl);
  }

  public void itemStateChanged(ItemEvent ie) {
    BitSet frequencies = new BitSet(Harmonics.NFREQUENCIES);
    for(int i = 0; i < Harmonics.NFREQUENCIES; i++) {
      if(list.isIndexSelected(i)) {
        frequencies.set(i);
      }
    }
    harmonics.setFrequencies(frequencies);
  }
}
```

A Bean-Descriptor object associates a customizer with a Bean.

The following listing shows the code for **HarmonicsBeanInfo**. It extends **SimpleBeanInfo** and overrides the **getBeanDescriptor( )** method to return a **BeanDescriptor** object for this Bean. The **BeanDescriptor** constructor that is used in the program accepts two arguments. The first is the class of the Bean and the second is the class of the customizer.

```
package harmonics;
import java.beans.*;

public class HarmonicsBeanInfo extends SimpleBeanInfo {

  public BeanDescriptor getBeanDescriptor() {
    return new BeanDescriptor(Harmonics.class,
```

```
                    HarmonicsCustomizer.class);
      }
}
```

Another Customizer Example

This section provides another example of a Bean customizer. The Bean
displays a pie chart with its associated title and legend. Figure 9-5 shows
both the component and its customizer.

You can test the example by selecting the **Pie** Bean from the ToolBox
window. It initially appears as an empty circle. To invoke the customizer,
select Edit | Customize from the BeanBox menu. This causes the customizer
to appear. Notice that there is space for a maximum of five entries. For each
data entry, you can specify a name, value, and color.

There are five classes in this example. First, **Pie** is a Bean that displays a pie
chart. A title and legend are also presented. Second, **PieCustomizer** presents
a graphical user interface that allows one to define the names, values, and
colors used to produce the pie chart. Third, **PieBeanInfo** associates
PieCustomizer and **Pie**. Fourth, **Data** is a class that encapsulates the

9

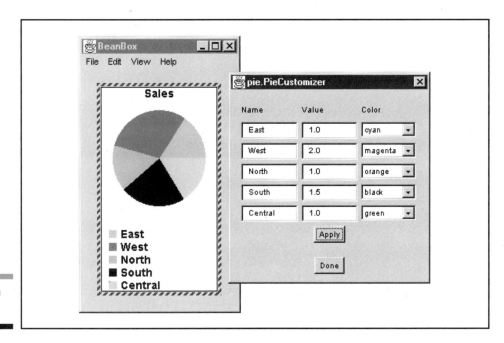

The **Pie** Bean
Figure 9-5.

name, value, and color information associated with one data point. Finally, **ColorChoice** is a subclass of **Choice**. It is used to build the graphical user interface of the customizer.

The following listing shows the code for the **Pie** Bean. It defines two properties named **title** and **data**. The former is the string that is displayed at the top of the Bean. The latter is a vector of **Data** objects that contain the information needed to generate the pie chart.

The constructor initializes the properties and sets the initial size of the Bean. The access methods for the properties follow the constructor. Notice that the **adjustSize( )** method is invoked if the **title** or **data** properties are changed. Also, the **setFont( )** method calls the same method of the superclass and also invokes **adjustSize( )**.

The **paint( )** method produces the display. It has four primary functions: (a) draw a border around the Bean, (b) display the title, (c) draw the colored wedges of the pie chart, and (d) draw the legend. Notice that the precise position of each element which is drawn (namely string, arc, or rectangle) must be calculated by using the current font size.

Finally, the **getPreferredSize( )** and **adjustSize( )** methods are similar to what has been seen before in this book. In this example, the former method computes a **Dimension** object by using information about the current font and the number of entries in **data**.

```
package pie;
import java.awt.*;
import java.util.*;

public class Pie extends Canvas {
  private String title;
  private Vector data;

  public Pie() {
    title = "";
    data = new Vector();
    setSize(150, 150);
  }

  public String getTitle() {
    return title;
  }

  public void setTitle(String title) {
```

```
    this.title = title;
    adjustSize();
  }

  public Vector getData() {
    return data;
  }

  public void setData(Vector data) {
    this.data = data;
    adjustSize();
    repaint();
  }

  public void setFont(Font font) {
    super.setFont(font);
    adjustSize();
  }

  public void paint(Graphics g) {

    // Determine dimensions of Bean
    Dimension size = getSize();
    int height = size.height;
    int width = size.width;

    // Draw border around the component
    g.setColor(Color.black);
    g.drawRect(0, 0, width - 1, height - 1);

    // Draw title of chart
    FontMetrics fm = g.getFontMetrics();
    int fmHeight = fm.getHeight();
    int fmWidth = fm.stringWidth(title);
    int x = (width - fmWidth)/2;
    int y = fm.getAscent();
    g.drawString(title, x, y);

    // Compute placement of Bean
    int radius = (int)(width * 0.4);
    int centerx = (int)(width * 0.5);
    x = centerx - radius;
    y += fmHeight;

    // Compute total of all data values
```

```
double total = 0;
Enumeration e = data.elements();
while(e.hasMoreElements()) {
  Data d = (Data)e.nextElement();
  total += d.getValue();
}

// Draw a circle if total is zero
if(total == 0) {
  g.drawOval(x, y, 2 * radius, 2 * radius);
}

// Draw wedges
int startAngle = 0;
e = data.elements();
while(e.hasMoreElements()) {
  Data d = (Data)e.nextElement();
  double value = d.getValue();
  if(value == 0) {
    continue;
  }
  Color color = d.getColor();
  g.setColor(color);
  int angle = (int)(360 * value/total);
  g.fillArc(x, y, 2 * radius, 2 * radius,
    startAngle, angle);
  startAngle += angle;
}
if(total > 0 && startAngle < 360) {
  g.fillArc(x, y, 2 * radius, 2 * radius,
    startAngle, 360 - startAngle);
}

// Draw legend
e = data.elements();
x = 10;
y += width;
while(e.hasMoreElements()) {
  Data d = (Data)e.nextElement();
  String name = d.getName();
  double value = d.getValue();
  Color color = d.getColor();
  g.setColor(color);
  g.fillRect(x, y, 10, 10);
  g.setColor(Color.black);
```

```
        g.drawString(name, x + 15, y + 10);
        y += fmHeight;
    }
}

public Dimension getPreferredSize() {
    Graphics g = getGraphics();
    FontMetrics fm = g.getFontMetrics();
    int fmHeight = fm.getHeight();
    Dimension d = getSize();
    int n = data.size();
    return new Dimension(d.width,
        fmHeight + d.width + fmHeight * n + 10);
}

private void adjustSize() {
    Dimension d = getPreferredSize();
    setSize(d.width, d.height);
    Component parent = getParent();
    if(parent != null) {
        parent.invalidate();
        parent.doLayout();
    }
}
}
```

The following listing shows the code for **PieCustomizer**. This is a subclass of **Panel** that allows a user to edit the name, value, and color of each of the five **Data** objects that are used to generate the pie chart.

The **NUMITEMS** constant defines the number of rows in the grid displayed by the customizer. The user interface elements in that grid are saved in the **names**, **values**, and **colors** variables. There is a button named "Apply" below the grid. When that button is pressed, the Bean is updated. The **apply** variable holds a reference to the **Button** object. The variable **pcsupport** holds a reference to a **PropertyChangeSupport** object. A reference to the Bean itself is held in the variable **pie**.

The constructor has two primary functions. First, it builds the graphical user interface by creating and arranging all of the necessary elements. Notice that the customizer is registered to receive any action events that are generated by the "Apply" button. Second, it creates a **PropertyChangeSupport** object and holds a reference to that object in the **pcsupport** variable.

The **getInsets( )** method establishes the margins for this customizer.

9

The **setObject( )** method is called by the builder tool to provide the customizer with a reference to the Bean. This is passed as the argument to that method. The customizer then reads the properties of that Bean and uses this information to update the elements in the graphical user interface.

addPropertyChangeListener( ) and **removePropertyChange Listener( )** are two methods used to register and unregister listeners that want to receive property change notifications.

The **actionPerformed( )** method is invoked when the "Apply" button is pressed. Information from the various user interface elements is used to build a new vector of **Data** objects. This vector is passed to the **setData( )** method of the Bean.

Finally, the **translate( )** method is used to process string entries from fields in the grid. Data is read from such a text field. If the user has entered a string in an incorrect format or if a negative value has been entered, this method returns zero. Otherwise, the **double** equivalent of this string is returned.

```java
package pie;
import java.awt.*;
import java.awt.event.*;
import java.beans.*;
import java.util.*;

public class PieCustomizer extends Panel
implements ActionListener, Customizer {
  private final static int NUMITEMS = 5;
  private TextField names[], values[];
  private ColorChoice colors[];
  private Button apply;
  private PropertyChangeSupport pcsupport;
  private Pie pie;

  public PieCustomizer() {

    // Initialize labels
    Label labels[] = new Label[3];
    labels[0] = new Label("Name");
    labels[1] = new Label("Value");
    labels[2] = new Label("Color");

    // Initialize names
    names = new TextField[NUMITEMS];
    for(int i = 0; i < NUMITEMS; i++) {
```

```
      names[i] = new TextField("");
   }

   // Initialize values
   values = new TextField[NUMITEMS];
   for(int i = 0; i < NUMITEMS; i++) {
      values[i] = new TextField("");
   }

   // Initialize colors
   colors = new ColorChoice[NUMITEMS];
   for(int i = 0; i < NUMITEMS; i++) {
      colors[i] = new ColorChoice();
   }

   // Initialize the "Apply" button
   apply = new Button("Apply");
   apply.addActionListener(this);

   // Arrange GUI elements
   setLayout(new BorderLayout());
   Panel pc = new Panel();
   pc.setLayout(new GridLayout(NUMITEMS + 1, 3, 5, 5));
   pc.add(labels[0]);
   pc.add(labels[1]);
   pc.add(labels[2]);
   for(int i = 0; i < NUMITEMS; i++) {
      pc.add(names[i]);
      pc.add(values[i]);
      pc.add(colors[i]);
   }
   add("Center", pc);
   Panel ps = new Panel();
   ps.add(apply);
   add("South", ps);
   setSize(300, 180);

   // Create a PropertyChangeSupport object
   pcsupport = new PropertyChangeSupport(this);
}

public Insets getInsets() {
   return new Insets(10, 10, 10, 10);
}
```

9

```java
public void setObject(Object object) {

  // Save reference to the Pie object
  pie = (Pie)object;

  // Get data from the pie object
  Vector data = pie.getData();
  Enumeration e = data.elements();
  int i = 0;
  while(e.hasMoreElements()) {
    Data d = (Data)e.nextElement();
    names[i].setText(d.getName());
    values[i].setText("" + d.getValue());
    colors[i].setColor(d.getColor());
    i++;
  }
}

public void
addPropertyChangeListener(PropertyChangeListener pcl) {
  pcsupport.addPropertyChangeListener(pcl);
}

public void
removePropertyChangeListener(PropertyChangeListener pcl) {
  pcsupport.removePropertyChangeListener(pcl);
}

public void actionPerformed(ActionEvent ae) {
  if(ae.getSource() == apply) {

    // Process the information from the GUI elements
    Vector data = new Vector();
    for(int i = 0; i < NUMITEMS; i++) {
      String name = names[i].getText();
      double value = translate(values[i]);
      Color color = colors[i].getColor();
      data.addElement(new Data(name, value, color));
    }

    // Update the Bean
    pie.setData(data);
  }
}
```

```
private double translate(TextField tf) {
  // Convert the string entry in a text field
  // to a double
  String s = tf.getText();
  double d;
  try {
    d = Double.valueOf(s).doubleValue();
  }
  catch(NumberFormatException e) {
    tf.setText("0");
    return 0;
  }
  if(d < 0) {
    tf.setText("0");
    return 0;
  }
  return d;
}
}
```

The following listing shows the code for the **ColorChoice** class. You have already seen that this was one of the elements used to build the user interface of the customizer. It allowed the user to select the color of a wedge in the pie chart.

The static variable **colorMap** holds a **Hashtable** that is used to map from a user-friendly string to a **Color** object. The static variable **n** is used to select an initial value for each **ColorChoice** object.

The constructor obtains the keys of the hash table and invokes the **addItem( )** method of the superclass to add this string to the set of available colors. It then selects a color to initialize the choice element. (Note: If this was not done, all **ColorChoice** elements would always be initialized to the first entry. This is inconvenient for the user because he or she would need to manually change some of these colors so that the different wedges in the pie chart are distinguishable.)

The **getColor( )** method returns a **Color** object that corresponds to the selection made by the user. This is invoked when the customizer generates a vector of **Data** objects for the Bean.

The **setColor( )** method is invoked after the customizer reads a vector of **Data** objects from the Bean. The private **findKey( )** method is used to search the hash table entries for the string corresponding to a specific **Color** object.

9

```
package pie;
import java.awt.*;
import java.util.*;

public class ColorChoice extends Choice {
  private static Hashtable colorMap;
  static {
    colorMap = new Hashtable();
    colorMap.put("black", Color.black);
    colorMap.put("blue", Color.blue);
    colorMap.put("cyan", Color.cyan);
    colorMap.put("dark gray", Color.darkGray);
    colorMap.put("gray", Color.gray);
    colorMap.put("green", Color.green);
    colorMap.put("light gray", Color.lightGray);
    colorMap.put("magenta", Color.magenta);
    colorMap.put("orange", Color.orange);
    colorMap.put("pink", Color.pink);
    colorMap.put("red", Color.red);
    colorMap.put("white", Color.white);
    colorMap.put("yellow", Color.yellow);
  }
  private static int n = 0;

  public ColorChoice() {

    // Initialize the entries in the choice
    Enumeration e = colorMap.keys();
    while(e.hasMoreElements()) {
      String str = (String)e.nextElement();
      addItem(str);
    }

    // Select a color
    select(n++);
    if(n >= colorMap.size()) {
      n = 0;
    }
  }

  public Color getColor() {
    return (Color)colorMap.get(getSelectedItem());
  }

  public void setColor(Color color) {
```

```
      select(findKey(color));
  }

  private String findKey(Color color) {
    Enumeration e = colorMap.keys();
    while(e.hasMoreElements()) {
      Object key = e.nextElement();
      if(color.equals(colorMap.get(key))) {
        return (String)key;
      }
    }
    return null;
  }
}
```

The following listing shows the code for **PieBeanInfo**. It extends
SimpleBeanInfo and overrides the **getBeanDescriptor( )** method to
return a **BeanDescriptor** object for this Bean. The **BeanDescriptor**
constructor used in the program accepts two arguments. The first is the
class of the Bean and the second is the class of the customizer. This is the
mechanism used to associate a customizer with a component.

```
package pie;
import java.beans.*;

public class PieBeanInfo extends SimpleBeanInfo {

  public BeanDescriptor getBeanDescriptor() {
    return new BeanDescriptor(Pie.class,
      PieCustomizer.class);
  }
}
```

9

The code for the **Data** class is shown in the following listing. Its purpose is
to encapsulate all of the information (namely name, value, and color) for an
entry in the pie chart. This information is held in the **name**, **value**, and
color variables which are initialized by the constructor. Notice that the class
implements the **Serializable** interface. This is required because the Bean
holds references to **Data** objects.

```
package pie;
import java.awt.*;
import java.io.*;
```

```
public class Data implements Serializable {
  private String name;
  private double value;
  private Color color;

  public Data(String name, double value, Color color) {
    this.name = name;
    this.value = value;
    this.color = color;
  }

  public String getName() {
    return name;
  }

  public double getValue() {
    return value;
  }

  public Color getColor() {
    return color;
  }

  public void setName(String name) {
    this.name = name;
  }

  public void setValue(double value) {
    this.value = value;
  }

  public void setColor(Color color) {
    this.color = color;
  }
}
```

You may wish to enhance the customizer for this Bean so that it includes the other properties used by this Bean (for example, font, background, and foreground colors).

CHAPTER 10

Remote Method Invocation (RMI)

Remote Method Invocation (RMI) allows a Java object that executes on one machine to invoke a method of a Java object that executes on another machine. This is an important feature because it allows you to build distributed applications.

The chapter begins by providing a brief overview of the architecture of RMI. A simple client/server application illustrates how to write such programs. Another example demonstrates how objects can be passed as arguments to remote method calls or returned as values. A broadcast application is then constructed that allows a server to initiate communication to a set of listeners. These examples lead you step by step through the entire process of using RMI to build and test distributed Java applications. After this introduction is complete, you are then ready to build a Bean that uses RMI to communicate with a server. Finally, some concluding comments about other RMI capabilities are included.

An Overview of RMI

A remote object implements one or more remote interfaces.

To understand how RMI works, you must appreciate the roles of *stubs* and *skeletons* as depicted in Figure 10-1. Here, an object C on machine 1 wants to call a method provided by object S on machine 2. Object S is a *remote object*. In other words, it implements one or more *remote interfaces* that contain methods which can be invoked by Java objects on other machines.

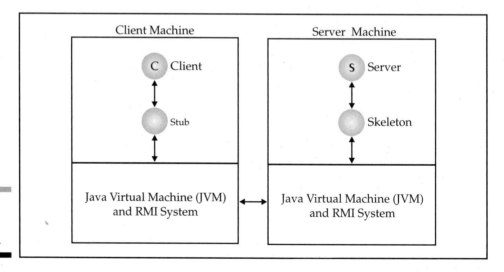

Stubs and skeletons

Figure 10-1.

A stub executes on a client machine and acts as a proxy for a remote object.

However, because object S is in a different address space on a separate machine, object C cannot simply invoke such a method directly. Instead, a stub is provided that executes in the same address space as object C. This acts as a proxy or surrogate for the remote object S. The stub has three primary responsibilities. First, it presents the same remote interfaces as object S. Therefore, from the perspective of object C, the stub is equivalent to the remote object. Second, the stub works with the JVM and RMI system on machine 1 to serialize any arguments to a remote method call and send this information to machine 2. Finally, the stub receives any result from the remote method invocation and returns this to object C.

A skeleton executes on a server machine.

On machine 2, the skeleton has three primary responsibilities. First, it receives the remote method call and any associated arguments. It works with the JVM and RMI system on machine 2 to deserialize any arguments for this remote method call. Second, it invokes the appropriate method of object S with these arguments. Finally, the skeleton receives any return value from this method call and works with the JVM and RMI system on machine 2 to serialize this return value and send this information back to machine 1.

The object serialization facilities examined earlier in this book are used here to send objects from one machine to another. Objects can be supplied as arguments to a remote method call or returned as results from it.

Stubs and skeletons are generated by a utility called the RMI compiler. The examples in this chapter show you how to use this tool.

At this point, you may be asking: How does object C get a reference to the correct stub for object S? There are two parts to the answer.

First, an object called the *Registry* maintains the mapping from names to remote object references. For example, object S can register itself with the name "DivideServer."

10

Second, a remote object is named via a URL that uses the **rmi** protocol. The form of such a URL is:

rmi://*host:port*/*server*

Here, *host* is the IP address or name of the server machine on which object S resides, *port* is the optional port number of the Registry on that machine, and *server* is the name of the remote server.

Therefore, if object C wants to contact object S on the machine with IP address a.b.c.d, it can obtain a stub for that remote object by asking the Registry for a reference to the URL shown here:

rmi://a.b.c.d/DivideServer

Once object C has a reference to the stub for object S, it can issue method calls to the stub.

The Registry maps names to remote object references.

The Java garbage collection facilities also work in a distributed application. Remote objects that are no longer referenced are automatically deleted.

Let us look at some of the classes and interfaces that provide this functionality.

The Remote Interface

The **Remote** interface in the **java.rmi** package defines no constants or methods. It exists only to designate which interfaces are remote. Every remote interface must directly or indirectly extend **java.rmi.Remote**. Only remote interfaces can be invoked via RMI. Local interfaces cannot be called in this manner.

The Naming Class

The **Naming** class in the **java.rmi** package provides three methods to associate names with remote objects. These are:

static void bind(String *name*, Remote *robj*)
  throws AlreadyBoundException, MalformedURLException

static void rebind(String *name*, Remote *robj*)
  throws RemoteException

static void unbind(String *name*)
  throws MalformedURLException, NotBoundException, RemoteException

Here, *name* is the name of the remote object and *robj* is a reference to that object. The **bind( )** method associates a name with a remote object. However, if the name is already used in the Registry, an **AlreadyBoundException** is thrown. The **rebind( )** method also associates a name with a remote object. If the name is already used in the Registry, the existing binding is replaced. Finally, the **unbind( )** method removes the binding for *name*.

In addition, the **lookup( )** method is used to obtain a reference for a remote object. It has the form:

    static Remote lookup(String *url*)
      throws MalformedURLException, NotBoundException,
      RemoteException, UnknownHostException

Here, *url* is the string equivalent of a URL that uses the **rmi** protocol.

The RemoteObject Class

The **RemoteObject** class in the **java.rmi.server** package extends **java.lang.Object** and overrides the **equals( )**, **hashCode( )**, and **toString( )** methods to provide correct behavior for remote objects.

The RemoteServer Class

The **RemoteServer** class in the **java.rmi.server** package extends **RemoteObject**. It is an abstract class that defines the methods needed to create and export remote objects.

The UnicastRemoteObject Class

The **UnicastRemoteObject** class in the **java.rmi.server** package is a concrete subclass of **RemoteServer**. To make a remote object, you extend this class.

10

The RemoteException Class

There are numerous problems that can be encountered at run time by a distributed application. For example, communication between machines can fail, a stub or skeleton may be missing, or difficulty can be encountered when serializing or deserializing arguments or return values. These and other types of faults cause the RMI subsystem to generate an exception.

The **RemoteException** class in the **java.rmi** package is a subclass of **IOException**. More than one dozen subclasses of **RemoteException** exist to express the various problems that can be encountered. Although there is not space in this chapter to look at these subclasses in detail, it is valuable to know they exist.

Building a Simple Client/Server Application

This section describes how to build a simple client/server application by using RMI. The server receives a request from a client, processes it, and returns a result. In this example, the request includes two **double** numbers. The server divides these and returns the result. Follow the steps described in the following sections to build and test this software.

Enter and Compile the Source Code

There are four source files for this example. The file DivideServer.java defines the remote interface that is provided by the server. It contains one method that accepts two **double** arguments and returns the value computed by dividing the first argument by the second argument. All remote interfaces must extend the **Remote** interface and all remote methods can throw a **RemoteException**.

```
package divide;
import java.rmi.*;

public interface DivideServer extends Remote {

  double divide(double d1, double d2) throws RemoteException;
}
```

The file DivideServerImpl.java implements the remote interface. The implementation of the **divide( )** method is straightforward. All remote objects must extend **UnicastRemoteObject**. That class provides functionality which is needed to make objects available from remote machines.

```
package divide;
import java.rmi.*;
import java.rmi.server.*;

public class DivideServerImpl
extends UnicastRemoteObject implements DivideServer {

  public DivideServerImpl()
  throws RemoteException {
  }
```

```
  public double divide(double d1, double d2)
  throws RemoteException {
    return d1 / d2;
  }
}
```

The file DivideServerApp.java contains the main program for the server machine. Its primary function is to update the RMI registry on that machine. This is done by using the **rebind( )** method of the **Naming** class. That method associates a name with an object reference. The first argument to the **rebind( )** method is a string that names the server as "DivideServer." Its second argument is an instance of **DivideServerImpl**.

```
package divide;
import java.net.*;
import java.rmi.*;

public class DivideServerApp {

  public static void main(String args[]) {
    try {
      DivideServerImpl divideServerImpl;
      divideServerImpl = new DivideServerImpl();
      Naming.rebind("DivideServer", divideServerImpl);
    }
    catch(Exception ex) {
      ex.printStackTrace();
    }
  }
}
```

10

The file DivideClient.java implements the client side of this distributed application. It requires three command line arguments. The first is the IP address or name of the server machine. The second and third arguments are the numbers to be divided.

The application begins by forming a string that follows the URL syntax. This URL uses the **rmi** protocol. It includes the IP address or name of the server and the string "DivideServer." It then invokes the **lookup( )** method of the **Naming** class. This accepts one argument that is the **rmi** URL and returns a reference to an object of type **Remote** which is then cast to a **DivideServer**. All remote method invocations can then be directed to this object.

The program continues by displaying its arguments and then invokes the remote **divide( )** method. The result returned from this method is displayed.

```
package divide;
import java.rmi.*;

public class DivideClient {

  public static void main(String args[]) {
    try {

      // Make rmi URL to name DivideServer
      String divideServerURL;
      divideServerURL = "rmi://" + args[0] + "/DivideServer";

      // Obtain a reference to that remote object
      DivideServer divideServer;
      divideServer = (DivideServer)Naming.lookup(divideServerURL);

      // Display numbers
      System.out.println("The first number is: " + args[1]);
      double d1 = Double.valueOf(args[1]).doubleValue();
      System.out.println("The second number is: " + args[2]);
      double d2 = Double.valueOf(args[2]).doubleValue();

      // Invoke remote method and display result
      double result = divideServer.divide(d1, d2);
      System.out.println("The result is: " + result);
    }
    catch(Exception ex) {
      ex.printStackTrace();
    }
  }
}
```

Use **javac** to compile the four source files you created.

Generate Stubs and Skeletons

To generate stubs and skeletons, you use a tool called the RMI compiler. To generate the stub and skeleton for **DivideServerImpl**, use this command line:

```
rmic -d . divide.DivideServerImpl
```

The -d option specifies the root of the class directory. In this case, the current directory is the root.

This command generates files named DivideServerImpl_Skel.class and DivideServerImpl_Stub.class in the divide subdirectory.

Install Files on the Client and Server Machines

At this point, six .class files have been created. Copy these files to a directory named "divide" on the server and to a directory named "divide" on the client. Not all of these .class files are actually needed on both the client and server machines. But, for the simple examples presented in this chapter, it is easier to just copy all the .class files and avoid any problem.

NOTE: The preferred configuration for testing this example requires two machines connected to a LAN. However, it is easy to execute this software with one stand-alone machine. Use IP address 127.0.0.1 to refer to your local machine.

Start the RMI Registry on the Server Machine

The RMI Registry maps names to object references. Start the RMI Registry on the server machine from the command line as shown here:

```
start rmiregistry
```

An empty window appears. Its title is the path of the rmiregistry.exe file.

10

Start the Server

Start the server code from the command line as shown here:

```
java divide.DivideServerApp
```

Recall that **DivideServerApp** instantiates **DivideServerImpl** and registers that object with the name "DivideServer."

Start the Client

The **DivideClient** software requires three arguments: the name or IP address of the server machine and the two numbers to be divided. You may invoke it from the command line by using one of the two formats shown here:

```
java divide.DivideClient server1 8 2
```

```
java divide.DivideClient 127.0.0.1 8 2
```

In the first line, the name of the server is provided. The second line uses its IP address (e.g. 127.0.0.1).

In either case, sample output from this program is shown here:

```
The first number is: 8
The second number is: 2
The result is: 4.0
```

Note that if you divide 0 by 0 the result is "NaN" which means "Not a Number." If you divide 1 by 0 the result is "Infinity."

Remote Method Arguments and Return Values

The server in the previous example had one remote interface. Its one method accepted two **double** arguments and returned a **double** result. Simple types such as these are passed by value from one machine to another.

What happens if a remote method accepts objects as arguments or returns an object as a result? The answer depends on whether the object is a remote object or a local object. (Remote objects are defined as those that implement remote interfaces. Local objects do not.) You will see that local objects are exchanged by value but remote objects are exchanged by reference.

This section presents an example that shows how a local object can be passed from one machine to another as a return value. It is also a client/server configuration. The client prompts the user for the three coefficients to a quadratic equation of the form shown here:

$$ax^2 + bx + c = 0.$$

The coefficients are sent as arguments to a remote method on the server. The server solves the quadratic equation and returns an array of two objects. Each of these objects is a complex number and represents a root of the quadratic equation. The quadratic equation is solved using the quadratic formula shown next:

$$d = \text{Math.sqrt}(b^2 - 4 \times a \times c)$$
$$x0 = (-b + d)/(2 \times a)$$
$$x1 = (-b - d)/(2 \times a)$$

Here, x0 and x1 are the complex roots of the quadratic equation.

In this example, you will also see that local objects exchanged between machines must be serializable. Follow the steps described in the following sections to build and test this software.

Enter and Compile the Source Code

There are five source files for this example. The file QuadraticServer.java defines one remote interface provided by the server. It contains one method that accepts three **double** arguments and returns an array of two **Complex** objects that are the roots of the quadratic equation.

```
package quadratic;
import java.rmi.*;

public interface QuadraticServer extends Remote {

  Complex[] solve(double a, double b, double c)
  throws RemoteException;
}
```

10

The file **Complex.java** encapsulates the real and imaginary components of a complex number. The **toString( )** method returns a **String** object that represents a complex number. Note that this class implements the **Serializable** interface. This is necessary because **Complex** objects generated on the server must be returned to the client.

```
package quadratic;
import java.io.*;

public class Complex implements Serializable {
  private double real, imaginary;

  public Complex(double real, double imaginary) {
    this.real = real;
```

```
    this.imaginary = imaginary;
  }

  public String toString() {
    String sr = "" + real;
    String si = "" + imaginary;
    if(si.startsWith("-")) {
      return sr + si + "i";
    }
    else {
      return sr + "+" + si + "i";
    }
  }
}
```

The file QuadraticServerImpl.java implements the remote interface. The implementation of the **solve( )** method is straightforward. All remote objects must extend **UnicastRemoteObject**. It provides functionality that is needed to make objects available from remote machines.

```
package quadratic;
import java.rmi.*;
import java.rmi.server.*;

public class QuadraticServerImpl
extends UnicastRemoteObject implements QuadraticServer {

  public QuadraticServerImpl()
  throws RemoteException {
  }

  public Complex[] solve(double a, double b, double c)
  throws RemoteException {
    Complex roots[] = new Complex[2];
    double d = b * b - 4 * a * c;
    if(d > 0) {
      d = Math.sqrt(d);
      roots[0] = new Complex((-b + d)/(2 * a), 0);
      roots[1] = new Complex((-b - d)/(2 * a), 0);
    }
    else {
      d = Math.sqrt(-d);
      double e = -b/(2 * a);
      double f = d/(2 * a);
```

```
      roots[0] = new Complex(e, f);
      roots[1] = new Complex(e, -f);
    }
    return roots;
  }
}
```

The file QuadraticServerApp.java contains the main program for the server machine. Its primary function is to update the RMI registry on that machine. This is done by using the **rebind( )** method of the **Naming** class. That method associates a name with an object reference. The first argument to the **rebind( )** method is a string that names the server as "QuadraticServer." Its second argument is a reference to an instance of **QuadraticServerImpl**.

```
package quadratic;
import java.rmi.*;

public class QuadraticServerApp {

  public static void main(String args[]) {
    try {
      QuadraticServerImpl quadraticServerImpl;
      quadraticServerImpl = new QuadraticServerImpl();
      Naming.rebind("QuadraticServer", quadraticServerImpl);
    }
    catch(Exception ex) {
      ex.printStackTrace();
    }
  }
}
```

10

The file QuadraticClient.java implements the client side of this distributed application. It requires four command line arguments. The first is the IP address or name of the server machine. The second, third, and fourth arguments are the coefficients of the x^2, x^1, and x^0 terms of the quadratic equation.

The application begins by forming a string that follows the URL syntax. This URL uses the **rmi** protocol. It includes the IP address or name of the server and the string "QuadraticServer." It then invokes the **lookup( )** method of the **Naming** class. This accepts one argument that is the **rmi** URL and returns a reference to an object of type **Remote** which is then cast to a **QuadraticServer**. All remote method invocations can then be directed to this object.

The program continues by displaying its arguments and then invokes the remote **solve( )** method. Results from this method are displayed.

```java
package quadratic;
import java.rmi.*;

public class QuadraticClient {

  public static void main(String args[]) {
    try {

      // Make rmi URL to name QuadraticServer
      String quadraticServerURL;
      quadraticServerURL =
        "rmi://" + args[0] + "/QuadraticServer";

      // Obtain a reference to that remote object
      QuadraticServer quadraticServer;
      quadraticServer =
        (QuadraticServer)Naming.lookup(quadraticServerURL);

      // Display coefficients
      double a = Double.valueOf(args[1]).doubleValue();
      double b = Double.valueOf(args[2]).doubleValue();
      double c = Double.valueOf(args[3]).doubleValue();
      System.out.println("The coefficients are:");
      System.out.println("\ta = " + a);
      System.out.println("\tb = " + b);
      System.out.println("\tc = " + c);

      // Invoke remote method and display results
      Complex results[] = quadraticServer.solve(a, b, c);
      System.out.println("The results are:");
      System.out.println("\t" + results[0]);
      System.out.println("\t" + results[1]);
    }
    catch(Exception ex) {
      ex.printStackTrace();
    }
  }
}
```

Use **javac** to compile the four source files you created.

Generate Stubs and Skeletons

To generate stubs and skeletons for **QuadraticServerImpl** use the command line here:

    rmic -d . quadratic.QuadraticServerImpl

This command generates files named QuadraticServerImpl_Skel.class and QuadraticServerImpl_Stub.class in the quadratic subdirectory.

Install Files on the Client and Server Machines

At this point, seven .class files have been created. Copy these files to a directory named "quadratic" on the server and to a directory named "quadratic" on the client.

Start the RMI Registry on the Server Machine

The RMI Registry maps names to object references. Start the RMI Registry on the server machine from the command line as shown here:

    start rmiregistry

Start the Server

Start the server code from the command line as shown here:

    java quadratic.QuadraticServerApp

Recall that **QuadraticServerApp** instantiates **QuadraticServerImpl** and registers that object with the name "QuadraticServer."

10

Start the Client

The **QuadraticClient** software requires four arguments: the IP address or name of the server machine and the three numbers that are the coefficients of the quadratic equation. You may invoke it from the command line by using one of the two formats shown here:

    java quadratic.QuadraticClient server1 8 2 7

    java quadratic.QuadraticClient 127.0.0.1 8 2 7

In the first line, the name of the server is provided. The second line uses its IP address (e.g., 127.0.0.1).

In either case, sample output from this program is shown here:

```
The coefficients are:
   a = 8.0
   b = 2.0
   c = 7.0
The results are:
   -0.125+0.9270248108869579i
   -0.125-0.9270248108869579i
```

Building a Broadcast Application

The previous examples showed how to build an application in which clients initiate communication with the server. There was one remote interface that was implemented by the server. It defined a method that clients could invoke.

This section shows how to build an application in which a server broadcasts messages to a set of clients. The example uses two remote interfaces. Clients implement an interface to receive messages from a server. The server implements an interface so clients may register to receive those messages. Follow the steps described in the following sections to build and test this software.

Enter and Compile the Source Code

There are six source files for this example. The file BroadcastServer.java defines the remote interface that is provided by the server. It contains two methods that allow clients to add and remove themselves from the set of listeners that receive broadcast messages.

```java
package broadcast;
import java.rmi.*;

public interface BroadcastServer extends Remote {

  void addBroadcastListener(BroadcastListener bl)
  throws RemoteException;

  void removeBroadcastListener(BroadcastListener bl)
  throws RemoteException;
}
```

The file BroadcastListener.java defines the remote interface that is provided by the client. It contains one method that allows the client to receive messages from the server.

```
package broadcast;
import java.rmi.*;

public interface BroadcastListener extends Remote {

  public void receiveBroadcast(String message)
  throws RemoteException;
}
```

The file BroadcastServerImpl.java implements the remote interface of the server. References to the clients that register to receive messages are held in the variable **listeners**. A reference to the thread that continually prompts the user for a message to be broadcast is held in the variable **thread**. The constructor initializes both of these variables and starts the thread.

The **addBroadcastlistener( )** and **removeBroadcastListener( )** methods update the set of clients that are registered to receive messages.

The **run( )** method executes an infinite loop that prompts the user for a message and broadcasts that string to the clients. Most of the work is done by the **sendMessage( )** method. It first makes a clone of the **listeners** vector. This is done in a **synchronized** block to avoid problems if a client is concurrently trying to register or unregister as a listener. Then it invokes the **receiveBroadcast( )** method of each client and passes the message as an argument to this method.

```
package broadcast;
import java.io.*;
import java.rmi.*;
import java.rmi.server.*;
import java.util.*;

public class BroadcastServerImpl
extends UnicastRemoteObject
implements BroadcastServer, Runnable {
  private Vector listeners;
  private Thread thread;

  public BroadcastServerImpl() throws RemoteException {
    listeners = new Vector();
```

10

```
  thread = new Thread(this);
  thread.start();
}

public void addBroadcastListener(BroadcastListener bl)
throws RemoteException {
  listeners.addElement(bl);
}

public void removeBroadcastListener(BroadcastListener bl)
throws RemoteException {
  listeners.removeElement(bl);
}

public void run() {
  try {
    InputStreamReader isr;
    isr = new InputStreamReader(System.in);
    BufferedReader br;
    br = new BufferedReader(isr);
    while(true) {
      String p = "Enter the message to be broadcast:";
      System.out.println(p);
      String s = br.readLine();
      if(s == null) {
        return;
      }
      sendMessage(s);
    }
  }
  catch(Exception ex) {
    ex.printStackTrace();
  }
}

protected void sendMessage(String message) {

  // v1 = a clone of the listeners vector
  // v2 = a new vector
  Vector v1, v2;
  synchronized(this) {
    v1 = (Vector)listeners.clone();
  }
  v2 = new Vector();
```

```
      // Broadcast the message to these listeners
      Enumeration e1 = v1.elements();
      while(e1.hasMoreElements()) {
        BroadcastListener b1;
        b1 = (BroadcastListener)e1.nextElement();
        try {
          b1.receiveBroadcast(message);
        }
        catch(Exception ex) {
          v2.addElement(b1);
        }
      }

      // Remove listeners that caused exceptions
      Enumeration e2 = v2.elements();
      while(e2.hasMoreElements()) {
        listeners.removeElement(e2.nextElement());
      }
    }
  }
}
```

The file BroadcastListenerImpl.java implements the remote interface of the client. It displays any message that is received.

```
package broadcast;
import java.rmi.*;
import java.rmi.server.*;

public class BroadcastListenerImpl
extends UnicastRemoteObject
implements BroadcastListener {

  public BroadcastListenerImpl()
  throws RemoteException {
  }

  public void receiveBroadcast(String message)
  throws RemoteException {
    System.out.println("Message = " + message);
  }
}
```

10

The file BroadcastServerApp.java contains the main program for the server machine. Its primary function is to update the RMI registry on that machine.

This is done by using the **rebind( )** method of the **Naming** class. That method associates a name with an object reference. The first argument to the **rebind( )** method is a string that names the server as "BroadcastServer." Its second argument is a reference to an instance of **BroadcastServerImpl**.

```
package broadcast;
import java.net.*;
import java.rmi.*;

public class BroadcastServerApp {

  public static void main(String args[]) {
    try {
      BroadcastServerImpl bsi;
      bsi = new BroadcastServerImpl();
      Naming.rebind("BroadcastServer", bsi);
    }
    catch(Exception ex) {
      ex.printStackTrace();
    }
  }
}
```

The file BroadcastClient.java implements the client side of this distributed application. It requires one command line argument. That is the IP address or name of the server machine.

The application begins by forming a string that follows the URL syntax. This URL uses the **rmi** protocol. It includes the IP address or name of the server and the string "BroadcastServer." It then invokes the **lookup( )** method of the **Naming** class. This accepts one argument that is the **rmi** URL and returns a reference to an object of type **Remote** which is then cast to a **BroadcastServer**. All remote method invocations can then be directed to this object.

The program then instantiates **BroadcastListenerImpl**. This is the object that implements the remote interface of the client. Finally, the client registers to receive messages by calling the **addBroadcastListener( )** method of the server and passing a reference to the **BroadcastListenerImpl** object.

```
package broadcast;
import java.rmi.*;

public class BroadcastClient {
```

```
    private static BroadcastListenerImpl bli;

    public static void main(String args[]) {
      try {

// Make rmi URL to BroadcastServer
        String broadcastServerURL;
        broadcastServerURL =
          "rmi://" + args[0] + "/BroadcastServer";

        // Obtain a reference to that remote object
        BroadcastServer broadcastServer =
          (BroadcastServer)Naming.lookup(broadcastServerURL);
        bli = new BroadcastListenerImpl();
        broadcastServer.addBroadcastListener(bli);
      }
      catch(Exception ex) {
        ex.printStackTrace();
      }
    }
}
```

Use **javac** to compile the six source files you created.

Generate Stubs and Skeletons

You must generate stubs and skeletons for both the remote client and remote
server objects. This can be done via the following commands:

> rmic -d . Broadcast.BroadcastListenerImpl

> rmic -d . broadcast.BroadcastServerImpl

10

This command generates files named BroadcastListenerImpl_Skel.class,
BroadcastListenerImpl_Stub.class, BroadcastServerImpl_Skel.class, and
BroadcastServerImpl_Stub.class in the broadcast subdirectory.

Install Files on the Client and Server Machines

At this point, ten .class files have been created. Copy these files to a directory
named "broadcast" on the server and to a directory named "broadcast" on
the client.

Start the RMI Registry on the Server Machine

The RMI Registry maps names to object references. Start the RMI Registry on the server machine from the command line as shown here:

    start rmiregistry

Start the Server

Start the server code from the command line as shown here:

    java broadcast.BroadcastServerApp

Recall that **BroadcastServerApp** instantiates **BroadcastServerImpl** and registers that object with the name "BroadcastServer."

The server software then prompts the user for a message to broadcast. The prompt appears as:

```
Enter the message to be broadcast:
```

When the user types a string and presses the ENTER key, the message is transmitted and another prompt is presented. This continues indefinitely. The program terminates when an empty string is entered.

Start the Client

The **BroadcastClient** software requires one argument: the name or IP address of the server machine. You may invoke it from the command line by using one of the two formats shown here:

    java broadcast.BroadcastClient server1

    java broadcast.BroadcastClient 127.0.0.1

In the first line, the name of the server is provided. The second line uses its IP address (e.g., 127.0.0.1).

In either case, sample output from this program is shown here:

```
Message = 12345
```

Using RMI in a Bean

This section develops a Bean named **NetworkCanvas**. The component displays a map and shows a set of links connecting some of the major cities. These links can represent telecommunication links, train routes, utility lines, or any other connectivity between the cities. Each link is colored either green or red. A green link is operational and a red one has some problem. The Bean has one property named **address**. This is the IP address or name of the server from which both link configuration and status information is obtained. As the operational status of these links change, the map is dynamically updated with this information. Figure 10-2 shows how this component appears.

In addition, this section develops an application named **NetworkServerApp** which simulates a maintenance center. It provides a simple command line interface through which an administrator can change the operational status of any link.

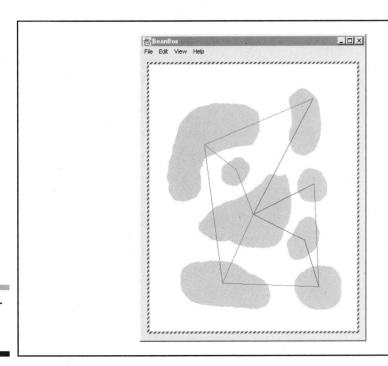

The **Network-Canvas** Bean

Figure 10-2.

10

Both the Bean and the server application in this example are RMI servers. Follow the steps described in the following sections to build and test this software.

Enter Configuration Files

There are two text files that define locations of the major cities on the map and the links that connect them.

The file cities.txt is shown in the following listing. Each line contains the name of a city followed by the x and y coordinates where it is located on the map. (The map itself is in the file map.gif.)

```
A,314,64
B,316,224
C,325,417
D,297,329
E,140,410
F,199,281
G,167,197
H,106,150
```

The file links.txt is shown in the following listing. Each line contains the name of two cities that are connected by a link.

```
A,F
B,F
D,F
D,C
B,C
E,C
E,F
E,H
G,F
G,H
A,H
```

Enter and Compile the Source Code

There are eleven source files for this example. The file NetworkServer.java defines the remote interface provided by the server. It contains two methods that allow clients to add and remove themselves from the set of listeners that receive broadcast messages. In addition, the **getLinks( )** method can be called by a client to get the configuration and status information for all links.

```
package network;
import java.rmi.*;
import java.util.*;

public interface NetworkServer extends Remote {

    public void addNetworkListener(NetworkListener nl)
    throws RemoteException;

    public void removeNetworkListener(NetworkListener nl)
    throws RemoteException;

    public Vector getLinks()
    throws RemoteException;
}
```

The file NetworkListener.java defines the remote interface that is provided by the client. It contains one method that allows the client to receive notifications about link changes from the server.

```
package network;
import java.rmi.*;

public interface NetworkListener extends Remote {

    void linkChange(LinkEvent le) throws RemoteException;
}
```

The file LinkEvent.java defines a custom event. Its constructor accepts three arguments: the source of the event, the ID of the link, and the operational status of the link. The link ID is contained in the variable **linkId** and the operational status is contained in the **boolean** variable **operational**.

```
package network;
import java.util.*;

public class LinkEvent extends EventObject {
    private int linkId;
    private boolean operational;

    public LinkEvent(NetworkServer source,
    int linkId, boolean operational) {
        super(source);
        this.linkId = linkId;
        this.operational = operational;
```

10

```
  }

  public int getLinkId() {
    return linkId;
  }

  public boolean getOperational() {
    return operational;
  }
}
```

The file Link.java defines a link between two cities. The static variable **links** is a vector that holds references to all of the **Link** objects. (This technique of having the class keep track of its instances is one that has been seen previously in this book.) The variables **city1** and **city2** are the names of two cities connected by a link and the **operational** variable records the status of that link. The static **getLinks( )** method returns the **links** variable.

The constructor accepts three arguments: the names of the two cities and the operational status of the link. These are saved in the variables **city1**, **city2**, and **operational**. The access methods for these variables follow the constructor. Note that **city1** and **city2** are read-only but **operational** can also be written.

```
package network;
import java.io.*;
import java.util.*;

public class Link implements Serializable {
  private static Vector links = new Vector();
  private String city1, city2;
  private boolean operational;

  public static Vector getLinks() {
    return links;
  }

  public Link(String city1, String city2,
  boolean operational) {
    this.city1 = city1;
    this.city2 = city2;
    this.operational = operational;
    links.addElement(this);
  }
```

```
public String getCity1() {
  return city1;
}

public String getCity2() {
  return city2;
}

public boolean getOperational() {
  return operational;
}

public void setOperational(boolean operational) {
  this.operational = operational;
}
}
```

The file NetworkServerImpl.java implements the remote interface of the server. The variable **listeners** holds references to the clients that register to receive notifications about link changes.

The **addNetworkListener( )** and **removeNetworkListener( )** methods update the set of clients that are registered to receive link updates. The **getLinks( )** method returns a vector of all **Link** objects. This is obtained by calling the static **getLinks( )** method of the **Link** class.

The **generateLinkEvent( )** method is called when a user of the server application updates the status of a link. A **LinkEvent** object is created and **fireLinkEvent( )** is invoked to multicast it.

The **fireLinkEvent( )** method multicasts a **LinkEvent** object to all registered listeners. A clone of the **listeners** vector is made inside a **synchronized** block. This avoids problems in case an attempt is made to register or unregister a listener at the same time. The **LinkEvent** object is then multicast to these listeners. Note the remote **linkChange( )** method is invoked for each **NetworkListener**. If an exception occurs during this remote method invocation, that listener is added to vector **v2**. Finally, the listeners in **v2** are removed from the **listeners** vector. (If a remote Bean terminates, a reference to that **NetworkListener** is still contained in the **listeners** vector. By removing such an entry, you can avoid generating repeated exceptions.)

```
package network;
import java.rmi.*;
import java.rmi.server.*;
```

```
import java.util.*;

public class NetworkServerImpl
extends UnicastRemoteObject implements NetworkServer {
  private Vector listeners;

  public NetworkServerImpl()
  throws RemoteException {
    listeners = new Vector();
  }

  public void addNetworkListener(NetworkListener nl)
  throws RemoteException {
    listeners.addElement(nl);
  }

  public void removeNetworkListener(NetworkListener nl)
  throws RemoteException {
    listeners.removeElement(nl);
  }

  public Vector getLinks()
  throws RemoteException {
    return Link.getLinks();
  }

  public void generateLinkEvent(int id, boolean operational) {
    Vector links = Link.getLinks();
    Link link = (Link)links.elementAt(id);
    link.setOperational(operational);
    LinkEvent le = new LinkEvent(this, id, operational);
    fireLinkEvent(le);
  }

  private void fireLinkEvent(LinkEvent le) {

    // v1 = a clone of the listeners vector
    // v2 = a new vector
    Vector v1, v2;
    synchronized(this) {
      v1 = (Vector)listeners.clone();
    }
    v2 = new Vector();

    // Broadcast the message to these listeners
```

```
Enumeration e1 = v1.elements();
while(e1.hasMoreElements()) {
  NetworkListener nl = (NetworkListener)e1.nextElement();
  try {
    nl.linkChange(le);
  }
  catch(Exception ex) {
    v2.addElement(nl);
  }
}

// Remove listeners that caused exceptions
Enumeration e2 = v2.elements();
while(e2.hasMoreElements()) {
  listeners.removeElement(e2.nextElement());
}
  }
}
```

The file NetworkServerApp.java contains the main program for the server machine. Its first function is to update the RMI registry on that machine. This is done by using the **rebind( )** method of the **Naming** class. That method associates a name with an object reference. The first argument to the **rebind( )** method is a string that names the server as "NetworkServer." The second argument is a reference to an instance of **NetworkServerImpl**.

Its second function is to read and process the link definitions from the links.txt file. Each line in that file contains the information needed to create a new **Link** object. Information about each link is displayed on the standard output.

Finally, an infinite loop is executed to prompt the user for changes to the link status. The user enters a link ID and changes the operational status to either **true** or **false**. This causes the method **generateLinkEvent( )** of the **NetworkServerImpl** object to be called.

10

```
package network;
import java.io.*;
import java.rmi.*;
import java.util.*;

public class NetworkServerApp {

  public static void main(String args[]) {
    try {
```

```
// Create and register a NetworkServerImpl object
NetworkServerImpl nsi = new NetworkServerImpl();
Naming.rebind("NetworkServer", nsi);

// Read and process link definitions from links.txt
Vector links = new Vector();
FileReader fr = new FileReader("network/links.txt");
BufferedReader br = new BufferedReader(fr);
String line;
int id = 0;
System.out.println("Links:");
while((line = br.readLine()) != null) {
  StringTokenizer st = new StringTokenizer(line, ",");
  String city1 = st.nextToken();
  String city2 = st.nextToken();
  new Link(city1, city2, true);
  String str = "\t" + id + ": " + city1 + "," + city2;
  System.out.println(str);
  ++id;
}
System.out.println("");

// Prompt user for changes to link status
InputStreamReader isr;
isr = new InputStreamReader(System.in);
br = new BufferedReader(isr);
while(true) {
  System.out.print("Link number? ");
  int linkNum = Integer.parseInt(br.readLine());
  if(linkNum >= id) {
    System.out.println("Error:  Invalid link number");
    continue;
  }
  System.out.print("Operational (true/false)? ");
  String status = br.readLine();
  boolean operational;
  operational = Boolean.valueOf(status).booleanValue();
  nsi.generateLinkEvent(linkNum, operational);
  System.out.println("");
}
}
catch(Exception ex) {
  ex.printStackTrace();
}
```

```
    }
}
```

The file NetworkListenerImpl.java implements the remote interface of the client. Its **linkChange( )** method receives a **LinkEvent** object and passes this to the Bean.

```
package network;
import java.rmi.*;
import java.rmi.server.*;

public class NetworkListenerImpl
extends UnicastRemoteObject implements NetworkListener {
  private NetworkCanvas nc;

  public NetworkListenerImpl(NetworkCanvas nc)
  throws RemoteException {
    this.nc = nc;
  }

  public void linkChange(LinkEvent le)
  throws RemoteException {
    nc.linkChange(le);
  }
}
```

The file NetworkCanvas.java has the source code for the Bean. A reference to the country map is held in the **image** variable. The dimensions in pixels of that image are saved in variables **height** and **width**. References to **City** and **Link** objects are held in the vectors **cities** and **links**. A reference to the remote **NetworkServer** object is held in the variable **networkServer**. The **nli** variable holds a reference to the **NetworkListenerImpl** object. All of these variables are **transient** because you either cannot serialize that type of object or do not need to do so. Finally, the **address** variable is a **String** that is the one property of this Bean. It contains the IP address or name of the server machine.

The constructor calls the **init( )** method to perform three primary functions. First, the **cities** and **links** variables are initialized. Second, the file map.gif is read from the JAR file and an **Image** object is created from this data. The dimensions of this image are determined and saved in variables named **width** and **height**. Finally, the cities.txt file is read from the JAR file and a set of **City** objects is created from this data.

10

The **getPreferredSize( )** method is overriden to return the overall dimensions of this Bean. A **Dimension** object is returned whose size is equivalent to that of the map.gif file. The **adjustSize( )** method has been seen in previous chapters of this book.

Read and write access to the **address** property of the Bean is provided by the **getAddress( )** and **setAddress( )** methods.

The **linkChange( )** method is invoked by the **NetworkListenerImpl** object when the operational status of a link changes.

The **paint( )** and **drawLink( )** methods generate the appearance of this Bean. The image is drawn first. Then the colored lines that represent the links connecting the cities are drawn. To draw a link, the **city1** and **city2** fields of the **Link** object are obtained. These are strings that name the cities. A search is made to find the **City** objects. The coordinates of a city are determined by the **getX( )** and **getY( )** methods of **City**.

The **apply( )** method is called by the Bean customizer when the **address** property of the Bean is set. It begins by updating the **address** variable. If the **networkServer** variable is not **null**, the Bean unregisters the **NetworkListenerInterface** object from that server. A **String** is then formed that follows the URL syntax. This URL uses the **rmi** protocol. It includes the IP address or name of the server and the string "NetworkServer." It then invokes the **lookup( )** method of the **Naming** class. This accepts one argument that is the rmi URL and returns a reference to an object of type **Remote** which is then cast to a **NetworkServer**. A **NetworkListenerImpl** object is created and registered to receive link events from the server. The **getLinks( )** method is then used to initialize the **links** vector. The **repaint( )** method is then called to update the display.

Finally, the **readObject( )** method performs the actions necessary so this Bean may be correctly deserialized. The **defaultReadObject( )** method restores the nonstatic and nontransient variables of this object. Some additional processing is then necessary to make the Bean fully operational. First, the **init( )** method is called to read the map.gif and cities.txt files from the JAR file. Second, the **adjustSize( )** method is called to adjust the size of the Bean so it can contain the map. Third, the display is updated via a call to **repaint( )**. Finally, the **apply( )** method is invoked so that the Bean registers itself with the server to receive the latest status about the links.

```
package network;
import java.awt.*;
import java.awt.image.*;
```

```java
import java.io.*;
import java.net.*;
import java.rmi.*;
import java.util.*;

public class NetworkCanvas extends Canvas {
  private transient Image image;
  private transient int height, width;
  private transient Vector cities;
  private transient Vector links;
  private transient NetworkServer networkServer;
  private transient NetworkListenerImpl nli;
  private String address = "";

  public NetworkCanvas() {
    init();
  }

  private void init() {
    try {

      // Initialize the cities and links vectors
      cities = new Vector();
      links = new Vector();

      // Get map image from 'map.gif'
      MediaTracker mt = new MediaTracker(this);
      URL url = getClass().getResource("map.gif");
      image = createImage((ImageProducer)url.getContent());
      mt.addImage(image, 0);
      mt.waitForAll();
      height = image.getHeight(this);
      width = image.getWidth(this);

      // Read and process entries from 'cities.txt'
      Class cls = getClass();
      String r = "cities.txt";
      InputStream is = cls.getResourceAsStream(r);
      InputStreamReader isr = new InputStreamReader(is);
      BufferedReader br = new BufferedReader(isr);
      String line;
      while((line = br.readLine()) != null) {
        StringTokenizer st = new StringTokenizer(line, ",");
        String name = st.nextToken();
        int x = Integer.parseInt(st.nextToken());
```

```
        int y = Integer.parseInt(st.nextToken());
        City city = new City(name, x, y);
        cities.addElement(city);
      }
    }
    catch(Exception ex) {
      ex.printStackTrace();
    }
  }

  public Dimension getPreferredSize() {
    return new Dimension(width, height);
  }

  private void adjustSize() {
    Dimension d = getPreferredSize();
    setSize(d.width, d.height);
    Component parent = getParent();
    if(parent != null) {
      parent.invalidate();
      parent.doLayout();
    }
  }

  public String getAddress() {
    return address;
  }

  public void setAddress(String address) {
    this.address = address;
  }

  public void linkChange(LinkEvent le) {
    int linkId = le.getLinkId();
    Link link = (Link)links.elementAt(linkId);
    link.setOperational(le.getOperational());
    repaint();
  }

  public void paint(Graphics g) {
    g.drawImage(image, 0, 0, this);
    Enumeration e = links.elements();
    while(e.hasMoreElements()) {
      drawLink(g, (Link)e.nextElement());
    }
```

```
    }

    private void drawLink(Graphics g, Link link) {

      // Determine link color
      if(link.getOperational()) {
        g.setColor(new Color(0, 128, 0));
      }
      else {
        g.setColor(new Color(128, 0, 0));
      }

      // Determine location of first city
      int x1, y1;
      x1 = y1 = 0;
      Enumeration e = cities.elements();
      while(e.hasMoreElements()) {
        City city = (City)e.nextElement();
        if(city.getName().equals(link.getCity1())) {
          x1 = city.getX();
          y1 = city.getY();
          break;
        }
      }

      // Determine location of second city
      int x2, y2;
      x2 = y2 = 0;
      e = cities.elements();
      while(e.hasMoreElements()) {
        City city = (City)e.nextElement();
        if(city.getName().equals(link.getCity2())) {
          x2 = city.getX();
          y2 = city.getY();
          break;
        }
      }
      g.drawLine(x1, y1, x2, y2);
    }

    public void apply(String address) {

      // Save server address
      this.address = address;
```

```java
      // Remove existing NetworkListenerImpl
      if(networkServer != null) {
        try {
          networkServer.removeNetworkListener(nli);
        }
        catch(Exception ex) {
          ex.printStackTrace();
        }
        networkServer = null;
      }

      // Lookup existing NetworkServer,
      // Create a NetworkListenerImpl object,
      // and update display
      String networkServerURL =
        "rmi://" + address + "/NetworkServer";
      try {
        networkServer =
          (NetworkServer)Naming.lookup(networkServerURL);
        nli = new NetworkListenerImpl(this);
        networkServer.addNetworkListener(nli);
        links = networkServer.getLinks();
        repaint();
      }
      catch(Exception ex) {
        ex.printStackTrace();
      }
    }

    private void readObject(ObjectInputStream ois)
    throws IOException, ClassNotFoundException {
      try {
        ois.defaultReadObject();
        init();
        adjustSize();
        repaint();
        apply(address);
      }
      catch(Exception ex) {
        ex.printStackTrace();
      }
    }
  }
```

The file City.java encapsulates information about a city.

```
package network;

public class City {
  private String name;
  private int x, y;

  public City(String name, int x, int y) {
    this.name = name;
    this.x = x;
    this.y = y;
  }

  public String getName() {
    return name;
  }

  public int getX() {
    return x;
  }

  public int getY() {
    return y;
  }
}
```

The file NetworkCanvasBeanInfo.java associates a customizer with this Bean.

```
package network;
import java.beans.*;

public class NetworkCanvasBeanInfo
extends SimpleBeanInfo {

  public BeanDescriptor getBeanDescriptor() {
    return new BeanDescriptor(NetworkCanvas.class,
      NetworkCanvasCustomizer.class);
  }
}
```

10

The file NetworkCanvasCustomizer.java provides the customization function.
The interface presented by the customizer has a label, text field, and button.
It allows the user to enter the IP address or name of the machine on which
the server is executing. When the user presses the Apply button, the **apply( )**
method of the Bean is invoked and the data in the text field is passed as an

argument to this method. (As seen previously, the **apply( )** method causes
the Bean to contact the server and obtain the latest link status.)

```java
package network;
import java.awt.*;
import java.awt.event.*;
import java.beans.*;

public class NetworkCanvasCustomizer
extends Panel implements ActionListener, Customizer {
  private PropertyChangeSupport pcsupport =
    new PropertyChangeSupport(this);
  private NetworkCanvas networkCanvas;
  private Label l;
  private TextField tf;
  private Button b;

  public NetworkCanvasCustomizer() {
  }

  public void setObject(Object object) {
    networkCanvas = (NetworkCanvas)object;
    l = new Label("Server Address");
    add(l);
    tf = new TextField("", 15);
    tf.setText(networkCanvas.getAddress());
    add(tf);
    b = new Button("Apply");
    add(b);
    b.addActionListener(this);
  }

  public Dimension getPreferredSize() {
    return new Dimension(200, 70);
  }

  public void
  addPropertyChangeListener(PropertyChangeListener pcl) {
    pcsupport.addPropertyChangeListener(pcl);
  }

  public void
  removePropertyChangeListener(PropertyChangeListener pcl) {
    pcsupport.removePropertyChangeListener(pcl);
```

```
  }

  public void actionPerformed(ActionEvent ae) {
    networkCanvas.apply(tf.getText());
  }
}
```

Use **javac** to compile the eleven source files you created.

Generate Stubs and Skeletons

Enter the following commands to generate the necessary stubs and skeletons:

    rmic -d . network.NetworkListenerImpl

    rmic -d . network.NetworkServerImpl

These commands generate files named NetworkListenerImpl_Skel.class, NetworkListenerImpl_Stub.class, NetworkServerImpl_Skel.class, and NetworkServerImpl_Stub.class in the network subdirectory.

Generate and Install a JAR File

Enter the following command on one line to generate a JAR file:

    jar cfm c:\bdk\jars\network.jar network*.mft network*.class
        network*.txt network*.gif

This command is a fast way to make a JAR file for the client. However, not all of these files are actually used on the client.

10

Install Files on the Client and Server Machines

If necessary, copy the JAR file to the directory c:\bdk\jars on the client machine. Also copy the .class and .txt files to a directory named **network** on the server machine.

Start the RMI Registry on the Server Machine

Enter the following command to start the RMI registry:

    start rmiregistry

Start the Server

Enter the following command to start the server:

```
java network.NetworkServerApp
```

You should see the following output from the server:

```
Links:
    0: A,F
    1: B,F
    2: D,F
    3: D,C
    4: B,C
    5: E,C
    6: E,F
    7: E,H
    8: G,F
    9: G,H
   10: A,H

Link number?
```

Start and Customize the Client

Follow these steps to experiment with this software:

1. Start the BDK and create an instance of the **NetworkCanvas** Bean.
2. Select Edit | Customize from the BeanBox menu bar. Observe that a small dialog box appears prompting you for the IP address of the machine on which the server is executing. This is shown in Figure 10-3. You can enter 127.0.0.1 if the server is executing on your PC or workstation. Then press the Apply button.
3. Observe that the links appear.

Modify Link Status via the Server

Use the interface provided by the server to change the operational status of some links and observe that these changes are reflected on the **NetworkCanvas** Bean.

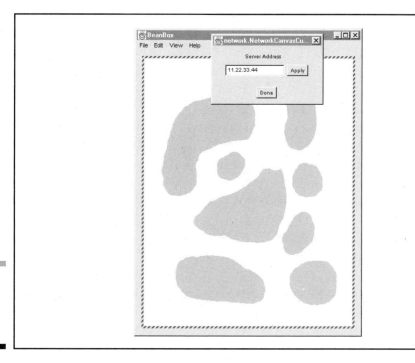

The **Network-Canvas-Customizer**
Figure 10-3.

More About RMI

The examples in this chapter cover only the basics of RMI. There are other RMI features which you may wish to explore further. For example, it is possible to dynamically load the classes involved in making remote method calls. The stubs, skeletons, and other classes used in a distributed application can be loaded at run time. This capability is known as *dynamic class loading*. A complete treatment of this topic requires some discussion of class loaders and security managers.

10

Finally, work is being done to provide interoperability with CORBA objects. CORBA is the Common Object Request Broker Architecture that has been defined by the Object Management Group (OMG). It is one standard for building distributed applications. This is an important development because it will allow software designers to build enterprise-wide solutions which incorporate both JavaBeans and CORBA components that may be written in other languages. You should remain informed about developments in this area.

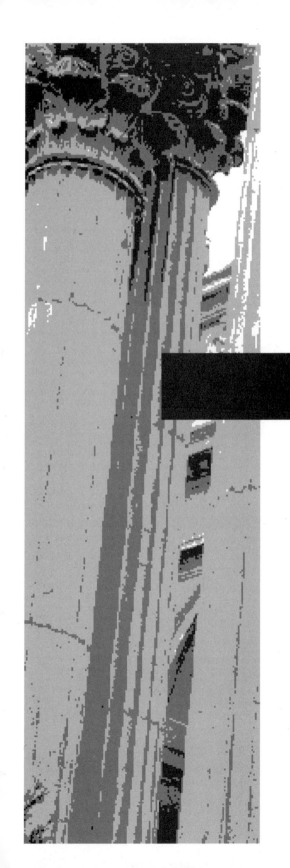

CHAPTER 11

Building Multicast Beans

The previous chapter showed how to build distributed applications by using Remote Method Invocation (RMI). RMI uses TCP/IP to send data from one machine to another. The TCP protocol is designed to ensure reliable, sequenced delivery of packets from a source to a destination. If a packet is lost, the protocol software on the two machines arranges to retransmit the missing information.

This chapter discusses a different way to develop distributed applications. It makes use of a technology called IP multicasting. A server sends only one copy of a packet. The network infrastructure can then efficiently distribute this packet to many receivers. An example is developed to illustrate how to write Beans that make use of IP multicasting.

An Overview of Multicasting

IP multicasting provides a way to efficiently transmit information from a sender to many receivers.

If a sender wants to transmit a packet to many receivers, it can send a separate copy of the packet to each one of them. This technique is called *unicasting*. It has the advantage that the TCP protocol can be used to ensure a sequenced, reliable flow of packets from the sender. However, it has the disadvantage that the processing load on the server increases as the number of recipients grows. The maximum number of receivers is limited by the available resources on the server machine. In addition, the bandwidth and processing demand on the network resources also grows. These can present additional limiting factors.

IP multicasting provides a way to efficiently transmit information from a sender to receivers. Only one copy of a datagram packet is sent into the network. The network infrastructure then sends that information to all of the receivers. In some respects, this is analogous to broadcast radio or television. The sender simply transmits one copy of the data and has no knowledge of which receivers are listening.

Each multicast group is a distinct IP address and port.

This technology provides an efficient way to broadcast information from a sender to many receivers. It can be used, for example, to transmit news updates, weather reports, multimedia entertainment, or classroom lectures. Multicasting can also be an efficient way to share information among a set of users, such as the members of a video conference. Note, however, that the information exchange must be able to tolerate some loss of packets.

A *multicast group* is a set of senders and receivers that exchange data using the multicast protocols. Each group has a distinct IP address and port. An IP address for multicasting must be in the range from 224.0.0.0 to

239.255.255.255. (Messages addressed to 224.0.0.1 are not forwarded beyond the local subnet.)

NOTE: IP multicasting requires that servers, clients, and the network infrastructure support the multicasting protocols. The protocol stack on a Windows 95 PC provides this functionality. Therefore, you may use this technique to communicate among a group of such machines connected to the same LAN segment. However, if you want to use multicasting to communicate among a set of Windows 95 PCs connected to different LAN segments, the routers that connect these different segments must also support multicasting. Check with your local system administrator to confirm that your network supports this feature.

Classes

To write Beans that use the multicast technology, you will use the **DatagramPacket** and **MulticastSocket** classes in the **java.net** package. This section provides a brief overview of their functionality.

The DatagramPacket Class

The **DatagramPacket** class encapsulates information about a User Datagram Protocol (UDP) packet. This protocol does not guarantee a reliable, sequenced exchange of data between two machines. Nonetheless, it can be useful in some situations. You create instances of this class to both transmit and receive information from a multicast group.

The class has the two constructors shown here:

DatagramPacket(byte *buffer*[ ], int *size*)

DatagramPacket(byte *buffer*[ ], int *size*, InetAddress *ia*, int *port*)

The first form of the constructor is used to handle incoming packets and the second form is used to handle outgoing packets. Here, *buffer* is a byte array that holds the data to be transmitted or received, *size* is the number of bytes in the packet, *ia* is the destination address, and *port* is the destination port. Table 11-1 summarizes the methods of this class. All of them are **synchronized**.

11

Method	Description
InetAddress getAddress( )	Returns an **InetAddress** object encapsulating information about an IP address.
byte[ ] getData( )	Returns a byte array with the packet data.
int getLength( )	Returns the length of the packet data.
int getPort( )	Returns the port for the packet.
void setAddress(InetAddress *ia*)	Sets the address for the packet to *ia*.
void setData(byte *buffer*[ ])	Sets the data for the packet to *buffer*.
void setLength(int *size*)	Sets the length of the packet to *size*.
void setPort(int *port*)	Sets the port for the packet to *port*.

The Methods Defined by **Datagram-Packet**
Table 11-1.

The MulticastSocket Class

The **MulticastSocket** class extends **DatagramSocket** and encapsulates information about a socket used for communication with a multicast group. It has these two constructors:

MulticastSocket( ) throws IOException

MulticastSocket(int *port*) throws IOException

The second form of the constructor binds the socket to a port.

In this book, we will use only three of the methods provided by this class. They are shown here:

void joinGroup(InetAddress *ia*) throws IOException

void send(DatagramPacket *dp*) throws IOException

synchronized void receive(DatagramPacket *dp*) throws IOException

The **joinGroup( )** method is called to join the multicast group whose IP address is represented by *ia*. A datagram packet represented by *dp* is transmitted via **send( )**. The **receive( )** method reads a datagram packet from a multicast group into *dp*. This method waits until data is available.

A Multicast Example

This section develops two Beans named **GaussianSender** and **GaussianReceiver**. The former component generates random **double** numbers that have a Gaussian distribution. That is, their average value is zero and their standard deviation is one. These random numbers are transmitted to a multicast group. The latter component reads these numbers from that multicast group and updates a graph showing a frequency distribution of these numbers.

When the **GaussianReceiver** begins execution, it has no data that can be used to generate its plot. Instead, it acquires this information over time by reading many numbers from the multicast group. It should not be surprising that the curve becomes smoother as more data is collected. Figure 11-1 shows how these components appear after two hours of execution. **GaussianSender** is in the top part of that screenshot and **GaussianReceiver** is in the bottom part. The UDP protocol used for multicasting does not guarantee that a datagram packet will reach its destination. However, in this application, you can see that the loss of some packets does not visibly affect the shape of the curve.

Each frequency distribution is centered at zero. The x-axis of the graph ranges from –3 to +3. Its y-axis ranges from 0 to +1.

Customizers are included for each of these Beans. Figure 11-2 shows how the **address**, **port**, and the **msec** properties of **GaussianSender** can be

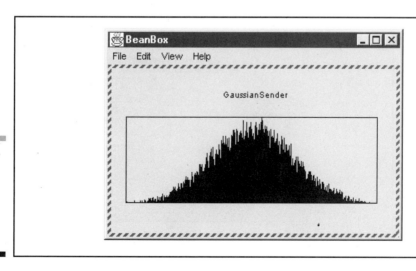

The **Gaussian-Sender** and **Gaussian-Receiver** Beans

Figure 11-1.

11

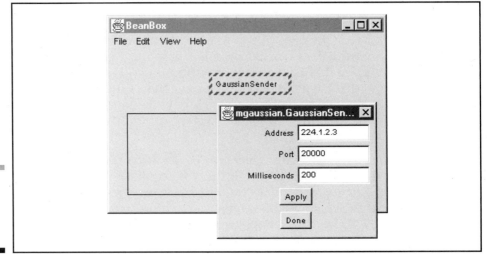

The **Gaussian-Sende**r Customizer
Figure 11-2.

adjusted. The first two properties designate the multicast group to which the random numbers are transmitted. The last property determines the number of milliseconds between transmissions.

Figure 11-3 shows how the **address** and **port** properties of **GaussianReceiver** can be adjusted.

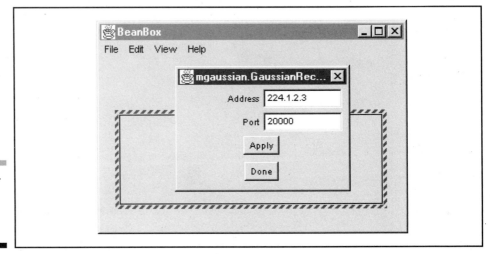

The **Gaussian-Receiver** Customizer
Figure 11-3.

For both of these Beans, the Apply button is pressed to update the properties in the Bean.

You may test these components on one PC by following these steps:

1. Create an instance of **GaussianSender**.
2. Use its customizer to select a multicast group and set the number of milliseconds between transmissions. You must use an address in the range of 224.0.0.0 to 239.255.255.255 (for example, 224.1.2.3).
3. Create an instance of **GaussianReceiver**.
4. Use its customizer to select a multicast group. Use the same address/port values as set for **GaussianSender**. Observe that a histogram now begins to appear.

If you have a LAN with several PCs, create an instance of **GaussianSender** on one machine and create instances of **GaussianReceiver** on several different machines. This configuration demonstrates the power of IP multicasting.

The classes used in this example are summarized in the following table.

GaussianSender	Generates and multicasts random numbers that have a Gaussian distribution.
GaussianSenderBeanInfo	Designates the properties, events, and methods of **GaussianSender**.
GaussianSenderCustomizer	Customizes **GaussianSender**.
GaussianReceiver	Receives the random numbers and uses these to update a frequency distribution plot.
GaussianReceiverBeanInfo	Designates the properties, events, and methods of **GaussianReceiver**.
GaussianReceiverCustomizer	Customizes **GaussianReceiver**.

11

The source code for **GaussianSender** is shown in the next listing. This is an invisible Bean that implements the **Runnable** and **Serializable** interfaces. Its properties are saved in the **address**, **port**, and **msec** variables. A reference to the thread that generates and transmits the random numbers is held in the **transient** variable **t**.

The constructor initializes the **address** property. Access methods for all properties follow the constructor. The **apply( )** method is called by the customizer to update the properties. This method also starts a thread.

The **run( )** method begins by creating a **Random** object. This is a pseudorandom number generator. A **MulticastSocket** object is created for the port and an **InetAddress** object is created for the address. The thread then enters an infinite loop to generate and transmit random numbers. After sleeping for **msec** milliseconds, the thread invokes the **nextGaussian( )** method of the **Random** object to obtain a random **double** number. A **byte** array is formed from this number. This is used to construct a **DatagramPacket** object for the multicast group. Finally, the **send( )** method of the **MulticastSocket** is used to transmit the datagram packet.

The **readObject( )** method provides custom deserialization for this object. It calls **defaultReadObject( )** to restore the properties of this Bean and starts a thread.

```java
package mgaussian;
import java.io.*;
import java.net.*;
import java.util.*;

public class GaussianSender
implements Runnable, Serializable {
  private String address;
  private int port, msec;
  private transient Thread t;

  public GaussianSender() {
    address = "";
  }

  public String getAddress() {
    return address;
  }

  public void setAddress(String address) {
    this.address = address;
  }

  public int getPort() {
    return port;
  }
```

```java
public void setPort(int port) {
  this.port = port;
}

public int getMsec() {
  return msec;
}

public void setMsec(int msec) {
  this.msec = msec;
}

public void apply(String address, int port, int msec) {

  // Set the address, port, and msec properties
  setAddress(address);
  setPort(port);
  setMsec(msec);

  // Start a new thread
  t = new Thread(this);
  t.start();
}

public void run() {
  try {

    // Create a pseudorandom number generator
    Random r = new Random();

    // Create a MulticastSocket object for the port
    MulticastSocket ms = new MulticastSocket(port);

    // Create an InetAddress object for the address
    InetAddress ia = InetAddress.getByName(address);

    while(true) {

      // Sleep for msec milliseconds
      Thread.sleep(msec);

      // Generate the next random number
      double d = r.nextGaussian();

      // Convert the number to an array of bytes
```

11

```
        String s = "" + d;
        byte buffer[] = s.getBytes();

        // Create a DatagramPacket object and send it on
        // the multicast socket
        DatagramPacket dp;
        dp = new DatagramPacket(buffer, buffer.length, ia, port);
        ms.send(dp);
      }
    }
    catch(Exception ex) {
      ex.printStackTrace();
    }
  }

  private void readObject(ObjectInputStream ois)
  throws ClassNotFoundException, IOException {
    ois.defaultReadObject();
    // Start a new thread
    t = new Thread(this);
    t.start();
  }
}
```

The source code for **GaussianSenderBeanInfo** is shown in the following
listing. It extends **SimpleBeanInfo** and overrides **getBeanDescriptor( )**
to associate a customizer with this component.

```
package mgaussian;
import java.beans.*;

public class GaussianSenderBeanInfo extends SimpleBeanInfo {

  public BeanDescriptor getBeanDescriptor() {
    return new BeanDescriptor(GaussianSender.class,
      GaussianSenderCustomizer.class);
  }
}
```

The source code for **GaussianSenderCustomizer** is shown in the next
listing. It extends **Panel** and implements the **ActionListener** and
Customizer interfaces. A reference to the **PropertyChangeSupport**
object is held in the **pcsupport** variable. The text fields for the customizer

are **taddress**, **tport**, and **tmseconds**. A reference to the **GaussianSender** object that is being customized is held in **gsender**.

The constructor begins by creating and arranging all of the necessary GUI elements. It then creates a **PropertyChangeSupport** object.

The **setObject( )** method is called by the builder tool. It reads the **address**, **port**, and **msec** properties from the **GaussianSender** object and uses their values to initialize the text fields in the customizer GUI.

The **actionPerformed( )** method is called when the Apply button is pressed. It reads the values from the text values and calls the **apply( )** method of the **GaussianSender** object to update its properties.

Finally, the **addPropertyChangeListener( )** and **removePropertyChangeListener( )** methods are used to register and unregister listeners for property change events.

```
package mgaussian;
import java.awt.*;
import java.awt.event.*;
import java.beans.*;

public class GaussianSenderCustomizer
extends Panel implements ActionListener, Customizer {
  private PropertyChangeSupport pcsupport;
  private TextField taddress, tport, tmseconds;
  private GaussianSender gsender;

  public GaussianSenderCustomizer() {

    // Create GUI
    setLayout(new BorderLayout());
    Panel pc = new Panel();
    pc.setLayout(new GridLayout(3, 2, 5, 5));
    Label laddress = new Label("Address");
    laddress.setAlignment(Label.RIGHT);
    pc.add(laddress);
    taddress = new TextField("");
    pc.add(taddress);
    Label lport = new Label("Port");
    lport.setAlignment(Label.RIGHT);
    pc.add(lport);
    tport = new TextField("");
    pc.add(tport);
    Label lmseconds = new Label("Milliseconds");
```

11

```
        lmseconds.setAlignment(Label.RIGHT);
        pc.add(lmseconds);
        tmseconds = new TextField("");
        pc.add(tmseconds);
        add("Center", pc);
        Panel ps = new Panel();
        Button bapply = new Button("Apply");
        ps.add(bapply);
        bapply.addActionListener(this);
        add("South", ps);
        setSize(300, 400);

        // Create PropertyChangeSupport object
        pcsupport = new PropertyChangeSupport(this);
    }

    public void setObject(Object o) {
        // Called by builder tool
        gsender = (GaussianSender)o;
        taddress.setText(gsender.getAddress());
        tport.setText("" + gsender.getPort());
        tmseconds.setText("" + gsender.getMsec());
    }

    public void actionPerformed(ActionEvent ae) {
        // Called when "apply" button is pressed
        int port = Integer.parseInt(tport.getText());
        int msec = Integer.parseInt(tmseconds.getText());
        gsender.apply(taddress.getText(), port, msec);
    }

    public void addPropertyChangeListener(
    PropertyChangeListener pcl) {
        pcsupport.addPropertyChangeListener(pcl);
    }

    public void removePropertyChangeListener(
    PropertyChangeListener pcl) {
        pcsupport.removePropertyChangeListener(pcl);
    }
}
```

The source code for **GaussianReceiver** is shown in the next listing. It extends **Canvas** and implements the **Runnable** interface. The x-axis ranges from **–MAXGAUSSIAN** to **+MAXGAUSSIAN**. The constant **BUFSIZE** defines the size of a buffer in which datagram packets are read. Overall dimensions of the graph are stored in **width** and **height**. Variables **address** and **port** contain the properties of the Bean. A reference to the **Thread** object is stored in variable **t**. This variable must be **transient** because **Thread** objects cannot be serialized. The number of entries in the array **data** is equal to the width of the Bean in pixels. Each of these entries represents a specific value between **–MAXGAUSSIAN** and **+MAXGAUSSIAN**. When a random number is received, a check is first made to see if it is between **–MAXGAUSSIAN** and **+MAXGAUSSIAN**. If not, the value is ignored. Otherwise, the entry representing the value closest to the random number is incremented by one. In this manner, the information required to generate the frequency distribution graph is acquired. Notice that this array is **transient** because we have chosen not to preserve its values during the serialization and deserialization process.

The constructor initializes the instance variables. All of the entries in the **data** array are set to zero. Access methods for the properties follow the constructor.

The **apply( )** method is called by the customizer to update the properties. It stops any current thread, sets the **data** entries to zero, updates the properties, and starts a new thread.

The **run( )** method begins by creating a **MulticastSocket** object for the port and an **InetAddress** object for the address. The **joinGroup( )** method of **MulticastSocket** is called so the object can join the multicast group. An infinite loop is then started. It calls the **receive( )** method of the **MulticastSocket** object to read the next datagram packet from the multicast group. This method waits until such a packet is available. Data in the packet is then processed by calling **receive( )** and the display is updated by calling **repaint( )**.

The **receive( )** method has one argument which is the random number. Values outside the range **–MAXGAUSSIAN** and **+MAXGAUSSIAN** are ignored. The remaining code in this method determines which entry in the **data** array represents a value closest to the random number. That element is then incremented by one.

11

The **update( )** method is overridden to avoid screen flicker. The **paint( )** method generates the plot. It begins by creating a background buffer. Drawing operations are done to this buffer. The buffer is filled with the background color and a border is drawn around the component. The maximum count in the **data** array is determined. This is needed in the next step to calculate the height of the various lines that represent the histogram. Finally, the background buffer is copied to the foreground.

The **readObject( )** method provides custom deserialization. The **defaultReadObject( )** method restores the non-static and non-transient variables. Space is allocated for a **data** array and its elements are initialized to zero. A new thread is started.

```java
package mgaussian;
import java.awt.*;
import java.io.*;
import java.net.*;

public class GaussianReceiver extends Canvas
implements Runnable {
  private final static int MAXGAUSSIAN = 3;
  private final static int BUFSIZE = 10;
  private int width, height;
  private String address;
  private int port;
  private transient Thread t;
  private transient long data[];

  public GaussianReceiver() {
    width = 300;
    height = 100;
    address = "";
    port = 0;
    data = new long[width];
    for(int i = 0; i < width; i++) {
      data[i] = 0;
    }
    setSize(width, height);
  }

  public String getAddress() {
    return address;
  }

  public void setAddress(String address) {
    this.address = address;
  }

  public int getPort() {
    return port;
```

```java
  }

  public void setPort(int port) {
    this.port = port;
  }

  public void apply(String address, int port) {

    // Set data elements to zero
    for(int i = 0; i < width; i++) {
      data[i] = 0;
    }

    // Set address and port
    setAddress(address);
    setPort(port);

    // Start thread
    t = new Thread(this);
    t.start();
  }

  public void run() {
    try {

      // Join the multicast group defined by address and port
      MulticastSocket ms = new MulticastSocket(port);
      InetAddress ia = InetAddress.getByName(address);
      ms.joinGroup(ia);

      while(true) {

        // Receive a datagram packet
        byte buffer[] = new byte[BUFSIZE];
        int n = buffer.length;
        DatagramPacket dp = new DatagramPacket(buffer, n);
        ms.receive(dp);

        // Get data from datagram packet
        String str = new String(dp.getData());
        double d = Double.valueOf(str).doubleValue();
        receive(d);

        // Update the frequency distribution graph
        repaint();
```

```
    }
  }
  catch(Exception ex) {
    ex.printStackTrace();
  }
}

public void receive(double d) {

  // Ignore values outside of the range
  if(d < -MAXGAUSSIAN || d > MAXGAUSSIAN)
    return;

  // Increment one of the elements in data[]
  double deltax =
    2 * MAXGAUSSIAN/((double)(getSize().width));
  int x = -MAXGAUSSIAN;
  for(int i = 1; i < width; i++) {
    if(-MAXGAUSSIAN + deltax * i > d) {
      // Determine which entry to increment
      double xa = -MAXGAUSSIAN + deltax * (i - 1);
      double xb = -MAXGAUSSIAN + deltax * i;
      double a = d - xa;
      double b = xb - d;
      if(a < b) {
        ++data[i - 1];
      }
      else {
        ++data[i];
      }
      break;
    }
  }
}

public void update(Graphics g) {
  paint(g);
}

public void paint(Graphics g) {

  // Create background buffer
  Image buffer = createImage(width, height);
  Graphics bg = buffer.getGraphics();
  bg.setColor(getBackground());
```

```
    bg.fillRect(0, 0, width - 1, height - 1);

    // Draw border around the Bean
    bg.setColor(getForeground());
    bg.drawRect(0, 0, width - 1, height - 1);

    // Determine the maximum entry
    long max = 0;
    for(int i = 0; i < width; i++) {
      max = (data[i] > max) ? data[i] : max;
    }

    // Draw lines to represent the frequency distribution
    if(max != 0) {
      for(int i = 0; i < width; i++) {
        long hd = (int)(height * data[i]);
        int y = (int)(height - hd/max);
        bg.drawLine(i, height, i, y);
      }
    }

    // Copy background buffer to foreground
    g.drawImage(buffer, 0, 0, null);
  }

  private void readObject(ObjectInputStream ois)
  throws ClassNotFoundException, IOException {
    ois.defaultReadObject();
    // Initialize data[]
    data = new long[width];
    for(int i = 0; i < width; i++) {
      data[i] = 0;
    }
    // Start thread
    t = new Thread(this);
    t.start();
  }
}
```

The source code for **GaussianReceiverBeanInfo** is shown in the following
listing. It extends **SimpleBeanInfo** and overrides **getBeanDescriptor( )**
to associate a customizer with this component.

```
package mgaussian;
import java.beans.*;
```

11

```
public class GaussianReceiverBeanInfo extends SimpleBeanInfo {

  public BeanDescriptor getBeanDescriptor() {
    BeanDescriptor bd = new BeanDescriptor(GaussianReceiver.class,
      GaussianReceiverCustomizer.class);
    return bd;
  }
}
```

The source code for **GaussianReceiverCustomizer** is shown in the
following listing. It is similar to what has been seen previously for
GaussianSenderCustomizer.

```
package mgaussian;
import java.awt.*;
import java.awt.event.*;
import java.beans.*;

public class GaussianReceiverCustomizer
extends Panel implements ActionListener, Customizer {
  private PropertyChangeSupport pcsupport;
  TextField taddress, tport;
  GaussianReceiver greceiver;

  public GaussianReceiverCustomizer() {

    // Create GUI
    setLayout(new BorderLayout());
    Panel pc = new Panel();
    pc.setLayout(new GridLayout(2, 2, 5, 5));
    Label laddress = new Label("Address");
    laddress.setAlignment(Label.RIGHT);
    pc.add(laddress);
    taddress = new TextField("");
    pc.add(taddress);
    Label lport = new Label("Port");
    lport.setAlignment(Label.RIGHT);
    pc.add(lport);
    tport = new TextField("");
    pc.add(tport);
    add("Center", pc);
    Panel ps = new Panel();
    Button bapply = new Button("Apply");
    ps.add(bapply);
```

```
      bapply.addActionListener(this);
      add("South", ps);
      setSize(300, 400);

      // Create a PropertyChangeSupport object
      pcsupport = new PropertyChangeSupport(this);
  }

  public void setObject(Object o) {
    // Called by builder tool
    greceiver = (GaussianReceiver)o;
    taddress.setText(greceiver.getAddress());
    tport.setText("" + greceiver.getPort());
  }

  public void actionPerformed(ActionEvent ae) {
    // Called when "apply" button is pressed
    int port = Integer.parseInt(tport.getText());
    greceiver.apply(taddress.getText(), port);
    pcsupport.firePropertyChange("", null, null);
  }

  public void
  addPropertyChangeListener(PropertyChangeListener pcl) {
    pcsupport.addPropertyChangeListener(pcl);
  }

  public void
  removePropertyChangeListener(PropertyChangeListener pcl) {
    pcsupport.removePropertyChangeListener(pcl);
  }
}
```

This example illustrates how to use IP multicasting to efficiently broadcast data to many users. However, there is one possible disadvantage to this technique. You saw that it took some time for the **GaussianReceiver** Bean to accumulate enough data to display a reasonable frequency distribution. If this is an issue in your application, one solution may be to use an approach that combines both RMI and IP multicasting. When a client begins execution, it can use RMI to initialize itself with all of the current data. Any subsequent updates can be received from multicast sockets.

11

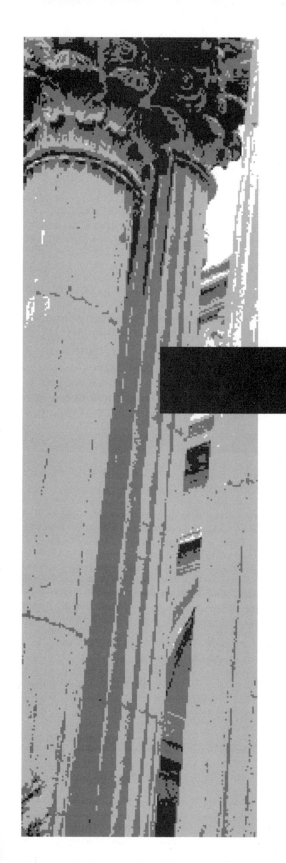

CHAPTER 12

Internationalization

T his chapter describes how to build Beans that operate correctly for an international audience. It shows how to format dates, numbers, currencies, and percentages according to different local conventions.

The concept of a resource bundle is then introduced. This is a set of objects that are selected at run time so your Bean operates correctly in a specific geographic or cultural region. For example, resource bundles can define which images and strings are used by a component. This selection is based on the location and preferences of the user. Examples illustrate how to write Beans that use resource bundles.

Locales

A *locale* is a geographic or cultural region in which a specific language and customs are used. For example, the people of France speak the French language and follow conventions for formatting dates, numbers, currencies, and percentages. However, it is important to realize that geography or language alone does not uniquely identify a locale. People in other regions of the world such as Quebec, Canada, also speak French but follow different customs. Similarly, the English language is spoken by people in Australia, the United Kingdom, and the United States. However, some conventions followed in these countries may be dissimilar.

A locale is a
geographic or
cultural region.

The **Locale** class in the **java.util** package allows you to identify a locale. It has these two constructors:

Locale(String *language*, String *country*)

Locale(String *language*, String *country*, String *variant*)

Here, *language* is a lowercase two letter code that defines the language used in the locale. These codes are defined by the ISO-639 standard. The *country* argument is an uppercase two letter code that defines the country. These codes are defined by the ISO-3166 standard. Finally, the *variant* argument provides a way to designate information specific to a browser or vendor. (Use your favorite web search tool to obtain ISO-639 and ISO-3166.)

Some examples of language codes are: da for Danish, de for German, en for English, fr for French, ga for Irish, ja for Japanese, ru for Russian, and vi for Vietnamese. Some examples of country codes are: CA for Canada, CN for China, DE for Germany, FR for France, JP for Japan, RU for the Russian Federation, GB for the United Kingdom, and US for the United States.

The following items are some examples that illustrate the use of these constructors:

Locale("fr", "CA")

Locale("fr", "FR")

The **Locale** class defines several constants that hold references to **Locale** objects for a specific language. These are: **CHINESE**, **ENGLISH**, **FRENCH**, **ITALIAN**, **JAPANESE**, **KOREAN**, **SIMPLIFIED_CHINESE**, and **TRADITIONAL_CHINESE**. There are also several constants that hold references to **Locale** objects for a specific country. These are: **CANADA**, **CANADA_FRENCH**, **CHINA**, **FRANCE**, **GERMANY**, **ITALY**, **JAPAN**, **KOREA**, **PRC** (People's Republic of China), **TAIWAN**, **UK**, and **US**.

Table 12-1 summarizes some of the commonly used methods of **Locale**.

It is important to realize that **Locale** objects only identify a locale. They do not provide locale-sensitive behavior.

There are several classes in the Java class libraries that do adjust their behavior based on the setting of the default locale. This is the mechanism by which your software components automatically behave differently based on the default locale setting.

The remaining sections of this chapter provide examples that illustrate the operation of some locale-sensitive classes.

Formatting Dates

This section develops an example that illustrates how a Bean can operate in a locale-sensitive manner when it displays dates. Since the precise format of a date differs from locale to locale, a professionally written Bean takes this into consideration. The Bean is named **CalendarViewer** and appears as shown in Figure 12-1. Notice that the name of the month and the names of the weekdays are displayed in Italian. The buttons at the bottom of the screen allow a user to display the previous or next month.

There are four classes in this example. The Bean itself is **CalendarViewer**. Month and year information is presented at the top of the screen by **CalendarLabel**. Buttons at the bottom of the screen that allow one to move to the previous or next month are managed by **CalendarButtons**. Finally, the grid in which the days of the month are displayed is generated by **CalendarCanvas**.

12

Method	Description
String getCountry( )	Returns the uppercase, two-letter country code.
String getDisplayCountry( )	Returns a string equivalent of the country for the default locale.
String getDisplayCountry(Locale *locale*)	Returns a string equivalent of the country for *locale*.
String getDisplayLanguage( )	Returns a string equivalent of the language for the default locale.
String getDisplayLanguage(Locale *locale*)	Returns a string equivalent of the language for *locale*.
String getDisplayName( )	Returns a string equivalent of the default locale.
String getDisplayName(Locale *locale*)	Returns a string equivalent of *locale*.
String getDisplayVariant( )	Returns a string equivalent of the variant for the default locale.
String getDisplayVariant(Locale *locale*)	Returns a string equivalent of the variant for *locale*.
String getLanguage( )	Returns the lowercase, two-letter language code.
String getVariant( )	Returns the code for the variant.

Some Methods
Defined by
Locale
Table 12-1.

The next listing shows the source code for **CalendarViewer**. The variable **gCalendar** refers to a **GregorianCalendar** object. References to the other three objects that comprise this Bean are held in variables **calendarLabel**, **calendarCanvas**, and **calendarButtons**.

The constructor begins by setting the default locale to **Locale.ITALY**. This is done for testing purposes only. In a production quality component, such a line would not be included. Instead, the default locale would be dynamically determined by the configuration settings of the user's PC or workstation. You are free to experiment with this Bean and try other locale options such **Locale.FRANCE**, **Locale.GERMANY**, and **Locale.CANADA**. Observe that the strings displayed by the **CalendarLabel** and **CalendarCanvas** objects change to reflect the different languages in those regions. In addition, the

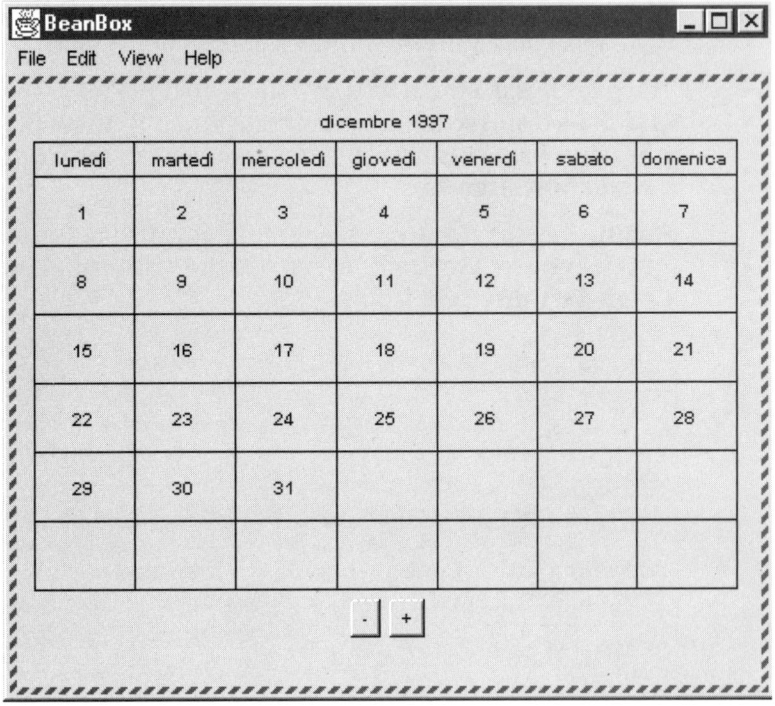

The **Calendar-Viewer** Bean

Figure 12-1.

first day of the week can also vary. For example, Monday is considered the first day of the week in France.

The next step in the constructor initializes the **gCalendar** variable by creating a **GregorianCalendar** object. This calendar object is created with the current date and time. The date of the **GregorianCalendar** object is then set to the first day of the current month. (This is done so it is easier for the program to move from one month to another.) Finally, the constructor creates **CalendarLabel**, **CalendarCanvas**, and **CalendarButtons** objects and adds these to the graphical user interface.

The **getPreferredSize( )** method sets the overall dimensions of the Bean and **getGCalendar( )** is the access method for the **gCalendar** variable.

The **next( )** method is invoked when the user requests that the next month be displayed. It begins by getting the month and year components of the calendar date and initializing the **daysInMonths** array. This array holds the

12

number of days in each calendar month. Notice the check for a leap year. To move ahead one month, the **add( )** method of **GregorianCalendar** is used. Its argument is the number of days to be added to the calendar date.

The **previous( )** method is invoked when the user requests that the previous month be displayed. It is somewhat similar to the **next( )** method. However, a negative value is supplied as an argument to the **add( )** method of **GregorianCalendar**.

Finally, the **dateChanged( )** method is called at the end of both the **next( )** and **previous( )** methods to repaint the **CalendarLabel** and **CalendarCanvas** objects.

```java
package icalendar;
import java.awt.*;
import java.util.*;

public class CalendarViewer extends Panel {
  private GregorianCalendar gCalendar;
  private CalendarLabel calendarLabel;
  private CalendarCanvas calendarCanvas;
  private CalendarButtons calendarButtons;

  public CalendarViewer() {

    // Set locale for testing purposes
    Locale.setDefault(Locale.ITALY);

    // Create a calendar initialized with the
    // current date/time in the default locale
    gCalendar = new GregorianCalendar();

    // Adjust the date of this calendar to
    // the first of the current month
    int date = gCalendar.get(Calendar.DATE);
    gCalendar.add(Calendar.DATE, -(date - 1));

    // Create GUI
    setLayout(new BorderLayout());
    calendarLabel = new CalendarLabel(this);
    add("North", calendarLabel);
    calendarCanvas = new CalendarCanvas(this);
    add("Center", calendarCanvas);
    calendarButtons = new CalendarButtons(this);
    add("South", calendarButtons);
```

```
  }

  public Dimension getPreferredSize() {
    return new Dimension(400, 300);
  }

  public GregorianCalendar getGCalendar() {
    return gCalendar;
  }

  public void next() {
    int month = gCalendar.get(Calendar.MONTH);
    int year = gCalendar.get(Calendar.YEAR);
    int daysInMonths[] = { 31, 28, 31, 30, 31, 30,
      31, 31, 30, 31, 30, 31 };
    daysInMonths[1] +=
      gCalendar.isLeapYear(year) ? 1 : 0;
    gCalendar.add(Calendar.DATE, daysInMonths[month]);
    dateChanged();
  }

  public void previous() {
    int month = gCalendar.get(Calendar.MONTH);
    int year = gCalendar.get(Calendar.YEAR);
    int daysInMonths[] = { 31, 28, 31, 30, 31, 30,
      31, 31, 30, 31, 30, 31 };
    daysInMonths[1] +=
      gCalendar.isLeapYear(year) ? 1 : 0;
    if(--month < 0) {
      month = 11;
    }
    gCalendar.add(Calendar.DATE, -daysInMonths[month]);
    dateChanged();
  }

  private void dateChanged() {
    calendarLabel.repaint();
    calendarCanvas.repaint();
  }
}
```

12

The source code for **CalendarLabel** is shown in the next listing. A reference to the **CalendarViewer** object is held in the variable **cv**. This variable is initialized by the constructor and **setAlignment( )** is called to center the text of the label.

The **SimpleDate-Format** object operates in a locale-sensitive manner. It determines the current locale and uses the information in the **DateFormat-Symbols** object for that locale.

The **paint( )** method begins by instantiating a **SimpleDateFormat** object to display both the month and year information. The argument to its constructor indicates that the full form of both the month and year should be displayed. A reference to the **GregorianCalendar** object held by the Bean is then obtained via the **getGCalendar( )** object. The **getTime( )** method returns a **Date** object. This is passed as an argument to the **format( )** method of the **SimpleDateFormat** object. A string is returned that is used to set the text of the label.

```
package icalendar;
import java.awt.*;
import java.text.*;
import java.util.*;

public class CalendarLabel extends Label {
  private CalendarViewer cv;

  public CalendarLabel(CalendarViewer cv) {
    this.cv = cv;
    setAlignment(Label.CENTER);
  }

  public void paint(Graphics g) {
    // Format month and year information
    SimpleDateFormat sdf = new SimpleDateFormat("MMMM yyyy");
    GregorianCalendar gc = cv.getGCalendar();
    String s = sdf.format(gc.getTime());
    setText(s);
  }
}
```

The source code for **CalendarButtons** is shown in the following listing. A reference to the **CalendarViewer** object is held in the variable **cv**. This variable is initialized by the constructor and the previous and next buttons are created. The **actionPerformed( )** method calls either the **previous( )** or **next( )** method of the Bean.

```
package icalendar;
import java.awt.*;
import java.awt.event.*;

public class CalendarButtons extends Panel
implements ActionListener {
  private CalendarViewer cv;
  private Button previous, next;
```

```
public CalendarButtons(CalendarViewer cv) {
  this.cv = cv;
  previous = new Button("-");
  previous.addActionListener(this);
  add(previous);
  next = new Button("+");
  next.addActionListener(this);
  add(next);
}

public void actionPerformed(ActionEvent ae) {
  if(ae.getSource() == previous) {
    cv.previous();
  }
  else {
    cv.next();
  }
}
}
```

The source code for **CalendarCanvas** is shown in the next listing. A reference to the **CalendarViewer** object is held in the variable **cv**. The constructor initializes this variable and creates a **DateFormatSymbols** object. This is done so that the **getWeekdays( )** method can be used to initialize the **dayNames** array. The **DateFormatSymbols** object operates in a locale-sensitive manner. It returns strings that are appropriate for the current locale.

The **paint( )** method generates a grid showing the information for a month. It begins by getting a reference to the **GregorianCalendar** object of the Bean. The year, month, date, and day-of-week parameters are then determined. The **daysInMonths** array is initialized as previously described. A rectangle is then drawn around the canvas border. Lines are drawn to create the grid cells. The columns are labeled with the names of the weekdays. Notice that the **getFirstDayOfWeek( )** method of **GregorianCalendar** is used to determine how the columns should be labeled.

Two nested **for** loops are used to display the dates in the grid cells. The variable **dom** represents a day of the month and is incremented each time through the inner loop. If **dom** is less than zero, no number is written to the grid. If **dom** is greater than the last day in that month, no further numbers are written to the grid. In order for this design to work, **dom** must be initialized before the loops are encountered. If the first day of the month is

12

not equal to the first day of the week, **dom** may be set to a negative value so
that the correct number of days are skipped by the inner **for** loop.

```java
package icalendar;
import java.awt.*;
import java.text.*;
import java.util.*;

public class CalendarCanvas extends Canvas {
  private CalendarViewer cv;
  private String dayNames[];

  public CalendarCanvas(CalendarViewer cv) {
    this.cv = cv;
    DateFormatSymbols dfs = new DateFormatSymbols();
    dayNames = dfs.getWeekdays();
  }

  public void paint(Graphics g) {

    // Get year, month, date, and day-of-week information
    GregorianCalendar gc = cv.getGCalendar();
    int year = gc.get(Calendar.YEAR);
    int month = gc.get(Calendar.MONTH);
    int date = gc.get(Calendar.DATE);
    int dow = gc.get(Calendar.DAY_OF_WEEK);
    int daysInMonths[] = { 31, 28, 31, 30, 31, 30,
      31, 31, 30, 31, 30, 31 };
    daysInMonths[1] +=
      gc.isLeapYear(year) ? 1 : 0;

    // Draw rectangle around the canvas boundaries
    Dimension d = getSize();
    int h = d.height;
    int w = d.width;
    g.drawRect(0, 0, w - 1, h - 1);

    // Draw lines for the grid columns
    int c = w/7;
    for(int i = 1; i < 7; i++) {
      g.drawLine(i * c, 0, i * c, h);
    }

    // Draw lines for the grid rows
    int r = h/13;
```

```
for(int i = 1; i <= 11; i = i + 2) {
  g.drawLine(0, i * r, w, i * r);
}

// Draw the names of the days on the grid
int j = gc.getFirstDayOfWeek();
for(int i = 0; i < 7; i++) {
  String s = dayNames[j];
  FontMetrics fm = g.getFontMetrics();
  int ascent = fm.getAscent();
  int width = fm.stringWidth(s);
  int x = i * c + (c - width)/2;
  int y = (r - ascent)/2 + ascent;
  g.drawString(s, x, y);
  if(++j > 7) {
    j = 1;
  }
}

// Compute the variable dom
// (If necessary, this will be a negative value)
int fdow = gc.getFirstDayOfWeek();
int dom = (fdow <= dow) ? fdow - dow + 1 : fdow - 8 + dow;

// Draw numbers into the grid cells
for(int row = 0; row < 6; row++) {
  for(int col = 0; col < 7; col++) {
    if(dom > daysInMonths[month]) {
      break;
    }
    if(dom > 0) {
      // Display date in the grid cell
      String s = "" + dom;
      FontMetrics fm = g.getFontMetrics();
      int ascent = fm.getAscent();
      int width = fm.stringWidth(s);
      int x = c * col + (c - width)/2;
      int y = 2 * r * row +
        (2 * r - ascent)/2 + ascent + r;
      g.drawString(s, x, y);
    }
    ++dom;
  }
}
}
}
```

12

In this simple example, the overall size of the Bean was statically determined by the **getPreferredSize( )** method of **CalendarViewer**. If you use the Properties window to adjust the **font** property, you will observe that the strings displayed in the grid can overlap each other. An enhanced design would dynamically modify the size of the grid so the weekdays and numbers always fit within the cells. With large font sizes, abbreviated names for the weekdays could be used. You could invoke the **getShortWeekdays( )** method of **DateFormatSymbols** to accomplish this.

Formatting Numbers, Currencies, and Percentages

Different conventions are used to format numerical quantities in various locales. This section develops a Bean named **Numbers** that illustrates how to display numbers, currencies, and percentages. It uses the **NumberFormat** class to provide the correct formatting of numerical quantities based upon the specified locale. As you probably know, both country and language determine how this data is represented.

Figure 12-2 shows how this component appears in BeanBox. It generates a table with four rows and five columns. Each column shows how a number, currency, and percentage appear when displayed according to the conventions of a particular country. The names of the countries are displayed in the first row.

The next listing shows the source code for the **Numbers** Bean. An array of **Locale** objects is held in the **locales** variable. There is one entry for each of the five locales. The constructor calls the **initLocales( )** method to allocate storage for the **locales** array and initialize its elements. Overall dimensions of the component are then established via the **setSize( )** method.

The **paint( )** method generates the table and its elements. The first row contains the names of the five countries. These strings are obtained via a call to the **getDisplayCountry( )** method of the **Locale** object.

The second row shows how the number one million appears when using the different formatting conventions of these countries. The static **getNumberInstance( )** method of the **NumberFormat** class is used to obtain a **NumberFormat** object for a specific locale. The argument to **getNumberInstance( )** designates the locale for which formatting is to be done. A string equivalent of a number may be generated via the **format( )**

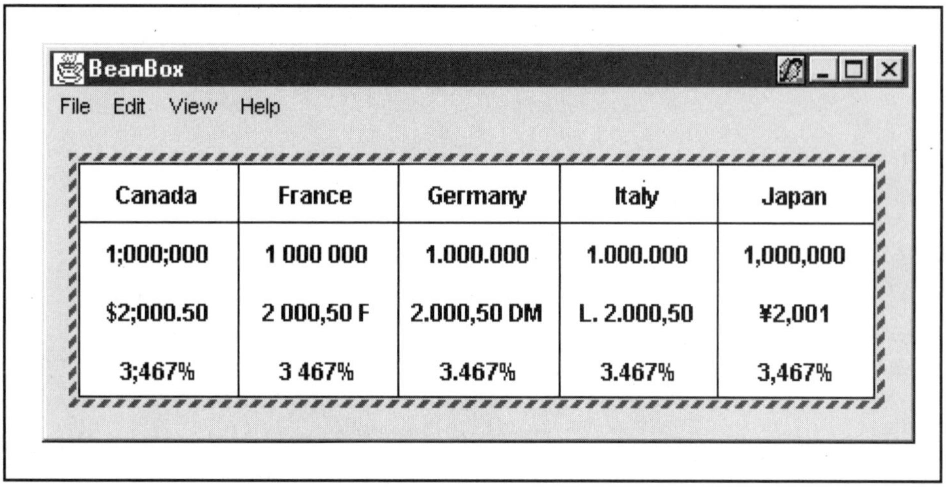

Canada	France	Germany	Italy	Japan
1;000;000	1 000 000	1.000.000	1.000.000	1,000,000
$2;000.50	2 000,50 F	2.000,50 DM	L. 2.000,50	¥2,001
3;467%	3 467%	3.467%	3.467%	3,467%

The **Numbers**
Bean
Figure 12-2.

*The **Number-**
Format object
operates in a
locale-sensitive
manner.*

method of the **NumberFormat** object. Notice that the entries in the second row use different characters (or spaces) to group sets of digits.

The third row shows how the currency value 2000.5 appears when using the different formatting conventions of these countries. The static **getCurrencyInstance( )** method of the **NumberFormat** class is used to obtain a **NumberFormat** object for a specific locale. The argument to **getCurrencyInstance( )** designates the locale for which formatting is to be done. A string equivalent of a currency value may be generated via the **format( )** method of the **NumberFormat** object. Notice that the entries in the third row contain either a prefix or suffix to represent the dollar, franc, mark, lira, or yen.

The fourth row shows how the percentage value 34.67% appears when using the different formatting conventions of these countries. The static **getPercentInstance( )** method of the **NumberFormat** class is used to obtain a **NumberFormat** object for a specific locale. The argument to **getPercentInstance( )** designates the locale for which formatting is to be done. A string equivalent of a percent value may be generated via the **format( )** method of the **NumberFormat** object. Notice that the entries in the fourth row use different characters (or spaces) to group sets of digits.

12

```
package numbers;
import java.awt.*;
import java.text.*;
import java.util.*;
```

```
public class Numbers extends Canvas {
 private Locale locales[];

 public Numbers() {
   initLocales();
   setSize(420, 120);
 }

 private void initLocales() {
   locales = new Locale[5];
   locales[0] = Locale.CANADA;
   locales[1] = Locale.FRANCE;
   locales[2] = Locale.GERMANY;
   locales[3] = Locale.ITALY;
   locales[4] = Locale.JAPAN;
 }

 public void paint(Graphics g) {

   // Draw rectangle around the canvas boundaries
   Dimension d = getSize();
   int h = d.height;
   int w = d.width;
   g.drawRect(0, 0, w - 1, h - 1);

   // Draw lines for the grid columns
   int c = w/locales.length;
   for(int i = 1; i < locales.length; i++) {
     g.drawLine(i * c, 0, i * c, h);
   }

   // Draw a line under the first row
   int r = h/4;
   g.drawLine(0, r, w, r);

   // Determine font ascent
   FontMetrics fm = g.getFontMetrics();
   int ascent = fm.getAscent();

   // Draw the names of the countries on the first row
   for(int i = 0; i < locales.length; i++) {
     String s = locales[i].getDisplayCountry();
     int width = fm.stringWidth(s);
     int x = i * c + (c - width)/2;
     int y = (r - ascent)/2 + ascent;
```

```
      g.drawString(s, x, y);
    }

    // Draw the number 1000000 on the second row
    for(int i = 0; i < locales.length; i++) {
      NumberFormat nf;
      nf = NumberFormat.getNumberInstance(locales[i]);
      String s = nf.format(1000000);
      int width = fm.stringWidth(s);
      int x = i * c + (c - width)/2;
      int y = r + (r - ascent)/2 + ascent;
      g.drawString(s, x, y);
    }

    // Draw the currency value 2000.5 on the third row
    for(int i = 0; i < locales.length; i++) {
      NumberFormat nf;
      nf = NumberFormat.getCurrencyInstance(locales[i]);
      String s = nf.format(2000.5);
      int width = fm.stringWidth(s);
      int x = i * c + (c - width)/2;
      int y = 2 * r + (r - ascent)/2 + ascent;
      g.drawString(s, x, y);
    }

    // Draw the percentage value 34.67% on the fourth row
    for(int i = 0; i < locales.length; i++) {
      NumberFormat nf;
      nf = NumberFormat.getPercentInstance(locales[i]);
      String s = nf.format(34.67);
      int width = fm.stringWidth(s);
      int x = i * c + (c - width)/2;
      int y = 3 * r + (r - ascent)/2 + ascent;
      g.drawString(s, x, y);
    }
  }
}
```

12

Resource Bundles

A resource
bundle is a set
of objects that
provide
locale-sensitive
information.

A *resource bundle* is a set of objects that provide locale-sensitive information. For example, assume that you write a Bean which presents a graphical user interface. It displays images and uses strings for labels on buttons, lists, and other elements. These images and strings must be different based on the locale in which that component executes.

One way to accomplish this is to program your Bean so it selects the appropriate image or string by using a series of "if-else" statements. However, there is a serious disadvantage to such a design. It requires that you change the source code for your component each time a new locale must be handled.

It would be preferable if you could separate the locale-sensitive part of your code from the locale-independent part. New locales could then be accommodated easily. This is the advantage provided by using resource bundles.

Let us look at some of the classes that provide this functionality.

The ResourceBundle Class

The **ResourceBundle** class in the **java.util** package provides two static methods that allow you to get a reference to a resource bundle for a specific locale. These methods are:

    static final ResourceBundle getBundle(String *name*)
       throws MissingResourceException

    static final ResourceBundle getBundle(String *name*, Locale *locale*)
       throws MissingResourceException

Here, *name* identifies the requested resource which is needed and *locale* identifies the locale for which it is needed. The first form of this method returns a **ResourceBundle** object for the default locale and the second form returns a **ResourceBundle** object for the specified locale.

In order to use this functionality, you must understand how the **getBundle( )** method searches for a bundle. The search proceeds in the sequence shown in the following list:

1. A file named *bundle_language_country_identifier*.class
2. A file named *bundle_language_country*.class
3. A file named *bundle_language*.class
4. A file named *bundle*.class
5. A file named *bundle_language_country_identifier*.properties
6. A file named *bundle_language_country*.properties
7. A file named *bundle_language*.properties
8. A file named *bundle*.properties

Here, *bundle* is the name of the requested resource bundle. The *language*, *country*, and *identifier* parameters are determined by either the default or specified locale.

As you can see, the locale-sensitive information for a resource bundle can be stored in either a .class or a .properties file. The use of .class files to store resource bundle information is beyond the scope of this book. The examples provided in this chapter illustrate only how to use .properties files for this data.

For example, you might define resource bundles for Italy and Japan by creating files named CountryResources_it.properties and CountryResources_ja.properties, respectively. The file named CountryResources.properties is used if a resource bundle for a more specific file cannot be located.

A .properties file that defines a resource bundle contains lines that define key-value pairs. For example, your CountryResources_it.properties file might contain the following:

```
FlagFile=italy.gif
```

Here, the string **FlagFile** is a key and italy.gif is its value. Other files each define **FlagFile** to reference a different GIF file.

A **ResourceBundle** object contains a set of key-value pairs. The keys can be obtained by calling this method:

Enumeration getKeys( )

The objects corresponding to these keys can be obtained with any of the following methods:

String getString(String *key*) throws MissingResourceException

String[ ] getStringArray(String *key*) throws MissingResourceException

Object getObject(String *key*) throws MissingResourceException

Here, *key* is a string that uniquely names the requested resource. This is the mechanism you use to read locale-sensitive values from a resource bundle.

12

Using Locale-Sensitive Images from Resource Bundles

This section develops a component to illustrate how locale-sensitive images may be retrieved from a resource bundle. The Bean is named **Flag** and it displays an image representing the flag of the country for the default locale. Figure 12-3 shows how this component appears in the BeanBox when the default locale is set to **Locale.JAPAN**.

The next listing shows the source code for the **Flag** Bean. This class extends **Applet** and defines a variable named **image** that holds a reference to the flag image. Notice that this variable must be designated as **transient** because the **Image** class cannot be serialized.

The **init( )** method begins by setting the default locale for the country Japan. The next line obtains the default locale. The resource bundle for that locale is returned from the static **getBundle( )** method of the **ResourceBundle** class. The first argument to this method is the name of the bundle (that is, "flag.CountryResources") and the second argument is the **Locale** object.

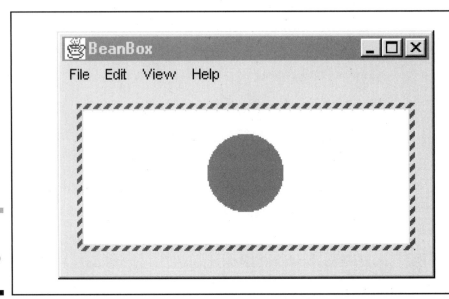

The **Flag**
Bean (for
Locale.JAPAN)
Figure 12-3.

The **getString( )** method of the **ResourceBundle** object is used to obtain the locale-sensitive value for the key "FlagFile."

Once the name of the GIF file is known, the **getResource( )** method of **Class** is called to obtain a **URL** object for this file. The **getContent( )** method of the **URL** object retrieves the data from the image and the **createImage( )** method of **Component** returns an **Image** object that is saved in the **image** variable.

The **paint( )** method displays the image.

In order to correctly deserialize this Bean, it is necessary to provide the **readObject( )** method shown at the end of the listing. It calls **defaultReadObject( )** on the **ObjectInputStream** object to restore the nonstatic and nontransient variables for this **Flag** object. Then the **init( )** method is called to create the **Image** object for the flag.

```
package flag;
import java.applet.*;
import java.awt.*;
import java.awt.image.*;
import java.io.*;
import java.net.*;
import java.util.*;

public class Flag extends Applet {
  private transient Image image;

  public void init() {

    // Set locale for testing purposes
    Locale.setDefault(Locale.JAPAN);

    // Get the default locale
    Locale locale = Locale.getDefault();

    // Get the resource bundle
    String name = "flag.CountryResources";
    ResourceBundle rb =
      ResourceBundle.getBundle(name, locale);

    // Get name of the flag file
    String flagFile = rb.getString("FlagFile");

    // Get the resource
```

12

```
      URL flagURL = getClass().getResource(flagFile);

      // Get the image
      try{
        image =
          createImage((ImageProducer)flagURL.getContent());
      }
      catch(Exception ex) {
        ex.printStackTrace();
      }

      // Set size of the Bean
      setSize(250, 100);
    }

  public void paint(Graphics g) {
    g.drawImage(image, 0, 0, this);
  }

  private void readObject(ObjectInputStream ois)
  throws ClassNotFoundException, IOException {
    ois.defaultReadObject();
    init();
  }
}
```

This example requires that several .properties files be included in the JAR file. These files are named CountryResources_XX.properties where **XX** identifies the locale as previously described. The GIF files with the flag images must also be packaged into the JAR file. Use the following command to generate the JAR file:

jar cfm c:\bdk\jars\flag.jar flag*.mft flag*.class flag*.properties flag*.gif

To observe how this Bean operates in a different locale, modify the first line of the **init( )** method, recompile the component, rebuild the JAR file, and restart the BDK.

Using Locale-Sensitive Strings from Resource Bundles

This section illustrates how to use locale-sensitive strings from resource bundles. The Beans developed here are revised editions of the **Painter** and

Selector Beans from Chapter 2. Figure 12-4 shows how these components appear in the BeanBox for when the default locale is set to **Locale.ITALY**. Notice that the labels for the three scroll bars are locale-sensitive.

The revised code for **Painter** is shown in the following listing. This Bean has one property named **color**. The **paint( )** method uses this value to fill a square on the display.

```
package icselector;
import java.awt.*;

public class Painter extends Canvas {
  private Color color;

  public Painter() {
    color = Color.white;
    setSize(50, 50);
  }

  public Color getColor() {
    return color;
  }

  public void setColor(Color color) {
    this.color = color;
    repaint();
  }

  public void paint(Graphics g) {
    Dimension d = getSize();
    int w = d.width;
    int h = d.height;
    g.setColor(color);
    g.fillRect(0, 0, w - 1, h - 1);
    g.setColor(Color.black);
    g.drawRect(0, 0, w - 1, h - 1);
  }
}
```

12

The revised code for **Selector** is shown in the next listing. Its **color** variable represents the color chosen by the three slider elements. A **PropertyChangeSupport** object is referenced by the variable **pcs**. The other variables hold references to the three scroll bars.

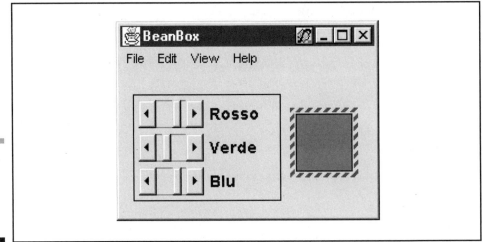

The constructor begins by setting the default locale for testing purposes and initializing the **color** and **pcs** variables. Next, the static **getBundle( )** method of **ResourceBundle** is called to obtain a **ResourceBundle** object for the bundle named "icselector.Resources" for the specified locale. Once the **ResourceBundle** object has been obtained, its **getString( )** method can be called to obtain the locale-sensitive value associated with a specific key.

The GUI elements are then created and initialized. Notice that the **Selector** object is registered to receive adjustment events generated by the scroll bars. A border for this object is established by **getInsets( )**.

Access methods for the **color** property are next in the listing. The **paint( )** method draws a border around the Bean.

The **adjustmentValueChanged( )** method receives adjustment events generated by the scroll bars. It gets the values from these three elements and creates a **Color** object. The **firePropertyChange( )** method of the **PropertyChangeSupport** object is invoked to notify any listeners that registered to receive property change notifications.

Listeners register and unregister to receive property change events via **addPropertyChangeListener( )** and **removePropertyChangeListener( )**.

```
package icselector;
import java.awt.*;
import java.awt.event.*;
import java.beans.*;
import java.util.*;

public class Selector extends Panel
implements AdjustmentListener {
  private Color color;
  private PropertyChangeSupport pcs;
  private Scrollbar rScrollbar, gScrollbar, bScrollbar;

  public Selector() {

    // Set locale for testing purposes
    Locale.setDefault(Locale.ITALY);

    // Get the default locale
    Locale locale = Locale.getDefault();

    // Initialize variables
    color = Color.white;
    pcs = new PropertyChangeSupport(this);

    // Get the resource bundle
    ResourceBundle rb =
      ResourceBundle.getBundle("icselector.Resources",
        locale);

    // Get labels for the sliders
    String red = rb.getString("Red");
    String green = rb.getString("Green");
    String blue = rb.getString("Blue");

    // Initialize GUI elements
    setLayout(new GridLayout(3, 2, 5, 5));
    rScrollbar =
      new Scrollbar(Scrollbar.HORIZONTAL, 255, 10, 0, 265);
    add(rScrollbar);
    rScrollbar.addAdjustmentListener(this);
    Label rLabel = new Label(red, Label.LEFT);
    add(rLabel);
    gScrollbar =
      new Scrollbar(Scrollbar.HORIZONTAL, 255, 10, 0, 265);
    add(gScrollbar);
```

12

```
  gScrollbar.addAdjustmentListener(this);
  Label gLabel = new Label(green, Label.LEFT);
  add(gLabel);
  bScrollbar =
    new Scrollbar(Scrollbar.HORIZONTAL, 255, 10, 0, 265);
  add(bScrollbar);
  bScrollbar.addAdjustmentListener(this);
  Label bLabel = new Label(blue, Label.LEFT);
  add(bLabel);
}

public Insets getInsets() {
  return new Insets(5, 5, 5, 5);
}

public Color getColor() {
  return color;
}

public void setColor(Color color) {
  this.color = color;
}

public void paint(Graphics g) {
  Dimension d = getSize();
  g.drawRect(0, 0, d.width - 1, d.height - 1);
}

public void adjustmentValueChanged(AdjustmentEvent ae) {
  Scrollbar source = (Scrollbar)ae.getSource();
  int value = ae.getValue();
  source.setValue(value);
  int r = rScrollbar.getValue();
  int g = gScrollbar.getValue();
  int b = bScrollbar.getValue();
  Color oldColor = color;
  color = new Color(r, g, b);
  pcs.firePropertyChange("color", oldColor, color);
}

public void
addPropertyChangeListener(PropertyChangeListener pcl) {
  pcs.addPropertyChangeListener(pcl);
}
```

```
public void
removePropertyChangeListener(PropertyChangeListener pcl) {
  pcs.removePropertyChangeListener(pcl);
}
}
```

This example requires that several .properties files be included in the JAR file. These files are named Resources_XX.properties where **XX** identifies the locale as previously described. You provide these files. For example, Resources_de.properties defines the labels for the German language:

```
Red=Rot
Green=Gr\u00fcn
Blue=Blau
```

Notice the use of a Unicode character in one of the entries.

The English versions are defined in Resources_en.properties as shown here:

```
Red=Red
Green=Green
Blue=Blue
```

The French versions are defined in Resources_fr.properties as shown here:

```
Red=Rouge
Green=Vert
Blue=Bleu
```

The Italian versions are defined in Resources_it.properties as shown here:

```
Red=Rosso
Green=Verde
Blue=Blu
```

Now use the following command to generate the correct JAR file:

```
jar cfm c:\bdk\jars\icselector.jar icselector\*.mft
icselector\*.class icselector\*.properties
```

To observe how this Bean operates in a different locale, modify the first line of the **init( )** method, recompile the component, rebuild the JAR file, and restart the BDK.

12

CHAPTER 13

Building Electronic Mail Beans

This chapter shows how to build components that send and receive electronic mail. The Simple Mail Transport Protocol (SMTP) and Post Office Protocol—Version 3 (POP3) are Internet application protocols used for these purposes. An overview is presented for each protocol and Beans are developed to implement it. Other components provide graphical user interfaces through which messages can be sent and received.

An Overview of the Simple Mail Transport Protocol

Electronic mail can be sent via SMTP.

The Simple Mail Transport Protocol (SMTP) defines how an electronic mail message can be sent from one machine to another on the Internet. This section provides a brief overview of its primary features. You can find an official definition of this protocol by searching for the document named RFC 821 on the Internet.

Commands are sent from a client machine to an SMTP server. Each command must be terminated by a carriage return and line feed. The SMTP server generates a response for each command. Each response begins with a three-digit numeric code and is followed by a text string.

The following sections describe five commands that are used in this chapter and some of the responses which can be issued by an SMTP server. Additional details about other types of server responses can be found in RFC 821.

NOTE: You may examine this interaction between a client and server by opening a telnet session with an SMTP server. On a Windows 95/NT machine, open a DOS window and type **telnet *smtpserver* 25** at the command prompt. Here, *smtpserver* is the IP address or name of the machine that runs the SMTP server. Port 25 is typically used for SMTP servers. Type commands to the server and observe the responses.

HELO

The HELO command is sent by a client to begin a session with an SMTP server. It has the following format:

HELO *domain*

Here, *domain* is the domain name of the client. An example of such a command is shown here:

HELO mycompany.com

If there are no problems, the response from the SMTP server begins with the numeric code 250. An example of such a response is shown here:

250 smtpserver.com Helo mycompany.com

MAIL FROM

The MAIL FROM command is sent by a client to identify the sender of this message. It has the following format:

MAIL FROM: *sender*

Here, *sender* is the electronic mail address of the sender. An example of such a command is:

MAIL FROM: joe@mycompany.com

If there are no problems, the response from the SMTP server begins with the numeric code 250. An example of such a response is shown here:

250 joe@mycompany.com... Sender ok

RCPT TO

The RCPT TO command is sent by a client to identify a recipient of this message. It has the following format:

RCPT TO: sue@othercompany.com

If there are no problems, the response from the server begins with the numeric code 250. An example of such a response is:

250 sue@othercompany.com... Recipient ok

If there is a format error, the response from the server begins with the numeric code 501. An example of such a response is:

501 Syntax error

13

The SMTP protocol allows a client to send multiple RCPT TO commands for a single message. In this manner, several recipients can be designated.

(However, the components developed in this chapter are limited to only one recipient.)

DATA

The DATA command is sent by a client to indicate the beginning of the message itself. It has the following format:

DATA

If there are no problems, the response from the server begins with the numeric code 354. An example of such a response is:

354 Enter mail, end with "." on a line by itself

Multiple lines are then sent from the client to the server to transmit the message header and body. The client must then send a single line containing only a period followed by a carriage return and line feed. This indicates to the SMTP server that all of the data has been transmitted.

If there is a line in the message body which begins with a period, the protocol requires the sender to replace this character with two periods. This is the mechanism used to escape that character. For simplicity, this step is omitted from the components developed in this chapter.

An example of an email message is shown here:

Date: 22 Feb 98 14:22:45
From: <joe@mycompany.com>
To: <sue@othercomany.com>
Would you like to meet for lunch on Friday?

.

If there are no problems, the response from the SMTP server begins with the numeric code 250. An example of such a response is:

250 Mail accepted

QUIT

The QUIT command is sent by a client to indicate the end of the session. It has the following format:

QUIT

If there are no problems, the response from the server begins with the numeric code 221. An example of such a response is:

221 emailserver.com delivering mail

Classes and Interfaces

This section develops some components to send electronic mail via the SMTP protocol. Let us briefly look at the classes and interfaces used in this example.

First, **SmtpClient** is an invisible Bean that handles the details of the SMTP protocol. It opens a socket to the SMTP server and then writes commands and reads responses from that machine. This component has two properties named **hostname** and **port** that identify the IP name or address of the host and the software port to which the SMTP server is connected.

Second, **SmtpGui** is a visible Bean that presents a user interface by which a person can enter the information required for a message. Figure 13-1 shows how this component appears in the BeanBox. Text fields are provided for the email address of the sender and the recipient. A text area allows one to enter the message body. When these elements have been completed, the user presses the Send button.

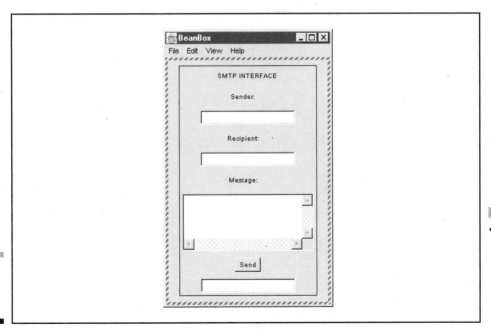

The **SmtpGui**
Bean
Figure 13-1.

13

Third, **SmtpEvent** is a custom event that is generated by **SmtpGui** when the user presses the Send button. This object contains the information that was entered into the GUI elements of that component.

Fourth, **SmtpListener** is an interface implemented by **SmtpClient**. It defines one method to receive the **SmtpEvent** objects generated by **SmtpGui**.

Fifth, **SmtpSource** is an interface implemented by **SmtpGui**. It defines one method called by **SmtpClient** to pass responses back to **SmtpGui**.

These classes and interfaces are discussed in the following sections. Note that the separation of user interface logic and protocol logic into two separate Beans has several important advantages. First, the user interface can be changed without affecting the protocol Bean. Second, you may wish to build applications that generate and send electronic messages based on conditions in your program. For example, a message can be generated by a calendar program to remind a person about an appointment. This can be done by generating an **SmtpEvent** and sending it directly to an **SmtpClient**.

The SmtpEvent Class

The source code for the **SmtpEvent** class is shown in the following listing. This class extends **EventObject** and encapsulates the information needed to generate an electronic mail message.

```
package smtp;
import java.util.*;

public class SmtpEvent extends EventObject {
  private String sender;
  private String recipient;
  private String message;

  public SmtpEvent(Object source, String sender,
  String recipient, String message) {
    super(source);
    this.sender = sender;
    this.recipient = recipient;
    this.message = message;
  }

  public String getSender() {
    return sender;
  }
```

```
public String getRecipient() {
  return recipient;
}

public String getMessage() {
  return message;
}
}
```

The SmtpListener Interface

The source code for the **SmtpListener** interface is shown in the following listing. Its **send( )** method accepts an **SmtpEvent** object as an argument. The method is invoked when the **SmtpGui** object fires this custom event.

```
package smtp;
import java.util.*;

public interface SmtpListener extends EventListener {

  public void send(SmtpEvent smtpe);
}
```

The SmtpSource Interface

The source code for the **SmtpSource** interface is shown in the following listing. Its **respond( )** method is called by the **SmtpClient** object to respond to a command request from the **SmtpGui**. The **int** argument indicates the success or failure of the command.

```
package smtp;

public interface SmtpSource {

  public void respond(int code);
}
```

The SmtpGui Class

The source code for the **SmtpGui** class is shown in the next listing. This class extends **Panel** and implements the **ActionListener**, **SmtpSource**, and **TextListener** interfaces. The variable **listener** holds a reference to the **SmtpListener** that receives **SmtpEvent** objects. The other instance

13

variables hold references to the three text fields and one text area of the user interface.

The constructor first creates the GUI elements. Notice that the **SmtpGui** object is registered to receive text events from the text fields and action events from the button. A **GridBagLayout** object is then created. This serves as the layout manager for the Bean. (The **GridBagLayout** class is more complex than the other layout managers you have seen. However, it provides more control over the placement of components within a container and generates a platform-independent user interface.) A **GridBagConstraints** object is also created. This has a variety of fields that control how the **GridBagLayout** object arranges the components within a container.

To understand the operation of the **GridBagLayout** and **GridBagConstraints** objects, imagine that the **SmtpGui** is divided into a grid of nine rows and one column. The **add( )** method is used to add each of the GUI elements to the container. This is similar to what you have seen with the other layout managers. However, the fields of the **GridBagConstraints** object determine the size and placement of that element.

The **gridx** and **gridy** fields determine the row and column of the grid in which the upper-left corner of the element is located. In this example, **gridx** is always zero and **gridy** is adjusted before adding the next element. The **gridwidth** and **gridheight** fields determine the number of columns and rows that are used by this component. In this example, the **gridwidth** and **gridheight** are always set to one. The **insets** field holds an **Insets** object that determines the margin around each component. The constructor concludes by adding each of the elements to the **SmtpGui** object.

The **paint( )** method draws a border around the Bean. The **textValueChanged( )** method is called when either the sender or recipient text field is changed. It clears the result text field. The **actionPerformed( )** method is called when the Send button is pressed. It creates an **SmtpEvent** object from the values in the GUI elements and passes this object as an argument to the **fireEmailEvent( )** method.

The **addEmailListener( )** and **removeEmailListener( )** methods provide the required registration and unregistration functionality. The **fireEmailEvent( )** calls the **send( )** event of the listener with the custom event object as its argument.

The **respond( )** method is called by the **SmtpClient** Bean to provide a response for a command. The response is encoded as an **int** that is passed as the argument to the **responsd( )** method. These **int** values are defined by the **SmtpClient** object. The function of the **responsd( )** method is to look at this **int** value and determine a string that should be displayed to the user in the result text field.

Finally, the **readObject( )** method is called during the deserialization process. It clears the text fields and text area.

```
package smtp;
import java.awt.*;
import java.awt.event.*;
import java.io.*;
import java.util.*;

public class SmtpGui extends Panel
implements ActionListener, SmtpSource, TextListener {
  private SmtpListener listener;
  private TextField senderTf, recipientTf, resultTf;
  private TextArea messageTa;

  public SmtpGui() {

    // Create GUI elements
    Label title = new Label("SMTP INTERFACE", Label.CENTER);
    Label senderLabel = new Label("Sender:");
    senderTf = new TextField(20);
    senderTf.addTextListener(this);
    Label recipientLabel = new Label("Recipient:");
    recipientTf = new TextField(20);
    recipientTf.addTextListener(this);
    Label messageLabel = new Label("Message:");
    messageTa = new TextArea(5, 30);
    messageTa.addTextListener(this);
    Button sendButton = new Button("Send");
    sendButton.addActionListener(this);
    resultTf = new TextField(20);

    // Create and set layout manager
    GridBagLayout gbl = new GridBagLayout();
    setLayout(gbl);

    // Create and initialize GridBagConstraints object
    GridBagConstraints gbc = new GridBagConstraints();
    gbc.gridx = 0;
    gbc.gridwidth = 1;
    gbc.gridheight = 1;
```

13

```
gbc.insets = new Insets(5, 5, 5, 5);

// Add title to the GUI
gbc.gridy = 0;
gbl.setConstraints(title, gbc);
add(title);

// Add sender label to the GUI
gbc.gridy = 1;
gbl.setConstraints(senderLabel, gbc);
add(senderLabel);

// Add sender text field to the GUI
gbc.gridy = 2;
gbl.setConstraints(senderTf, gbc);
add(senderTf);

// Add recipient label to the GUI
gbc.gridy = 3;
gbl.setConstraints(recipientLabel, gbc);
add(recipientLabel);

// Add recipient text field to the GUI
gbc.gridy = 4;
gbl.setConstraints(recipientTf, gbc);
add(recipientTf);

// Add message label to the GUI
gbc.gridy = 5;
gbl.setConstraints(messageLabel, gbc);
add(messageLabel);

// Add message text area to the GUI
gbc.gridy = 6;
gbl.setConstraints(messageTa, gbc);
add(messageTa);

// Add send button to the GUI
gbc.gridy = 7;
gbl.setConstraints(sendButton, gbc);
add(sendButton);

// Add result text field to the GUI
gbc.gridy = 8;
gbl.setConstraints(resultTf, gbc);
```

```
    add(resultTf);
  }

  public void paint(Graphics g) {
    Dimension d = getSize();
    g.drawRect(0, 0, d.width - 1, d.height - 1);
  }

  public void textValueChanged(TextEvent te) {
    resultTf.setText("");
  }

  public void actionPerformed(ActionEvent ae) {
    String s = senderTf.getText();
    String r = recipientTf.getText();
    String m = messageTa.getText();
    SmtpEvent smtpe = new SmtpEvent(this, s, r, m);
    fireEmailEvent(smtpe);
  }

  public void addEmailListener(SmtpListener smtpl)
  throws TooManyListenersException {
    if(listener == null) {
      listener = smtpl;
    }
    else {
      throw new TooManyListenersException();
    }
  }

  public void removeEmailListener(SmtpListener smtpl) {
    listener = null;
  }

  public void fireEmailEvent(SmtpEvent smtpe) {
    listener.send(smtpe);
  }

  public void respond(int code) {
    String str = "Smtp Problem";
    if(code == SmtpClient.SENDOK) {
      str = "Sent";
    }
    else if(code == SmtpClient.FAILEDCOMMUNICATION) {
      str = "Failed Communication";
```

13

```
      }
      else if(code == SmtpClient.FAILEDHANDSHAKE) {
        str = "Failed Handshake";
      }
      else if(code == SmtpClient.BADSENDERADDRESS) {
        str = "Bad Sender Address";
      }
      else if(code == SmtpClient.BADRECIPIENT) {
        str = "Bad Recipient";
      }
      else if(code == SmtpClient.FAILEDDATA) {
        str = "Failed Data Transfer";
      }
      else if(code == SmtpClient.FAILEDEMAIL) {
        str = "Failed Email";
      }
      else if(code == SmtpClient.FAILEDQUIT) {
        str = "Failed Quit";
      }
      resultTf.setText(str);
    }

    private void readObject(ObjectInputStream ois)
    throws ClassNotFoundException, IOException {

      // Read non-static and non-transient information from stream
      ois.defaultReadObject();

      // Clear all information from the GUI elements
      senderTf.setText("");
      recipientTf.setText("");
      messageTa.selectAll();
      messageTa.replaceRange("", 0, messageTa.getSelectionEnd());
      resultTf.setText("");
    }
}
```

The SmtpClient Class

The source code for the **SmtpClient** class is shown in the next listing. This class implements the **Serializable** and **SmtpListener** interfaces. It also defines several **int** constants to represent the various types of responses that can be received from the SMTP server. The variables **hostname** and **port** are the two properties of this Bean. They contain the IP address or name of the host and the software port to which the SMTP process is connected, respectively. The variables **pw** and **br** hold references to **PrintWriter** and **BufferedReader** objects, respectively, that are used to communicate with the SMTP server. The **smtpe** and **smtps** variables hold references to the custom event and the object that generated it. These last four variables are **transient** because we do not want to store them in the serial stream.

The constructor initializes the properties and their access methods follow the constructor.

The **send( )** method performs all of the steps to send an electronic mail message. It accepts an **SmtpEvent** object as its argument and initializes **smtpe** and **smtps** from that information. A **Socket** object is created for the machine and port specified by the Bean properties. Its input and output streams are obtained and wrapped as **BufferedReader** and **PrintWriter** objects. The **smtpProtocolHandler( )** method handles all of the steps necessary to communicate with the SMTP server. When this method returns, the socket is closed and the **respond( )** method is called to inform the source of this message that the operation completed successfully. If an exception occurs, the source is informed of this problem.

The **smtpProtocolHandler( )** method sends commands to the SMTP server and interprets its responses. It begins by calling the **init( )** method to read the initialization string from the server. If a problem is encountered, that method returns **false** and **smtpProtocolHandler( )** returns. Otherwise, the **helo( )**, **mailFrom( )**, **rcptTo( )**, **data( )**, **email( )**, and **quit( )** methods are called in sequence to perform the steps necessary to send this message. Each of these methods returns **false** if a problem is encountered.

The **init( )** method reads the string which is sent by the SMTP server when it begins operation. If this string begins with the code 220, the method returns **true**. Otherwise, **respond( )** is called to inform the source that the handshake failed.

The **helo ( )** method sends the HELO command. If the response begins with the code 250, the method returns **true**. Otherwise, **respond( )** is called to inform the source that the handshake failed.

The **mailFrom( )** method sends the MAIL FROM command. If the response begins with the code 250, the method returns **true**. Otherwise, **respond( )** is called to inform the source that there is a problem with the originator email address.

13

The **rcptTo( )** method sends the RCPT TO command. If the response begins with the code 250, the method returns **true**. Otherwise, **respond( )** is called to inform the source that there is a problem with the email address of the recipient.

The **data( )** method sends the DATA command. If the response begins with the code 354, the method returns **true**. Otherwise, **respond( )** is called to inform the source that there is a problem.

The **email( )** method sends the body of the electronic message. It calls **date( )**, **from( )**, **to( )**, and **message( )** to send the various parts of the message header and body. If the response begins with code 250, the method returns **true**. Otherwise, **respond( )** is called to inform the source that this attempt to send email failed.

The date and time information in the email message is sent by the **date( )** method. It uses a **SimpleDateFormat** object to correctly format the date and time information.

The **from( )** and **to( )** methods identify the originator and recipient of this message from the information in the **SmtpEvent** object.

The **message( )** method completes the body of the electronic mail. This information is also obtained from the **SmtpEvent** object. Notice that the body is terminated by a line containing only a period.

The **quit( )** method sends the QUIT command. If the response begins with the code 221, the method returns **true**. Otherwise, **respond( )** is called to inform the source that a problem was encountered.

The **writeCommand( )** method is used to send commands to the SMTP server. It terminates each command with a carriage return and new line and flushes the **PrintWriter** to ensure that the command is sent immediately.

The **readResponse( )** method is used to read responses from the SMTP server. An empty string is returned from this method if an exception is thrown by the **readLine( )** method of the **BufferedReader** object.

```
package smtp;
import java.io.*;
import java.net.*;
import java.text.*;
import java.util.*;

public class SmtpClient implements
Serializable, SmtpListener {
  public final static int SENDOK = 0;
  public final static int FAILEDCOMMUNICATION = 1;
  public final static int FAILEDHANDSHAKE = 2;
```

```java
public final static int BADSENDERADDRESS = 3;
public final static int BADRECIPIENT = 4;
public final static int FAILEDDATA = 5;
public final static int FAILEDEMAIL = 6;
public final static int FAILEDQUIT = 7;
private String hostname;
private int port;
private transient PrintWriter pw;
private transient BufferedReader br;
private transient SmtpEvent smtpe;
private transient SmtpSource smtps;

public SmtpClient() {
  hostname = "";
  port = 25;
}

public String getHostname() {
  return hostname;
}

public int getPort() {
  return port;
}

public void setHostname(String hostname) {
  this.hostname = hostname;
}

public void setPort(int port) {
  this.port = port;
}

public void send(SmtpEvent smtpe) {
  this.smtpe = smtpe;
  smtps = (SmtpSource)smtpe.getSource();
  try {

    // Create BufferedReader and PrintWriter
    Socket socket = new Socket(hostname, port);
    InputStream is = socket.getInputStream();
    InputStreamReader isr = new InputStreamReader(is);
    br =  new BufferedReader(isr);
    OutputStream os = socket.getOutputStream();
    BufferedOutputStream bos = new BufferedOutputStream(os);
```

13

```
      pw = new PrintWriter(bos);

      // Use the SMTP protocol to send the message
      smtpProtocolHandler();

      // Close the socket
      socket.close();

      // Display result for sender
      smtps.respond(SENDOK);
    }
    catch(Exception ex) {
      // Inform sender about problem
      smtps.respond(FAILEDCOMMUNICATION);
    }
  }

  private void smtpProtocolHandler() {
    if(!init()) {
      return;
    }
    if(!helo()) {
      return;
    }
    if(!mailFrom()) {
      return;
    }
    if(!rcptTo()) {
      return;
    }
    if(!data()) {
      return;
    }
    if(!email()) {
      return;
    }
    if(!quit()) {
      return;
    }
  }

  private boolean init() {
    if(!readResponse().startsWith("220")) {
      smtps.respond(FAILEDHANDSHAKE);
      return false;
```

```
      }
    return true;
  }

  private boolean helo() {
    writeCommand("HELO");
    if(!readResponse().startsWith("250")) {
      smtps.respond(FAILEDHANDSHAKE);
      return false;
    }
    return true;
  }

  private boolean mailFrom() {
    writeCommand("MAIL FROM:" + smtpe.getSender());
    if(!readResponse().startsWith("250")) {
      smtps.respond(BADSENDERADDRESS);
      return false;
    }
    return true;
  }

  private boolean rcptTo() {
    String recipient = smtpe.getRecipient();
    writeCommand("RCPT TO:" + recipient);
    if(!readResponse().startsWith("250")) {
      smtps.respond(BADRECIPIENT);
      return false;
    }
    return true;
  }

  private boolean data() {
    writeCommand("DATA");
    if(!readResponse().startsWith("354"))  {
      smtps.respond(FAILEDDATA);
      return false;
    }
    return true;
  }

  private boolean email() {
    date();
    from();
    to();
```

13

```
  message();
  if(!readResponse().startsWith("250")) {
    smtps.respond(FAILEDEMAIL);
    return false;
  }
  return true;
}

private void date() {
  SimpleDateFormat sdf;
  sdf = new SimpleDateFormat("dd MMM yy hh:mm:ss");
  writeCommand("Date: " + sdf.format(new Date()));
}

private void from() {
  writeCommand("From: " + smtpe.getSender());
}

private void to() {
  writeCommand("To: " + smtpe.getRecipient());
}

private void message() {
  writeCommand(smtpe.getMessage());
  writeCommand(".");
}

private boolean quit() {
  writeCommand("QUIT");
  if(!readResponse().startsWith("221")) {
    smtps.respond(FAILEDQUIT);
    return false;
  }
  return true;
}

private void writeCommand(String command) {
  pw.print(command);
  pw.print("\r\n");
  pw.flush();
}

private String readResponse() {
  String line = "";
  try {
```

```
      line = br.readLine();
    }
    catch(Exception ex) {
    }
    return line;
  }
}
```

Testing the SMTP Beans

To test the SMTP components, follow these steps:

1. Create instances of the **SmtpGui** and **SmtpClient** components in BeanBox.
2. Select the **SmtpClient** Bean and use the Properties window to set its **hostname** and **port** properties.
3. Select the **SmtpGui** Bean. Map its email event to the appropriate method call on the **SmtpClient** Bean. (Specifically, select Edit | Events | email | send from the menu bar in BeanBox. Map this event to the **send( )** method of **SmtpClient**.)
4. Complete the sender, recipient, and message fields.
5. Press the Send button. The result text field should display "Sent."

An Overview of the
Post Office Protocol— Version 3 (POP3)

Electronic mail can be received via POP3.

The Post Office Protocol—Version 3 (POP3) defines how an electronic mail message can be retrieved from one machine by another on the Internet. This section provides a brief overview of its primary features. You can find an official definition of this protocol by searching for the document named RFC 822 on the Internet.

Commands are sent from a client machine to a POP3 server. Each command must be terminated by a carriage return and line feed. The POP3 server generates a response for each command. Each response begins with "+OK" if the command was executed successfully or "-ERR" if an error was encountered.

13

The following sections describe five commands that are used in this chapter and some of the responses which can be issued by a POP3 server. Additional details about other types of server responses can be found in RFC 822. It must also be noted that there is a software timer associated with this protocol.

Therefore, if there is no activity for some period of time, the session times out.

NOTE: You may examine this interaction between a client and server by opening a telnet session with a POP3 server. On a Windows 95/NT machine, open a DOS window and type **telnet *pop3server* 110** at the command prompt. Here, *pop3server* is the IP address or name of the machine that runs the POP3 server. Port 110 is typically used for POP3 servers. Type commands to the server and observe the responses.

USER

The USER command is sent by a client to identify the recipient. It has the following format:

> USER *username*

Here, *username* is the email address of the person who wants to retrieve messages. An example of such a command is shown here:

> USER joe@mycompany.com

If there are no problems, the response from the server begins with the substring "+OK." An example of such a response is:

> +OK password required for joe@mycompany.com

If there are problems, the response from the server begins with the substring "-ERR".

PASS

The PASS command is sent by a client to supply a password for the recipient. It has the following format:

> PASS *password*

Here, *password* is the password of the recipient. An example of such a command is shown here:

PASS a1b2c3

If there are no problems, the response from the server begins with the substring "+OK." An example of such a response is:

+OK joe@mycompany.com has 4 messages (s) (3675 octets)

If there are problems, the response from the server begins with the substring "-ERR." An example of such a response is:

-ERR Password supplied by joe@mycompany.com is incorrect.

RETR

The RETR command is sent by a client to retrieve a specific message. It has the following format:

RETR *index*

Here, *index* is the index of the message to be retrieved. An example of such a command is shown here:

RETR 3

If there are no problems, the response from the server begins with the substring "+OK." An example of such a response is shown here:

```
+OK 120 octets
From:  sue@othercompany.com
Date:  22 Nov 97 12:10:08
To:  joe@mycompany.com
I can meet you on Friday.
.
```

Notice that the end of the message is identified by a line containing only a period.

If there are problems, the response from the server begins with the substring "-ERR." An example of such a response is:

-ERR Message 3 does not exist.

13

DELE

The DELE command is sent by a client to delete a specific message. It has the following format:

DELE *index*

Here, *index* is the index of the message to be retrieved. An example of such a command is shown here:

DELE 3

If there are no problems, the response from the server begins with the substring "+OK." An example of such a response is:

+OK Message 3 has been deleted.

If there are problems, the response from the server begins with the substring "-ERR." An example of such a response is:

-ERR Message 3 does not exist.

QUIT

The QUIT command is sent by a client to retrieve a specific message. It has the following format:

QUIT

If there are no problems, the response from the server begins with the substring "+OK." An example of such a response is shown here:

+OK Pop server at mycompany.com signing off.

If there are problems, the response from the server begins with the substring "-ERR."

Classes and Interfaces

This section develops some components to retrieve electronic mail via the POP3 protocol. Let us briefly look at the classes and interfaces used in this example.

First, **Pop3Client** is an invisible Bean that handles the details of the POP3 protocol. It opens a socket to the POP3 server and then writes commands and reads responses from that machine. This component has two properties named **hostname** and **port** that identify the IP name or address of the POP3 host and the software port to which that server is connected. Port 110 is generally used for the POP3 process.

Second, **Pop3Gui** is a visible Bean that presents a user interface that allows a person to enter the information required to retrieve a message. Figure 13-2 shows how this component appears in the BeanBox. You can see that there are text fields for the user name and password. The Connect button must then be pressed to login to the POP3 server. If this login attempt is successful, the label on the button changes to "Disconnect." The Retrieve button must be pressed to retrieve the next message. The message is displayed in the text area and can be deleted by pressing the Delete button.

Third, **Pop3Event** is a custom event that is generated by **Pop3Gui** when the user presses any of its three buttons. This object contains the information that was entered into the GUI elements of that component.

Fourth, **Pop3Listener** is an interface implemented by **Pop3Client**. It defines four methods to receive the **Pop3Event** objects generated by

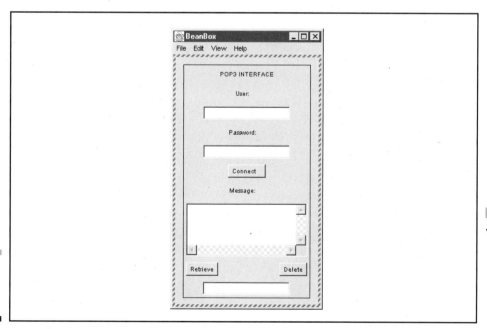

The **Pop3Gui**
Bean
Figure 13-2.

13

Pop3Gui. These provide the connect, retrieve, delete, and disconnect functionality.

Fifth, **Pop3Source** is an interface implemented by **Pop3Gui**. It defines one method called by **Pop3Client** to pass responses back to **Pop3Gui**.

These classes and interfaces are discussed in the following sections. Note that the separation of user interface logic and protocol logic into two separate Beans has several important advantages. First, the user interface can be changed without affecting the protocol Bean. Second, you may wish to build applications that periodically check the electronic messages. This can be done by generating a **Pop3Event** and sending it directly to a **Pop3Client**.

The Pop3Event Class

The source code for the **Pop3Event** class is shown in the following listing. This class extends **EventObject** and encapsulates the information needed to send one or more commands to a POP3 server. The **user**, **pass**, and **msgId** variables hold the user name, user password, and the ID of the message to be retrieved or deleted.

There are three forms for the constructor. The first form is used to login to the POP3 server. The second form is used to retrieve or delete a specific message. The last form is used to disconnect from the server.

```
package pop3;
import java.util.*;

public class Pop3Event extends EventObject {
  private String user, pass;
  private int msgId;

  public Pop3Event(Object source, String user, String pass) {
    super(source);
    this.user = user;
    this.pass = pass;
  }

  public Pop3Event(Object source, int msgId) {
    super(source);
    this.msgId = msgId;
  }

  public Pop3Event(Object source) {
    super(source);
```

```
    }

    public String getUser() {
      return user;
    }

    public String getPass() {
      return pass;
    }

    public int getMsgId() {
      return msgId;
    }
}
```

The Pop3Listener Interface

The source code for the **Pop3Listener** interface is shown in the following listing. It defines four methods that allow a user to connect to a POP3 server, retrieve a message, delete a message, or disconnect.

```
package pop3;
import java.util.*;

public interface Pop3Listener extends EventListener {

    public void connect(Pop3Event pop3e);

    public void retr(Pop3Event pop3e);

    public void dele(Pop3Event pop3e);

    public void disconnect(Pop3Event pop3e);
}
```

The Pop3Source Interface

The source code for the **Pop3Source** interface is shown in the following listing. Its **respond( )** method is called by the **Pop3Client** object to respond to a command request from the **Pop3Gui**. The **message( )** method is called by the **Pop3Client** object to provide a message to the **Pop3Gui**.

13

```
package pop3;
```

```
public interface Pop3Source {

  public void respond(int code);

  public void message(String msg);
}
```

The Pop3Gui Class

The source code for the **Pop3Gui** class is shown in the next listing. This class extends **Panel** and implements the **ActionListener**, **Pop3Source**, and **TextListener** interfaces. The variable **listeners** is a vector that holds references to the adapter objects that receive **Pop3Event** objects and forward these to the **Pop3Client**. The other instance variables hold references to the three text fields, one text area, and three buttons of the user interface. A **transient** variable named **msgId** identifies which message is currently displayed in the text area.

The constructor first creates the GUI elements. Notice that the **Pop3Gui** object is registered to receive text events from the text fields and action events from the button. **GridBagLayout** and **GridBagConstraints** objects are then created.

The **gridx** and **gridy** fields determine the row and column of the grid in which the upper-left corner of the element is located. In this example, **gridx** is equal to zero for all elements except the Delete button. In that case, **gridx** is equal to one. The variable **gridy** is adjusted before adding the next element. The **gridwidth** and **gridheight** fields determine the number of columns and rows that are used by this component. In this example, **gridwidth** is equal to two for all rows except the one which contains the Retrieve and Delete buttons. In that case, **gridwidth** is set to one. The **insets** field holds an **Insets** object that determines the margin around each component. The constructor concludes by adding each of the elements to the **SmtpGui** object.

The **paint( )** method draws a border around the Bean. The **textValueChanged( )** method is called when either the user or password text field is changed. It clears the result text field.

The **actionPerformed( )** method is called when any button is pressed. It clears the message area and calls the **connectOrDisconnect( )**, **retrieve( )**, or **delete( )** method.

The **connectOrDisconnect( )** method examines the current label on that button. If it is equal to "Connect," a **Pop3Event** object is created with the user name and password and this object is passed as an argument to **fireMethod( )**. Otherwise, a **Pop3Event** object is created by using a different constructor. In either case, the second argument to **fireMethod( )** is the name of the method to be invoked.

The **retrieve( )** and **delete( )** methods generate **Pop3Event** objects to retrieve and delete specific messages. In both cases, **fireMethod( )** is invoked to send this custom event to the **Pop3Client** object. Its second argument is the name of the **Pop3Listener** method that should be invoked.

The **addPop3Listener( )** and **removePop3Listener( )** methods provide the required registration and unregistration functionality.

Specific methods in the **Pop3Listener** interface are invoked via **fireMethod( )**. Its first argument is the **Pop3Event** object and its second argument is the name of the method to be invoked. The **listeners** vector is cloned in a **synchronized** block as previously described in this book. Then, the Java reflection capabilities are used to obtain a **Method** object for the method named in the second argument. This method is part of the **Pop3Listener** interface and accepts one argument of type **Pop3Event**. The method is then invoked for all listeners by using the **invoke( )** method of the **Method** object.

The **respond( )** method is called by the **Pop3Client** Bean to provide a response for a command. The response is encoded as an **int** that is passed as the argument to that method. These **int** values are defined by the **Pop3Client** object. The function of the **responsd( )** method is to examine this **int** value and determine a string that should be displayed to the user in the result text field. Some additional processing is done for certain types of responses. For example, the label on the Connect/Disconnect button is changed to "Connect" if either a **FAILEDCONNECT** or **FAILEDLOGIN** response is received. If the connect attempt was successful, the label on this button is changed to "Disconnect." The label on the button is also changed to "Connect" for **QUITOK**, **FAILEDQUIT**, and **TIMEOUT** responses.

Finally, the **readObject( )** method is called during the deserialization process. It clears the text fields and text area and sets the label on the Connect/Disconnect button to "Connect."

```
package pop3;
import java.awt.*;
import java.awt.event.*;
import java.io.*;
import java.lang.reflect.*;
import java.util.*;
```

13

```
public class Pop3Gui extends Panel
implements ActionListener, Pop3Source, TextListener {
  private Vector listeners;
  private TextField userTf, passTf, resultTf;
  private TextArea messageTa;
  private Button connectButton, deleteButton, retrieveButton;
  private transient int msgId;

  public Pop3Gui() {

    // Create listeners vector
    listeners = new Vector();

    // Create GUI elements
    Label title = new Label("POP3 INTERFACE", Label.CENTER);
    Label userLabel = new Label("User:");
    userTf = new TextField(20);
    userTf.addTextListener(this);
    Label passLabel = new Label("Password:");
    passTf = new TextField(20);
    passTf.setEchoChar('*');
    passTf.addTextListener(this);
    connectButton = new Button("Connect    ");
    connectButton.addActionListener(this);
    Label messageLabel = new Label("Message:");
    messageTa = new TextArea(5, 30);
    retrieveButton = new Button("Retrieve");
    retrieveButton.addActionListener(this);
    deleteButton = new Button("Delete");
    deleteButton.addActionListener(this);
    resultTf = new TextField(20);

    // Create and set layout manager
    GridBagLayout gbl = new GridBagLayout();
    setLayout(gbl);

    // Create and initialize GridBagConstraints object
    GridBagConstraints gbc = new GridBagConstraints();
    gbc.gridx = 0;
    gbc.gridwidth = 2;
    gbc.gridheight = 1;
    gbc.insets = new Insets(5, 5, 5, 5);

    // Add title to the GUI
```

```
gbc.gridy = 0;
gbl.setConstraints(title, gbc);
add(title);

// Add user label to the GUI
gbc.gridy = 1;
gbl.setConstraints(userLabel, gbc);
add(userLabel);

// Add user text field to the GUI
gbc.gridy = 2;
gbl.setConstraints(userTf, gbc);
add(userTf);

// Add password label to the GUI
gbc.gridy = 3;
gbl.setConstraints(passLabel, gbc);
add(passLabel);

// Add password text field to the GUI
gbc.gridy = 4;
gbl.setConstraints(passTf, gbc);
add(passTf);

// Add connect button to the GUI
gbc.gridy = 5;
gbl.setConstraints(connectButton, gbc);
add(connectButton);

// Add message label area to the GUI
gbc.gridy = 6;
gbl.setConstraints(messageLabel, gbc);
add(messageLabel);

// Add message text area to the GUI
gbc.gridy = 7;
gbl.setConstraints(messageTa, gbc);
add(messageTa);

// Add retrieve button to the GUI
gbc.gridy = 8;
gbc.gridwidth = 1;
gbl.setConstraints(retrieveButton, gbc);
add(retrieveButton);
```

13

```
  // Add delete button to the GUI
  gbc.gridx = 1;
  gbc.gridy = 8;
  gbc.gridwidth = 1;
  gbc.anchor = GridBagConstraints.EAST;
  gbl.setConstraints(deleteButton, gbc);
  add(deleteButton);

  // Add result text field to the GUI
  gbc.gridx = 0;
  gbc.gridy = 9;
  gbc.gridwidth = 2;
  gbc.anchor = GridBagConstraints.CENTER;
  gbl.setConstraints(resultTf, gbc);
  add(resultTf);
}

public void paint(Graphics g) {
  Dimension d = getSize();
  g.drawRect(0, 0, d.width - 1, d.height - 1);
}

public void textValueChanged(TextEvent te) {
  resultTf.setText("");
}

public void actionPerformed(ActionEvent ae) {
  messageTa.selectAll();
  messageTa.replaceRange("", 0, messageTa.getSelectionEnd());
  resultTf.setText("");
  Button button = (Button)ae.getSource();
  if(button == connectButton) {
    connectOrDisconnect();
  }
  else if(button == retrieveButton) {
    retrieve();
  }
  else if(button == deleteButton) {
    delete();
  }
}

private void connectOrDisconnect() {
  // Connect or disconnect based on button label
  if(connectButton.getLabel().equals("Connect    ")) {
```

```
      String user = userTf.getText();
      String pass = passTf.getText();
      Pop3Event pop3e = new Pop3Event(this, user, pass);
      fireMethod(pop3e, "connect");
    }
    else {
      Pop3Event pop3e = new Pop3Event(this);
      fireMethod(pop3e, "disconnect");
    }
  }

  private void retrieve() {
    Pop3Event pop3e = new Pop3Event(this, ++msgId);
    fireMethod(pop3e, "retr");
  }

  private void delete() {
    Pop3Event pop3e = new Pop3Event(this, msgId);
    fireMethod(pop3e, "dele");
  }

  public void addPop3Listener(Pop3Listener pop3l) {
    listeners.addElement(pop3l);
  }

  public void removePop3Listener(Pop3Listener pop3l) {
    listeners.removeElement(pop3l);
  }

  public void fireMethod(Pop3Event p3e, String mname) {

    // Clone the listeners vector in a synchronized block
    Vector v;
    synchronized(this) {
      v = (Vector)listeners.clone();
    }

    // Obtain a Method object for the method named 'mname'
    // in the Pop3Listener interface which accepts one
    // parameter of type Pop3Event
    Class cls = Pop3Listener.class;
    Class pTypes[] = { Pop3Event.class };
    Method method;
    try {
      method = cls.getMethod(mname, pTypes);
```

13

```
    }
  catch(Exception ex) {
    return;
  }

  // Initialize an array with the arguments for
  // this method
  Object args[] = { p3e };

  // Invoke the method for all listeners
  for(int i = 0; i < v.size(); i++) {
    Pop3Listener p3l = (Pop3Listener)v.elementAt(i);
    try {
      method.invoke(p3l, args);
    }
    catch(Exception ex) {
    }
  }
}

public void respond(int code) {
  String str = "Pop3 Problem";
  if(code == Pop3Client.FAILEDCONNECT) {
    str = "Failed Connect";
    connectButton.setLabel("Connect   ");
  }
  else if(code == Pop3Client.FAILEDLOGIN) {
    str = "Failed Login";
    connectButton.setLabel("Connect   ");
  }
  else if(code == Pop3Client.CONNECTOK) {
    str = "Connected";
    connectButton.setLabel("Disconnect");
    msgId = 0;
  }
  else if(code == Pop3Client.RETRIEVEOK) {
    str = "Retrieved";
  }
  else if(code == Pop3Client.BADMSGINDEX) {
    str = "No message";
  }
  else if(code == Pop3Client.MSGDELETED) {
    str = "Message Deleted";
  }
```

```java
    else if(code == Pop3Client.FAILEDRETRIEVE) {
      str = "Failed Retrieve";
    }
    else if(code == Pop3Client.DELETEOK) {
      str = "Deleted";
    }
    else if(code == Pop3Client.FAILEDDELETE) {
      str = "Failed Delete";
    }
    else if(code == Pop3Client.QUITOK) {
      str = "Quit";
      connectButton.setLabel("Connect    ");
    }
    else if(code == Pop3Client.FAILEDQUIT) {
      str = "Failed Quit";
      connectButton.setLabel("Connect    ");
    }
    else if(code == Pop3Client.TIMEOUT) {
      str = "Timeout";
      connectButton.setLabel("Connect    ");
    }
    resultTf.setText(str);
  }

  public void message(String s) {
    messageTa.selectAll();
    messageTa.replaceRange(s, 0, messageTa.getSelectionEnd());
  }

  private void readObject(ObjectInputStream ois)
  throws ClassNotFoundException, IOException {

    // Read non-static and non-transient information from stream
    ois.defaultReadObject();

    // Clear all information from the GUI elements
    userTf.setText("");
    passTf.setText("");
    connectButton.setLabel("Connect    ");
    messageTa.selectAll();
    messageTa.replaceRange("", 0, messageTa.getSelectionEnd());
    resultTf.setText("");
  }
}
```

13

The Pop3Client Class

The source code for the **Pop3Client** class is shown in the next listing. This class implements the **Pop3Listener** and **Serializable** interfaces. It also defines several **int** constants to represent the various types of responses that can be received from the POP3 server. The variables named **hostname** and **port** are the two properties of this Bean. They contain the IP address or name of the POP3 host and the software port to which it is connected, respectively. The variables **pw** and **br** hold references to **PrintWriter** and **BufferedReader** objects, respectively, that are used to communicate with the POP3 server.

The constructor initializes the properties and the access methods for the properties follow the constructor.

The **connect( )** method performs all of the steps required to login to a POP3 server. It accepts a **Pop3Event** object as its argument. The **pop3s** variable identifies the source of the custom event. A **Socket** object is created for the machine and port specified by the Bean properties. Its input and output streams are obtained and wrapped as **BufferedReader** and **PrintWriter** objects. The initialization message sent by the server is checked to confirm that it begins with the substring "+OK." If so, the user name and password are supplied. Again, the responses from the server are checked. If no errors are encountered, the **respond( )** method of the **Pop3Source** object is called with the **CONNECTOK** argument.

The **retr( )** and **dele( )** methods perform all of the steps required to retrieve and delete messages from a POP3 server. The **disconnect( )** method performs all of the steps to disconnect from a POP3 server. These three methods each accept a **Pop3Event** object as their argument. They send a command to the POP3 server, interpret the response, and return a result to the **Pop3Source** object by invoking its **respond( )** method. The **retr( )** method also calls the **message( )** method of the **Pop3Source** object.

The **writeCommand( )** method is used to send commands to the POP3 server. It terminates each command with a carriage return and new line and flushes the **PrintWriter** to ensure that the command is sent immediately.

The **readResponse( )** method is used to read responses from the POP3 server. An empty string is returned from this method if an exception is thrown by the **readLine( )** method of the **BufferedReader** object.

Messages are read from the POP3 server by calling **readMessage( )**. Notice that this method interprets a line starting with a period as the end of a message.

```
package pop3;
import java.io.*;
import java.net.*;

public class Pop3Client implements Pop3Listener, Serializable {
  public final static int FAILEDCONNECT = 0;
  public final static int FAILEDLOGIN = 1;
  public final static int CONNECTOK = 2;
  public final static int RETRIEVEOK = 3;
  public final static int BADMSGINDEX = 4;
  public final static int MSGDELETED = 5;
  public final static int FAILEDRETRIEVE = 6;
  public final static int DELETEOK = 7;
  public final static int FAILEDDELETE = 8;
  public final static int QUITOK = 9;
  public final static int FAILEDQUIT = 10;
  public final static int TIMEOUT = 11;
  private String hostname;
  private int port;
  private transient PrintWriter pw;
  private transient BufferedReader br;

  public Pop3Client() {
    hostname = "";
    port = 110;
  }

  public String getHostname() {
    return hostname;
  }

  public int getPort() {
    return port;
  }

  public void setHostname(String hostname) {
    this.hostname = hostname;
  }

  public void setPort(int port) {
    this.port = port;
  }

  public void connect(Pop3Event pop3e) {
    Pop3Source pop3s = (Pop3Source)pop3e.getSource();
```

```
try {

  // Create BufferedReader and PrintWriter
  Socket socket = new Socket(hostname, port);
  InputStream is = socket.getInputStream();
  InputStreamReader isr = new InputStreamReader(is);
  br = new BufferedReader(isr);
  OutputStream os = socket.getOutputStream();
  BufferedOutputStream bos = new BufferedOutputStream(os);
  pw = new PrintWriter(bos);

  // Check return code
  if(!readResponse().startsWith("+OK")) {
    pop3s.respond(FAILEDCONNECT);
    return;
  }

  // Supply user and password information
  writeCommand("USER " + pop3e.getUser());
  if(!readResponse().startsWith("+OK")) {
    pop3s.respond(FAILEDLOGIN);
    return;
  }
  writeCommand("PASS " + pop3e.getPass());
  if(!readResponse().startsWith("+OK")) {
    pop3s.respond(FAILEDLOGIN);
    return;
  }
  pop3s.respond(CONNECTOK);

}
catch(Exception ex) {
  pop3s.respond(FAILEDCONNECT);
}
}

public void retr(Pop3Event pop3e) {
  Pop3Source pop3s = (Pop3Source)pop3e.getSource();
  try {
    writeCommand("RETR " + pop3e.getMsgId());
    String line = br.readLine();
    if(line.startsWith("+OK")) {
      pop3s.respond(RETRIEVEOK);
      pop3s.message(readMessage());
    }
```

```
      else if(line.indexOf("does not exist") != -1) {
        pop3s.respond(BADMSGINDEX);
      }
      else if(line.indexOf("has been deleted") != -1) {
        pop3s.respond(MSGDELETED);
      }
      else if(line.indexOf("timeout") != -1) {
        pop3s.respond(TIMEOUT);
      }
      else {
        pop3s.respond(FAILEDRETRIEVE);
      }
    }
  catch(Exception ex) {
    pop3s.respond(FAILEDRETRIEVE);
  }
}

public void dele(Pop3Event pop3e) {
  Pop3Source pop3s = (Pop3Source)pop3e.getSource();
  try {
    writeCommand("DELE " + pop3e.getMsgId());
    String response = readResponse();
    if(response.startsWith("+OK")) {
      pop3s.respond(DELETEOK);
      return;
    }
    else if(response.indexOf("timeout") != -1) {
      pop3s.respond(TIMEOUT);
      return;
    }
  }
  catch(Exception ex) {
  }
  pop3s.respond(FAILEDDELETE);
}

public void disconnect(Pop3Event pop3e) {
  Pop3Source pop3s = (Pop3Source)pop3e.getSource();
  try {
    writeCommand("QUIT");
    String response = readResponse();
    if(response.startsWith("+OK")) {
      pop3s.respond(QUITOK);
      return;
```

13

```
      }
      else if(response.indexOf("timeout") != -1) {
        pop3s.respond(TIMEOUT);
        return;
      }
    }
    catch(Exception ex) {
    }
    pop3s.respond(FAILEDQUIT);
  }

  private void writeCommand(String command) {
    pw.print(command);
    pw.print("\r\n");
    pw.flush();
  }

  private String readResponse() {
    String line = "";
    try {
      line = br.readLine();
    }
    catch(Exception ex) {
    }
    return line;
  }

  private String readMessage() {
    String message = "";
    while(true) {
      try {
        String line = br.readLine();
        message += line + "\n";
        if(line.startsWith(".")) {
          break;
        }
      }
      catch(Exception ex) {
        break;
      }
    }
    return message;
  }
}
```

Testing the POP3 Beans

To test the POP3 components, follow these steps:

1. Create instances of the **POP3Gui** and **POP3Client** components in BeanBox.

2. Select the **POP3Client** Bean and use the Properties window to set its **hostname** and **port** properties.

3. Select the **Pop3Gui** Bean. Map its four POP3 events to the appropriate method calls on the **Pop3Client** Bean. (For example, select Edit | Events | pop3 | connect from the menu bar in BeanBox. Map this event to the **connect( )** method of **Pop3Client**.)

4. Complete the user and password fields.

5. Press the Connect button. The result text field should display "Connected" and the label on the button should now be "Disconnect."

6. Press the Retrieve button. The result text field should display "Retrieved" and the text area should display the message.

7. Press the Delete button to delete the message. The result text field should display "Deleted."

8. You may continue retrieving and deleting messages. When you want to terminate your session with the POP3 server, press the Disconnect button.

Concluding Comments

This chapter illustrates how to design a set of Beans that allow an application to communicate with other users. The protocol handlers are separated from the user interface components. Therefore, the same protocol handlers can be used with different user interfaces. You can apply the principles in this chapter to build Beans that handle other Internet protocols such as the File Transfer Protocol (FTP) or Network News Transfer Protocol (NNTP).

13

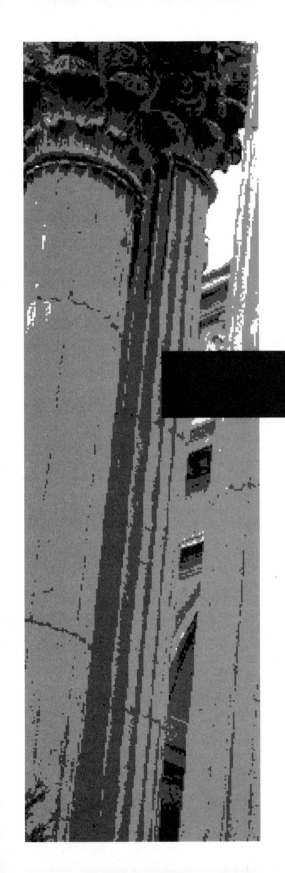

CHAPTER 14

Integrating Key Concepts

The preceding chapters examined the various techniques that are required to develop Beans. In those chapters, we examined some key concepts. Here you will see how the pieces fit together. In this final chapter, an application is developed that integrates many of the elements required to create professional-quality components. The example is a graphical tool that allows you to instantiate and connect Beans. Among other things, it illustrates how the reflection and introspection classes introduced in Chapter 5 can be used to dynamically obtain information about components. A class loader is also developed to use Beans and their supporting classes from JAR files.

User Interface

The user interface for this tool is deliberately kept simple. An empty window is initially presented. This provides a layout area to which you may add Beans. These can then be connected together.

In order to hold the source code for this example to a manageable size, several restrictions apply. The Beans to be used by this tool must be placed in the beantool\jars directory. Only Beans that are subclasses of **java.lang.Component** are processed. Non-visible components are ignored. Beans that are applets do not work here. Also, the class loader does not handle any resource files associated with Beans and the program does not provide any capability to configure Beans. You may find it an interesting exercise to remove these restrictions.

Enter the following command to start the program:

    java beantool.BeanTool

An empty frame titled "BeanTool" should appear. The following sections describe how to use this tool.

Adding a Bean to the Layout Area

Follow these steps to add a Bean to the layout area:

1. Position the cursor at the point where you want to add a Bean. (The cursor position indicates where you want to locate the upper-left corner of the Bean.)
2. Press and hold the ALT key.
3. Click the left mouse button. Observe that a modal dialog box appears. This is labeled "Add Dialog" and contains a list of the available Beans, as shown in Figure 14-1.

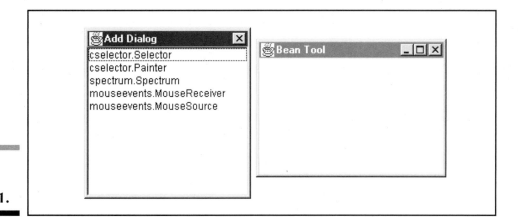

The Add
Dialog box
Figure 14-1.

4. Release the ALT key.

5. Select one of the entries in the list. Observe that the modal dialog box disappears and that a new instance of the Bean has been created.

Connecting Two Beans in the Layout Area

Follow these steps to connect two Beans in the layout area:

1. Position the cursor at a point slightly above the top border of the Bean that is to be the event source.

2. Hold the SHIFT key.

3. Click the left mouse button.

4. Position the cursor at a point slightly above the top border of the Bean that is to be the event listener.

5. Click the left mouse button. Observe that a modal dialog box appears as shown in Figure 14-2. This is labeled "Connect Dialog" and it contains a list of event set names. These are the event sets generated by the source.

6. Release the SHIFT key.

7. Select one of the entries in the list. Observe that the modal dialog box disappears. As the source generates the designated events, these are received and processed by the listener.

14

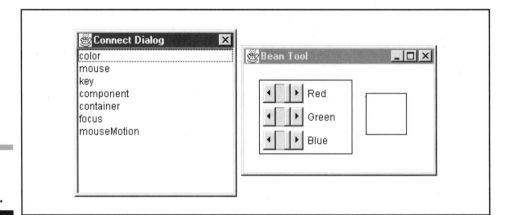

The Connect
Dialog box
Figure 14-2.

Source Code

There are seven classes in this example. Their primary functions are summarized in the following table:

Class	Function
AddDialog	Displays a dialog box that allows the user to add a Bean to the layout area.
Bean	Contains the names of the available Beans.
BeanInstance	Contains information about an instance of a Bean in the layout area.
BeanTool	Provides the layout area in which Beans are contained.
ConnectDialog	Displays a dialog box that allows the user to connect two Beans.
Jar	Processes the entries from a JAR file.
JarClassLoader	Loads .class entries from the JAR files.

The following sections discuss the source code for each of these classes. These are considered in a logical, not alphabetic, order.

The BeanTool Class

The source code for **BeanTool** is shown in the next listing. Its **x** and **y** variables identify the position of the mouse when it is clicked. The **bean1** variable is used when you are connecting two Beans. It holds a reference to the first Bean that is selected (that is, the event source).

The **main( )** method processes the JAR files in the beantool\jars subdirectory by invoking the **process( )** method of **Jar**. An instance of **BeanTool** is then created.

The constructor calls the superclass constructor to provide a title for the frame. It then creates instances of **MyMouseAdapter** and **MyWindowAdapter** and registers these to receive mouse and window events. The size of the frame is set and it is made visible.

The **MyMouseAdapter** class extends **MouseAdapter** and overrides **mouseClicked( )**. This method saves the mouse position in **x** and **y**. If the ALT key is pressed, the **add( )** method is called. If the SHIFT key is pressed, the **connect( )** method is called. The layout area is then repainted.

The **MyWindowAdapter** class extends **WindowAdapter** and overrides **windowClosing( )** to exit from the application.

An **AddDialog** object is created by the **add( )** method to allow a user to select a Bean. Because the user is not connecting components, **bean1** is set to **null**.

The **connect( )** method determines which Bean has been selected by the user. If **selectBeanInstance( )** returns **null**, the cursor is not positioned slightly above the top border of any Bean. If **bean1** is **null**, this means that the user is selecting the first of two Beans to be connected. In that case, a reference to that component is saved in **bean1** and the method returns. Otherwise, the user is selecting the second of two Beans to be connected. In that case, a **ConnectDialog** object is created that allows the user to identify the events for which the listener should be registered. When this operation is complete, **bean1** is set to **null**.

The **selectBeanContainer( )** method determines which of the Beans in the frame has been selected by the user. A component is selected if the mouse is clicked within a small, invisible rectangle along the top of a Bean. This rectangle is ten pixels in height.

All of the Bean instances are arranged in the frame via the **doLayout( )** method.

A Bean is added to the frame via the **insertBean( )** method. This is called from the **AddDialog** object. A **BeanInstance** object is created for the component. This object contains a reference to the Bean and its position in the frame. Finally, the **doLayout( )** method is called to layout all of the components.

```java
package beantool;
import java.awt.*;
import java.awt.event.*;
import java.beans.*;
import java.util.*;

public class BeanTool extends Frame {
  private int x, y;
  private Object bean1;

  public static void main(String args[]) {
    Jar.process();
    new BeanTool();
  }

  public BeanTool() {
    super("Bean Tool");
    addMouseListener(new MyMouseAdapter());
    addWindowListener(new MyWindowAdapter());
    setSize(400, 400);
    setVisible(true);
  }

  class MyMouseAdapter extends MouseAdapter {
    public void mouseClicked(MouseEvent me) {
      x = me.getX();
      y = me.getY();
      if(me.isAltDown()) {
        add();
      }
      else if(me.isShiftDown()) {
        connect();
      }
      repaint();
    }
  }
}
```

```
class MyWindowAdapter extends WindowAdapter {
  public void windowClosing(WindowEvent we) {
    System.exit(0);
  }
}

public void add() {
  new AddDialog(this);
  bean1 = null;
}

public void connect() {
  BeanInstance bi = selectBeanInstance();
  if(bi != null) {
    if(bean1 == null) {
      bean1 = bi.getBean();
      return;
    }
    Object bean2 = bi.getBean();
    new ConnectDialog(this, "Title", bean1, bean2);
  }
  bean1 = null;
}

public BeanInstance selectBeanInstance() {
  // Determine which component is being selected
  Vector v = BeanInstance.getBeanInstances();
  Enumeration e = v.elements();
  while(e.hasMoreElements()) {
    BeanInstance bi = (BeanInstance)e.nextElement();
    Component c = (Component)bi.getBean();
    Point p = c.getLocation();
    Dimension d = c.getSize();
    Rectangle r =
      new Rectangle(p.x, p.y - 10, d.width - 1, 10);
    if(r.contains(x, y)) {
      return bi;
    }
  }
  return null;
}

public void doLayout() {
  // Layout all of the components
```

14

```
    Vector v = BeanInstance.getBeanInstances();
    Enumeration e = v.elements();
    while(e.hasMoreElements()) {
      BeanInstance bi = (BeanInstance)e.nextElement();
      Component c = (Component)bi.getBean();
      Dimension d = c.getPreferredSize();
      c.setBounds(bi.getX(), bi.getY(), d.width, d.height);
      c.doLayout();
    }
  }

  public void insertBean(String beanName) {

    // Create a new instance of the Bean
    // named beanName
    BeanInstance bi = new BeanInstance(this, beanName, x, y);

    // Layout all components
    doLayout();
  }
}
```

The Jar Class

The source code for **Jar** is shown in the following listing. This is very similar
to the **Jar** class seen in Chapter 6. The primary difference is that the
processManifestFile( ) method reads and processes the entries in the
manifest file. A **Bean** object is created for each .class file in the JAR file that is
designated as a Bean. (This information is used later by **AddDialog** to list all
of the available Beans.)

```
package beantool;
import java.io.*;
import java.util.*;
import java.util.zip.*;

public class Jar {
  private static Hashtable data = new Hashtable();
  private String filename;

  public static void putData(String clsName, byte[] buffer) {
    data.put(clsName, buffer);
  }

  public static Object getData(String clsName) {
```

```
      return data.get(clsName);
  }

  public static void process() {
    try {
      char c = File.separatorChar;
      File dir = new File("beantool" + c + "jars");
      String entries[] = dir.list();
      for(int i = 0; i < entries.length; i++) {
        if(entries[i].endsWith(".jar")) {
          new Jar("beantool" + c + "jars" + c + entries[i]);
        }
      }
    }
    catch(Exception ex) {
      ex.printStackTrace();
    }
  }

  public Jar(String filename) {
    // Read and process the .class entries in the JAR file
    this.filename = filename;
    try {
      FileInputStream fis = new FileInputStream(filename);
      ZipInputStream zis = new ZipInputStream(fis);
      ZipEntry ze = null;
      while((ze = zis.getNextEntry()) != null) {
        String name = ze.getName();
        if(name.equals("META-INF/MANIFEST.MF")) {
          processManifestFile(zis);
        }
        else if(name.endsWith(".class")) {
          processClassFile(name, zis);
        }
      }
      zis.close();
    }
    catch(Exception ex) {
      ex.printStackTrace();
    }
  }

  private void processManifestFile(ZipInputStream zis) {

    try {
```

14

```
      // Create a BufferedReader for the zip input stream
      InputStreamReader isr = new InputStreamReader(zis);
      BufferedReader br = new BufferedReader(isr);

      // Read lines from the manifest file
      // and create Bean objects
      String name = null;
      String line = null;
      while((line = br.readLine()) != null) {

        // Process lines starting with .class
        if(line.startsWith("Name: ") &&
        line.endsWith(".class")) {
          name = line.substring(line.indexOf(":") + 2);
        }
        else if(line.startsWith("Java-Bean: ")) {
          if(name != null) {

            // Determine class name
            String name2 = name.replace('/', '.');
            int i = name2.indexOf(".class");
            name2 = name2.substring(0, i);

            // Create a Bean object for that class
            new Bean(name2);
            name = null;
          }
        }
      }
    }
    catch(Exception ex) {
      ex.printStackTrace();
    }
}

private void processClassFile(String name1,
ZipInputStream zis) {

  // Determine class name
  String name2 = name1.replace('/','.');
  int i = name2.indexOf(".class");
  if(i != -1) {
    name2 = name2.substring(0, i);
  }
```

```
    try {

      // Read bytecodes from the zip input stream
      ByteArrayOutputStream baos =
        new ByteArrayOutputStream();
      for(;;) {
        byte block[] = new byte[1024];
        int len = zis.read(block);
        if(len < 0) {
          break;
        }
        baos.write(block, 0, len);
      }
      byte buffer[] = baos.toByteArray();

      // Save these bytecodes
      putData(name2, buffer);
    }
    catch(Exception ex) {
      ex.printStackTrace();
    }
  }
}
```

The JarClassLoader Class

The source code for **JarClassLoader** is shown in the following listing. It is identical to the class loader in Chapter 6 and is reproduced here for your convenience.

```
package beantool;

public class JarClassLoader extends ClassLoader {
  public static JarClassLoader singleton =
    new JarClassLoader();

  protected Class loadClass(String clsName, boolean resolve)
  throws ClassNotFoundException {

    // Check the System class loader
    Class cls;
    try {
      cls = super.findSystemClass(clsName);
      return cls;
```

14

```
    }
    catch(ClassNotFoundException ex) {
    }
    catch(NoClassDefFoundError err) {
    }

    // Check if this class has already
    // been loaded
    cls = findLoadedClass(clsName);
    if(cls != null) {
      return cls;
    }

    // Get the bytecodes for this class
    byte buffer[] = (byte[])Jar.getData(clsName);
    if(buffer == null) {
      throw new ClassNotFoundException();
    }

    // Parse the data
    cls = defineClass(clsName, buffer, 0, buffer.length);
    if(cls == null) {
      throw new ClassFormatError();
    }

    // Resolve the class if necessary
    if(resolve) {
      resolveClass(cls);
    }

    // Return the class
    return cls;
  }
}
```

The Bean Class

The source code for **Bean** is shown in the following listing. Instances of this class are created for each Bean that is read from the JAR files in the beantool\jars directory. This information is needed by **AddDialog**.

```
package beantool;
import java.util.*;

public class Bean {
```

```
private static Vector beans = new Vector();
private String name;

public static Vector getBeans() {
  return beans;
}

public Bean(String name) {
  this.name = name;
  beans.addElement(this);
}

public String getName() {
  return name;
}
}
```

The AddDialog Class

The source code for **AddDialog** is shown in the next listing. A reference to the **BeanTool** object is held in **beanTool** and a reference to the list element is held in **list**. The constructor invokes the superclass constructor, initializes the instance variables, calls **initializeList( )** to fill the list with the names of the available Beans, registers a **MyWindowAdapter** object to receive window events, sets the size of the dialog, and makes it visible.

The **initializeList( )** method invokes the **getBeans( )** method of the **Bean** class to obtain the names of the Beans and add these to the list.

When a user selects a Bean from the list, **itemStateChanged( )** is invoked. This method calls the **insertBean( )** method of the **BeanTool** object to add the Bean to the frame and invokes **dispose( )** to relinquish the resources used by the dialog box.

```
package beantool;
import java.awt.*;
import java.awt.event.*;
import java.util.*;

public class AddDialog extends Dialog
implements ItemListener {
  private BeanTool beanTool;
  private java.awt.List list;

  public AddDialog(BeanTool beanTool) {
```

14

```java
    // Invoke superclass constructor
    super(beanTool, "Add Dialog", true);

    // Initialize beanTool
    this.beanTool = beanTool;

    // Create and initialize list
    // and add it to dialog box
    list = new java.awt.List();
    initializeList();
    list.addItemListener(this);
    add("Center", list);

    // Register to receive window events
    addWindowListener(new MyWindowAdapter());

    // Set size of dialog and make it visible
    setSize(200, 200);
    show();
  }

  private void initializeList() {
    // Initialize list
    Vector beans = Bean.getBeans();
    Enumeration e = beans.elements();
    while(e.hasMoreElements()) {
      Bean bean = (Bean)e.nextElement();
      list.add(bean.getName());
    }
  }

  public void itemStateChanged(ItemEvent ie) {
    // Process list selection
    String beanName = list.getSelectedItem();
    beanTool.insertBean(beanName);
    dispose();
  }

  class MyWindowAdapter extends WindowAdapter {
    public void windowClosing(WindowEvent we) {
      dispose();
    }
  }
}
```

The BeanInstance Class

The source code for **BeanInstance** is shown in the next listing. There is one **BeanInstance** object for each Bean in the layout area. It holds a reference to the component and also records its location in the frame. (The location is stored as the x and y coordinates of the upper-left corner of the Bean.) This information is stored in the **bean**, **x**, and **y** variables. The static variable, **bean Instances**, holds references to all of the **BeanInstance** objects.

The **getBeanInstances( )** method returns the value of **beanInstances**.

The constructor begins by saving the location data. It then uses the **instantiate( )** method of the **Beans** class to create an instance of the Bean. The first argument to this method is the **JarClassLoader** object and the second argument is the name of the Bean. Beans that are not a subclass of **Component** are ignored in this tool. Otherwise, the component is added to the **beanInstances** vector. The component is then positioned via **setLocation( )**. Layout operations are done via **doLayout( )** and the Bean is added to the **BeanTool** frame.

Access methods for the instance variables follow the constructor.

```
package beantool;
import java.awt.*;
import java.beans.*;
import java.util.*;

public class BeanInstance {
  private static Vector beanInstances = new Vector();
  private Object bean;
  private int x, y;

  public static Vector getBeanInstances() {
    return beanInstances;
  }

  public BeanInstance(BeanTool beanTool,
  String beanName, int x, int y) {

    // Save the location of the component
    this.x = x;
    this.y = y;

    // Instantiate the component named beanName
    try {
```

14

```
    bean = Beans.instantiate(JarClassLoader.singleton,
      beanName);
  }
  catch(Exception ex) {
    return;
  }

  // Ignore invisible components
  if(!Beans.isInstanceOf(bean, Component.class)) {
    return;
  }

  // Add the component to beanInstances
  beanInstances.addElement(this);

  // Position and layout the component
  Component c = (Component)bean;
  c.setLocation(x, y);
  c.doLayout();

  // Add the component to the BeanTool frame
  beanTool.add(c);
}

public Object getBean() {
  return bean;
}

public int getX() {
  return x;
}

public int getY() {
  return y;
}
}
```

The ConnectDialog Class

The source code for **ConnectDialog** is shown in the next listing. References to the event source and listener are held in **bean1** and **bean2**, respectively. An array of the **EventSetDescriptor** objects for the source is held in **esds**.

The constructor invokes its superclass constructor. A title is assigned to the modal dialog box. Both **bean1** and **bean2** are updated from the constructor arguments. The list element is initialized by calling **initializeList( )** and a **MyWindowAdapter** object is created and registered to process window events. The size of the dialog box is set and it is made visible.

The **initializeList( )** method gets the **BeanInfo** object for **bean1**. The names of the event sets generated by **bean1** are obtained via **getEventSetDescriptors( )**. An event set name is obtained by using **getName( )**.

When a user selects an entry in the list, **itemStateChange( )** is called. The **EventSetDescriptor** object is obtained from the **esds** array and the **Method** object for the registration method is obtained via **getAddListener( )**. The **invoke( )** method is used to call this registration method. The net effect is to register **bean2** to receive a set of events generated by **bean1**.

Note this important point: This tool is not constructed with any prior knowledge of these two Beans. However, it can still dynamically connect them because it makes use of the introspection facilities. The **invoke( )** method of the **Method** object makes this possible.

```
package beantool;
import java.awt.*;
import java.awt.event.*;
import java.beans.*;
import java.lang.reflect.*;
import java.util.*;

public class ConnectDialog extends Dialog
implements ItemListener {
  private Object bean1, bean2;
  private java.awt.List list;
  EventSetDescriptor esds[];

  public ConnectDialog(Frame frame, String title,
  Object bean1, Object bean2) {

    // Invoke superclass constructor
    super(frame, "Connect Dialog", true);

    // Save bean1 and bean2
    this.bean1 = bean1;
```

14

```
  this.bean2 = bean2;

  // Create and initialize list
  list = new java.awt.List();
  initializeList();
  list.addItemListener(this);
  add("Center", list);

  // Register to receive window events
  addWindowListener(new MyWindowAdapter());

  // Set size of dialog and make it visible
  setSize(200, 200);
  show();
}

private void initializeList() {

  // Get the BeanInfo object for bean1
  Class cls1 = bean1.getClass();
  BeanInfo bi1;
  try {
    bi1 = Introspector.getBeanInfo(cls1);
  }
  catch(Exception ex) {
    return;
  }

  // Get the EventSetDescriptor objects for
  // bean1 and add these to the list
  esds = bi1.getEventSetDescriptors();
  for(int i = 0; i < esds.length; i++) {
    list.add(esds[i].getName());
  }
}

public void itemStateChanged(ItemEvent ie) {

  // Obtain the EventSetDescriptor object
  int index = list.getSelectedIndex();
  EventSetDescriptor esd = esds[index];

  // Obtain the registration method
```

```
Method method = esd.getAddListenerMethod();

// Invoke the registration method of
// bean1 to register bean2
Object args[] = new Object[1];
args[0] = bean2;
try {
  method.invoke(bean1, args);
}
catch(Exception ex) {
  ex.printStackTrace();
}

// Dispose of this dialog box
dispose();
}

class MyWindowAdapter extends WindowAdapter {
  public void windowClosing(WindowEvent we) {
    dispose();
  }
}
}
```

Possible Enhancements

This example can serve as a starting point for your own experiments. For example, you may wish to enhance this tool so a Bean can be configured. This could be requested by holding the CTRL key and clicking the mouse in the rectangle along the top of the component. If a customizer is associated with the Bean, a modal dialog box can be opened with that user interface. Otherwise, a modal dialog box can appear that lists the properties of the Bean. When the user selects one of these properties, the appropriate property editor can be presented.

Concluding Comments

This book addresses the fundamentals of JavaBeans programming. You should frequently check the web page at **http://java.sun.com** for the latest information about this evolving technology. In particular, watch for announcements about Enterprise JavaBeans. These will allow you to build mission-critical applications by assembling a set of server-based components. **14**

Also read about the JavaBeans Bridge for ActiveX™. This allows you to use JavaBeans in applications such as Microsoft Word, Excel, VisualBasic, or Internet Explorer. A related tool is the JavaBeans Migration Assistant for ActiveX™. This helps you convert an ActiveX™ control to a Bean.

Finally, check the online directory of JavaBeans components. By taking advantage of this software, you can substantially accelerate the development of your next application.

Index

NOTE: Page numbers in *italics* refer to illustrations or tables.